FRANCIS SCHAEFFER STUDY CENTER

BRITISH AND AMERICAN LITERATURE

1550-1900 SOURCE BOOK

YEAR 3

Published by

Greenleaf Press
1570 Old Laguardo Rd
Lebanon, TN 37087

Table of Contents

Introduction

This course is an inductive study of English and American Literature from 1560's to 1900. While it is not by any means comprehensive, it does attempt to give you an introduction to the major periods, genres, and writers of the time.

Inductive study has three basic components: observation, interpretation, application. Those of you who have already done any of Precept Ministries' inductive Bible study courses, will be familiar with the process. Inductive method can be used in any kind of study. In an inductive study you ask questions of the text AND expect to find the answers to those questions in the text. You do not begin with commentaries, critiques, or summaries. While it is true that other very gifted scholars have much that is helpful to say about a literary work, you will be asked to go to them only after YOU have done your own work.

The foundation of inductive study is ***observation***. The more carefully and accurately you observe your subject, the more accurate your interpretation will be. If your house has a faulty foundation, everything built on top of it will be faulty. Careless observations will produce questionable interpretation.

By inductive study, I mean, that you focus your attention primarily on the texts of the works themselves. Most of your time will be spent here. In this step you will ask, "What does the text **say**?"

To determine the answer to this question you will ask questions of the text:

- What kind of literature is this?
- Is it a poem, a short story, a novel, a play, a work of non-fiction?
- Does it primarily a narrative, that is, does it set out to tell a story.
- Does it primarily describe a person, place, or event?
- Does the writer want to convince you of some truth and stir you up to think or act as he or she does?

As you study inductively you will ask questions like the following.

- **Who** is it about (Who are the characters, supporting characters, protagonist, and antagonist)?
- **What** do they do? (plot?)
- **When** does the action take place?
- **Where** does the action take place (setting)?
- **Why** do things happen as they do?
- **How** do things work out the way they do?

Once you have thoroughly observed the text, you can begin the process of putting it all together – of ***interpreting*** what you have read. In this step you ask, "What does this **mean**?" What is the point the writer is trying to make? Does the writer successfully make that point?

When you are studying literature inductively, you will also ask another kind of *how* question. **How** does the writer communicate all this to the reader?

- What literary devices or techniques are used?
- How does a writer use the sounds of words to reinforce meaning?
- How does the structure, the imagery, and the physical layout on the page reinforce meaning?

Once you feel that you have a pretty good handle on what the work says and what the work means, you move to the ***application*** stage. At this point you look at the relevance of the work –

- what did it have to say to those alive when it was written?
- Does it have anything important to say to you personally or to contemporary culture?
- Is it *true?* Does it accurately or inaccurately describe human nature, the nature of the universe, and/or God?
- Even if you don't agree with the writer's conclusions or worldview, is there some truth in the piece anyway?
- Has the writer accurately observed some things about man, nature, society, or God.?
- Even those who may have reached unbiblical or inaccurate conclusions about the nature of these things, may still have some useful insights. Do you know people who think like the writer?
- Do you know people who behave like (or think like) the characters you read about?
- What would the Gospel have to say to these situations or viewpoints? Ideas have consequences – personally, culturally, and eternally.

You can use your study of literature to develop your ability to analyze and evaluate the ideas and values promoted by your culture.

Often literature study guides or text books will take a different approach. Sometimes the study guide will tell you what the work is going to say and then tell you what the work means. After you have read the text, you might be asked to reproduce all you were told the work says and means. I am not going to observe or interpret the text for you. That is your job. As you read and observe and interpret the work for yourself, you will find out for yourself what the writer says and means. After that you can compare you conclusions with what others have written and see if you agree of disagree.

The other thing I do not want to do is interrupt your reading unnecessarily. After reading any necessary background information, you should jump right into the text. Read the whole thing. After you have read through the piece (or if it is a longer work, the section of a selection) once, then go back and work through the questions. The questions found here are intended to guide you through careful observation of the text. If you are an avid reader you might not need much help, and you may find yourself using the questions simply as a reminder of what to look for. If you haven't read much in the way of literature, you may find that you need to rely on the questions more heavily. Either way, focus on the text, itself.

Finally, have fun.

The Kings and Queens of England

Willy, Willy, Henry, Stee

Henry, Dick, John, Henry 3,

I, 2, 3, Neds, Richard 2

Henry 4, 5, 6, then Who?

Edward 4, 5, Dick the Bad

Henrys twain and Ned the Lad

Mary, Bessy, James the Vain

Charlie, Charlie, James again.

William and Mary, Anne Gloria

4 Georges, William, Victoria.

-Unknown

(William 1, William 2, Henry 1, Stephen,

Henry 2, Richard 1, John, Henry 3,

Edward 1,2,3, Richard 2

Henry 4, 5, 6,

Henry 7. 8. Edward 4,

Mary, Elisabeth 1, James 1,

Charles 1, Charles 2, James 2,

William and Mary, Anne Gloria,

George 1,2,3,4, William 3, Victoria)

LESSON 1: *Foxe's Book of Martyrs*

Foxe's Book of Martyrs **was published in England in 1563 under the title of** ***Actes and Monuments of Matters Most Speciall and Memorable*****, but from the beginning it was popularly known as** ***Foxe's Book of Martyrs*****. Originally the book focused on the persecution of the Reformers – mostly Wyclif, but was expanded significantly to include the martyrs of the early Christian Church as well. Foxe is said to have painstakingly researched the stories of those martyrs included in the book. The book ends with the stories of those who were persecuted and martyred under the bloody reign of Henry VIII's oldest daughter, Queen Mary.**

The English people rejoiced at the end of Mary's reign of terror, and embraced the work. Dedicated to the newly crowned Queen Elizabeth, ***Foxe's*** **was an instant best seller. Its influence was also long-lived. Three books were most commonly found in the majority of American**

households even into the twentieth century – The Bible, Pilgrim's Progress, and Foxe's Book of Martyrs.

Read the excerpts from *Foxe's* found on the next few pages. As you read, note the periods of time covered, and the subjects of the major sections. Write these in the margins of the text.

After you have finished reading, answer the following questions:

1. **What stories stuck out most in your mind, and why? (If nothing stuck with you, it may be God's way of saying, "You need to read it again.")**

2. **What impression do you have of Hus? Of Wyclif? Of the martyrs under Mary?**

3. **How would you expect the English people (generally) to feel about the Catholic church after either living through Queen Mary's reign OR after reading Foxe's account of life under Queen Mary? Would you expect them to welcome another Catholic monarch?**

4. **What is the effect of beginning his history of martyrdom with the early Church and ending with contemporary reformers (and those martyred under Mary)?**

Foxe's Book of Martyrs

CHAPTER II

The Ten Primitive Persecutions

The First Persecution, Under Nero, A.D. 67

The first persecution of the Church took place in the year 67, under Nero, the sixth emperor of Rome. This monarch reigned for the space of five years, with tolerable credit to himself, but then gave way to the greatest extravagancy of temper, and to the most atrocious barbarities. Among other diabolical whims, he ordered that the city of Rome should be set on fire, which order was executed by his officers, guards, and servants. While the imperial city was in flames, he went up to the tower of Macaenas, played upon his harp, sung the song of the burning of Troy, and openly declared that 'he wished the ruin of all things before his death.' Besides the noble pile, called the Circus, many other palaces and houses were consumed; several thousands perished in the flames, were smothered in the smoke, or buried beneath the ruins.

This dreadful conflagration continued nine days; when Nero, finding that his conduct was greatly blamed, and a severe odium cast upon him, determined to lay the whole upon the Christians, at once to excuse himself, and have an opportunity of glutting his sight with new cruelties. This was the occasion of the first persecution; and the barbarities exercised on the Christians were such as even excited the commiseration of the Romans themselves. Nero even refined upon cruelty, and contrived all manner of punishments for the Christians that the most infernal imagination could design. In particular, he had some sewed up in skins of wild beasts, and then worried by dogs until they expired; and others dressed in shirts made stiff with wax, fixed to axletrees, and set on fire in his gardens, in order to illuminate them. This persecution was general throughout the whole Roman Empire; but it rather increased than diminished the spirit of Christianity. In the course of it, St. Paul and St. Peter were martyred.

To their names may be added, Erastus, chamberlain of Corinth; Aristarchus, the Macedonian, and Trophimus, an Ephesians, converted by St. Paul, and fellow-laborer with him, Joseph, commonly called Barsabas, and Ananias, bishop of Damascus; each of the Seventy.

The Second Persecution, Under Domitian, A.D. 81

The emperor Domitian, who was naturally inclined to cruelty, first slew his brother, and then raised the second persecution against the Christians. In his rage he put to death some of the Roman senators, some through malice; and others to confiscate their estates. He then commanded all the lineage of David be put to death.

Among the numerous martyrs that suffered during this persecution was Simeon, bishop of Jerusalem, who was crucified; and St. John, who was boiled in oil, and afterward banished to Patmos. Flavia, the daughter of a Roman senator, was likewise banished to Pontus; and a law was made, "That no Christian, once brought before the tribunal, should be exempted from punishment without renouncing his religion."

A variety of fabricated tales were, during this reign, composed in order to injure the Christians. Such was the infatuation of the pagans, that, if famine, pestilence, or earthquakes afflicted any of the Roman provinces, it was laid upon the Christians. These persecutions among the Christians increased the number of informers and many, for the sake of gain, swore away the lives of the innocent.

Another hardship was, that, when any Christians were brought before the magistrates, a test oath was proposed, when, if they refused to take it, death was pronounced against them; and if they confessed themselves Christians, the sentence was the same.

The following were the most remarkable among the numerous martyrs who suffered during this persecution.

Dionysius, the Areopagite, was an Athenian by birth, and educated in all the useful and ornamental literature of Greece. He then travelled to Egypt to study astronomy, and made very particular observations on the great and supernatural eclipse, which happened at the time of our Savior's crucifixion.

The sanctity of his conversation and the purity of his manners recommended him so strongly to the Christians in general, that he was appointed bishop of Athens.

Nicodemus, a benevolent Christian of some distinction, suffered at Rome during the rage of Domitian's persecution.

Protasius and Gervasius were martyred at Milan.

Timothy was the celebrated disciple of St. Paul, and bishop of Ephesus, where he zealously governed the Church until A.D. 97. At this period, as the pagans were about to celebrate a feast called Catagogion, Timothy, meeting the procession, severely reproved them for their ridiculous idolatry, which so exasperated the people that they fell upon him with their clubs, and beat him in so dreadful a manner that he expired of the bruises two days later.

The Third Persecution, Under Trajan, A.D. 108

In the third persecution Pliny the Second, a man learned and famous, seeing the lamentable slaughter of Christians, and moved therewith to pity, wrote to Trajan, certifying him that there were many thousands of them daily put to death, of which none did any thing contrary to the Roman laws worthy of persecution. "The whole account they gave of their crime or error (whichever it is to be called) amounted only to this-viz. that they were accustomed on a stated day to meet before daylight, and to repeat together a set form of prayer to Christ as a God, and to bind themselves by an obligation-not indeed to commit wickedness; but, on the contrary-never to commit theft, robbery, or adultery, never to falsify their word, never to defraud any man: after which it was their custom to separate, and reassemble to partake in common of a harmless meal."

In this persecution suffered the blessed martyr, Ignatius, who is held in famous reverence among very many. This Ignatius was appointed to the bishopric of Antioch next after Peter in succession. Some do say, that he, being sent from Syria to Rome, because he professed Christ, was given to the wild beasts to be devoured. It is also said of him, that when he passed through Asia, being under the most strict custody of his keepers, he strengthened and confirmed the churches through all the cities as he went, both with his exhortations and preaching of the Word of God. Accordingly, having come to Smyrna, he wrote to the Church at Rome, exhorting them not to use means for his deliverance from martyrdom, lest they should deprive him of that which he most longed and hoped for. "Now I begin to be a disciple. I care for nothing, of visible or invisible things, so that I may but win Christ. Let fire and the cross, let the companies of wild beasts, let breaking of bones and tearing of limbs, let the grinding of the whole body, and all the malice of the devil, come upon me; be it so, only may I win Christ Jesus!" And even when he was sentenced to be thrown to the beasts, such as the burning desire that he had to suffer, that he spake, what time he heard the lions roaring, saying: "I am the wheat of Christ: I am going to be ground with the teeth of wild beasts, that I may be found pure bread."

Trajan being succeeded by Adrian, the latter continued this third persecution with as much severity as his predecessor. About this time Alexander, bishop of Rome, with his two deacons, were martyred; as were Quirinus and Hernes, with their families;

Zenon, a Roman nobleman, and about ten thousand other Christians.

In Mount Ararat many were crucified, crowned with thorns, and spears run into their sides, in imitation of Christ's passion. Eustachius, a brave and successful Roman commander, was by the emperor ordered to join in an idolatrous sacrifice to celebrate some of his own victories; but his faith (being a Christian in his heart) was so much greater than his vanity, that he nobly refused it. Enraged at the denial, the ungrateful emperor forgot the service of this skilful commander, and ordered him and his whole family to be martyred.

At the martyrdom of Faustines and Jovita, brothers and citizens of Brescia, their torments were so many, and their patience so great, that Calocerius, a pagan, beholding them, was struck with admiration, and exclaimed in a kind of ecstasy, "Great is the God of the Christians!" for which he was apprehended, and suffered a similar fate.

Many other similar cruelties and rigors were exercised against the Christians, until Quadratus, bishop of Athens, made a learned apology in their favor before the emperor, who happened to be there and Aristides, a philosopher of the same city, wrote an elegant epistle, which caused Adrian to relax in his severities, and relent in their favor.

Adrian dying A.D. 138, was succeeded by Antoninus Pius, one of the most amiable monarchs that ever reigned, and who stayed the persecutions against the Christians.

The Fourth Persecution, Under Marcus Aurelius Antoninus, A.D. 162

Marcus Aurelius, followed about the year of our Lord 161, a man of nature more stern and severe; and, although in study of philosophy and in civil government no less commendable, yet, toward the Christians sharp and fierce; by whom was moved the fourth persecution.

The cruelties used in this persecution were such that many of the spectators shuddered with horror at the sight, and were astonished at the intrepidity of the sufferers. Some of the martyrs were obliged to pass, with their already wounded feet, over thorns, nails, sharp shells, etc. upon their points, others were scourged until their sinews and veins lay bare, and after suffering the most excruciating tortures that could be devised, they were destroyed by the most terrible deaths.

Germanicus, a young man, but a true Christian, being delivered to the wild beasts on account of his faith, behaved with such astonishing courage that several pagans became converts to a faith which inspired such fortitude.

Polycarp, the venerable bishop of Smyrna, hearing that persons were seeking for him, escaped, but was discovered by a child. After feasting the guards who apprehended him, he desired an hour in prayer, which being allowed, he prayed with such fervency, that his guards repented that they had been instrumental in taking him. He was, however, carried before the proconsul, condemned, and burnt in the market place.

The proconsul then urged him, saying, "Swear, and I will release thee;--reproach Christ."

Polycarp answered, "Eighty and six years have I served him, and he never once wronged me; how then shall I blaspheme my King, Who hath saved me?" At the stake to which he was only tied, but not nailed as usual, as he assured them he should stand immovable, the flames, on their kindling the fagots, encircled his body, like an arch, without touching him; and the executioner, on seeing this, was ordered to pierce him with a sword, when so great a quantity of blood flowed out as extinguished the fire. But his body, at the instigation of the enemies of the Gospel, especially Jews, was ordered to be consumed in the pile, and the request of his friends, who wished to give it Christian burial, rejected. They nevertheless collected his bones and as much of his remains as possible, and caused them to be decently interred.

Metrodorus, a minister, who preached boldly, and Pionius, who made some excellent apologies for the Christian faith, were likewise burnt. Carpus and Papilus, two worthy Christians, and Agatonica, a pious woman, suffered martyrdom at Pergamopolis, in Asia.

Felicitatis, an illustrious Roman lady, of a considerable family, and the most shining virtues, was a devout Christian. She had seven sons, whom she had educated with the most exemplary piety.

Januarius, the eldest, was scourged, and pressed to death with weights; Felix and Philip, the two next had their brains dashed out with clubs; Silvanus, the fourth, was murdered by being thrown from a precipice; and the three younger sons, Alexander, Vitalis, and Martial, were beheaded. The mother was beheaded with the same sword as the three latter.

Justin, the celebrated philosopher, fell a martyr in this persecution. He was a native of Neapolis, in Samaria, and was born A.D. 103. Justin was a great lover of truth, and a universal scholar; he investigated the Stoic and Peripatetic philosophy, and attempted the Pythagorean; but the behavior of our of its professors disgusting him, he applied himself to the Platonic, in which he took great delight. About the year 133, when he was thirty years of age, he became a convert to Christianity, and then, for the first time, perceived the real nature of truth.

He wrote an elegant epistle to the Gentiles, and employed his talents in convincing the Jews of the truth of the Christian rites; spending a great deal of time in traveling, until he took up his abode in Rome, and fixed his habitation upon the Viminal mount.

He kept a public school, taught many who afterward became great men, and wrote a treatise to confuse heresies of all kinds. As the pagans began to treat the Christians with great severity, Justin wrote his first apology in their favor. This piece displays great learning and genius, and occasioned the emperor to publish an edict in favor of the Christians.

Soon after, he entered into frequent contests with Crescens, a person of a vicious life and conversation, but a celebrated cynic philosopher; and his arguments appeared so powerful, yet disgusting to the cynic, that he resolved on, and in the sequel accomplished, his destruction.

The second apology of Justin, upon certain severities, gave Crescens the cynic an opportunity of prejudicing the emperor against the writer of it; upon which Justin, and six of his companions, were apprehended. Being commanded to sacrifice to the pagan idols, they refused, and were condemned to be scourged, and then beheaded; which sentence was executed with all imaginable severity.

Several were beheaded for refusing to sacrifice to the image of Jupiter; in particular Concordus, a deacon of the city of Spolito.

Some of the restless northern nations having risen in arms against Rome, the emperor marched to encounter them. He was, however, drawn into an ambuscade, and dreaded the loss of his whole army. Enveloped with mountains, surrounded by enemies, and perishing with thirst, the pagan deities were invoked in vain; when the men belonging to the militine, or thundering legion, who were all Christians, were commanded to call upon their God for succor. A miraculous deliverance immediately ensued; a prodigious quantity of rain fell, which, being caught by the men, and filling their dykes, afforded a sudden and astonishing relief. It appears that the storm which miraculously flashed in the face of the enemy so intimidated them, that part deserted to the Roman army; the rest were defeated, and the revolted provinces entirely recovered.

This affair occasioned the persecution to subside for some time, at least in those parts immediately under the inspection of the emperor; but we find that it soon after raged in France, particularly at Lyons, where the tortures to which many of the Christians were put, almost exceed the powers of description.

The principal of these martyrs were Vetius Agathus, a young man; Blandina, a Christian lady, of a weak constitution; Sanctus, a deacon of Vienna; red hot plates of brass were placed upon the tenderest parts of his body; Biblias, a weak woman, once an apostate. Attalus, of Pergamus; and Pothinus, the venerable bishop of Lyons, who was ninety years of age. Blandina, on the day when she and the three other champions were first brought into the amphitheater, she was suspended on a piece of wood fixed in the ground, and exposed as food for the wild beasts; at which time, by her earnest prayers, she encouraged others. But none of the wild beasts would touch her, so that she was remanded to prison. When she was again produced for the third and last time, she was accompanied by Ponticus, a youth of fifteen, and the constancy of their faith so enraged the multitude that neither the sex of the one nor the youth of the other were respected, being exposed to all manner of punishments and tortures. Being strengthened by Blandina, he persevered unto death; and she, after enduring all the torments heretofore mentioned, was at length slain with the sword.

When the Christians, upon these occasions, received martyrdom, they were ornamented, and crowned with garlands of flowers; for which they, in heaven, received eternal crowns of glory.

It has been said that the lives of the early Christians consisted of "persecution above ground and prayer below ground." Their lives are expressed by the Coliseum and the catacombs. Beneath Rome are the excavations which we call the catacombs, which were at once temples and tombs. The early Church of Rome might well be called the Church of the Catacombs. There are some sixty catacombs near Rome, in which some six hundred miles of galleries have been traced, and these are not all. These galleries are about eight feet high and from three to five feet wide, containing on either side several rows of long, low, horizontal recesses, one above another like berths in a ship. In these the dead bodies were placed and the front closed, either by a single marble slab or several great tiles laid in mortar. On these slabs or tiles, epitaphs or symbols are graved or painted. Both pagans and Christians buried their dead in these catacombs. When the Christian graves have been opened the skeletons tell their own terrible tale. Heads are found severed from the body, ribs and shoulder blades are broken, bones are often calcined from fire. But despite the awful story of persecution that we may read here, the inscriptions breathe forth peace and joy and triumph. Here are a few:

"Here lies Marcia, put to rest in a dream of peace."

"Lawrence to his sweetest son, borne away of angels."

"Victorious in peace and in Christ."

"Being called away, he went in peace."

Remember when reading these inscriptions the story the skeletons tell of persecution, of torture, and of fire.

But the full force of these epitaphs is seen when we contrast them with the pagan epitaphs, such as:

"Live for the present hour, since we are sure of nothing else."

"I lift my hands against the gods who took me away at the age of twenty though I had done no harm."

"Once I was not. Now I am not. I know nothing about it, and it is no concern of mine."

"Traveler, curse me not as you pass, for I am in darkness and cannot answer."

The most frequent Christian symbols on the walls of the catacombs, are, the good shepherd with the lamb on his shoulder, a ship under full sail, harps, anchors, crowns, vines, and above all the fish.

[. . .]

The Tenth Persecution, Under Diocletian, A.D. 303

Under the Roman emperors, commonly called the Era of the Martyrs, was occasioned partly by the increasing number and luxury of the Christians, and the hatred of Galerius, the adopted son of Diocletian, who, being stimulated by his mother, a bigoted pagan, never ceased persuading the emperor to enter upon the persecution, until he had accomplished his purpose.

The fatal day fixed upon to commence the bloody work, was the twenty-third of February, A.D. 303, that being the day in which the Terminalia were celebrated, and on which, as the cruel pagans boasted, they hoped to put a termination to Christianity. On the appointed day, the persecution began in Nicomedia, on the morning of which the prefect of that city repaired, with a great number of officers and assistants, to the church of the Christians, where, having forced open the doors, they seized upon all the sacred books, and committed them to the flames.

The whole of this transaction was in the presence of Diocletian and Galerius, who, not contented with burning the books, had the church leveled with the ground. This was followed by a severe edict, commanding the destruction of all other Christian churches and books; and an order soon succeeded, to render Christians of all denomination outlaws.

The publication of this edict occasioned an immediate martyrdom, for a bold Christian not only tore it down from the place to which it was affixed, but execrated the name of the emperor for his injustice. A provocation like this was sufficient to call down pagan vengeance upon his head; he was accordingly seized, severely tortured, and then burned alive.

All the Christians were apprehended and imprisoned; and Galerius privately ordered the imperial palace to be set on fire, that the Christians might be charged as the incendiaries, and a plausible pretence given for carrying on the persecution with the greater severities. A general sacrifice was commenced, which occasioned various martyrdoms. No distinction was made of age or sex; the name of Christian was so obnoxious to the pagans that all indiscriminately fell sacrifices to their opinions. Many houses were set on fire, and whole Christian families perished in the flames; and others had stones fastened about their necks, and being tied together were driven into the sea. The persecution became general in all the Roman provinces, but more particularly in the east; and as it lasted ten years, it is impossible to ascertain the numbers martyred, or to enumerate the various modes of martyrdom.

Racks, scourges, swords, daggers, crosses, poison, and famine, were made use of in various parts to dispatch the Christians; and invention was exhausted to devise tortures against such as had no crime, but thinking differently from the votaries of superstition.

A city of Phrygia, consisting entirely of Christians, was burnt, and all the inhabitants perished in the flames.

Tired with slaughter, at length, several governors of provinces represented to the imperial court, the impropriety of such conduct. Hence many were respited from execution, but, though they were not put to death, as much as possible was done to render their lives miserable, many of them having their ears cut off, their noses slit, their right eyes put out, their limbs rendered useless by dreadful dislocations, and their flesh seared in conspicuous places with red-hot irons.

It is necessary now to particularize the most conspicuous persons who laid down their lives in martyrdom in this bloody persecution.

Sebastian, a celebrated martyr, was born at Narbonne, in Gaul, instructed in the principles of Christianity at Milan, and afterward became an officer of the emperor's guard at Rome. He remained a true Christian in the midst of idolatry;

unallured by the splendors of a court, untainted by evil examples, and uncontaminated by the hopes of preferment. Refusing to be a pagan, the emperor ordered him to be taken to a field near the city, termed the Campus Martius, and there to be shot to death with arrows; which sentence was executed accordingly. Some pious Christians coming to the place of execution, in order to give his body burial, perceived signs of life in him, and immediately moving him to a place of security, they, in a short time effected his recovery, and prepared him for a second martyrdom; for, as soon as he was able to go out, he placed himself intentionally in the emperor's way as he was going to the temple, and reprehended him for his various cruelties and unreasonable prejudices against Christianity. As soon as Diocletian had overcome his surprise, he ordered Sebastian to be seized, and carried to a place near the palace, and beaten to death; and, that the Christians should not either use means again to recover or bury his body, he ordered that it should be thrown into the common sewer. Nevertheless, a Christian lady named Lucina, found means to remove it from the sewer, and bury it in the catacombs, or repositories of the dead.

The Christians, about this time, upon mature consideration, thought it unlawful to bear arms under a heathen emperor. Maximilian, the son of Fabius Victor, was the first beheaded under this regulation.

Vitus, a Sicilian of considerable family, was brought up a Christian; when his virtues increased with his years, his constancy supported him under all afflictions, and his faith was superior to the most dangerous perils. His father, Hylas, who was a pagan, finding that he had been instructed in the principles of Christianity by the nurse who brought him up, used all his endeavors to bring him back to paganism, and at length sacrificed his son to the idols, June 14, A.D. 303.

Victor was a Christian of a good family at Marseilles, in France; he spent a great part of the night in visiting the afflicted, and confirming the weak; which pious work he could not, consistently with his own safety, perform in the daytime; and his fortune he spent in relieving the distresses of poor Christians. He was at length, however, seized by the emperor Maximian's decree, who ordered him to be bound, and dragged through the streets. During the execution of this order, he was treated with all manner of cruelties and indignities by the enraged populace. Remaining still inflexible, his courage was deemed obstinacy. Being by order stretched upon the rack, he turned his eyes toward heaven, and prayed to God to endue him with patience, after which he underwent the tortures with most admirable fortitude. After the executioners were tired with inflicting torments on him, he was conveyed to a dungeon. In his confinement, he converted his jailers, named Alexander, Felician, and Longinus. This affair coming to the ears of the emperor, he ordered them immediately to be put to death, and the jailers were accordingly beheaded. Victor was then again put to the rack, unmercifully beaten with batoons, and again sent to prison. Being a third time examined concerning his religion, he persevered in his principles; a small altar was then brought, and he was commanded to offer incense upon it immediately. Fired with indignation at the request, he boldly stepped forward, and with his foot overthrew both altar and idol. This so enraged the emperor Maximian, who was present, that he ordered the foot with which he had kicked the altar to be immediately cut off; and Victor was thrown into a mill, and crushed to pieces with the stones, A.D. 303.

We shall conclude our account of the tenth and last general persecution with the death of St. George, the titular saint and patron of England. St. George was born in Cappadocia, of Christian parents; and giving proofs of his courage, was promoted in the army of the emperor Diocletian. During the persecution, St. George threw up his command, went boldly to the senate house, and avowed his being a Christian, taking occasion at the same time to remonstrate against paganism, and point out the absurdity of worshipping idols. This freedom so greatly provoked the senate that St. George was ordered to be tortured, and by the emperor's orders was dragged through the streets, and beheaded the next day.

The legend of the dragon, which is associated with this martyr, is usually illustrated by representing St. George seated upon a charging horse and transfixing the monster with his spear. This fiery dragon symbolizes the devil, who was vanquished by St. George's steadfast faith in Christ, which remained unshaken in spite of torture and death.

CHAPTER VIII

An Account of the Persecutions in Bohemia Under the Papacy

The Roman pontiffs having usurped a power over several churches were particularly severe on the Bohemians, which occasioned them to send two ministers and four lay-brothers to Rome, in the year 977, to obtain redress of the pope. After some delay, their request was granted, and their grievances redressed. Two things in particular they were permitted to do, viz., to have divine service performed in their own language, and to give the cup to the laity in the Sacrament.

The disputes, however, soon broke out again, the succeeding popes exerting their whole power to impose on the minds of the Bohemians; and the latter, with great spirit, aiming to preserve their religious liberties.

In A.D. 1375, some zealous friends of the Gospel applied to Charles, king of Bohemia, to call an ecumenical Council, for an inquiry into the abuses that had crept into the Church, and to make a full and thorough reformation. The king, not knowing how to proceed, sent to the pope for directions how to act; but the pontiff was so incensed at this affair that his only reply was, "Severely punish those rash and profane heretics." The monarch, accordingly banished every one who had been concerned in the application, and, to oblige the pope, laid a great number of additional restraints upon the religious liberties of the people.

The victims of persecution, however, were not so numerous in Bohemia, until after the burning of John Huss and Jerome of Prague. These two eminent reformers were condemned and executed at the instigation of the pope and his emissaries, as the reader will perceive by the following short sketches of their lives.

Persecution of John Huss

John Huss was born at Hussenitz, a village in Bohemia, about the year 1380. His parents gave him the best education their circumstances would admit; and having acquired a tolerable knowledge of the classics at a private school, he was removed to the university of Prague, where he soon gave strong proofs of his mental powers, and was remarkable for his diligence and application to study.

In 1398, Huss commenced bachelor of divinity, and was after successively chosen pastor of the Church of Bethlehem, in Prague, and dean and rector of the university. In these stations he discharged his duties with great fidelity; and became, at length, so conspicuous for his preaching, which was in conformity with the doctrines of Wickliffe, that it was not likely he could long escape the notice of the pope and his adherents, against whom he inveighed with no small degree of asperity.

The English reformist, Wickliffe, had so kindled the light of reformation, that it began to illumine the darkest corners of popery and ignorance. His doctrines spread into Bohemia, and were well received by great numbers of people, but by none so particularly as John Huss, and his zealous friend and fellow martyr, Jerome of Prague.

The archbishop of Prague, finding the reformists daily increasing, issued a decree to suppress the further spreading of Wickliffe's writings: but this had an effect quite different to what he expected, for it stimulated the friends of those doctrines to greater zeal, and almost the whole university united to propagate them.

Being strongly attached to the doctrines of Wickliffe, Huss opposed the decree of the archbishop, who, however, at length, obtained a bull from the pope, giving him commission to prevent the publishing of Wickliffe's doctrines in his province. By virtue of this bull, the archbishop condemned the writings of Wickliffe: he also proceeded against four doctors, who had not delivered up the copies of that divine, and prohibited them, notwithstanding their privileges, to preach to any congregation. Dr. Huss, with some other members of the university, protested against these proceedings, and entered an appeal from the sentence of the archbishop.

The affair being made known to the pope, he granted a commission to Cardinal Colonna, to cite John Huss to appear personally at the court of Rome, to answer the accusations laid against him, of preaching both errors and heresies. Dr. Huss desired to be excused from a personal appearance, and was so greatly favored in Bohemia, that King Winceslaus, the queen, the nobility, and the university, desired the pope to dispense with such an appearance; as also that he would not suffer the kingdom of Bohemia to lie under the accusation of heresy, but permit them to preach the Gospel with freedom in their places of worship.

Three proctors appeared for Dr. Huss before Cardinal Colonna. They endeavored to excuse his absence, and said they were ready to answer in his behalf. But the cardinal declared Huss contumacious, and excommunicated him accordingly. The proctors appealed to the pope, and appointed four cardinals to examine the process: these commissioners confirmed the former sentence, and extended the excommunication not only to Huss but to all his friends and followers.

From this unjust sentence Huss appealed to a future Council, but without success; and, notwithstanding so severe a decree, and an expulsion in consequence from his church in Prague, he retired to Hussenitz, his native place, where he continued to promulgate his new doctrine, both from the pulpit and with the pen.

The letters which he wrote at this time were very numerous; and he compiled a treatise in which he maintained, that reading the books of Protestants could not be absolutely forbidden. He wrote in defense of Wickliffe's book on the Trinity; and boldly declared against the vices of the pope, the cardinals, and clergy, of those corrupt times. He wrote also many other books, all of which were penned with a strength of argument that greatly facilitated the spreading of his doctrines.

In the month of November, 1414, a general Council was assembled at Constance, in Germany, in order, as was pretended, for the sole purpose of determining a dispute then pending between three persons who contended for the papacy; but the real motive was to crush the progress of the Reformation.

John Huss was summoned to appear at this Council; and, to encourage him, the emperor sent him a safe-conduct: the civilities, and even reverence, which Huss met with on his journey were beyond imagination. The streets, and sometimes the very roads, were lined with people, whom respect, rather than curiosity, had brought together.

He was ushered into the town with great acclamations, and it may be said that he passed through Germany in a kind of triumph. He could not help expressing his surprise at the treatment he received: "I thought (said he) I had been an outcast. I now see my worst friends are in Bohemia."

As soon as Huss arrived at Constance, he immediately took lodgings in a remote part of the city. A short time after his arrival, came one Stephen Paletz, who was employed by the clergy at Prague to manage the intended prosecution against him. Paletz was afterwards joined by Michael de Cassis, on the part of the court of Rome. These two declared themselves his accusers, and drew up a set of articles against him, which they presented to the pope and the prelates of the Council.

When it was known that he was in the city he was immediately arrested, and committed prisoner to a chamber in the palace. This violation of common law and justice was particularly noticed by one of Huss's friends, who urged the imperial safe-conduct; but the pope replied he never granted any safe-conduct, nor was he bound by that of the emperor.

While Huss was in confinement, the Council acted the part of inquisitors.

They condemned the doctrines of Wickliffe, and even ordered his remains to be dug up and burned to ashes; which orders were strictly complied with. In the meantime, the nobility of Bohemia and Poland strongly interceded for Huss; and so far prevailed as to prevent his being condemned unheard, which had been resolved on by the commissioners appointed to try him.

When he was brought before the Council, the articles exhibited against him were read: they were upwards of forty in number, and chiefly extracted from his writings.

John Huss's answer was this: "I did appeal unto the pope; who being dead, and the cause of my matter remaining undetermined, I appealed likewise unto his successor John XXIII: before whom when, by the space of two years, I could not be admitted by my advocates to defend my cause, I appealed unto the high judge Christ."

When John Huss had spoken these words, it was demanded of him whether he had received absolution of the pope or no? He answered, "No." Then again, whether it was lawful for him to appeal unto Christ or no? Whereunto John Huss answered: "Verily I do affirm here before you all, that there is no more just or effectual appeal, than that appeal which is made unto Christ, forasmuch as the law doth determine, that to appeal is no other thing than in a cause of grief or wrong done by an inferior judge, to implore and require aid at a higher Judge's hand. Who is then a higher Judge than Christ? Who, I say, can know or judge the matter more justly, or with more equity? when in Him there is found no deceit, neither can He be deceived; or, who can better help the miserable and oppressed than He?" While John Huss, with a devout and sober countenance, was speaking and pronouncing those words, he was derided and mocked by all the whole Council.

These excellent sentences were esteemed as so many expressions of treason, and tended to inflame his adversaries. Accordingly, the bishops appointed by the Council stripped him of his priestly garments, degraded him, put a paper miter on his head, on which was painted devils, with this inscription, "A ringleader of heretics." Which when he saw, he said: "My Lord Jesus Christ, for my sake, did wear a crown of thorns; why should not I then, for His sake, again wear this light crown, be it ever so ignominious? Truly I will do it, and that willingly." When it was set upon his head, the bishop said: "Now we commit thy soul unto the devil." "But I," said John Huss, lifting his eyes towards the heaven, "do commend into Thy hands, O Lord Jesus Christ! my spirit which Thou has redeemed."

When the chain was put about him at the stake, he said, with a smiling countenance, "My Lord Jesus Christ was bound with a harder chain than this for my sake, and why then should I be ashamed of this rusty one?"

When the fagots were piled up to his very neck, the duke of Bavaria was so officious as to desire him to abjure. "No, (said Huss;) I never preached any doctrine of an evil tendency; and what I taught with my lips I now seal with my blood." He then said to the executioner, "You are now going to burn a goose, (Huss signifying goose in the Bohemian language:) but in a century you will have a swan which you can neither roast nor boil." If he were prophetic, he must have meant Martin Luther, who shone about a hundred years after, and who had a swan for his arms.

The flames were now applied to the fagots, when our martyr sung a hymn with so loud and cheerful a voice that he was heard through all the cracklings of the combustibles, and the noise of the multitude. At length his voice was interrupted by the severity of the flames, which soon closed his existence.

Then, with great diligence, gathering the ashes together, they cast them into the river Rhine, that the least remnant of that man should not be left upon the earth, whose memory, notwithstanding, cannot be abolished out of the minds of the godly, neither by fire, neither by water, neither by any kind of torment.

Persecution of Jerome of Prague

This reformer, who was the companion of Dr. Huss, and may be said to be a co-martyr with him, was born at Prague, and educated in that university, where he particularly distinguished himself for his great abilities and learning. He likewise visited several other learned seminaries in Europe, particularly the universities of Paris, Heidelburg, Cologne and Oxford. At the latter place he became acquainted with the works of Wickliffe, and being a person of uncommon application, he translated many of them into his native language, having, with great pains, made himself master of the English tongue.

On his return to Prague, he professed himself an open favorer of Wickliffe, and finding that his doctrines had made considerable progress in Bohemia, and that Huss was the principal promoter of them, he became an assistant to him in the great work of reformation.

On the fourth of April, 1415, Jerome arrived at Constance, about three months before the death of Huss. He entered the town privately, and consulting with some of the leaders of his party, whom he found there, was easily convinced he could not be of any service to his friends.

Finding that his arrival in Constance was publicly known, and that the Council intended to seize him, he thought it most prudent to retire. Accordingly, the next day he went to Iberling, an imperial town, about a mile from Constance. From this place he wrote to the emperor, and proposed his readiness to appear before the Council, if he would give him a safe-conduct; but this was refused.

He then applied to the Council, but met with an answer no less unfavorable than that from the emperor.

After this, he set out on his return to Bohemia. He had the precaution to take with him a certificate, signed by several of the Bohemian nobility, then at Constance, testifying that he had used all prudent means in his power to procure a hearing.

Jerome, however, did not thus escape. He was seized at Hirsaw by an officer belonging to the duke of Sultsbach, who, though unauthorized so to act, made little doubt of obtaining thanks from the Council for so acceptable a service.

The duke of Sultsbach, having Jerome now in his power, wrote to the Council for directions how to proceed. The Council, after expressing their obligations to the duke, desired him to send the prisoner immediately to Constance. The elector palatine met him on the way, and conducted him into the city, himself riding on horseback, with a numerous retinue, who led Jerome in fetters by a long chain; and immediately on his arrival he was committed to a loathsome dungeon.

Jerome was treated nearly in the same manner as Huss had been, only that he was much longer confined, and shifted from one prison to another. At length, being brought before the Council, he desired that he might plead his own cause, and exculpate himself: which being refused him, he broke out into the following exclamation:

"What barbarity is this! For three hundred and forty days have I been confined in a variety of prisons. There is not a misery, there is not a want, that I have not experienced. To my enemies you have allowed the fullest scope of accusation: to me you deny the least opportunity of defense. Not an hour will you now indulge me in preparing for my trial. You have swallowed the blackest calumnies against me. You have represented me as a heretic, without knowing my doctrine; as an enemy of the faith, before you knew what faith I professed: as a persecutor of priests before you could have an opportunity of understanding my sentiments on that head. You are a General Council: in you center all this world can communicate of gravity, wisdom, and sanctity: but still you are men, and men are seducible by appearances. The higher your character is for wisdom, the greater ought your care to be not to deviate into folly. The cause I now plead is not my own cause: it is the cause of men, it is the cause of Christians; it is a cause which is to affect the rights of posterity, however the experiment is to be made in my person."

This speech had not the least effect; Jerome was obliged to hear the charge read, which was reduced under the following heads: 1. That he was a derider of the papal dignity. 2. An opposer of the pope. 3. An enemy to the cardinals. 4. A persecutor of the prelates. 5. A hater of the Christian religion.

The trial of Jerome was brought on the third day after his accusation and witnesses were examined in support of the charge. The prisoner was prepared for his defense, which appears almost incredible, when we consider he had been three hundred and forty days shut up in loathsome prisons, deprived of daylight, and almost starved for want of common necessaries. But his spirit soared above these disadvantages, under which a man less animated would have sunk; nor was he more at a loss of quotations from the fathers and ancient authors than if he had been furnished with the finest library.

The most bigoted of the assembly were unwilling he should be heard, knowing what effect eloquence is apt to have on the minds of the most prejudiced. At length, however, it was carried by the majority that he should have liberty to proceed in his defense, which he began in such an exalted strain of moving elocution that the heart of obdurate zeal was seen to melt, and the mind of superstition seemed to admit a ray of conviction. He made an admirable distinction between evidence as resting upon facts, and as supported by malice and calumny. He laid before the assembly the whole tenor of his life and conduct. He observed that the greatest and most holy men had been known to differ in points of speculation, with a view to distinguish truth, not to keep it concealed. He expressed a noble contempt of all his enemies, who would have induced him to retract the cause of virtue and truth. He entered upon a high encomium of Huss; and declared he was ready to follow him in the glorious task of martyrdom. He then touched upon the most defensible doctrines of Wickliffe; and concluded with observing that it was far from his intention to advance anything against the state of the Church of God; that it was only against the abuse of the clergy he complained; and that he could not help saying, it was certainly impious that the patrimony of the Church, which was originally intended for the purpose of charity and universal benevolence, should be prostituted to the pride of the eye, in feasts, foppish vestments, and other reproaches to the name and profession of Christianity.

The trial being over, Jerome received the same sentence that had been passed upon his martyred countryman. In consequence of this, he was, in the usual style of popish affectation, delivered over to the civil power: but as he was a layman, he had not to undergo the ceremony of degradation. They had prepared a cap of paper painted with red devils, which being put upon his head, he said, "Our Lord Jesus Christ, when He suffered death for me a most miserable sinner, did wear a crown of thorns upon His head, and for His sake will I wear this cap."

Two days were allowed him in hopes that he would recant; in which time the cardinal of Florence used his utmost endeavors to bring him over. But they all proved ineffectual. Jerome was resolved to seal the doctrine with his blood; and he suffered death with the most distinguished magnanimity.

In going to the place of execution he sang several hymns, and when he came to the spot, which was the same where Huss had been burnt, he knelt down, and prayed fervently. He embraced the stake with great cheerfulness, and when they went behind him to set fire to the fagots, he said, "Come here, and kindle it before my eyes; for if I had been afraid of it, I had not come to this place." The fire being kindled, he sang a hymn, but was soon interrupted by the flames; and the last words he was heard to say these, "This soul in flames I offer Christ, to Thee."

The elegant Pogge, a learned gentleman of Florence, secretary to two popes, and a zealous but liberal Catholic, in a letter to Leonard Arotin, bore ample testimony of the extraordinary powers and virtues of Jerome whom he emphatically styles, A prodigious man!

CHAPTER XII

The Life and Story of the True Servant and Martyr of God,

William Tyndale

We have now to enter into the story of the good martyr of God, William Tyndale; which William Tyndale, as he was a special organ of the Lord appointed, and as God's mattock to shake the inward roots and foundation of the pope's proud prelacy, so the great prince of darkness, with his impious imps, having a special malice against him, left no way unsought how craftily to entrap him, and falsely to betray him, and maliciously to spill his life, as by the process of his story here following may appear.

William Tyndale, the faithful minister of Christ, was born about the borders of Wales, and brought up from a child in the University of Oxford, where he, by long continuance, increased as well in the knowledge of tongues, and other liberal arts, as especially in the knowledge of the Scriptures, whereunto his mind was singularly addicted; insomuch that he, lying then in Magdalen Hall, read privily to certain students and fellows of Magdalen College some parcel of divinity; instructing them in the knowledge and truth of the Scriptures. His manners and conversation being correspondent to the same, were such that all they that knew him reputed him to be a man of most virtuous disposition, and of life unspotted.

Thus he, in the University of Oxford, increasing more and more in learning, and proceeding in degrees of the schools, spying his time, removed from thence to the University of Cambridge, where he likewise made his abode a certain space. Being now further ripened in the knowledge of God's Word, leaving that university, he resorted to one Master Welch, a knight of Gloucestershire, and was there schoolmaster to his children, and in good favor with his master. As this gentleman kept a good ordinary commonly at his table, there resorted to him many times sundry abbots, deans, archdeacons, with divers other doctors, and great beneficed men; who there, together with Master Tyndale sitting at the same table, did use many times to enter communication, and talk of learned men, as of Luther and of Erasmus; also of divers other controversies and questions upon the Scripture.

Then Master Tyndale, as he was learned and well practiced in God's matters, spared not to show unto them simply and plainly his judgment, and when they at any time did vary from Tyndale in opinions, he would show them in the Book, and lay plainly before them the open and manifest places of the Scriptures, to confute their errors, and confirm his sayings. And thus continued they for a certain season, reasoning and contending together divers times, until at length they waxed weary, and bare a secret grudge in their hearts against him.

As this grew on, the priests of the country, clustering together, began to grudge and storm against Tyndale, railing against him in alehouses and other places, affirming that his sayings were heresy; and accused him secretly to the chancellor, and others of the bishop's officers.

It followed not long after this that there was a sitting of the bishop's chancellor appointed, and warning was given to the priests to appear, amongst whom Master Tyndale was also warned to be there. And whether he had any misdoubt by their threatenings, or knowledge given him that they would lay some things to his charge, it is uncertain; but certain this is (as he himself declared), that he doubted their privy accusations; so that he by the way, in going thitherwards, cried in his mind heartily to God, to give him strength fast to stand in the truth of His Word.

When the time came for his appearance before the chancellor, he threatened him grievously, reviling and rating him as though he had been a dog, and laid to his charge many things whereof no accuser could be brought forth, notwithstanding that the priests of the country were there present. Thus Master Tyndale, escaping out of their hands, departed home, and returned to his master again.

There dwelt not far off a certain doctor, that he been chancellor to a bishop, who had been of old, familiar acquaintance with Master Tyndale, and favored him well; unto whom Master Tyndale went and opened his mind upon divers questions of the Scripture: for to him he durst be bold to disclose his heart. Unto whom the doctor said, "Do you not know that the pope is very Antichrist, whom the Scripture speaketh of? But beware what you say; for if you shall be perceived to be of that opinion, it will cost you your life."

Not long after, Master Tyndale happened to be in the company of a certain divine, recounted for a learned man, and, in communing and disputing with him, he drove him to that issue, that the said great doctor burst out into these blasphemous words, "We were better to be without God's laws than the pope's." Master Tyndale, hearing this, full of godly zeal, and not bearing that blasphemous saying, replied, "I defy the pope, and all his laws;" and added, "If God spared him life, ere many years he would cause a boy that driveth the plough to know more of the Scripture than he did."

The grudge of the priests increasing still more and more against Tyndale, they never ceased barking and rating at him, and laid many things sorely to his charge, saying that he was a heretic. Being so molested and vexed, he was constrained to leave that country, and to seek another place; and so coming to Master Welch, he desired him, of his good will, that he might depart from him, saying: "Sir, I perceive that I shall not be suffered to tarry long here in this country, neither shall you be able, though you would, to keep me out of the hands of the spirituality; what displeasure might grow to you by keeping me, God knoweth; for the which I should be right sorry."

So that in fine, Master Tyndale, with the good will of his master, departed, and eftsoons came up to London, and there preached a while, as he had done in the country.

Bethinking himself of Cuthbert Tonstal, then bishop of London, and especially of the great commendation of Erasmus, who, in his annotations, so extolleth the said Tonstal for his learning, Tyndale thus cast with himself, that if he might attain unto his service, he were a happy man. Coming to Sir Henry Guilford, the king's comptroller, and bringing with him an oration of Isocrates, which he had translated out of Greek into English, he desired him to speak to the said bishop of London for him; which he also did; and willed him moreover to write an epistle to the bishop, and to go himself with him. This he did, and delivered his epistle to a servant of his, named William Hebilthwait, a man of his old acquaintance. But God, who secretly disposeth the course of things, saw that was not best for Tyndale's purpose, nor for the profit of His Church, and therefore gave him to find little favor in the bishop's sight; the answer of whom was this: his house was full; he had more than he could well find: and he advised him to seek in London abroad, where, he said, he could lack no service.

Being refused of the bishop he came to Humphrey Mummuth, alderman of London, and besought him to help him: who the same time took him into his house, where the said Tyndale lived (as Mummuth said) like a good priest, studying both night and day. He would eat but sodden meat by his good will, nor drink but small single beer. He was never seen in the house to wear linen about him, all the space of his being there.

And so remained Master Tyndale in London almost a year, marking with himself the course of the world, and especially the demeanor of the preachers, how they boasted themselves, and set up their authority; beholding also the pomp of the prelates, with other things more, which greatly misliked him; insomuch that he understood not only that there was no room in the bishop's house for him to translate the New Testament, but also that there was no place to do it in all England.

Therefore, having by God's providence some aid ministered unto him by Humphrey Mummuth, and certain other good men, he took his leave of the realm, and departed into Germany, where the good man, being inflamed with a tender care and zeal of his country, refused no travail nor diligence, how, by all means possible, to reduce his brethren and countrymen of England to the same taste and understanding of God's holy Word and verity, which the Lord had endued him withal. Whereupon, considering in his mind, and conferring also with John Frith, Tyndale thought with himself no way more to conduce thereunto, than if the Scripture were turned into the vulgar speech, that the poor people might read and see the simple plain Word of God. He perceived that it was not possible to establish the lay people in any truth, except the Scriptures were so plainly laid before their eyes in their mother tongue that they might see the meaning of the text; for else, whatsoever truth should be taught them, the enemies of the truth would quench it, either with reasons of sophistry, and traditions of their own making, founded without all ground of Scripture; or else juggling with the text, expounding it in such a sense as it were impossible to gather of the text, if the right meaning thereof were seen.

Master Tyndale considered this only, or most chiefly, to be the cause of all mischief in the Church, that the Scriptures of God were hidden from the people's eyes; for so long the abominable doings and idolatries maintained by the pharisaical clergy could not be espied; and therefore all their labor was with might and main to keep it down, so that either it should not be read at all, or if it were, they would darken the right sense with the mist of their sophistry, and so entangle those who rebuked or despised their abominations; wresting the Scripture unto their own purpose, contrary unto the meaning of the text, they would so delude the unlearned lay people, that though thou felt in thy heart, and were sure that all were false that they said, yet couldst thou not solve their subtle riddles.

For these and such other considerations this good man was stirred up of God to translate the Scripture into his mother tongue, for the profit of the simple people of his country; first setting in hand with the New Testament, which came forth in print about A.D. 1525. Cuthbert Tonstal, bishop of London, with Sir Thomas More, being sore aggrieved, despised how to destroy that false erroneous translation, as they called it.

It happened that one Augustine Packington, a mercer, was then at Antwerp, where the bishop was. This man favored Tyndale, but showed the contrary unto the bishop. The bishop, being desirous to bring his purpose to pass, communed how that he would gladly buy the New Testaments. Packington hearing him say so, said, "My lord! I can do more in this matter than most merchants that be here, if it be your pleasure; for I know the Dutchmen and strangers that have brought them of Tyndale, and have them here to sell; so that if it be your lordship's pleasure, I must disburse money to pay for them, or else I cannot have them: and so I will assure you to have every book of them that is printed and unsold." The bishop, thinking he had God "by the toe," said, "Do your diligence, gentle Master Packington! get them for me, and I will pay whatsoever they cost; for I intend to burn and destroy them all at Paul's Cross." This Augustine Packington went unto William Tyndale, and declared the whole matter, and so, upon compact made between them, the bishop of London had the books, Packington had the thanks, and Tyndale had the money.

After this, Tyndale corrected the same New Testaments again, and caused them to be newly imprinted, so that they came thick and threefold over into England. When the bishop perceived that, he sent for Packington, and said to him, "How cometh this, that there are so many New Testaments abroad? You promised me that you would buy them all." Then answered Packington, "Surely, I bought all that were to be had, but I perceive they have printed more since. I see it will never be better so long as they have letters and stamps: wherefore you were best to buy the stamps too, and so you shall be sure," at which answer the bishop smiled, and so the matter ended.

In short space after, it fortuned that George Constantine was apprehended by Sir Thomas More, who was then chancellor of England, as suspected of certain heresies. Master More asked of him, saying, "Constantine! I would have thee be plain with me in one thing that I will ask; and I promise thee I will show thee favor in all other things whereof thou art accused. There is beyond the sea, Tyndale, Joye, and a great many of you: I know they cannot live without help. There are some that succor them with money; and thou, being one of them, hadst thy part thereof, and therefore knowest whence it came. I pray thee, tell me, who be they that help them thus?" "My lord," quoth Constantine, "I will tell you truly: it is the bishop of London that hath helped us, for he hath bestowed among us a great deal of money upon New Testaments to burn them; and that hath been, and yet is, our only succor and comfort." "Now by my troth," quoth More, "I think even the same; for so much I told the bishop before he went about it."

After that, Master Tyndale took in hand to translate the Old Testament, finishing the five books of Moses, with sundry most learned and godly prologues most worthy to be read and read again by all good Christians. These books being sent over into England, it cannot be spoken what a door of light they opened to the eyes of the whole English nation, which before were shut up in darkness.

At his first departing out of the realm he took his journey into Germany, where he had conference with Luther and other learned men; after he had continued there a certain season he came down into the Netherlands, and had his most abiding in the town of Antwerp.

The godly books of Tyndale, and especially the New Testament of his translation, after that they began to come into men's hands, and to spread abroad, wrought great and singular profit to the godly; but the ungodly (envying and disdaining that the people should be anything wiser than they and, fearing lest by the shining beams of truth, their works of darkness should be discerned) began to sir with no small ado.

At what time Tyndale had translated Deuteronomy, minding to print the same at Hamburg, he sailed thitherward; upon the coast of Holland he suffered shipwreck, by which he lost all his books, writings, and copies, his money and his time, and so was compelled to begin all again. He came in another ship to Hamburg, where, at his appointment, Master Coverdale tarried for him, and helped him in the translating of the whole five books of Moses, from Easter until December, in the house of a worshipful widow, Mistress Margaret Van Emmerson, A.D. 1529; a great sweating sickness being at the same time in the town. So, having dispatched his business at Hamburg, he returned to Antwerp.

When God's will was, that the New Testament in the common tongue should come abroad, Tyndale, the translator thereof, added to the latter end a certain epistle, wherein he desired them that were learned to amend, if ought were found amiss. Wherefore if there had been any such default deserving correction, it had been the part of courtesy and gentleness, for men of knowledge and judgment to have showed their learning therein, and to have redressed what was to be amended. But the clergy, not willing to have that book prosper, cried out upon it, that there were a thousand heresies in it, and that it was not to be corrected, but utterly to be suppressed. Some said it was not possible to translate the Scriptures into English; some that it was not lawful for the lay people to have it in their mother tongue; some, that it would make them all heretics. And to the intent to induce the temporal rulers unto their purpose, they said it would make the people to rebel against the king.

All this Tyndale himself, in his prologue before the first book of Moses, declareth; showing further what great pains were taken in examining that translation, and comparing it with their own imaginations, that with less labor, he supposeth, they might have translated a great part of the Bible; showing moreover that they scanned and examined every title and point in such sort, and so narrowly, that there was not one therein, but if it lacked a prick over his head, they did note it, and numbered it unto the ignorant people for a heresy.

So great were then the froward devices of the English clergy (who should have been the guides of light unto the people), to drive the people from the knowledge of the Scripture, which neither they would translate themselves, nor yet abide it to be translated of others; to the intent (as Tyndale saith) that the world being kept still in darkness, they might sit in the consciences of the people through vain superstition and false doctrine, to satisfy their ambition, and insatiable covetousness, and to exalt their own honor above king and emperor.

The bishops and prelates never rested before they had brought the king to their consent; by reason whereof, a proclamation in all haste was devised and set forth under public authority, that the Testament of Tyndale's translation was inhibited-which was about A.D. 1537. And not content herewith, they proceeded further, how to entangle him in their nets, and to bereave him of his life; which how they brought to pass, now it remaineth to be declared.

In the registers of London it appeareth manifest how that the bishops and Sir Thomas More having before them such as had been at Antwerp, most studiously would search and examine all things belonging to Tyndale, where and with whom he hosted, whereabouts stood the house, what was his stature, in what apparel he went, what resort he had; all which things when they had diligently learned then began they to work their feats.

William Tyndale, being in the town of Antwerp, had been lodged about one whole year in the house of Thomas Pointz, an Englishman, who kept a house of English merchants. Came thither one out of England, whose name was Henry Philips, his father being customer of Poole, a comely fellow, like as he had been a gentleman having a servant with him: but wherefore he came, or for what purpose he was sent thither, no man could tell.

Master Tyndale divers times was desired forth to dinner and support amongst merchants; by means whereof this Henry Philips became acquainted with him, so that within short space Master Tyndale had a great confidence in him, and brought him to his lodging, to the house of Thomas Pointz; and had him also once or twice with him to dinner and supper, and further entered such friendship with him, that through his procurement he lay in the same house of the said Pointz; to whom he showed moreover his books, and other secrets of his study, so little did Tyndale then mistrust this traitor.

But Pointz, having no great confidence in the fellow, asked Master Tyndale how he came acquainted with this Philips. Master Tyndale answered, that he was an honest man, handsomely learned, and very conformable. Pointz, perceiving that he bare such favor to him, said no more, thinking that he was brought acquainted with him by some friend of his. The said Philips, being in the town three or four days, upon a time desired Pointz to walk with him forth of the town to show him the commodities thereof, and in walking together without the town, had communication of divers things, and some of the king's affairs; by which talk Pointz as yet suspected nothing. But after, when the time was past, Pointz perceived this to be the mind of Philips, to feel whether the said Pointz might, for lucre of money, help him to his purpose, for he perceived before that Philips was monied, and would that Pointz should think no less. For he had desired Pointz before to help him to divers things; and such things as he named, he required might be of the best, "for," said he, "I have money enough."

Philips went from Antwerp to the court of Brussels, which is from thence twenty-four English miles, whence he brought with him to Antwerp, the procurator-general, who is the emperor's attorney, with certain other officers.

Within three or four days, Pointz went forth to the town of Barois, being eighteen English miles from Antwerp, where he had business to do for the space of a month or six weeks; and in the time of his absence Henry Philips came again to Antwerp, to the house of Pointz, and coming in, spake with his wife, asking whether Master Tyndale were within. Then went he forth again and set the officers whom he had brought with him from Brussels, in the street, and about the door. About noon he came again, and went to Master Tyndale, and desired him to lend him forty shillings; "for," said he, "I lost my purse this morning, coming over at the passage between this and Mechlin." So Master Tyndale took him forty shillings, which was easy to be had of him, if he had it; for in the wily subtleties of this world he was simple and inexpert. Then said Philips, "Master Tyndale! you shall be my guest here this day." "No," said Master Tyndale, "I go forth this day to dinner, and you shall go with me, and be my guest, where you shall be welcome."

So when it was dinner time, Master Tyndale went forth with Philips, and at the going forth of Pointz's house, was a long narrow entry, so that two could not go in front. Master Tyndale would have put Philips before him, but Philips would in no wise, but put Master Tyndale before, for that he pretended to show great humanity. So Master Tyndale, being a man of no great stature, went before, and Philips, a tall, comely person, followed behind him; who had set officers on either side of the door upon two seats, who might see who came in the entry. Philips pointed with his finger over Master Tyndale's head down to him, that the officers might see that it was he whom they should take. The officers afterwards told Pointz, when they had laid him in prison, that they pitied to see his simplicity. They brought him to the emperor's attorney, where he dined. Then came the procurator-general to the house of Pointz, and sent away all that was there of Master Tyndale's, as well his books as other things; and from thence Tyndale was had to the castle of Vilvorde, eighteen English miles from Antwerp.

Master Tyndale, remaining in prison, was proffered an advocate and a procurator; the which he refused, saying that he would make answer for himself. He had so preached to them who had him in charge, and such as was there conversant with him in the Castle that they reported of him, that if he were not a good Christian man, they knew not whom they might take to be one.

At last, after much reasoning, when no reason would serve, although he deserved no death, he was condemned by virtue of the emperor's decree, made in the assembly at Augsburg. Brought forth to the place of execution, he was tied to the stake, strangled by the hangman, and afterwards consumed with fire, at the town of Vilvorde, A.D. 1536; crying at the stake with a fervent zeal, and a loud voice, "Lord! open the king of England's eyes."

Such was the power of his doctrine, and the sincerity of his life, that during the time of his imprisonment (which endured a year and a half), he converted, it is said, his keeper, the keeper's daughter, and others of his household.

As touching his translation of the New Testament, because his enemies did so much carp at it, pretending it to be full of heresies, he wrote to John Frith, as followeth, "I call God to record against the day we shall appear before our Lord Jesus, that I never altered one syllable of God's Word against my conscience, nor would do this day, if all that is in earth, whether it be honor, pleasure, or riches, might be given me."

CHAPTER XIV

An Account of the Persecutions in Great Britain and Ireland, Prior to the Reign of Queen Mary I

Gildas, the most ancient British writer extant, who lived about the time that the Saxons left the island of Great Britain, has drawn a most shocking instance of the barbarity of those people.

The Saxons, on their arrival, being heathens like the Scots and Picts, destroyed the churches and murdered the clergy wherever they came: but they could not destroy Christianity, for those who would not submit to the Saxon yoke, went and resided beyond the Severn. Neither have we the names of those Christian sufferers transmitted to us, especially those of the clergy.

The most dreadful instance of barbarity under the Saxon government, was the massacre of the monks of Bangor, A.D. 586. These monks were in all respects different from those men who bear the same name at present.

In the eighth century, the Danes, a roving crew of barbarians, landed in different parts of Britain, both in England and Scotland.

At first they were repulsed, but in A.D. 857, a party of them landed somewhere near Southampton, and not only robbed the people but burned down the churches, and murdered the clergy.

In A.D. 868, these barbarians penetrated into the center of England, and took up their quarters at Nottingham; but the English, under their king, Ethelred, drove them from their posts, and obligted them to retire to Northumberland.

In 870, another body of these barbarians landed at Norfolk, and engaged in battle with the English at Hertford. Victory declared in favor of the pagans, who took Edmund, king of the East Angles, prisoner, and after treating him with a thousand indignities, transfixed his body with arrows, and then beheaded him.

In Fifeshire, in Scotland, they burned many of the churches, and among the rest that belonging to the Culdees, at St. Andrews. The piety of these men made them objects of abhorrence to the Danes, who, wherever they went singled out the Christian priests for destruction, of whom no less than two hundred were massacred in Scotland.

It was much the same in that part of Ireland now called Leinster, there the Danes murdered and burned the priests alive in their own churches; they carried destruction along with them wherever they went, sparing neither age nor sex, but the clergy were the most obnoxious to them, because they ridiculed their idolatry, and persuaded their people to have nothing to do with them.

In the reign of Edward III the Church of England was extremely corrupted with errors and superstition; and the light of the Gospel of Christ was greatly eclipsed and darkened with human inventions, burthensome ceremonies and gross idolatry.

The followers of Wickliffe, then called Lollards, were become extremely numerous, and the clergy were so vexed to see them increase; whatever power or influence they might have to molest them in an underhand manner, they had no authority by law to put them to death. However, the clergy embraced the favorable opportunity, and prevailed upon the king to suffer a bill to be brought into parliament, by which all Lollards who remained obstinate, should be delivered over to the secular power, and burnt as heretics. This act was the first in Britain for the burning of people for their religious sentiments; it passed in the year 1401, and was soon after put into execution.

The first person who suffered in consequence of this cruel act was William Santree, or Sawtree, a priest, who was burnt to death in Smithfield.

Soon after this, Sir John Oldcastle, Lord Cobham, in consequence of his attachment to the doctrines of Wickliffe, was accused of heresy, and being condemned to be hanged and burnt, was accordingly executed in Lincoln's Inn Fields, A.D. 1419. In his written defense Lord Cobham said:

"As for images, I understand that they be not of belief, but that they were ordained since the belief of Christ was given by sufferance of the Church, to represent and bring to mind the passion of our Lord Jesus Christ, and martyrdom and good living of other saints: and that whoso it be, that doth the worship to dead images that is due to God, or putteth such hope or trust in help of them, as he should do to God, or hath affection in one more than in another, he doth in that, the greatest sin of idol worship.

"Also I suppose this fully, that every man in this earth is a pilgrim toward bliss, or toward pain; and that he that knoweth not, we will not know, we keep the holy commandments of God in his living here (albeit that he go on pilgrimages to all the world, and he die so), he shall be damned: he that knoweth the holy commandments of God, and keepeth them to his end, he shall be saved, though he never in his life go on pilgrimage, as men now use, to Canterbury, or to Rome, or to any other place."

Upon the day appointed, Lord Cobham was brought out of the Tower with his arms bound behind him, having a very cheerful countenance. Then was he laid upon a hurdle, as though he had been a most heinous traitor to the crown, and so drawn forth into St. Giles's field. As he was come to the place of execution, and was taken from the hurdle, he fell down devoutly upon his knees, desiring Almighty God to forgive his enemies. Then stood he up and beheld the multitude, exhorting them in most godly manner to follow the laws of God written in the Scriptures, and to beware of such teachers as they see contrary to Christ in their conversation and living. Then was he hanged up by the middle in chains of iron, and so consumed alive in the fire, praising the name of God, so long as his life lasted; the people, there present, showing great dolor. And this was done A.D. 1418.

How the priests that time fared, blasphemed, and accursed, requiring the people not to pray for him, but to judge him damned in hell, for that he departed not in the obedience of their pope, it were too long to write.

Thus resteth this valiant Christian knight, Sir John Oldcastle, under the altar of God, which is Jesus Christ, among that godly company, who, in the kingdom of patience, suffered great tribulation with the death of their bodies, for His faithful word and testimony.

In August, 1473, one Thomas Granter was apprehended in London; he was accused of professing the doctrines of Wickliffe, for which he was condemned as an obstinate heretic. This pious man, being brought to the sheriff's house, on the morning of the day appointed for his execution, desired a little refreshment, and having ate some, he said to the people present, "I eat now a very good meal, for I have a strange conflict to engage with before I go to supper"; and having eaten, he returned thanks to God for the bounties of His all-gracious providence, requesting that he might be instantly led to the place of execution, to bear testimony to the truth of those principles which he had professed. Accordingly he was chained to a stake on Tower-hill, where he was burnt alive, professing the truth with his last breath.

In the year 1499, one Badram, a pious man, was brought before the bishop of Norwich, having been accused by some of the priests, with holding the doctrines of Wickliffe. He confessed he did believe everything that was objected against him. For this, he was condemned as an obstinate heretic, and a warrant was granted for his execution; accordingly he was brought to the stake at Norwich, where he suffered with great constancy.

In 1506, one William Tilfrey, a pious man, was burnt alive at Amersham, in a close called Stoneyprat, and at the same time, his daughter, Joan Clarke, a married women, was obliged to light the fagots that were to burn her father.

This year also one Father Roberts, a priest, was convicted of being a Lollard before the bishop of Lincoln, and burnt alive at Buckingham.

In 1507 one Thomas Norris was burnt alive for the testimony of the truth of the Gospel, at Norwich. This man was a poor, inoffensive, harmless person, but his parish priest conversing with him one day, conjectured he was a Lollard. In consequence of this supposition he gave information to the bishop, and Norris was apprehended.

In 1508, one Lawrence Guale, who had been kept in prison two years, was burnt alive at Salisbury, for denying the real presence in the Sacrament. It appeared that this man kept a shop in Salisbury, and entertained some Lollards in his house; for which he was informed against to the bishop; but he abode by his first testimony, and was condemned to suffer as a heretic.

A pious woman was burnt at Chippen Sudburne, by order of the chancellor, Dr. Whittenham. After she had been consumed in the flames, and the people were returning home, a bull broke loose from a butcher and singling out the chancellor from all the rest of the company, he gored him through the body, and on his horns carried his entrails. This was seen by all the people, and it is remarkable that the animal did not meddle with any other person whatever.

October 18, 1511, William Succling and John Bannister, who had formerly recanted, returned again to the profession of the faith, and were burnt alive in Smithfield.

In the year 1517, one John Brown (who had recanted before in the reign of Henry VII and borne a fagot round St. Paul's,) was condemned by Dr. Wonhaman, archbishop of Canterbury, and burnt alive at Ashford. Before he was chained to the stake, the archbishop Wonhaman, and Yester, bishop of Rochester, caused his feet to be burnt in a fire until all the flesh came off, even to the bones. This was done in order to make him again recant, but he persisted in his attachment to the truth to the last.

Much about this time one Richard Hunn, a merchant tailor of the city of London, was apprehended, having refused to pay the priest his fees for the funeral of a child, and being conveyed to the Lollards' Tower, in the palace of Lambeth, was there privately murdered by some of the servants of the archbishop.

September 24, 1518, John Stilincen, who had before recanted, was apprehended, brought before Richard Fitz-James, bishop of London, and on the twenty-fifth of October was condemned as a heretic. He was chained to the stake in Smithfield amidst a vast crowd of spectators, and sealed his testimony to the truth with his blood. He declared that he was a Lollard, and that he had always believed the opinions of Wickliffe; and although he had been weak enough to recant his opinions, yet he was now willing to convince the world that he was ready to die for the truth.

In the year 1519, Thomas Mann was burnt in London, as was one Robert Celin, a plain, honest man for speaking against image worship and pilgrimages.

Much about this time, was executed in Smithfield, in London, James Brewster, a native of Colchester. His sentiments were the same as the rest of the Lollards, or those who followed the doctrines of Wickliffe; but notwithstanding the innocence of his life, and the regularity of his manners, he was obliged to submit to papal revenge.

During this year, one Christopher, a shoemaker, was burnt alive at Newbury, in Berkshire, for denying those popish articles which we have already mentioned. This man had gotten some books in English, which were sufficient to render him obnoxious to the Romish clergy.

Robert Silks, who had been condemned in the bishop's court as a heretic, made his escape out of prison, but was taken two years afterward, and brought back to Coventry, where he was burnt alive. The sheriffs always seized the goods of the martyrs for their own use, so that their wives and children were left to starve.

In 1532, Thomas Harding, who with his wife, had been accused of heresy, was brought before the bishop of Lincoln, and condemned for denying the real presence in the Sacrament. He was then chained to a stake, erected for the purpose, at Chesham in the Pell, near Botely; and when they had set fire to the fagots, one of the spectators dashed out his brains with a billet. The priests told the people that whoever brought fagots to burn heretics would have an indulgence to commit sins for forty days.

During the latter end of this year, Worham, archbishop of Canterbury, apprehended one Hitten, a priest at Maidstone; and after he had been long tortured in prison, and several times examined by the archbishop, and Fisher, bishop of Rochester, he was condemned as a heretic, and burnt alive before the door of his own parish church.

Thomas Bilney, professor of civil law at Cambridge, was brought before the bishop of London, and several other bishops, in the Chapter house, Westminster, and being several times threatened with the stake and flames, he was weak enough to recant; but he repented severely afterward.

For this he was brought before the bishop a second time, and condemned to death. Before he went to the stake he confessed his adherence to those opinions which Luther held; and, when at it, he smiled, and said, "I have had many storms in this world, but now my vessel will soon be on shore in heaven."

He stood unmoved in the flames, crying out, "Jesus, I believe"; and these were the last words he was heard to utter.

A few weeks after Bilney had suffered, Richard Byfield was cast into prison, and endured some whipping, for his adherence to the doctrines of Luther: this Mr. Byfield had been some time a monk, at Barnes, in Surrey, but was converted by reading Tyndale's version of the New Testament. The sufferings this man underwent for the truth were so great that it would require a volume to contain them. Sometimes he was shut up in a dungeon, where he was almost suffocated by the offensive and horrid smell of filth and stagnant water. At other times he was tied up by the arms, until almost all his joints were dislocated. He was whipped at the post several times, until scarcely any flesh was left on his back; and all this was done to make him recant. He was then taken to the Lollard's Tower in Lambeth palace, where he was chained by the neck to the wall, and once every day beaten in the most cruel manner by the archbishop's servants. At last he was condemned, degraded, and burnt in Smithfield.

The next person that suffered was John Tewkesbury. This was a plain, simple man, who had been guilty of no other offence against what was called the holy Mother Church, than that of reading Tyndale's translation of the New Testament. At first he was weak enough to adjure, but afterward repented, and acknowledged the truth. For this he was brought before the bishop of London, who condemned him as an obstinate heretic. He suffered greatly during the time of his imprisonment, so that when they brought him out to execution, he was almost dead. He was conducted to the stake in Smithfield, where he was burned, declaring his utter abhorrence of popery, and professing a firm belief that his cause was just in the sight of God.

The next person that suffered in this reign was James Baynham, a reputable citizen in London, who had married the widow of a gentleman in the Temple. When chained to the stake he embraced the fagots, and said, "Oh, ye papists, behold! ye look for miracles; here now may you see a miracle; for in this fire I feel no more pain than if I were in bed; for it is as sweet to me as a bed of roses." Thus he resigned his soul into the hands of his Redeemer.

Soon after the death of this martyr, one Traxnal, an inoffensive countryman, was burned alive at Bradford in Wiltshire, because he would not acknowledge the real presence in the Sacrament, nor own the papal supremacy over the consciences of men.

In the year 1533, John Frith, a noted martyr, died for the truth. When brought to the stake in Smithfield, he embraced the fagots, and exhorted a young man named Andrew Hewit, who suffered with him, to trust his soul to that God who had redeemed it. Both these sufferers endured much torment, for the wind blew the flames away from them, so that they were above two hours in agony before they expired.

In the year 1538, one Collins, a madman, suffered death with his dog in Smithfield. The circumstances were as follows: Collins happened to be in church when the priest elevated the host; and Collins, in derision of the sacrifice of the Mass, lifted up his dog above his head. For this crime Collins, who ought to have been sent to a madhouse, or whipped at the cart's tail, was brought before the bishop of London; and although he was really mad, yet such was the force of popish power, such the corruption in Church and state, that the poor madman, and his dog, were both carried to the stake in Smithfield, where they were burned to ashes, amidst a vast crowd of spectators.

There were some other persons who suffered the same year, of whom we shall take notice in the order they lie before us.

One Cowbridge suffered at Oxford; and although he was reputed to be a madman, yet he showed great signs of piety when he was fastened to the stake, and after the flames were kindled around him.

About the same time one Purderve was put to death for saying privately to a priest, after he had drunk the wine, "He blessed the hungry people with the empty chalice."

At the same time was condemned William Letton, a monk of great age, in the county of Suffolk, who was burned at Norwich for speaking against an idol that was carried in procession; and for asserting, that the Sacrament should be administered in both kinds.

Sometime before the burning of these men, Nicholas Peke was executed at Norwich; and when the fire was lighted, he was so scorched that he was as black as pitch. Dr. Reading standing before him, with Dr. Hearne and Dr. Spragwell, having a long white want in his hand, struck him upon the right shoulder, and said, "Peke, recant, and believe in the Sacrament." To this he answered, "I despise thee and it also;" and with great violence he spit blood, occasioned by the anguish of his sufferings. Dr. Reading granted forty days' indulgence for the sufferer, in order that he might recant his opinions. But he persisted in his adherence to the truth, without paying any regard to the malice of his enemies; and he was burned alive, rejoicing that Christ had counted him worthy to suffer for His name's sake.

On July 28, 1540, or 1541, (for the chronology differs) Thomas Cromwell, earl of Essex, was brought to a scaffold on Tower-hill, where he was executed with some striking instances of cruelty. He made a short speech to the people, and then meekly resigned himself to the axe.

It is, we think, with great propriety, that this nobleman is ranked among the martyrs; for although the accusations preferred against him, did not relate to anything in religion, yet had it not been for his zeal to demolish popery, he might have to the last retained the king's favor. To this may be added, that the papists plotted his destruction, for he did more towards promoting the Reformation, than any man in that age, except the good Dr. Cranmer.

Soon after the execution of Cromwell, Dr. Cuthbert Barnes, Thomas Garnet, and William Jerome, were brought before the ecclesiastical court of the bishop of London, and accused of heresy.

Being before the bishop of London, Dr. Barnes was asked whether the saints prayed for us? To this he answered, that "he would leave that to God; but (said he) I will pray for you."

On the thirteenth of July, 1541, these men were brought from the Tower to Smithfield, where they were all chained to one stake; and there suffered death with a constancy that nothing less than a firm faith in Jesus Christ could inspire.

One Thomas Sommers, an honest merchant, with three others, was thrown into prison, for reading some of Luther's books, and they were condemned to carry those books to a fire in Cheapside; there they were to throw them in the flames; but Sommers threw his over, for which he was sent back to the Tower, where he was stoned to death.

Dreadful persecutions were at this time carried on at Lincoln, under Dr. Longland, the bishop of that diocese. At Buckingham, Thomas Bainard, and James Moreton, the one for reading the Lord's Prayer in English, and the other for reading St. James' Epistles ion English, were both condemned and burnt alive.

Anthony Parsons, a priest, together with two others, was sent to Windsor, to be examined concerning heresy; and several articles were tendered to them to subscribe, which they refused. This was carried on by the bishop of Salisbury, who was the most violent persecutor of any in that age, except Bonner. When they were brought to the stake, Parsons asked for some drink, which being brought him, he drank to his fellow-sufferers, saying, "Be merry, my brethren, and lift up your hearts to God; for after this sharp breakfast I trust we shall have a good dinner in the Kingdom of Christ, our Lord and Redeemer." At these words Eastwood, one of the sufferers, lifteed up his eyes and hands to heaven, desiring the Lord above to receive his spirit. Parsons pulled the straw near to him, and then said to the spectators, "This is God's armor, and now I am a Christian soldier prepared for battle: I look for no mercy but through the merits of Christ;

He is my only Savior, in Him do I trust for salvation;" and soon after the fires were lighted, which burned their bodies, but could not hurt their precious and immortal souls. Their constancy triumphed over cruelty, and their sufferings will be held in everlasting remembrance.

Thus were Christ's people betrayed every way, and their lives bought and sold. For, in the said parliament, the king made this most blasphemous and cruel act, to be a law forever: that whatsoever they were that should read the Scriptures in the mother-tongue (which was then called "Wickliffe's learning"), they should forfeit land, cattle, body, life, and goods, from their heirs for ever, and so be condemned for heretics to God, enemies to the crown, and most arrant traitors to the land.

CHAPTER XV

An Account of the Persecutions in Scotland During the Reign of King Henry VIII

Like as there was no place, either of Germany, Italy, or France, wherein there were not some branches sprung out of that most fruitful root of Luther; so likewise was not this isle of Britain without his fruit and branches. Amongst whom was Patrick Hamilton, a Scotchman born of high and noble stock, and of the king's blood, of excellent towardness, twenty-three years of age, called abbot of Ferne. Coming out of his country with three companions to seek godly learning, he went to the University of Marburg in Germany, which university was then newly erected by Philip, Landgrave of Hesse.

During his residence here, he became intimately acquainted with those eminent lights of the Gospel, Martin Luther and Philip Melancthon; from whose writings and doctrines he strongly attached himself to the Protestant religion.

The archbishop of St. Andrews (who was a rigid papist) learning of Mr. Hamilton's proceedings, caused him to be seized, and being brought before him, after a short examination relative to his religious principles, he committed him a prisoner to the castle, at the same time ordering him to be confined in the most loathsome part of the prison.

The next morning Mr. Hamilton was brought before the bishop, and several others, for examination, when the principal articles exhibited against him were, his publicly disapproving of pilgrimages, purgatory, prayers to saints, for the dead, etc.

These articles Mr. Hamilton acknowledged to be true, in consequence of which he was immediately condemned to be burnt; and that his condemnation might have the greater authority, they caused it to be subscribed by all those of any note who were present, and to make the number as considerable as possible, even admitted the subscription of boys who were sons of the nobility.

So anxious was this bigoted and persecuting prelate for the destruction of Mr. Hamilton, that he ordered his sentence to be put in execution on the afternoon of the very day it was pronounced. He was accordingly led to the place appointed for the horrid tragedy, and was attended by a prodigious number of spectators. The greatest part of the multitude would not believe it was intended he should be put to death, but that it was only done to frighten him, and thereby bring him over to embrace the principles of the Romish religion.

When he arrived at the stake, he kneeled down, and, for some time prayed with great fervency. After this he was fastened to the stake, and the fagots placed round him. A quantity of gunpowder having been placed under his arms was first set on fire which scorched his left hand and one side of his face, but did no material injury, neither did it communicate with the fagots. In consequence of this, more powder and combustible matter were brought, which being set on fire took effect, and the fagots being kindled, he called out, with an audible voice: "Lord Jesus, receive my spirit! How long shall darkness overwhelm this realm? And how long wilt Thou suffer the tyranny of these men?"

The fire burning slow put him to great torment; but he bore it with Christian magnanimity. What gave him the greatest pain was, the clamor of some wicked men set on by the friars, who frequently cried, "Turn, thou heretic; call upon our Lady; say, Salve Regina, etc." To whom he replied, "Depart from me, and trouble me not, ye messengers of Satan." One Campbell, a friar, who was the ringleader, still continuing to interrupt him by opprobrious language; he said to him, "Wicked man, God forgive thee." After which, being prevented from further speech by the violence of the smoke, and the rapidity of the flames, he resigned up his soul into the hands of Him who gave it.

It was not long after the martyrdom of this blessed man of God, Master George Wishart, who was put to death by David Beaton, the bloody archbishop and cardinal of Scotland, A.D. 1546, the first day of March, that the said David Beaton, by the just revenge of God's mighty judgment, was slain within his own castle of St. Andrews, by the hands of one Leslie and other gentlemen, who, by the Lord stirred up, brake in suddenly upon him, and in his bed murdered him the said year, the last day of May, crying out, "Alas! alas! slay me not! I am a priest!" And so, like a butcher he lived, and like a butcher he died, and lay seven months and more unburied, and at last like a carrion was buried in a dunghill.

CHAPTER XVI

Persecutions in England

During the Reign of Queen Mary

The premature death of that celebrated young monarch, Edward VI, occasioned the most extraordinary and wonderful occurrences, which had ever existed from the times of our blessed Lord and Savior's incarnation in human shape. This melancholy event became speedily a subject of general regret. The succession to the British throne was soon made a matter of contention; and the scenes which ensued were a demonstration of the serious affliction in which the kingdom was involved. As his loss to the nation was more and more unfolded, the remembrance of his government was more and more the basis of grateful recollection. The very awful prospect, which was soon presented to the friends of Edward's administration, under the direction of his counselors and servants, was a contemplation which the reflecting mind was compelled to regard with most alarming apprehensions. The rapid approaches which were made towards a total reversion of the proceedings of the young king's reign, denoted the advances which were thereby represented to an entire resolution in the management of public affairs both in Church and state.

Alarmed for the condition in which the kingdom was likely to be involved by the king's death, an endeavor to prevent the consequences, which were but too plainly foreseen, was productive of the most serious and fatal effects. The king, in his long and lingering affliction, was induced to make a will, by which he bequeathed the English crown to Lady Jane, the daughter of the duke of Suffolk, who had been married to Lord Guilford, the son of the duke of Northumberland, and was the granddaughter of the second sister of King Henry, by Charles, duke of Suffolk. By this will, the succession of Mary and Elizabeth, his two sisters, was entirely superseded, from an apprehension of the returning system of popery; and the king's council, with the chief of the nobility, the lord-mayor of the city of London, and almost all the judges and the principal lawyers of the realm, subscribed their names to this regulation, as a sanction to the measure. Lord Chief Justice Hale, though a true Protestant and an upright judge, alone declined to unite his name in favor of the Lady Jane, because he had already signified his opinion that Mary was entitled to assume the reins of government. Others objected to Mary's being placed on the throne, on account of their fears that she might marry a foreigner, and thereby bring the crown into considerable danger. Her partiality to popery also left little doubt on the minds of any, that she would be induced to revive the dormant interests of the pope, and change the religion which had been used both in the days of her father, King Henry, and in those of her brother Edward: for in all his time she had manifested the greatest stubbornness and inflexibility of temper, as must be obvious from her letter to the lords of the council, whereby she put in her claim to the crown, on her brother's decease.

When this happened, the nobles, who had associated to prevent Mary's succession, and had been instrumental in promoting, and, perhaps, advising the measures of Edward, speedily proceeded to proclaim Lady Jane Gray, to be queen of England, in the city of London and various other populous cities of the realm. Though young, she possessed talents of a very superior nature, and her improvements under a most excellent tutor had given her many very great advantages.

Her reign was of only five days' continuance, for Mary, having succeeded by false promises in obtaining the crown, speedily commenced the execution of her avowed intention of extirpating and burning every Protestant. She was crowned at Westminster in the usual form, and her elevation was the signal for the commencement of the bloody persecution which followed.

Having obtained the sword of authority, she was not sparing in its exercise. The supporters of Lady Jane Gray were destined to feel its force. The duke of Northumberland was the first who experienced her savage resentment. Within a month after his confinement in the Tower, he was condemned, and brought to the scaffold, to suffer as a traitor. From his varied crimes, resulting out of a sordid and inordinate ambition, he died unpitied and unlamented.

The changes, which followed with rapidity, unequivocally declared that the queen was disaffected to the present state of religion. Dr. Poynet was displaced to make room for Gardiner to be bishop of Winchester, to whom she also gave the important office of lord-chancellor. Dr. Ridley was dismissed from the see of London, and Bonne introduced. J. Story was put out of the bishopric of Chichester, to admit Dr. Day. J. Hooper was sent prisoner to the Fleet, and Dr. Heath put into the see of Worcestor. Miles Coverdale was also excluded from Exeter, and Dr. Vesie placed in that diocese. Dr. Tonstall was also promoted to the see of Durham. These things being marked and perceived, great heaviness and discomfort grew more and more to all good men's hearts; but to the wicked great rejoicing. They that could dissemble took no great care how the matter went; but such, whose consciences were joined with the truth, perceived already coals to be kindled, which after should be the destruction of many a true Christian.

The Words and Behavior of the Lady Jane upon the Scaffold

The next victim was the amiable Lady Jane Gray, who, by her acceptance of the crown at the earnest solicitations of her friends, incurred the implacable resentment of the bloody Mary. When she first mounted the scaffold, she spoke to the specators in this manner: "Good people, I am come hither to die, and by a law I am condemned to the same. The fact against the queen's highness was unlawful, and the consenting thereunto by me: but, touching the procurement and desire thereof by me, or on my behalf, I do wash my hands thereof in innocence before God, and the face of you, good Christian people, this day:" and therewith she wrung her hands, wherein she had her book. Then said she, "I pray you all, good Christian people, to bear me witness, that I die a good Christian woman, and that I do look to be saved by no other mean, but only by the mercy of God in the blood of His only Son Jesus Christ: and I confess that when I did know the Word of God, I neglected the same, loved myself and the world, and therefore this plague and punishment is happily and worthily happened unto me for my sins; and yet I thank God, that of His goodness He hath thus given me a time and a respite to repent. And now, good people, while I am alive, I pray you assist me with your prayers." And then, kneeling down, she turned to Feckenham, saying, "Shall I say this Psalm?" and he said, "Yea." Then she said the Psalm of Miserere mei Deus, in English, in a most devout manner throughout to the end; and then she stood up, and gave her maid, Mrs. Ellen, her gloves and handkerchief, and her book to Mr. Bruges; and then she untied he gown, and the executioner pressed upon her to help her off with it: but she, desiring him to let her alone, turned towards her two gentlewomen, who helped her off therewith, and also with her frowes, paaft, and neckerchief, giving to her a fair handkerchief to put about her eyes.

Then the executioner kneeled down, and asked her forgiveness, whom she forgave most willingly. Then he desired her to stand upon the straw, which doing, she saw the block. Then she said, "I pray you, dispatch me quickly." Then she kneeled down, saying, "Will you take it off before I lay me down?" And the executioner said, "No, madam." Then she tied a handkerchief about her eyes, and feeling for the block, she said, "What shall I do? Where is it? Where is it?" One of the standers-by guiding her thereunto, she laid her head upon the block, and then stretched forth her body, and said, "Lord, into Thy hands I commend my spirit;" and so finished her life, in the year of our Lord 1554, the twelfth day of February, about the seventeenth year of her age.

Thus died Lady Jane; and on the same day Lord Guilford, her husband, one of the duke of Northumberland's sons, was likewise beheaded, two innocents in comparison with them that sat upon them. For they were both very young, and ignorantly accepted that which others had contrived, and by open proclamation consented to take from others, and give to them.

Touching the condemnation of this pious lady, it is to be noted that Judge Morgan, who gave sentence against her, soon after he had condemned her, fell mad, and in his raving cried out continually to have the Lady Jane taken away from him, and so he ended his life.

On the twenty-first day of the same month, Henry, duke of Suffolk, was beheaded on Tower-hill, the fourth day after his condemnation: about which time many gentlemen and yeomen were condemned, whereof some were executed at London, and some in the country. In the number of whom was Lord Thomas Gray, brother to the said duke, being apprehended not long after in North Wales, and executed for the same. Sir Nicholas Throgmorton, also, very narrowly escaped.

John Rogers, Vicar of St. Sepulchre's, and Reader of St. Paul's, London

John Rogers was educated at Cambridge, and was afterward many years chaplain to the merchant adventurers at Antwerp in Brabant. Here he met with the celebrated martyr William Tyndale, and Miles Coverdale, both voluntary exiles from their country for their aversion to popish superstition and idolatry. They were the instruments of his conversion; and he united with them in that translation of the Bible into English, entitled "The Translation of Thomas Matthew." From the Scriptures he knew that unlawful vows may be lawfully broken; hence he married, and removed to Wittenberg in Saxony, for the improvement of learning; and he there learned the Dutch language, and received the charge of a congregation, which he faithfully executed for many years. On King Edward's accession, he left Saxony to promote the work of reformation in England; and, after some time, Nicholas Ridley, then bishop of London, gave him a prebend in St. Paul's Cathedral, and the dean and chapter appointed him reader of the divinity lesson there. Here he continued until Queen Mary's succession to the throne, when the Gospel and true religion were banished, and the Antichrist of Rome, with his superstition and idolatry, introduced.

The circumstance of Mr. Rogers having preached at Paul's cross, after Queen Mary arrived at the Tower, has been already stated. He confirmed in his sermon the true doctrine taught in King Edward's time, and exhorted the people to beware of the pestilence of popery, idolatry, and superstition. For this he was called to account, but so ably defended himself that, for that time, he was dismissed. The proclamation of the queen, however, to prohibit true preaching, gave his enemies a new handle against him. Hence he was again summoned before the council, and commanded to keep his house. He did so, though he might have escaped; and though he perceived the state of the true religion to be desperate. Heknew he could not want a living in Germany; and he could not forget a wife and ten children, and to seek means to succor them. But all these things were insufficient to induce him to depart, and, when once called to answer in Christ's cause, he stoutly defended it, and hazarded his life for that purpose.

After long imprisonment in his own house, the restless Bonner, bishop of London, caused him to be committed to Newgate, there to be lodged among thieves and murderers.

After Mr. Rogers had been long and straitly imprisoned, and lodged in Newgate among thieves, often examined, and very uncharitably entreated, and at length unjustly and most cruelly condemned by Stephen Gardiner, bishop of Winchester, the fourth day of February, in the year of our Lord 1555, being Monday in the morning, he was suddenly warned by the keeper of Newgate's wife, to prepare himself for the fire; who, being then sound asleep, could scarce be awaked. At length being raised and awaked, and bid to make haste, then said he, "If it be so, I need not tie my points." And so was had down, first to bishop Bonner to be degraded: which being done, he craved of Bonner but one petition; and Bonner asked what that should be. Mr. Rogers replied that he might speak a few words with his wife before his burning, but that could not be obtained of him.

When the time came that he should be brought out of Newgate to Smithfield, the place of his execution, Mr. Woodroofe, one of the sheriffs, first came to Mr. Rogers, and asked him if he would revoke his abominable doctrine, and the evil opinion of the Sacrament of the altar. Mr. Rogers answered, "That which I have preached I will seal with my blood." Then Mr. Woodroofe said, "Thou art an heretic." "That shall be known," quoth Mr. Rogers, "at the Day of Judgment." "Well," said Mr. Woodroofe, "I will never pray for thee." "But I will pray for you," said Mr. Rogers; and so was brought the same day, the fourth of February, by the sheriffs, towards Smithfield, saying the Psalm Miserere by the way, all the people wonderfully rejoicing at his constancy; with great praises and thanks to God for the same. And there in the presence of Mr. Rochester, comptroller of the queen's household, Sir Richard Southwell, both the sheriffs, and a great number of people, he was burnt to ashes, washing his hands in the flame as he was burning. A little before his burning, his pardon was brought, if he would have recanted; but he utterly refused it. He was the first martyr of all the blessed company that suffered in Queen Mary's time that gave the first adventure upon the fire. His wife and children, being eleven in number, ten able to go, and one sucking at her breast, met him by the way, as he went towards Smithfield. This sorrowful sight of his own flesh and blood could nothing move him, but that he constantly and cheerfully took his death with wonderful patience, in the defense and quarrel of the Gospel of Christ."

Rev. John Bradford, and John Leaf, an Apprentice

Rev. John Bradford was born at Manchester, in Lancashire; he was a good Latin scholar, and afterward became a servant of Sir John Harrington, knight.

He continued several years in an honest and thriving way; but the Lord had elected him to a better function. Hence he departed from his master, quitting the Temple, at London, for the University of Cambridge, to learn, by God's law, how to further the building of the Lord's temple. In a few years after, the university gave him the degree of master of arts, and he became a fellow of Pembroke Hall.

Martin Bucer first urged him to preach, and when he modestly doubted his ability, Bucer was wont to reply, "If thou hast not fine wheat bread, yet give the poor people barley bread, or whatsoever else the Lord hath committed unto thee." Dr. Ridley, that worthy bishop of London, and glorious martyr of Christ, first called him to take the degree of a deacon and gave him a prebend in his cathedral Church of St. Paul.

In this preaching office Mr. Bradford diligently labored for the space of three years. Sharply he reproved sin, sweetly he preached Christ crucified, ably he disproved heresies and errors, earnestly he persuaded to godly life. After the death of blessed King Edward VI Mr. Bradford still continued diligent in preaching, until he was suppressed by Queen Mary.

An act now followed of the blackest ingratitude, and at which a pagan would blush. It has been recited, that a tumult was occasioned by Mr. Bourne's (then bishop of Bath) preaching at St. Paul's Cross; the indignation of the people placed his life in imminent danger; indeed a dagger was thrown at him. In this situation he entreated Mr. Bradford, who stood behind him. to speak in his place, and assuage the tumult. The people welcomed Mr. Bradford, and the latter afterward kept close to him, that his presence might prevent the populace from renewing their assaults.

The same Sunday in the afternoon, Mr. Bradford preached at Bow Church in Cheapside, and reproved the people sharply for their seditious misdemeanor. Notwithstanding this conduct, within three days after, he was sent for to the Tower of London, where the queen then was, to appear before the Council. There he was charged with this act of saving Mr. Bourne, which was called seditious, and they also objected against him for preaching. Thus he was committed, first to the Tower, then to other prisons, and, after his condemnation, to the Poultry Compter, where he preached twice a day continually, unless sickness hindered him. Such as his credit with the keeper of the king's Bench, that he permitted him in an evening to visit a poor, sick person near the steel-yard, upon his promise to return in time, and in this he never failed.

The night before he was sent to Newgate, he was troubled in his sleep by foreboding dreams, that on Monday after he should be burned in Smithfield. In the afternoon the keeper's wife came up and announced this dreadful news to him, but in him it excited only thankfulness to God. At night half a dozen friends came, with whom he spent all the evening in prayer and godly exercises.

When he was removed to Newgate, a weeping crowd accompanied him, and a rumor having been spread that he was to suffer at four the next morning, an immense multitude attended. At nine o'clock Mr. Bradford was brought into Smithfield. The cruelty of the sheriff deserves notice; for his brother-in-law, Roger Beswick, having taken him by the hand as he passed, Mr. Woodroffe, with his staff, cut his head open.

Mr. Bradford, being come to the place, fell flat on the ground, and putting off his clothes unto the shirt, he went to the stake, and there suffered with a young man of twenty years of age, whose name was John Leaf, an apprentice to Mr. Humphrey Gaudy, tallow-chandler, of Christ-church, London. Upon Friday before Palm Sunday, he was committed to the Compter in Bread-street, and afterward examined and condemned by the bloody bishop.

It is reported of him, that, when the bill of his confession was read unto him, instead of pen, he took a pin, and pricking his hand, sprinkled the blood upon the said bill, desiring the reader thereof to show the bishop that he had sealed the same bill with his blood already.

They both ended this mortal life, July 12, 1555, like two lambs, without any alteration of their countenances, hoping to obtain that prize they had long run for; to which may Almighty God conduct us all, through the merits of Christ our Savior!

We shall conclude this article with mentioning that Mr.

Sheriff Woodroffe, it is said, within half a year after, was struck on the right side with a palsy, and for the space of eight years after, (until his dying day,) he was unable to turn himself in his bed; thus he became at last a fearful object to behold.

The day after Mr. Bradford and John Leaf suffered in Smithfield William Minge, priest, died in prison at Maidstone. With as great constancy and boldness he yielded up his life in prison, as if it had pleased God to have called him to suffer by fire, as other godly men had done before at the stake, and as he himself was ready to do, had it pleased God to have called him to this trial.

Bishop Ridley and Bishop Latimer

These reverend prelates suffered October 17, 5555, at Oxford, on the same day Wolsey and Pygot perished at Ely. Pillars of the Church and accomplished ornaments of human nature, they were the admiration of the realm, amiably conspicuous in their lives, and glorious in their deaths.

Dr. Ridley was born in Northumberland, was first tauht grammar at Newcastle, and afterward removed to Cambridge, where his aptitude in education raised him gradually until he came to be the head of Pembroke College, where he received the title of Doctor of Divinity. Having returned from a trip to Paris, he was appointed chaplain by Henry VIII and bishop of Rochester, and was afterwards translated to the see of London in the time of Edward VI.

To his sermons the people resorted, swarming about him like bees, coveting the sweet flowers and wholesome juice of the fruitful doctrine, which he did not only preach, but showed the same by his life, as a glittering lanthorn to the eyes and senses of the blind, in such pure order that his very enemies could not reprove him in any one jot.

His tender treatment of Dr. Heath, who was a prisoner with him during one year, in Edward's reign, evidently proves that he had no Catholic cruelty in his disposition. In person he was erect and well proportioned; in temper forgiving; in self-mortification severe. His first duty in the morning was private prayer: he remained in his study until ten o'clock, and then attended the daily prayer used in his house. Dinner being done, he sat about an hour, conversing pleasantly, or playing at chess. His study next engaged his attention, unless business or visits occurred; about five o'clock prayers followed; and after he would recreate himself at chess for about an hour, then retire to his study until eleven o'clock, and pray on his knees as in the morning. In brief, he was a pattern of godliness and virtue, and such he endeavored to make men wherever he came.

His attentive kindness was displayed particularly to old Mrs.

Bonner, mother of Dr. Bonner, the cruel bishop of London. Dr. Ridley, when at his manor at Fulham, always invited her to his house, placed her at the head of his table, and treated her like his own mother; he did the same by Bonner's sister and other relatives; but when Dr. Ridley was under persecution, Bonner pursued a conduct diametrically opposite, and would have sacrificed Dr. Ridley's sister and her husband, Mr. George Shipside, had not Providence delivered him by the means of Dr. Heath, bishop of Worcester.

Dr. Ridley was first in part converted by reading Bertram's book on the Sacrament, and by his conferences with archbishop Cranmer and Peter Martyr.

When Edward VI was removed from the throne, and the bloody Mary succeeded, Bishop Ridley was immediately marked as an object of slaughter. He was first sent to the Tower, and afterward, at Oxford, was consigned to the common prison of Bocardo, with archbishop Cranmer and Mr. Latimer. Being separated from them, he was placed in the house of one Irish, where he remained until the day of his martyrdom, from 1554, until October 16, 1555.

It will easily be supposed that the conversations of these chiefs of the martyrs were elaborate, learned, and instructive. Such indeed they were, and equally beneficial to all their spiritual comforts. Bishop Ridley's letters to various Christian brethren in bonds in all parts, and his disputations with the mitred enemies of Christ, alike proved the clearness of his head and the integrity of his heart. In a letter to Mr. Grindal, (afterward archbishop of Canterbury,) he mentions with affection those who had preceded him in dying for the faith, and those who were expected to suffer; he regrets that popery is re-established in its full abomination, which he attributes to the wrath of God, made manifest in return for the lukewarmness of the clergy and the people in justly appreciating the blessed light of the Reformation.

This old practiced soldier of Christ, Master Hugh Latimer, was the son of one Hugh Latimer, of Thurkesson in the county of Leicester, a husbandman, of a good and wealthy estimation; where also he was born and brought up until he was four years of age, or thereabout: at which time his parents, having him as then left for their only son, with six daughters, seeing his ready, prompt, and sharp wit, purposed to train him up in erudition, and knowledge of good literature; wherein he so profited in his youth at the common schools of his own country, that at the age of fourteen years, he was sent to the University of Cambridge; where he entered into the study of the school divinity of that day, and was from principle a zealous observer of the Romish superstitions of the time. In his oration when he commenced bachelor of divinity, he inveighed against the reformer Melancthon, and openly declaimed against good Mr. Stafford, divinity lecturer in Cambridge.

Mr. Thomas Bilney, moved by a brotherly pity towards Mr.

Latimer, begged to wait upon him in his study, and to explain to him the groundwork of his (Mr. Bilney's) faith. This blessed interview effected his conversion: the persecutor of Christ became his zealous advocate, and before Dr. Stafford died he became reconciled to him.

Once converted, he became eager for the conversion of others, and commenced to be public preacher, and private instructor in the university. His sermons were so pointed against the absurdity of praying in the Latin tongue, and withholding the oracles of salvation from the people who were to be saved by belief in them, that he drew upon himself the pulpit animadversions of several of the resident friars and heads of houses, whom he subsequently silenced by his severe criticisms and eloquent arguments. This was at Christmas, 1529. At length Dr. West preached against Mr. Latimer at Barwell Abbey, and prohibited him from preaching again in the churches of the university, notwithstanding which, he continued during three years to advocate openly the cause of Christ, and even his enemies confessed the power of those talents he possessed. Mr. Bilney remained here some time with Mr. Latimer, and thus the place where they frequently walked together obtained the name of Heretics' Hill.

Mr. Latimer at this time traced out the innocence of a poor woman, accused by her husband of the murder of her child. Having preached before King Henry VIII at Windsor, he obtained the unfortunate mother's pardon. This, with many other benevolent acts, served only to excite the spleen of his adversaries. He was summoned before Cardinal Wolsey for heresy, but being a strenuous supporter of the king's supremacy, in opposition to the pope's, by favor of Lord Cromwell and Dr. Buts, (the king's physician,) he obtained the living of West Kingston, in Wiltshire. For his sermons here against purgatory, the immaculacy of the Virgin, and the worship of images, he was cited to appear before Warham, archbishop of Canterbury, and John, bishop of London. He was required to subscribe certain articles, expressive of his conformity to the accustomed usages; and there is reason to think, after repeated weekly examinations, that he did subscribe, as they did not seem to involve any important article of belief.

Guided by Providence, he escaped the subtle nets of his persecutors, and at length, through the powerful friends before mentioned, became bishop of Worcester, in which function he qualified or explained away most of the papal ceremonies he was for form's sake under the necessity of complying with. He continued in this active and dignified employment some years.

Beginning afresh to set forth his plow he labored in the Lord's harvest most fruitfully, discharging his talent as well in divers places of this realm, as before the king at the court. In the same place of the inward garden, which was before applied to lascivious and courtly pastimes, there he dispensed the fruitful Word of the glorious Gospel of Jesus Christ, preaching there before the king and his whole court, to the edification of many.

He remained a prisoner in the Tower until the coronation of Edward VI, when he was again called to the Lord's harvest in Stamford, and many other places: he also preached at London in the convocation house, and before the young king; indeed he lectured twice every Sunday, regardless of his great age (then above sixty-seven years,) and his weakness through a bruise received from the fall of a tree. Indefatigable in his private studies, he rose to them in winter and in summer at two o'clock in the morning.

By the strength of his own mind, or of some inward light from above, he had a prophetic view of what was to happen to the Church in Mary's reign, asserting that he was doomed to suffer for the truth, and that Winchester, then in the Tower, was preserved for that purpose. Soon after Queen Mary was proclaimed, a messenger was sent to summon Mr. Latimer to town, and there is reason to believe it was wished that he should make his escape.

Thus Master Latimer coming up to London, through Smithfield (where merrily he said that Smithfield had long groaned for him), was brought before the Council, where he patiently bore all the mocks and taunts given him by the scornful papists. He was cast into the Tower, where he, being assisted with the heavenly grace of Christ, sustained imprisonment a long time, notwithstanding the cruel and unmerciful handling of the lordly papists, which thought then their kingdom would never fall; he showed himself not only patient, but also cheerful in and above all that which they could or would work against him. Yea, such a valiant spirit the Lord gave him, that he was able not only to despise the terribleness of prisons and torments, but also to laugh to scorn the doings of his enemies.

Mr. Latimer, after remaining a long time in the Tower, was transported to Oxford, with Cranmer and Ridley, the disputations at which place have been already mentioned in a former part of this work. He remained imprisoned until October, and the principal objects of all his prayers were three-that he might stand faithful to the doctrine he had professed, that God would restore his Gospel to England once again, and preserve the Lady Elizabeth to be queen;

all of which happened. When he stood at the stake without the Bocardo gate, Oxford, with Dr. Ridley, and fire was putting to the pile of fagots, he raised his eyes benignantly towards heaven, and said, "God is faithful, who will not suffer you to be tempted above that ye are able." His body was forcibly penetrated by the fire, and the blood flowed abundantly from the heart; as if to verify his constant desire that his heart's blood might be shed in defense of the Gospel. His polemical and friendly letters are lasting monuments of his integrity and talents. It has been before said, that public disputation took place in April, 1554, new examinations took place in October, 1555, previous to the degradation and condemnation of Cranmer, Ridley, and Latimer. We now draw to the conclusion of the lives of the two last.

Dr. Ridley, the night before execution, was very facetious, had himself shaved, and called his supper a marriage feast; he remarked upon seeing Mrs. Irish (the keeper's wife) weep, "Though my breakfast will be somewhat sharp, my supper will be more pleasant and sweet."

The place of death was on the northside of the town, opposite Baliol College. Dr. Ridley was dressed in a black gown furred, and Mr. Latimer had a long shroud on, hanging down to his feet. Dr. Ridley, as he passed Bocardo, looked up to see Dr. Cranmer, but the latter was then engaged in disputation with a friar. When they came to the stake, Mr. Ridley embraced Latimer fervently, and bid him: "Be of good heart, brother, for God will either assuage the fury of the flame, or else strengthen us to abide it." He then knelt by the stake, and after earnestly praying together, they had a short private conversation. Dr. Smith then preached a short sermon against the martyrs, who would have answered him, but were prevented by Dr. Marshal, the vice-chancellor. Dr. Ridley then took off his gown and tippet, and gave them to his brother-in-law, Mr. Shipside. He gave away also many trifles to his weeping friends, and the populace were anxious to get even a fragment of his garments. Mr. Latimer gave nothing, and from the poverty of his garb, was soon stripped to his shroud, and stood venerable and erect, fearless of death.

Dr. Ridley being unclothed to his shirt, the smith placed an iron chain about their waists, and Dr. Ridley bid him fasten it securely; his brother having tied a bag of gunpowder about his neck, gave some also to Mr. Latimer.

Dr. Ridley then requested of Lord Williams, of Fame, to advocate with the queen the cause of some poor men to whom he had, when bishop, granted leases, but which the present bishop refused to confirm. A lighted fagot was now laid at Dr. Ridley's feet, which caused Mr. Latimer to say: "Be of good cheer, Ridley; and play the man. We shall this day, by God's grace, light up such a candle in England, as I trust, will never be put out."

When Dr. Ridley saw the fire flaming up towards him, he cried with a wonderful loud voice, "Lord, Lord, receive my spirit." Master Latimer, crying as vehemently on the other side, "O Father of heaven, receive my soul!" received the flame as it were embracing of it. After that he had stroked his face with his hands, and as it were, bathed them a little in the fire, he soon died (as it appeareth) with very little pain or none.

Well! dead they are, and the reward of this world they have already. What reward remaineth for them in heaven, the day of the Lord's glory, when he cometh with His saints, shall declare.

In the following month died Stephen Gardiner, bishop of Winchester and lord chancellor of England. This papistical monster was born at Bury, in Suffolk, and partly educated at Cambridge. Ambitious, cruel, and bigoted, he served any cause; he first espoused the king's part in the affair of Anne Boleyn: upon the establishment of the Reformation he declared the supremacy of the pope an execrable tenet; and when Queen Mary came to the crown, he entered into all her papistical bigoted views, and became a second time bishop of Winchester. It is conjectured it was his intention to have moved the sacrifice of Lady Elizabeth, but when he arrived at this point, it pleased God to remove him.

It was on the afternoon of the day when those faithful soldiers of Christ, Ridley and Latimer, perished, that Gardiner sat down with a joyful heart to dinner. Scarcely had he taken a few mouthfuls, when he was seized with illness, and carried to his bed, where he lingered fifteen days in great torment, unable in any wise to evacuate, and burnt with a devouring fever, that terminated in death. Execrated by all good Christians, we pray the Father of mercies, that he may receive that mercy above he never imparted below.

Upon entering Smithfield, the ground was so muddy that two officers offered to carry him to the stake, but he replied:

"Would you make me a pope? I am content to finish my journey on foot." Arriving at the stake, he said, "Shall I disdain to suffer at the stake, when my Redeemer did not refuse to suffer the most vile death upon the cross for me?" He then meekly recited the One hundred and seventh and One hundred and eighth Psalms, and when he had finished his prayers, was bound to the post, and fire applied to the pile. On December 18, 1555, perished this illustrious martyr, reverenced by man, and glorified in heaven!

Archbishop Cranmer

Dr. Thomas Cranmer was descended from an ancient family, and was born at the village of Arselacton, in the county of Northampton. After the usual school education he was sent to Cambridge, and was chosen fellow Jesus College. Here he married a gentleman's daughter, by which he forfeited his fellowship, and became a reader in Buckingham College, placing his wife at the Dolphin Inn, the landlady of which was a relation of hers, whence arose the idle report that he was an ostler. His lady shortly after dying in childbed; to his credit he was re-chosen a fellow of the college before mentioned. In a few years after, he was promoted to be Divinity Lecturer, and appointed one of the examiners over those who were ripe to become Bachelors or Doctors in Divinity. It was his principle to judge of their qualifications by the knowledge they possessed of the

Scriptures, rather than of the ancient fathers, and hence many popish priests were rejected, and others rendered much improved.

He was strongly solicited by Dr. Capon to be one of the fellows on the foundation of Cardinal Wolsey's college, Oxford, of which he hazarded the refusal. While he continued in Cambridge, the question of Henry VIII's divorce with Catharine was agitated. At that time, on account of the plague, Dr. Cranmer removed to the house of a Mr. Cressy, at Waltham Abbey, whose two sons were then educating under him. The affair of divorce, contrary to the king's approbation, had remained undecided above two or three years, from the intrigues of the canonists and civilians, and though the cardinals Campeius and Wolsey were commissioned from Rome to decide the question, they purposely protracted the sentence.

It happened that Dr. Gardiner (secretary) and Dr. Fox, defenders of the king in the above suit, came to the house of Mr. Cressy to lodge, while the king removed to Greenwich. At supper, a conversation ensued with Dr. Cranmer, who suggested that the question whether a man may marry his brother's wife or not, could be easily and speedily decided by the Word of God, and this as well in the English courts as in those of any foreign nation. The king, uneasy at the delay, sent for Dr. Gardiner and Dr. Fox to consult them, regretting that a new commission must be sent to Rome, and the suit be endlessly protracted. Upon relating to the king the conversation which had passed on the previous evening with Dr. Cranmer, his majesty sent for him, and opened the tenderness of conscience upon the near affinity of the queen. Dr. Cranmer advised that the matter should be referred to the most learned divines of Cambridge and Oxford, as he was unwilling to meddle in an affair of such weight; but the king enjoined him to deliver his sentiments in writing, and to repair for that purpose to the earl of Wiltshire's, who would accommodate him with books, and everything requisite for the occasion.

This Dr. Cranmer immediately did, and in his declaration not only quoted the authority of the Scriptures, of general councils, and the ancient writers, but maintained that the bishop of Rome had no authority whatever to dispense with the Word of God. The king asked him if he would stand by this bold declaration, to which replying in the affirmative, he was deputed ambassador to Rome, in conjunction with the earl of Wiltshire, Dr. Stokesley, Dr. Carne, Dr. Bennet, and others, previous to which, the marriage was discussed in most of the universities of Christendom and at home.

When the pope presented his toe to be kissed, as customary, the earl of Wiltshire and his party refused. Indeed, it is affirmed that a spaniel of the earl's attracted by the littler of the pope's toe, made a snap at it, whence his holiness drew in his sacred foot, and kicked at the offender with the other.

Upon the pope demanding the cause of their embassy, the earl presented Dr. Cranmer's book, declaring that his learned friends had come to defend it. The pope treated the embassy honorably, and appointed a day for the discussion, which he delayed, as if afraid of the issue of the investigation. The earl returned, and Dr. Cranmer, by the king's desire, visited the emperor, and was successful in bringing him over to his opinion. Upon the doctor's return to England, Dr. Warham, archbishop of Canterbury, having quitted this transitory life, Dr. Cranmer was deservedly, and by Dr. Warham's desire, elevated to that eminent station.

In this function, it may be said that he followed closely the charge of St. Paul. Diligent in duty, he rose at five in the morning, and continued in study and prayer until nine: between then and dinner, he devoted to temporal affairs. After dinner, if any suitors wanted hearing, he would determine their business with such an affability that even the defaulters were scarcely displeased. Then he would play at chess for an hour, or see others play, and at five o'clock he heard the Common Prayer read, and from this until supper he took the recreation of walking. At supper his conversation was lively and entertaining; again he walked or amused himself until nine o'clock, and then entered his study.

He ranked high in favor with King Henry, and even had the purity and the interest of the English Church deeply at heart. His mild and forgiving disposition is recorded in the following instance. An ignorant priest, in the country, had called Cranmer an ostler, and spoken very derogatory of his learning. Lord Cromwell receiving information of it, the man was sent to the Fleet, and his case was told to the archbishop by a Mr. Chertsey, a grocer, and a relation of the priest's. His grace, having sent for the offender, reasoned with him, and solicited the priest to question him on any learned subject. This the man, overcome by the bishop's good nature, and knowing his own glaring incapacity, declined, and entreated his forgiveness, which was immediately granted, with a charge to employ his time better when he returned to his parish. Cromwell was much vexed at the lenity displayed, but the bishop was ever more ready to receive injury than to retaliate in any other manner than by good advice and good offices.

At the time that Cranmer was raised to be archbishop, he was king's chaplain, and archdeacon of Taunton; he was also constituted by the pope the penitentiary general of England. It was considered by the king that Cranmer would be obsequious; hence the latter married the king to Anne Boleyn, performed her coronation, stood godfather to Elizabeth, the first child, and divorced the king from Catharine. Though Cranmer received a confirmation of his dignity from the pope, he always protested against acknowledging any other authority than the king's, and he persisted in the same independent sentiments when before Mary's commissioners in 1555.

One of the first steps after the divorce was to prevent preaching throughout his diocese, but this narrow measure had rather a political view than a religious one, as there were many who inveighed against the king's conduct. In his new dignity Cranmer agitated the question of supremacy, and by his powerful and just arguments induced the parliament to "render to Caesar the things that are Caesar's." During Cranmer's residence in Germany, 1531, he became acquainted with Ossiander, at Nuremberg, and married his niece, but left her with him while on his return to England. After a season he sent for her privately, and she remained with him until the year 1539, when the Six Articles compelled him to return her to her friends for a time.

It should be remembered that Ossiander, having obtained the approbation of his friend Cranmer, published the laborious work of the Harmony of the Gospels in 1537. In 1534 the archbishop completed the dearest wish of his heart, the removal of every obstacle to the perfection of the Reformation, by the subscription of the nobles and bishops to the king's sole supremacy. Only Bishop Fisher and Sir Thomas More made objection; and their agreement not to oppose the succession Cranmer was willing to consider at sufficient, but the monarch would have no other than an entire concession.

Not long after, Gardiner, in a private interview with the king, spoke inimically of Cranmer, (whom he maliciously hated) for assuming the title of primate of all England, as derogatory to the supremacy of the king. This created much jealousy against Cranmer, and his translation of the Bible was strongly opposed by Stokesley, bishop of London. It is said, upon the demise of Queen Catharine, that her successor Anne Boleyn rejoiced-a lesson this to show how shallow is the human judgment! since her own execution took place in the spring of the following year, and the king, on the day following the beheading of this sacrificed lady, married the beautiful Jane Seymour, a maid of honor to the late queen. Cranmer was ever the friend of Anne Boleyn, but it was dangerous to oppose the will of the carnal tyrannical monarch.

In 1538, the Holy Scriptures were openly exposed to sale; and the places of worship overflowed everywhere to hear its holy doctrines expounded. Upon the king's passing into a law the famous Six Articles, which went nearly again to establish the essential tenets of the Romish creed, Cranmer shone forth with all the luster of a Christian patriot, in resisting the doctrines they contained, and in which he was supported by the bishops of Sarum, Worcester, Ely, and Rochester, the two former of whom resigned their bishoprics. The king, though now in opposition to Cranmer, still revered the sincerity that marked his conduct. The death of Lord Cromwell in the Tower, in 1540, the good friend of Cranmer, was a severe blow to the wavering Protestant cause, but even now Cranmer, when he saw the tide directly adverse to the truth, boldly waited on the king in person, and by his manly and heartfelt pleading, caused the Book of Articles to be passed on his side, to the great confusion of his enemies, who had contemplated his fall as inevitable.

Cranmer now lived in as secluded a manner as possible, until the rancor of Winchester preferred some articles against him, relative to the dangerous opinion he taught in his family, joined to other treasonable charges. These the king himself delivered to Cranmer, and believing firmly the fidelity and assertions of innocence of the accused prelate, he caused the matter to be deeply investigated, and Winchester and Dr. Lenden, with Thornton and Barber, of the bishop's household, were found by the papers to be the real conspirators. The mild, forgiving Cranmer would have interceded for all remission of punishment, had not Henry, pleased with the subsidy voted by parliament, let them be discharged. These nefarious men, however, again renewing their plots against Cranmer, fell victims to Henry's resentment, and Gardiner forever lost his confidence. Sir G. Gostwick soon after laid charges against the archbishop, which Henry quashed, and the primate was willing to forgive.

In 1544, the archbishop's palace at Canterbury was burnt, and his brother-in-law with others perished in it. These various afflictions may serve to reconcile us to a humble state; for of what happiness could this great and good man boast, since his life was constantly harassed either by political, religious, or natural crosses? Again the inveterate Gardfiner laid high charges against the meek archbishop and would have sent him to the Tower; but the king was his friend, gave him his signet that he might defend him, and in the Council not only declared the bishop one of the best affected men in his realm, but sharply rebuked his accusers for their calumny.

A peace having been made, Henry, and the French king, Henry the Great, were unanimous to have the Mass abolished in their kingdom, and Cranmer set about this great work; but the death of the English monarch, in 1546, suspended the procedure, and King Edward his successor continued Cranmer in the same functions, upon whose coronation he delivered a charge that will ever honor his memory, for its purity, freedom, and truth. During this reign he prosecuted the glorious Reformation with unabated zeal, even in the year 1552, when he was seized with a severe ague, from which it pleased God to restore him that he might testify by his death the truth of that seed he had diligently sown.

The death of Edward, in 1553, exposed Cranmer to all the rage of his enemies. Though the archbishop was among those who supported Mary's accession, he was attainted at the meeting of parliament, and in November adjudged guilty of high treason at Guildhall, and degraded from his dignities. He sent a humble letter to Mary, explaining the cause of his signing the will in favor of Edward, and in 1554 he wrote to the Council, whom he pressed to obtain a pardon from the queen, by a letter delivered to Dr. Weston, but which the letter opened, and on seeing its contents, basely returned.

Treason was a charge quite inapplicable to Cranmer, who supported the queen's right; while others, who had favored Lady Jane were dismissed upon paying a small fine. A calumny was now spread against Cranmer that he complied with some of the popish ceremonies to ingratiate himself with the queen, which he dared publicly to disavow, and justified his articles of faith. The active part which the prelate had taken in the divorce of Mary's mother had ever rankled deeply in the heart of the queen, and revenge formed a prominent feature in the death of Cranmer.

We have in this work noticed the public disputations at Oxford, in which the talents of Cranmer, Ridley, and Latimer shone so conspicuously, and tended to their condemnation. The first sentence was illegal, inasmuch as the usurped power of the pope had not yet been re-established by law.

Being kept in prison until this was effected, a commission was dispatched from Rome, appointing Dr. Brooks to sit as the representative of his holiness, and Drs. Story and Martin as those of the queen. Cranmer was willing to bow to the authority of Drs. Story and Martin, but against that of Dr. Brooks he protested. Such were the remarks and replies of Cranmer, after a long examination, that Dr. Broks observed, "We come to examine you, and methinks you examine us."

Being sent back to confinement, he received a citation to appear at Rome within eighteen days, but this was impracticable, as he was imprisoned in England; and as he stated, even had he been at liberty, he was too poor to employ an advocate. Absurd as it must appear, Cranmer was condemned at Rome, and on February 14, 1556, a new commission was appointed, by which, Thirlby, bishop of Ely, and Bonner, of London, were deputed to sit in judgment at Christ-church, Oxford. By virtue of this instrument, Cranmer was gradually degraded, by putting mere rags on him to represent the dress of an archbishop; then stripping him of his attire, they took off his own gown, and put an old worn one upon him instead. This he bore unmoved, and his enemies, finding that severity only rendered him more determined, tried the opposite course, and placed him in the house of the dean of Christ-church, where he was treated with every indulgence.

This presented such a contrast to the three years' hard imprisonment he had received, that it threw him off his guard. His open, generous nature was more easily to be seduced by a liberal conduct than by threats and fetters. When Satan finds the Christian proof against one mode of attack, he tries another; and what form is so seductive as smiles, rewards, and power, after a long, painful imprisonment? Thus it was with Cranmer: his enemies promised him his former greatness if he would but recant, as well as the queen's favor, and this at the very time they knew that his death was determined in council. To soften the path to apostasy, the first paper brought for his signature was conceived in general terms; this once signed, five others were obtained as explanatory of the first, until finally he put his hand to the following detestable instrument:

"I, Thomas Cranmer, late archbishop of Canterbury, do renounce, abhor, and detest all manner of heresies and errors of Luther and Zuinglius, and all other teachings which are contrary to sound and true doctrine. And I believe most constantly in my heart, and with my mouth I confess one holy and Catholic Church visible, without which there is no salvation; and therefore I acknowledge the Bishop of Rome to be supreme head on earth, whom I acknowledge to be the highest bishop and pope, and Christ's vicar, unto whom all Christian people ought to be subject.

"And as concerning the sacraments, I believe and worship in the sacrament of the altar the body and blood of Christ, being contained most truly under the forms of bread and wine; the bread, through the mighty power of God being turned into the body of our Savior Jesus Christ, and the wine into his blood.

"And in the other six sacraments, also, (alike as in this) I believe and hold as the universal Church holdeth, and the Church of Rome judgeth and determineth.

"Furthermore, I believe that there is a place of purgatory, where souls departed be punished for a time, for whom the Church doth godily and wholesomely pray, like as it doth honor saints and make prayers to them.

"Finally, in all things I profess, that I do not otherwise believe than the Catholic Church and the Church of Rome holdeth and teacheth. I am sorry that I ever held or thought otherwise. And I beseech Almighty God, that of His mercy He will vouchsafe to forgive me whatsoever I have offended against God or His Church, and also I desire and beseech all Christian people to pray for me.

"And all such as have been deceived either by mine example or doctrine, I require them by the blood of Jesus Christ that they will return to the unity of the Church, that we may be all of one mind, without schism or division.

"And to conclude, as I submit myself to the Catholic Church of Christ, and to the supreme head thereof, so I submit myself unto the most excellent majesties of Philip and Mary, king and queen of this realm of England, etc., and to all other their laws and ordinances, being ready always as a faithful subject ever to obey them. And God is my witness, that I have not done this for favor or fear of any person, but willingly and of mine own conscience, as to the instruction of others."

"Let him that standeth take heed lest he fall!" said the apostle, and here was a falling off indeed! The papists now triumphed in their turn: they had acquired all they wanted short of his life. His recantation was immediately printed and dispersed, that it might have its due effect upon the astonished Protestants. But God counter worked all the designs of the Catholics by the extent to which they carried the implacable persecution of their prey. Doubtless, the love of life induced Cranmer to sign the above declaration: yet death may be said to have been preferable to life to him who lay under the stings of a goaded conscience and the contempt of every Gospel Christian; this principle he strongly felt in all its force and anguish.

The queen's revenge was only to be satiated by Cranmer's blood, and therefore she wrote an order to Dr. Pole, to prepare a sermon to be preached March 21, directly before his martyrdom, at St. Mary's, Oxford. Dr. Pole visited him the day previous, and was induced to believe that he would publicly deliver his sentiments in confirmation of the articles to which he had subscribed. About nine in the morning of the day of sacrifice, the queen's commissioners, attended by the magistrates, conducted the amiable unfortunate to St. Mary's Church. His torn, dirty garb, the same in which they habited him upon his degradation, excited the commiseration of the people. In the church he found a low mean stage, erected opposite to the pulpit, on which being placed, he turned his face, and fervently prayed to God.

The church was crowded with persons of both persuasions, expecting to hear the justification of the late apostasy: the Catholics rejoicing, and the Protestants deeply wounded in spirit at the deceit of the human heart. Dr. Pole, in his sermon, represented Cranmer as having been guilty of the most atrocious crimes; encouraged the deluded sufferer not to fear death, not to doubt the support of God in his torments, nor that Masses would be said in all the churches of Oxford for the repose of his soul. The doctor then noticed his conversion, and which he ascribed to the evident working of Almighty power and in order that the people might be convinced of its reality, asked the prisoner to give them a sign. This Cranmer did, and begged the congregation to pray for him, for he had committed many and grievous sins; but, of all, there was one which awfully lay upon his mind, of which he would speak shortly.

During the sermon Cranmer wept bitter tears: lifting up his hands and eyes to heaven, and letting them fall, as if unworthy to live: his grief now found vent in words: before his confession he fell upon his knees, and, in the following words unveiled the deep contrition and agitation which harrowed up his soul.

"O Father of heaven! O Son of God, Redeemer of the world! O Holy Ghost, three persons all one God! have mercy on me, most wretched caitiff and miserable sinner. I have offended both against heaven and earth, more than my tongue can express. Whither then may I go, or whither may I flee? To heaven I may be ashamed to lift up mine eyes and in earth I find no place of refuge or succor. To Thee, therefore, O Lord, do I run; to Thee do I humble myself, saying, O Lord, my God, my sins be great, but yet have mercy upon me for Thy great mercy. The great mystery that God became man, was not wrought for little or few offences. Thou didst not give Thy Son, O Heavenly Father, unto death for small sins only, but for all the greatest sins of the world, so that the sinner return to Thee with his whole heart, as I do at present. Wherefore, have mercy on me, O God, whose property is always to have mercy, have mercy upon me, O Lord, for Thy great mercy. I crave nothing for my own merits, but for Thy name's sake, that it may be hallowed thereby, and for Thy dear Son, Jesus Christ's sake. And now therefore, O Father of Heaven, hallowed be Thy name," etc.

Then rising, he said he was desirous before his death to give them some pious exhortations by which God might be glorified and themselves edified. He then descanted upon the danger of a love for the world, the duty of obedience to their majesties, of love to one another and the necessity of the rich administering to the wants of the poor. He quoted the three verses of the fifth chapter of James, and then proceeded, "Let them that be rich ponder well these three sentences: for if they ever had occasion to show their charity, they have it now at this present, the poor people being so many, and victual so dear.

"And now forasmuch as I am come to the last end of my life, whereupon hangeth all my life past, and all my life to come, either to live with my master Christ for ever in joy, or else to be in pain for ever with the wicked in hell, and I see before mine eyes presently, either heaven ready to receive me, or else hell ready to swallow me up; I shall therefore declare unto you my very faith how I believe, without any color of dissimulation: for now is no time to dissemble, whatsoever I have said or written in times past.

"First, I believe in God the Father Almighty, Maker of heaven and earth, etc. And I believe every article of the Catholic faith, every word and sentence taught by our Savior Jesus Christ, His apostles and prophets, in the New and Old Testament.

"And now I come to the great thing which so much troubleth my conscience, more than any thing that ever I did or said in my whole life, and that is the setting abroad of a writing contrary to the truth, which now here I renounce and refuse, as things written with my hand contrary to the truth which I thought in my heart, and written for fear of death, and to save my life, if it might be; and that is, all such bills or papers which I have written or signed with my hand since my degradation, wherein I have written many things untrue. And forasmuch as my hand hath offended, writing contrary to my heart, therefore my hand shall first be punished; for when I come to the fire it shall first be burned.

"And as for the pope, I refuse him as Christ's enemy, and Antichrist, with all his false doctrine."

Upon the conclusion of this unexpected declaration, amazement and indignation were conspicuous in every part of the church. The Catholics were completely foiled, their object being frustrated, Cranmer, like Samson, having completed a greater ruin upon his enemies in the hour of death, than he did in his life.

Cranmer would have proceeded in the exposure of the popish doctrines, but the murmurs of the idolaters drowned his voice, and the preacher gave an order to "lead the heretic away!" The savage command was directly obeyed, and the lamb about to suffer was torn from his stand to the place of slaughter, insulted all the way by the revilings and taunts of the pestilent monks and friars.

With thoughts intent upon a far higher object than the empty threats of man, he reached the spot dyed with the blood of Ridley and Latimer. There he knelt for a short time in earnest devotion, and then arose, that he might undress and prepare for the fire. Two friars who had been parties in prevailing upon him to abjure, now endeavored to draw him off again from the truth, but he was steadfast and immovable in what he had just professed, and publicly taught. A chain was provided to bind him to the stake, and after it had tightly encircled him, fire was put to the fuel, and the flames began soon to ascend.

Queen Mary's Treatment of Her Sister, the Princess Elizabeth

The preservation of Princess Elizabeth may be reckoned a remarkable instance of the watchful eye which Christ had over His Church. The bigotry of Mary regarded not the ties of consanguinity, of natural affection, of national succession. Her mind, physically morose, was under the dominion of men who possessed not the milk of human kindness, and whose principles were sanctioned and enjoined by the idolatrous tenets of the Romish pontiff. Could they have foreseen the short date of Mary's reign, they would have imbrued their hands in the Protestant blood of Elizabeth, and, as a sine qua non of the queen's salvation, have compelled her to bequeath the kingdom to some Catholic prince. The contest might have been attended with the horrors incidental to a religious civil war, and calamities might have been felt in England similar to those under Henry the Great in France, whom Queen Elizabeth assisted in opposing his priest-ridden Catholic subjects. As if Providence had the perpetual establishment of the Protestant faith in view, the difference of the duration of the two reigns is worthy of notice. Mary might have reigned many years in the course of nature, but the course of grace willed it otherwise. Five years and four months was the time of persecution allotted to this weak, disgraceful reign, while that of Elizabeth reckoned a number of years among the highest of those who have sat on the English throne, almost nine times that of her merciless sister!

Before Mary attained the crown, she treated Elizabeth with a sisterly kindness, but from that period her conduct was altered, and the most imperious distance substituted. Though Elizabeth had no concern in the rebellion of Sir Thomas Wyat, yet she was apprehended, and treated as a culprit in that commotion. The manner too of her arrest was similar to the mind that dictated it: the three cabinet members, whom she deputed to see the arrest executed, rudely entered the chamber at ten o'clock at night, and, though she was extremely ill, they could scarcely be induced to let her remain until the following morning. Her enfeebled state permitted her to be moved only by short stages in a journey of such length to London; but the princess, though afflicted in person, had a consolation in mind which her sister never could purchase: the people, through whom she passed on her way pitied her, and put up their prayers for her preservation.

Arrived at court, she was made a close prisoner for a fortnight, without knowing who was her accuser, or seeing anyone who could console or advise her. The charge, however, was at length unmasked by Gardiner, who, with nineteen of the Council, accused her of abetting Wyat's conspiracy, which she religiously affirmed to be false. Failing in this, they placed against her the transactions of Sir Peter Carew in the west, in which they were as unsuccessful as in the former. The queen now signified that it was her pleasure she should be committed to the Tower, a step which overwhelmed the princess with the greatest alarm and uneasiness. In vain she hoped the queen's majesty would not commit her to such a place; but there was no lenity to be expected; her attendants were limited, and a hundred northern soldiers appointed to guard her day and night.

On Palm Sunday she was conducted to the Tower. When she came to the palace garden, she cast her eyes towards the windows, eagerly anxious to meet those of the queen, but she was disappointed. A strict order was given in London that every one should go to church, and carry psalms, that she might be conveyed without clamor or commiseration to her prison.

At the time of passing under London Bridge the fall of the tide made it very dangerous, and the barge some time stuck fast against the starlings. To mortify her the more, she was landed at Traitors' Stairs. As it rained fast, and she was obliged to step in the water to land, she hesitated; but this excited no complaisance in the lord in waiting. When she set her foot on the steps, she exclaimed, "Here lands as true a subject, being prisoner, as ever landed at these stairs; and before Thee, O God, I speak it, having no friend but Thee alone!"

A large number of the wardens and servants of the Tower were arranged in order between whom the princess had to pass. Upon inquiring the use of this parade, she was informed it was customary to do so. "If," said she, "it is on account of me, I beseech you that they may be dismissed." On this the poor men knelt down, and prayed that God would preserve her grace, for which they were the next day turned out of their employments. The tragic scene must have been deeply interesting, to see an amiable and irreproachable princess sent like a lamb to languish in expectation of cruelty and death; against whom there was no other charge than her superiority in Christian virtues and acquired endowments. Her attendants openly wept as she proceeded with a dignified step to the frowning battlements of her destination. "Alas!" said Elizabeth, "what do you mean? I took you to comfort, not to dismay me; for my truth is such that no one shall have cause to weep for me."

The next step of her enemies was to procure evidence by means which, in the present day, are accounted detestable. Many poor prisoners were racked, to extract, if possible, any matters of accusation which might affect her life, and thereby gratify Gardiner's sanguinary disposition. He himself came to examine her, respecting her removal from her house at Ashbridge to Dunnington castle a long while before. The princess had quite forgotten this trivial circumstance, and Lord Arundel, after the investigation, kneeling down, apologized for having troubled her in such a frivolous matter. "You sift me narrowly," replied the princess, "but of this I am assured, that God has appointed a limit to your proceedings; and so God forgive you all."

Her own gentlemen, who ought to have been her purveyors, and served her provision, were compelled to give place to the common soldiers, at the command of the constable of the Tower, who was in every respect a servile tool of Gardiner; her grace's friends, however, procured an order of Council which regulated this petty tyranny more to her satisfaction.

After having been a whole month in close confinement, she sent for the lord chamberlain and Lord Chandois, to whom she represented the ill state of her health from a want of proper air and exercise. Application being made to the Council, Elizabeth was with some difficulty admitted to walk in the queen's lodgings, and afterwards in the garden, at which time the prisoners on that side were attended by their keepers, and not suffered to look down upon her. Their jealousy was excited by a child of four years, who daily brought flowers to the princess. The child was threatened with a whipping, and the father ordered to keep him from the princess's chambers.

On the fifth of May the constable was discharged from his office, and Sir Henry Benifield appointed in his room, accompanied by a hundred ruffian-looking soldiers in blue. This measure created considerable alarm in the mind of the princess, who imagined it was preparatory to her undergoing the same fate as Lady Jane Grey, upon the same block. Assured that this project was not in agitation, she entertained an idea that the new keeper of the Tower was commissioned to make away with her privately, as his equivocal character was in conformity with the ferocious inclination of those by whom he was appointed.

A report now obtained that her Grace was to be taken away by the new constable and his soldiers, which in the sequel proved to be true. An order of Council was made for her removal to the manor Woodstock, which took place on Trinity Sunday, May 13, under the authority of Sir Henry Benifield and Lord Tame. The ostensible cause of her removal was to make room for other prisoners. Richmond was the first place they stopped at, and here the princess slept, not however without much alarm at first, as her own servants were superseded by the soldiers, who were placed as guards at her chamber door. Upon representation, Lord Tame overruled this indecent stretch of power, and granted her perfect safety while under his custody.

In passing through Windsor, she saw several of her poor dejected servants waiting to see her. "Go to them," said she, to one of her attendants, "and say these words from me, tanquim ovis, that is, like a sheep to the slaughter."

The next night her Grace lodged at the house of a Mr. Dormer, in her way to which the people manifested such tokens of loyal affection that Sir Henry was indignant, and bestowed on them very liberally the names of rebels and traitors. In some villages they rang the bells for joy, imagining the princess's arrival among them was from a very different cause; but this harmless demonstration of gladness was sufficient with the persecuting Benifield to order his soldiers to seize and set these humble persons in the stocks.

The day following, her Grace arrived at Lord Tame's house, where she stayed all night, and was most nobly entertained. This excited Sir Henry's indignation, and made him caution Lord Tame to look well to his proceedings; but the humanity of Lord Tame was not to be frightened, and he returned a suitable reply. At another time, this official prodigal, to show his consequence and disregard of good manners, went up into a chamber, where was appointed for her Grace a chair, two cushions, and a foot carpet, wherein he presumptuously sat and called his man to pull off his boots. As soon as it was known to the ladies and gentlemen they laughed him to scorn. When supper was done, he called to his lordship, and directed that all gentlemen and ladies should withdraw home, marveling much that he would permit such a large company, considering the great charge he had committed to him. "Sir Henry," said his lordship, "content yourself; all shall be avoided, your men and all." "Nay, but my soldiers," replied Sir Henry, "shall watch all night." Lord Tame answered, "There is no need." "Well," said he, "need or need not, they shall so do."

The next day her Grace took her journey from thence to Woodstock, where she was enclosed, as before in the Tower of London, the soldiers keeping guard within and without the walls, every day, to the number of sixty; and in the night, without the walls were forty during all the time of her imprisonment.

At length she was permitted to walk in the gardens, but under the most severe restrictions, Sir Henry keeping the keys himself, and placing her always under many bolts and locks, whence she was induced to call him her jailer, at which he felt offended, and begged her to substitute the word officer. After much earnest entreaty to the Council, she obtained permission to write to the queen; but the jailer who brought her pen, ink, and paper stood by her while she wrote, and, when she left off, he carried the things away until they were wanted again. He also insisted upon carrying it himself to the queen, but Elizabeth would not suffer him to be the bearer, and it was presented by one of her gentlemen.

After the letter, Doctors Owen and Wendy went to the princess, as the state of her health rendered medical assistance necessary. They stayed with her five or six days, in which time she grew much better; they then returned to the queen, and spoke flatteringly of the princess' submission and humility, at which the queen seemed moved; but the bishops wanted a concession that she had offended her majesty. Elizabeth spurned this indirect mode of acknowledging herself guilty. "If I have offended," said she, "and am guilty, I crave no mercy but the law, which I am certain I should have had ere this, if anything could have been proved against me. I wish I were as clear from the peril of my enemies; then should I not be thus bolted and locked up within walls and doors."

Much question arose at this time respecting the propriety of uniting the princess to some foreigner, that she might quit the realm with a suitable portion. One of the Council had the brutality to urge the necessity of beheading her, if the king (Philip) meant to keep the realm in peace; but the Spaniards, detesting such a base thought, replied, "God forbid that our king and master should consent to such an infamous proceeding!" Stimulated by a noble principle, the Spaniards from this time repeatedly urged to the king that it would do him the highest honor to liberate the Lady Elizabeth, nor was the king impervious to their solicitation. He took her out of prison, and shortly after she was sent for to Hampton court. It may be remarked in this place, that the fallacy of human reasoning is shown in every moment. The barbarian who suggested the policy of beheading Elizabeth little contemplated the change of condition which his speech would bring about. In her journey from Woodstock, Benifield treated her with the same severity as before; removing her on a stormy day, and not suffering her old servant, who had come to Colnbrook, where she slept, to speak to her.

She remained a fortnight strictly guarded and watched, before anyone dared to speak with her; at length the vile Gardiner with three more of the Council, came with great submission. Elizabeth saluted them, remarked that she had been for a long time kept in solitary confinement, and begged they would intercede with the king and queen to deliver her from prison. Gardiner's visit was to draw from the princess a confession of her guilt; but she was guarded against his subtlety, adding, that, rather than admit she had done wrong, she would lie in prison all the rest of her life. The next day Gardiner came again, and kneeling down, declared that the queen was astonished she would persist in affirming that she was blameless-whence it would be inferred that the queen had unjustly imprisoned her grace. Gardiner further informed her that the queen had declared that she must tell another tale, before she could be set at liberty. "Then," replied the high-minded Elizabeth, "I had rather be in prison with honesty and truth, than have my liberty, and be suspected by her majesty. What I have said, I will stand to; nor will I ever speak falsehood!" The bishop and his friends then departed, leaving her locked up as before.

Seven days after the queen sent for Elizabeth at ten o'clock at night; two years had elapsed since they had seen each other. It created terror in the mind of the princess, who, at setting out, desired her gentlemen and ladies to pray for her, as her return to them again was uncertain.

Being conducted to the queen's bedchamber, upon entering it the princess knelt down, and having begged of God to preserve her majesty, she humbly assured her that her majesty had not a more loyal subject in the realm, whatever reports might be circulated to the contrary. With a haughty ungraciousness, the imperious queen replied: "You will not confess your offence, but stand stoutly to your truth. I pray God it may so fall out."

"If it do not," said Elizabeth, "I request neither favor nor pardon at your majesty's hands." "Well," said the queen, "you stiffly still persevere in your truth. Besides, you will not confess that you have not been wrongfully punished."

"I must not say so, if it please your majesty, to you."

"Why, then," said the queen, "belike you will to others."

"No, if it please your majesty: I have borne the burden, and must bear it. I humbly beseech your majesty to have a good opinion of me and to think me to be your subject, not only from the beginning hitherto, but for ever, as long as life lasteth." They departed without any heartfelt satisfaction on either side; nor can we think the conduct of Elizabeth displayed that independence and fortitude which accompanies perfect innocence. Elizabeth's admitting that she would not say, neither to the queen nor to others, that she had been unjustly punished, was in direct contradiction to what she had told Gardiner, and must have arisen from some motive at this time inexplicable. King Philip is supposed to have been secretly concealed during the interview, and to have been friendly to the princess.

In seven days from the time of her return to imprisonment, her severe jailer and his men were discharged, and she was set at liberty, under the constraint of being always attended and watched by some of the queen's Council. Four of her gentlemen were sent to the Tower without any other charge against them than being zealous servants of their mistress. This event was soon after followed by the happy news of Gardiner's death, for which all good and merciful men glorified God, inasmuch as it had taken the chief tiger from the den, and rendered the life of the Protestant successor of Mary more secure.

This miscreant, while the princess was in the Tower, sent a secret writ, signed by a few of the Council, for her private execution, and, had Mr. Bridges, lieutenant of the Tower, been as little scrupulous of dark assassination as this pious prelate was, she must have perished. The warrant not having the queen's signature, Mr. Bridges hastened to her majesty to give her information of it, and to know her mind. This was a plot of Winchester's, who, to convict her of treasonable practices, caused several prisoners to be racked; particularly Mr. Edmund Tremaine and Smithwicke were offered considerable bribes to accuse the guiltless princess.

Her life was several times in danger. While at Woodstock, fire was apparently put between the boards and ceiling under which she lay. It was also reported strongly that one Paul Penny, the keeper of Woodstock, a notorious ruffian, was appointed to assassinate her, but, however this might be, God counteracted in this point the nefarious designs of the enemies of the Reformation. James Basset was another appointed to perform the same deed: he was a peculiar favorite of Gardiner, and had come within a mile of Woodstock, intending to speak with Benifield on the subject. The goodness of God however so ordered it that while Basset was traveling to Woodstock, Benifield, by an order of Council, was going to London: in consequence of which, he left a positive order with his brother, that no man should be admitted to the princess during his absence, not even with a note from the queen; his brother met the murderer, but the latter's intention was frustrated, as no admission could be obtained.

When Elizabeth quitted Woodstock, she left the following lines written with her diamond on the window:

Much suspected by me,

Nothing proved can be. Quoth Elizabeth, prisoner.

With the life of Winchester ceased the extreme danger of the princess, as many of her other secret enemies soon after followed him, and, last of all, her cruel sister, who outlived Gardiner but three years.

The death of Mary was ascribed to several causes. The Council endeavored to console her in her last moments, imagining it was the absence of her husband that lay heavy at her heart, but though his treatment had some weight, the loss of Calais, the last fortress possessed by the English in France, was the true source of her sorrow. "Open my heart," said Mary, "when I am dead, and you shall find Calais written there." Religion caused her no alarm; the priests had lulled to rest every misgiving of conscience, which might have obtruded, on account of the accusing spirits of the murdered martyrs. Not the blood she had spilled, but the loss of a town excited her emotions in dying, and this last stroke seemed to be awarded, that her fanatical persecution might be paralleled by her political imbecility.

We earnestly pray that the annals of no country, Catholic or pagan, may ever be stained with such a repetition of human sacrifices to papal power, and that the detestation in which the character of Mary is holden, may be a beacon to succeeding monarchs to avoid the rocks of fanaticism!

God's Punishment upon Some of the Persecutors of His People in Mary's Reign

After that arch-persecutor, Gardiner, was dead, others followed, of whom Dr. Morgan, bishop of St. David's, who succeeded Bishop Farrar, is to be noticed. Not long after he was installed in his bishopric, he was stricken by the visitation of God; his food passed through the throat, but rose again with great violence. In this manner, almost literally starved to death, he terminated his existence.

Bishop Thornton, suffragan of Dover, was an indefatigable persecutor of the true Church. One day after he had exercised his cruel tyranny upon a number of pious persons at Canterbury, he came from the chapter-house to Borne, where as he stood on a Sunday looking at his men playing at bowls, he fell down in a fit of the palsy, and did not long survive.

After the latter, succeeded another bishop or suffragen, ordained by Gardiner, who not long after he had been raised to the see of Dover, fell down a pair of stairs in the cardinal's chamber at Greenwich, and broke his neck. He had just received the cardinal's blessing-he could receive nothing worse.

John Cooper, of Watsam, Suffolk, suffered by perjury; he was from private pique persecuted by one Fenning, who suborned two others to swear that they heard Cooper say, 'If God did not take away Queen Mary, the devil would.' Cooper denied all such words, but Cooper was a Proestant and a heretic, and therefore he was hung, drawn and quartered, his property confiscated, and his wife and nine children reduced to beggary. The following harvest, however, Grimwood of Hitcham, one of the witnesses before mentioned, was visited for his villainy: while at work, stacking up corn, his bowels suddenly burst out, and before relief could be obtained, her died. Thus was deliberate perjury rewarded by sudden death!

In the case of the martyr Mr. Bradford, the severity of Mr.

Sheriff Woodroffe has been noticed-he rejoiced at the death of the saints, and at Mr. Rogers' execution, he broke the carman's head, because he stopped the cart to let the martyr's children take a last farewell of him. Scarcely had Mr. Woodroffe's sheriffalty expired a week, when he was struck with a paralytic affection, and languished a few days in the most pitable and helpless condition, presenting a striking contrast to his former activity in the cause of blood.

Ralph Lardyn, who betrayed the martyr George Eagles, is believed to have been afterward arraigned and hanged in consequence of accusing himself. At the bar, he denounced himself in these words: "This has most justly fallen upon me, for betraying the innocent blood of that just and good man George Eagles, who was here condemned in the time of Queen Mary by my procurement, when I sold his blood for a little money."

As James Abbes was going to execution, and exhorting the pitying bystanders to adhere steadfastly to the truth, and like him to seal the cause of Christ with their blood, a servant of the sheriff's interrupted him, and blasphemously called his religion heresy, and the good man a lunatic. Scarcely however had the flames reached the martyr, before the fearful stroke of God fell upon the hardened wretch, in the presence of him he had so cruelly ridiculed. The man was suddenly seized with lunacy, cast off his clothes and shoes before the people, (as Abbes had done just before, to distribute among some poor persons,) at the same time exclaiming, "Thus did James Abbes, the true servant of God, who is saved by I am damned." Repeating this often, the sheriff had him secured, and made him put his clothes on, but no sooner was he alone, than he tore them off, and exclaimed as before. Being tied in a cart, he was conveyed to his master's house, and in about half a year he died; just before which a priest came to attend him, with the crucifix, etc., but the wretched man bade him take away such trumpery, and said that he and other priests had been the cause of his damnation, but that Abbes was saved.

One Clark, an avowed enemy of the Protestants in King Edward's reign, hung himself in the Tower of London.

Froling, a priest of much celebrity, fell down in the street and died on the spot.

Dale, an indefatigable informer, was consumed by vermin, and died a miserable spectacle.

Alexander, the severe keeper of Newgate, died miserably, swelling to a prodigious size, and became so inwardly putrid, that none could come near him. This cruel minister of the law would go to Bonner, Story, and others, requesting them to rid his prison, he was so much pestered with heretics! The son of this keeper, in three years after his father's death, dissipated his great property, and died suddenly in Newgate market. "The sins of the father," says the Decalogue, "shall be visited on the children." John Peter, son-in-law of Alexander, a horrid blasphemer and persecutor, died wretchedly. When he affirmed anything, he would say, "If it be not true, I pray I may rot ere I die." This awful state visited him in all its loathsomeness.

Sir Ralph Ellerker was eagerly desirous to see the heart taken out of Adam Damlip, who was wrongfully put to death. Shortly after Sir Ralph was slain by the French, who mangled him dreadfully, cut off his limbs, and tore his heart out.

When Gardiner heard of the miserable end of Judge Hales, he called the profession of the Gospel a doctrine of desperation; but he forgot that the judge's despondency arose after he had consented to the papistry. But with more reason may this be said of the Catholic tenets, if we consider the miserable end of Dr. Pendleton, Gardiner, and most of the leading persecutors. Gardiner, upon his death bed, was reminded by a bishop of Peter denying his master, "Ah," said Gardiner, "I have denied with Peter, but never repented with Peter."

After the accession of Elizabeth, most of the Catholic prelates were imprisoned in the Tower or the Fleet; Bonner was put into the Marshalsea.

Of the revilers of God's Word, we detail, among many others, the following occurrence. One William Maldon, living at Greenwich in servitude, was instructing himself profitably in reading an English primer one winter's evening. A serving man, named John Powell, sat by, and ridiculed all that Maldon said, who cautioned him not to make a jest of the Word of God. Powell nevertheless continued, until Maldon came to certain English Prayers, and read aloud, "Lord, have mercy upon us, Christ have mercy upon us," etc. Suddenly the reviler started, and exclaimed, "Lord, have mercy upon us!" He was struck with the utmost terror of mind, said the evil spirit could not abide that Christ should have any mercy upon him, and sunk into madness. He was remitted to Bedlam, and became an awful warning that God will not always be insulted with impunity.

Henry Smith, a student in the law, had a pious Protestant father, of Camben, in Gloucestershire, by whom he was virtuously educated. While studying law in the middle temple, he was induced to profess Catholicism, and, going to Louvain, in France, he returned with pardons, crucifixes, and a great freight of popish toys. Not content with these things, he openly reviled the Gospel religion he had been brought up in; but conscience one night reproached him so dreadfully, that in a fit of despair he hung himself in his garters. He was buried in a lane, without the Christian service being read over him.

Dr. Story, whose name has been so often mentioned in the preceding pages, was reserved to be cut off by public execution, a practice in which he had taken great delight when in power. He is supposed to have had a hand in most of the conflagrations in Mary's time, and was even ingenious in his invention of new modes of inflicting torture. When Elizabeth came to the throne, he was committed to prison, but unaccountably effected his escape to the continent, to carry fire and sword there among the Protestant brethren. From the duke of Alva, at Antwerp, he received a special commission to search all ships for contraband goods, and particularly for English heretical books.

Dr. Story gloried in a commission that was ordered by Providence to be his ruin, and to preserve the faithful from his sanguinary cruelty. It was contrived that one Parker, a merchant, should sail to Antwerp and information should be given to Dr. Story that he had a quantity of heretical books on board. The latter no sooner heard this, than he hastened to the vessel, sought everywhere above, and then went under the hatches, which were fastened down upon him. A prosperous gale brought the ship to England, and this traitorous, persecuting rebel was committed to prison, where he remained a considerable time, obstinately objecting to recant his Anti-christian spirit, or admit of Queen Elizabeth's supremacy. He alleged, though by birth and education an Englishman, that he was a sworn subject of the king of Spain, in whose service the famous duke of Alva was. The doctor being condemned, was laid upon a hurdle, and drawn from the Tower to Tyburn, where after being suspended about half an hour, he was cut down, stripped, and the executioner displayed the heart of a traitor.

Thus ended the existence of this Nimrod of England

BIBLE TRANSLATIONS

The Great Bible (1539-40)

Cramner's Bible, published by Coverdale just three years after Tyndall was burned at the stake at Henry Viii's command. It was the first Bible published, intended to be placed in all the churches in England and was called "The Great Bible" because of its size.

The Great Bible

Psalm 23

Dominus regit me.

1. THE Lord is my shepherd : therefore can I lack nothing.
2. He shall feed me in a green pasture : and lead me forth beside the waters of comfort.
3. He shall convert my soul : and bring me forth in the paths of righteousness, for his Name's sake.
4. Yea, thou I walk through the valley of the shadow of death, I will fear no evil : for thou art with me; thy rod and thy staff comfort me.
5. Thou shalt prepare a table before me against them that trouble me : thou hast anointed my head with oil, and my cup shall be full.
6. But thy loving-kindness and mercy shall follow me all the days of my life : and I will dwell in the house of the Lord for ever.

The Geneva Bible

Psalm 23

1 A Psalm of David. The Lord is my shepherd, I shall not want.
2 He maketh me to rest in green pasture, and leadeth me by the still waters.
3 He restoreth my soul, and leadeth me in the paths of righteousness for his Name's sake.
4 Yea, though I should walk through the valley of the shadow of death, I will fear no evil: for thou art with me: thy rod and thy staff, they comfort me.
5 Thou doest prepare a table before me in the sight of mine adversaries: thou doest anoint mine head with oil, and my cup runneth over.
6 Doubtless kindness and mercy shall follow me all the days of my life, and I shall remain a long season in the house of the Lord.

Douay-Rheims Version 1578

Psalm 23

1 A Psalm of David. The Lord ruleth me: and I shall want nothing.
2 He hath set me in a place of pasture. He hath brought me up, on the water of refreshment:
3 He hath converted my soul. He hath led me on the paths of justice, for his own name's sake.
4 For though I should walk in the midst of the shadow of death, I will fear no evils, for thou art with me. Thy rod and thy staff, they have comforted me.
5 Thou hast prepared a table before me against them that afflict me. Thou hast anointed my head with oil; and my chalice which inebreateth me, how goodly is it!
6 And thy mercy will follow me all the days of my life. And that I may dwell in the house of the Lord unto length of days.

The King James Version 1611

Psalm 23

1 The LORD is my shepherd; I shall not want.
2 He maketh me to lie down in green pastures: he leadeth me beside
the still waters.
3 He restoreth my soul: he leadeth me in the paths of righteousness for
his name's sake.
4 Yea, though I walk through the valley of the shadow of death, I will
fear no evil: for thou art with me; thy rod and thy staff they comfort
me.
5 Thou preparest a table before me in the presence of mine enemies:
thou anointest my head with oil; my cup runneth over.
6 Surely goodness and mercy shall follow me all the days of my life:
and I will dwell in the house of the LORD for ever.

Which of the translations do you like the best? The least? Tell why.

Harrys twain (Henry VIII), and Ned the Lad,/Mary, Bessy . . .

LESSON 2: READING POETRY

In this course we are going to make a mad dash through 300 years of literature. This particular 300 years can be broken down into a variety of literary schools and periods. A substantial part of the literature we will read will be poetry. Therefore, you are going to take a little time out to refine your poetry-reading skills. Some of you will like that more than others! Your work will broken down into daily assignments. PLEASE heed those divisions. If you try to cram it all into one day, you will not get it done. You might be able to skim it all, but skimming will not give you the foundation you are going to need. Skimming is not reading.

For your work this week, you will need a copy of the book, *Poetry for Dummies,* by The Poetry Center, John Timpane, and Maureen Watts. It was published by Wiley Publishing, Inc. in 2001. (A note for the sensitive among you: if you take the title personally, you're just being ridiculous!) (Maybe I should try that again, OF COURSE I'm not saying you're stupid! Where would you get such a ridiculous idea!) (Get the point? Good. Get the book.)

Day 1:

First Observation Skill: *read the text slowly and carefully.*

First, poetry reading is basically an inductive study skill. As with all inductive study (to repeat the information you should have read on the first pages of this guide), there are basically three steps. First you must **observe** what it says. Only after you have made careful observation of what the poem says, can you move to the second step, which is **interpretation.** As you begin to interpret the poem, you build on those observations you've made. I know what it says. Now, what does it mean? The final step involves make **application** of the poem to what you see happening around you.

In an inductive study of poetry, you spend most of your time looking at the text of the poem yourself. Later in your study, you might want to do a little research into what other people have said about the poem. You might find books or articles that tell you something about the poem's history, its form and structure, or its meaning.

Once you have studied the poem yourself, then you can compare your impressions of the poem and your interpretation of the poem with the impressions and interpretations of others. Sometimes you will agree with what a writer has to say, but sometimes, you will not agree at all. Sometimes the critic will see something that you didn't see at all and give you a new insight into the poem. If you go to those resources after you have drawn your own initial conclusions, the opinions of others will be much more useful to you.

I want you to be able to read a poem and understand it yourself. For that reason, we are going to learn how to be good observers – and then good interpreters of poetry. Excited? (O.K., humor me, I'm old.)

The first step in studying the poem is to actually READ the poem. Sounds obvious, doesn't it? Many times, though, we will not read the poem as much as we will *skim* the poem. That is why it is really best if you actually read the poem aloud. Remember, skimming is not reading.

Please read pp. 17-27, of *Poetry for Dummies,* for information on the right way to read a poem out loud. We will discuss this topic in class so read carefully (By the way, when you see the little "READ ALOUD" icon next to a poem, that means you should read it aloud).

Make notes on your reading. Summarize main points.

Day 2:

Second Observation skill: Answering who, what, when, where, why, and how.

Now that you know something of the mechanics of how to read a poem, let's talk about what you need to be looking for as you read. Read chapter two of *Poetry for Dummies*, "Subject Tone and Narrative," pp. 31-40. Pay careful attention to the section titled, "Figuring out a Poem's Narrative."

As you read, you will find reference to the following terms, *metaphor* and *protagonist*. The next chapter will spend a lot of time talking about metaphors, but the simple definition is an implied comparison between two things. Suppose you say, "My brother is a pig." Unless you have a very interesting family tree, you really are saying that your brother's behavior is pig-like. A protagonist is generally the main character of a story or a poem.

This is probably a good time to point out that a glossary can be found on pages 243-253 of your book.

You should be able to tell what each of the following terms (generally called, *literary terms*) mean and how they apply to poetry:

persona:

setting:

situation:

plot:

character

irony:

situational irony:

verbal irony:

metaphor

protagonist:

The wise student will anticipate that he or she might be asked to define these terms on a quiz at some point in the near future.

Day 3:

Third Observation Skill: Analyzing the text

Please turn your attention to chapter 3 of your text, *Tuning In to Language*. pp. 42-54. For today, we will focus only on the section beginning on page 44 titled, "Tools of Significance: Symbols, Similies, Metaphors, and Allusions."

The writers of your book are kind and gentle souls who say on page 50, "Knowing the names of these tools of language is not as important as being aware of all the ways poets can create them." It is true that just knowing the definitions of symbol, simile, metaphor and allusion is kind of pointless if that is ALL you know about them.

However, I am not a kind or gentle soul. I want you to know the names, the definitions of these terms so that you will know what I am talking about when I use them, and so that you will become confident in your use of them as well.

Therefore, please define these terms. While you're at it, give an example of each one, too.

symbol:

simile (pronounces SIM-i-lee):

metaphor:

allusion:

personification:

Tell some ways you would know that the poet is using a symbol?

Day 4:

Fourth Observation Skill: Observing structure and sound.

Please read "Music: What You Hear, Feel, and See," and "Orchestrating Sound," pages 51-55.

There is a lot of somewhat technical information in this section, so you might want to read with a highlighter in hand. Use it to mark the literary terms and their definitions as you read. When you have finished, please define the following terms and give examples for each.

STRUCTURE

These next literary terms have to do with the structure of a poem.

couplet:

trecets:

quatrains:

cinquains:

sestets:

septets:

octaves:

What is a stanza?

SOUNDS

Define and give examples of each of these terms:

alliteration

assonance

Tell how the use of these sounds "connect with the poem's meaning" (as your book says on page 54).

When most people think of poetry, they expect to see rhyme. You probably already know that a poem does not have to rhyme. The most common form of rhyme is *perfect rhyme*, sometimes called *complete rhyme*, but there are many variations of rhyme. Define each of the terms below and give the usual obligatory examples:

perfect rhyme

partial rhyme (sometimes called half-rhyme or off-rhyme):

vowel rhyme (a form of assonance):

end rhyme:

internal rhyme:

Explain how rhyme can benefit a poem.

Day 5

Interpretation Skills: Putting it all together.

After you have carefully observed the text of a poem you will find yourself naturally wanting to move beyond a focus on what the poet is literally saying. You will probably begin to ask, "Fine, so what does this thing MEAN?"

Chapter 4, "The Art of Interpretation," gives you quite a bit of information about interpretation skills. Please read pages 61-78 carefully. When you finish each section, use the following questions to make notes summarizing your reading.

The text defines *interpretation* as "the act of accounting for the feelings the poem gives you when you read it." But "feeling" is only part of the process. Read further in the paragraph – "When you look closely at a poem and see how it works, you find a way into it; you discover **feelings, meanings, and richness. . ."**

The process of looking "closely" at a text will generally be referred to as "making a close reading" of a text.

The *Poetry for Dummies* text goes on to say that "some of the feelings, meanings and richness" you will discover will be things created by the poet, but "some of [these]. . .you make for yourself." But a good reader must be careful not to "impose" his own interpretations on a text in a way that distorts the text itself. Obviously, as we read, we make connections between what the poet describes and our own experiences. And feeling is a part of that.

But don't stop there! You must also ask, as the text point out, "Why does this poem make me feel the way I do? What is the poem doing, and how does the poet do it?

Read the section following the heading, "Sense: Determining what a poem is saying." It is important to understand a writer's pupose for writing. A poet may intend to communicate many things –

List some of the things a poet may want to communicate with a reader:

Note the differences between differing levels of attention.

Explain the differences between what is explicitly stated and what is implied. Between what is literal and what is implied

Define *tone*. As you read *Richard Cory*, identify the tone. How do you identify the tone of a poem?

How do you recognize a symbol, metaphor, or image?

STRUCTURE

These next literary terms have to do with the structure of a poem.

couplet:

trecets:

quatrains:

cinquains:

sestets:

septets:

octaves:

What is a stanza?

SOUNDS

Define and give examples of each of these terms:

alliteration

assonance

Tell how the use of these sounds "connect with the poem's meaning" (as your book says on page 54).

When most people think of poetry, they expect to see rhyme. You probably already know that a poem does not have to rhyme. The most common form of rhyme is *perfect rhyme*, sometimes called *complete rhyme*, but there are many variations of rhyme. Define each of the terms below and give the usual obligatory examples:

perfect rhyme

partial rhyme (sometimes called half-rhyme or off-rhyme):

vowel rhyme (a form of assonance):

end rhyme:

internal rhyme:

Explain how rhyme can benefit a poem.

Time for a snack.

Lesson 3: Poetry of the Early English Renaissance: The Sonnet

Before we move on to specific English Renaissance Poets, we need to spend more time talked about the way poems are structured.

By way of review, define the following terms –

stanza

couplet

trecets

quatrains

cinquains

sestets

septets

octaves

The basic unit of a stanza would be a line. Meter determines the rhythm of a line. Meter is composed by the pattern of stressed (S) and non-stressed (n) syllables in each line.

The smallest unit of a line is called a *foot*. Each foot is made up of a determined number of syllables, and each syllable with have a set pattern of stressed and unstressed syllables.

Four of the basic metrical patterns are described in the chart below

Name	Number of Syllables	Stress Pattern	Example	Re-write and mark
DACTYL	**3 syllables**	**S! – n - n**	**DIN-o-saurs,**	**/ - -** **DI- no - saur**
ANAPEST	**3 syllables**	**n – n – S!**	**to the REAR!**	
TROCHEE	**2 syllables**	**S! – n**	**CAVE men,**	
IAMB	**2 syllables**	**n – S!**	**at – TACK!**	

Memorize these.

Number of Feet in a Line:

If the line is made up on one foot, we call it monometer.

Two feet – dimeter

Three feet – trimester

Four feet – tetrameter

Five feet – pentameter

Six feet – hexameter

A line made up of one iam only would be one foot long. And we would call it an ***iambic monometer line.***

A line made up of 5 iams would be five feet long. We would call it ***iambic pentameter.***

When a sentence ends at the end of a line, the line is said to be 'end-stopped.' Logical, no?

But when a sentence continues *without pausing,* beyond the end of a line, a couplet or a stanze, we call that enjambment.

Before going on, make sure you are able to explain what these terms mean:

rhythm

meter

feet

enjambment

Part II of Poetry of *Poetry for Dummies,* "In the Beginning Was a Poem," provides an overview of literary history. To start off our study, please ready the section, "The Renaissance (1450-1674) pp. 107-110. This section will summarize major characteristics of this period.

As the writers of your text point out, "The sonnet was an international craze" during this time period. We being our study of Renaissance literature with --

Sir Thomas Wyatt (1503-1542)

Thomas Wyatt was a served as courtier and diplomat for Henry VIII. His relationship with Anne Boleyn (the details of which are not entirely clear) eventual let to a brief imprisonment after her arrest. He was released some time after her execution. As Henry's diplomat, Wyatt traveled extensively throughout Europe and so became familiar with European literary styles – most notably the sonnets of Petrarch. Wyatt translated Petrarch sonnets into English. Using Petrarchan imagery and making some changes to the structure and rhyme scheme, he is considered the Father of the English sonnet.

Wyatt did not only write sonnets, however. In this lesson, we are going to start with some of these.

Use the Observation and Interpretation skills you practiced in the last lesson, read Wyatt's They Flee From Me that Sometimes Did Me Seek and answer the following questions:

1. **Who is the speaker?**

2. **Are other characters present, named, or described?**

3. **What is the setting?**

4. **What is the situation?**

5. What is the plot (that is, list the sequence of events)?

6. Paraphrase the poem. (Rewrite it in your own words.) You can use poetic form or prose.)

They flee from me that Sometime did me Seek

They flee from me that sometime did me seek
With naked foot, stalking in my chamber.
I have seen them gentle, tame, and meek,
That now are wild and do not remember.
That sometime they put themself in danger
To take bread at my hand; and now they range,
Busily seeking with a continual change.
Thanked be fortune it hath been otherwise
Twenty times better; but once in special,
In thin array after a pleasant guise,
When her loose gown from her shoulders did fall,
And she me caught in her arms long and small;
Therewithall sweetly did me kiss
And softly said, "dear heart, how like you this?"
It was no dream: I lay broad waking.
But all is turned thorough my gentleness
Into a strange fashion of forsaking;
And I have leave to go of her goodness,
And she also, to use newfangleness.
But since that I so kindly am served
I would fain know what she hath deserved.

-Thomas Wyatt

THE SONNET:

Sonnet is an Italian word which means, little song. A sonnet is a 14 line poem with a set meter (iambic pentameter) and a set rhyme scheme.

Read pp. 56-59, titled, "Feeling Rhythm and Measuring Meter." This section speaks specifically about sonnets.

Petrarchan (or Italian) Sonnets and English Sonnets:

The Italian Sonnet form:

Structure:

Fourteen lines made up of an ***octave*** (eight lines) and a **sestet** (six lines).

The octave states a theme or an experience.

The sestet answers or comments on the theme or experience stated or described in the octave. While the octave and the sestet technically are considered to be two stanzas, the stanzas are not usually separated by an extra space. The rhyme scheme is your clue to stanza breaks.

Rhyme scheme:

abbaabba cdecde

Petrarchan conceits:

When a poet uses an elaborate analogy or metaphor to express an imaginative idea you could say that he or she is using a ***poetic conceit***. Another way to think of a conceit is as a stock (or commonly used) image or idea.

If you were putting a newsletter together you might illustrate it with clip art – drawing or photographs of people or places commonly found in newsletter (a mother, a policeman, a picture of a landmark like Mt. Rushmore). We call those *stock images*. They are not created specifically for a one-time use, but intended to be used any time an editor needs a shot of a generic occupation or landmark. A very gifted editor might do something very fresh and creative with a stock image. A less gifted editor would just be slapping in a generic picture to fill the space. Poetic *conceits* can be used in the same ways. At one point those conceits were fresh and individual but over time they tend to become clichés. Petrachan conceits imitate the imagery and stylistic devices used by in Petrarch's poetry.

Petrarch wrote about his unrequited love for a lady named Laura. Forced to love her only from afar, Petrarch dwells on the ways in which his love pains him and is filled with images of misery, longing, despair – storming waves that toss and beat the lover, Love is idealized and her beauty is described is set ways – lips like cherries, ivory breasts, The beloved is often called by a generic classical name. The beloved has great power over the poet. She is able to wound him, even slay him with just one loving or one indifferent glance, In his sonnets you will find ***oxymorons*** (which has little to do with a big ox of a moronic lover) – things that a seemingly contractory. In additional to all this, true and lasting love can never be expressed physically – it is always platonic (of the mind, not the body) and is never fulfilled.

The English Sonnet's Form

Structure:

Fourteen lines made up of three quatrains (three sets of four lines units) followed by a rhyming couplet. As with the Italian Sonnet, even though each quatrain plus the couplet are considered to make up four stanza, there are usually not line extra spaces separating the stanzas. Again, the rhyme scheme is usually your clue to stanza breaks.

Rhyme scheme:

ababcdcdefef gg

Petrarchan Conceits:

The English sonnet (and you see this in Wyatt's sonnets) may also use Petrarchan conceits.

Now read the next poem. The following words may be unfamiliar to you, make sure you understand their definitions before you read.

eke: also

owre: oar/hour   cord: ship's ropes/lines   apace: swiftly

galley - A large, usually single-decked medieval ship of shallow draft, propelled by sails and oars and used as a merchant ship or warship in the Mediterranean

My Galley, Charged with Forgetfulness

My galley, chargèd with forgetfulness,
Thorough sharp seas in winter nights doth pass
'Tween rock and rock; and eke mine en'my, alas,
That is my lord, steereth with cruelness;
And every owre a thought in readiness, oar
As though that death were light in such a case.
An endless wind doth tear the sail apace
Of forced sighs and trusty fearfulness.
A rain of tears, a cloud of dark disdain,
Hath done the weared cords great hinderance;
Wreathèd with error and eke with ignorance.
The stars be hid that led me to this pain;
Drownèd is Reason that should me comfort,
And I remain despairing of the port.

Now that you have read the poem, "My Galley Charged with Forgetfulness," answer the following questions

What can you determine about the persona (or the speaker)?

Who else is mentioned in the poem?

What is the setting?

What is the situation?

What is the form? Is it an English sonnet or a Petrachan (Italian) sonnet?

Does the poet use Petrarchan conceits?

Does he seem to do anything different with them or does he just seem to use stock images?

What example of Petrarchan conceits do you find here?

Now read the next poem, also by Thomas Wyatt:

Whoso List to Hunt, I Know where is an Hind

Whoso list to hunt, I know where is an hind,

But as for me, *hélas*, I may no more.

The vain travail hath wearied me so sore,

I am of them that farthest cometh behind.

Yet may I by no means my wearied mind

Draw from the deer, but as she fleeth afore

Fainting I follow. I leave off therefore,

Sithens in a net I seek to hold the wind.

Who list her hunt, I put him out of doubt,

As well as I may spend his time in vain.

And graven with diamonds in letters plain

There is written, her fair neck round about:

Noli me tangere, for Caesar's I am,

And wild for to hold, though I seem tame.

Answer these questions about the poem "Whoso List to Hunt"

What can you determine about the persona (or the speaker)?

Who else is mentioned in the poem?

What is the setting?

What is the situation?

What is the form?

Does the poet use Petrarchan conceits?

Does he seem to do anything different with them or does he just seem to use stock images?

Now read the following poems by a variety of poets. Some are sonnets, Some are not. Read each one aloud. Use the observation and interpretation skills you've been using so far.

How many examples of poetic conceits can you find? (Any you would call, Petrarchan?)

Does the poet use stock images in the usual way or do something different with them?

HENRY HOWARD,
Earl of Surrey (1517?-1547)

Love that doth Reign and Live within my Thought

Love that doth reign and live within my thought
And built his seat within my captive breast,
Clad in the arms wherein with me he fought,
Oft in my face he doth his banner rest.
But she that taught me love and suffer pain,
My doubtful hope and eke my hot desire
With shamefast look to shadow and refrain,
Her smiling grace converteth straight to ire.
And coward Love then to the heart apace
Taketh his flight, where he doth lurk and plain
His purpose lost, and dare not show his face.
For my lord's guilt thus faultless bide I pain;
Yet from my lord shall not my foot remove:
Sweet is the death that taketh end by love.

CHRISTOPHER MARLOWE

Passionate Shepherd to his Love

Come live with me and be my love,
And we will all the pleasures prove,
That valleys, groves, hills, and fields,
Woods, or steepy mountain yields.

And we will sit upon the rocks,
Seeing the shepherds feed their flocks,
By shallow rivers, to whose falls
Melodious birds sing madrigals.

And I will make thee beds of roses,
And a thousand fragrant posies,
A cap of flowers and a kirtle
Embroider'd all with leaves of myrtle:

A gown made of the finest wool,
Which from our pretty lambs we pull;
Fair lined slippers for the cold,
With buckles of the purest gold:

A belt of straw and ivy buds,
With coral clasps and amber studs;
And if these pleasures may thee move,
Come live with me and be my love.

The shepherd swains shall dance and sing
For thy delight each May morning;
If these delights thy mind may move,
Then live with me and be my love.

William Shakespeare (1564-1616)

Sonnet XVIII:

Shall I Compare Thee to a Summer's Day?

Shall I compare thee to a summer's day?
Thou art more lovely and more temperate.
Rough winds do shake the darling buds of May,
And summer's lease hath all too short a date.
Sometime too hot the eye of heaven shines,
And often is his gold complexion dimm'd;
And every fair from fair sometime declines,
By chance or nature's changing course ntrimm'd;
But thy eternal summer shall not fade
Nor lose possession of that fair thou ow'st;
Nor shall Death brag thou wander'st in his shade,
When in eternal lines to time thou grow'st:
So long as men can breathe or eyes can see,
So long lives this, and this gives life to thee.

Sonnet XXIX:

When in Disgrace with Fortune and Men's Eyes

When, in disgrace with fortune and men's eyes,
I all alone beweep my outcast state
And trouble deaf heaven with my bootless cries
And look upon myself and curse my fate,
Wishing me like to one more rich in hope,
Featur'd like him, like him with friends possess'd,
Desiring this man's art and that man's scope,
With what I most enjoy contented least;
Yet in these thoughts myself almost despising,
Haply I think on thee, and then my state,
Like to the lark at break of day arising
From sullen earth, sings hymns at heaven's gate;
For thy sweet love remember'd such wealth brings
That then I scorn to change my state with kings.

Sonnet LXXI:

No Longer Mourn for me when I am Dead

No longer mourn for me when I am dead
Than you shall hear the surly sudden bell
Give warning to the world that I am fled
From this vile world, with vilest worms to dwell:
Nay, if you read this line, remember not
The hand that write it; for I love you so
That I in your sweet thoughts would be forgot
If thinking on me then should make you woe.
O, if, I say, you look upon this verse
When I perhaps compounded am with clay,
Do not so much as my poor name rehearse,
But let your love even with my life decay,
Lest the wise world should look into your moan
And mock you with me after I am gone.

Sonnet LXXIII:

That Time of Year thou mayst in me Behold

That time of year thou mayst in me behold
When yellow leaves, or none, or few, do hang
Upon those boughs which shake against the cold,
Bare ruin'd choirs, where late the sweet birds sang.
In me thou see'st the twilight of such day
As after sunset fadeth in the west,
Which by and by black night doth take away,
Death's second self, that seals up all in rest.
In me thou see'st the glowing of such fire
That on the ashes of his youth doth lie,
As the death-bed whereon it must expire,
Consum'd with that which it was nourish'd by.
This thou perceiv'st, which makes thy love more strong,
To love that well which thou must leave ere long.

Sonnet CXXX:

My Mistress' Eyes are Nothing like the Sun

My mistress' eyes are nothing like the sun;
Coral is far more red than her lips' red:
If snow be white, why then her breasts are dun;
If hairs be wires, black wires grow on her head.
I have seen roses damask'd, red and white,
But no such roses see I in her cheeks;
And in some perfumes is there more delight
Than in the breath that from my mistress reeks.
I love to hear her speak, yet well I know
That music hath a far more pleasing sound.
I grant I never saw a goddess go:
My mistress, when she walks, treads on the ground.
And yet, by heaven, I think my love as rare
As any she belied with false compare.

Sonnet CXVI:

Let me not to the Marriage of True Minds

Let me not to the marriage of true minds
Admit impediments. Love is not love
Which alters when it alteration finds,
Or bends with the remover to remove.
O no! it is an ever-fixed mark
That looks on tempests and is never shaken;
It is the star to every wand'ring bark,
Whose worth's unknown, although his height be taken.
Love's not Time's fool, though rosy lips and cheeks
Within his bending sickle's compass come;
Love alters not with his brief hours and weeks,
But bears it out even to the edge of doom.
If this be error and upon me prov'd,
I never writ, nor no man ever lov'd.

Good job. Review your work before class, and get ready for class discussion.

LESSON 4:

More RENAISSANCE Poets

Ben Jonson (1572-1637)

Ben Jonson wrote plays and lyric poetry. As a playwright, he was considered to be Shakespeare's chief rival. He was a contemporary of the Metaphysical poets that you will read about in the next couple of lessons, but his poetic style was much more straightforward. By all accounts, Jonson was one of those larger-than-life personalities who was much respected during his lifetime and whose influence was felt long after his death. His work greatly influence later poets, notably, Andrew Marvel and

After you have carefully read the following poem for yourself. Read pages 12-13 of your text, Poetry for Dummies, titled "Creating an Intense Emotional Experience." Then read the poem again.

Epigrams: On my First Son

Farewell, thou child of my right hand, and joy;
My sin was too much hope of thee, lov'd boy.
Seven years tho' wert lent to me, and I thee pay,
Exacted by thy fate, on the just day.
O, could I lose all father now! For why
Will man lament the state he should envy?
To have so soon 'scap'd world's and flesh's rage,
And if no other misery, yet age?
Rest in soft peace, and, ask'd, say, "Here doth lie
Ben Jonson his best piece of poetry.
For whose sake henceforth all his vows be such,
As what he loves may never like too much.

Who is the speaker and what is his situation? What is the tone of the poem? Read the poem again, looking at the ways the poet communicates that emotional tone?

Now read the following poems by Jonson, making notes as you read. Ask the usual who, who, what, when, where, why, and how questions of the poems. What can you learn about the speaker and the situation described in each poem. Note any other questions or observations as well.

To Heaven

Good and great God, can I not think of thee
But it must straight my melancholy be?
Is it interpreted in me disease
That, laden with my sins, I seek for ease?
Oh be thou witness, that the reins dost know
And hearts of all, if I be sad for show,
And judge me after; if I dare pretend
To ought but grace or aim at other end.
As thou art all, so be thou all to me,
First, midst, and last, converted one, and three;
My faith, my hope, my love; and in this state
My judge, my witness, and my advocate.
Where have I been this while exil'd from thee?
And whither rap'd, now thou but stoop'st to me?
Dwell, dwell here still. O, being everywhere,
How can I doubt to find thee ever here?

I know my state, both full of shame and scorn,
Conceiv'd in sin, and unto labour borne,
Standing with fear, and must with horror fall,
And destin'd unto judgment, after all.
I feel my griefs too, and there scarce is ground
Upon my flesh t' inflict another wound.
Yet dare I not complain, or wish for death
With holy Paul, lest it be thought the breath
Of discontent; or that these prayers be
For weariness of life, not love of thee.

Epicoene, or the Silent Woman: Still to be neat, still to be drest

Still to be neat, still to be drest,
As you were going to a feast;
Still to be powder'd, still perfum'd:
Lady, it is to be presum'd,
Though art's hid causes are not found,
All is not sweet, all is not sound.

Give me a look, give me a face,
That makes simplicity a grace;
Robes loosely flowing, hair as free:
Such sweet neglect more taketh me
Than all th' adulteries of art;
They strike mine eyes, but not my heart.

On My First Daughter

Here lies, to each her parents' Ruth,
Mary, the daughter of their youth;
Yet all heaven's gifts being heaven's due,
It makes the father less to rue.
At six months' end, she parted hence
With safety of her innocence;
Whose soul heaven's queen, whose name she bears,
In comfort of her mother's tears,
Hath placed amongst her virgin-train:
Where, while that severed doth remain,
This grave partakes the fleshly birth;
Which cover lightly, gentle earth!

HYMN TO THE BELLY

ROOM! room! make room for the bouncing Belly,
First father of sauce and deviser of jelly;
Prime master of arts and the giver of wit,
That found out the excellent engine, the spit,
The plough and the flail, the mill and the hopper,
The hutch and the boulter, the furnace and copper,
The oven, the bavin, the mawkin, the peel,
The hearth and the range, the dog and the wheel.
He, he first invented the hogshead and tun,
The gimlet and vice too, and taught 'em to run;
And since, with the funnel and hippocras bag,
He's made of himself that now he cries swag;
Which shows, though the pleasure be but of four inches,
Yet he is a weasel, the gullet that pinches
Of any delight, and not spares from his back
Whatever to make of the belly a sack.
Hail, hail, plump paunch! O the founder of taste,
For fresh meats or powdered, or pickle or paste!
Devourer of broiled, baked, roasted or sod!
And emptier of cups, be they even or odd!
All which have now made thee so wide i' the waist,
As scarce with no pudding thou art to be laced;
But eating and drinking until thou dost nod,
Thou break'st all thy girdles and break'st forth a god.

LESSON 5:

Poetry of the Late English Renaissance – The Metaphysical Poets

John Donne, George Herbert, Richard Crashaw, Abraham Cowley, Andrew Marvell and Henry Vaughan are the poets generally considered to belong to what is call the Metaphysical school of poetry. Herbert died in 1633 and Vaughn in 1695, so you can see that this school of poetry continued for seventy or so years. The late seventeenth century writer, John Dryden, applied the label *metaphysical* to their work – and he did not mean it as a compliment.

The metaphysical poets didn't feel obligated to write like the early Renaissance poets. They were happy to abandon conventional meters and rhythm and were often criticized for writing rough and jarring verse. The metaphysical poets were passionate about their pursuits – it they were in love, they were IN LOVE. If they mourned, they MOURNED.

The Metaphysical writers made use of *poetic conceits*, but the metaphysical conceit has specific characteristics –

They are tend to be highly intellectual, sometimes very complicated, and often grotesque. These extended metaphors usually compare very different things. A metaphysical poet seems to be happiest when his poems make use of paradoxical arguments and imagery.

There is a playfulness about these poets. You often may sense them winking at you, inviting you to go along with the game and join in the fun. Enjoy the fun.

Think

Paradoxical
Intellectual
Grotesque
Complicated
Argument
Playful

John Donne 1572-1631

John Donne converted from Catholicism to Anglicanism (i.e. he joined the Church of England) sometime in the 1590's and began to study law shortly after that. He took a position as an assistant to the Keeper of the Grteat Seal, Thomas Egerton. This position should have meant good things for Donne, but he spoiled things by falling in love with Egerton's niece, Anne. When their secret marriage was discovered, Donne was imprisoned. Did I mention that he also lost his job? Once he was released John worked as a lawyer. As you might guess,however, it would not necessarily work to the accused to be represented by a young lawyer who has greatly offended influential people in the court. Thus, financially the Donnes had a rough time of it.

His first book of poetry, *Divine Poems* was published in 1607. In 1615 he was appointed as the chaplain to King James, and in 1615 was named Dean of St. Paul's Church in London.

In his biography of John Donne, Izaac Walton described Donne like this:

> He was of stature moderately tall; of a straight and equally—proportioned body, to which all his words and actions gave an unexpressible addition of comeliness.
>
> The melancholy and pleasant humour were in him so contempered, that each gave advantage to the other, and made his company one of the delights of mankind
>
> His fancy was unimitably high, equalled only by his great wit; both being made useful by a commanding judgment
>
> His aspect was cheerful, and such as gave a silent testimony of a clear knowing soul, and of a conscience at peace with itself.

His melting eye showed that he had a soft heart, full of noble compassion; of too brave a soul to offer injuries, and too much a Christian not to pardon them in others.

He did much contemplate—especially after he entered into his sacred calling—the mercies of Almighty God, the immortality of the soul, and the joys of heaven: and would often say in a kind of sacred ecstasy,—"Blessed be God that he is God, only and divinely like himself."

He was by nature highly passionate, but more apt to reluct at the excesses of it. A great lover of the offices of humanity, and of so merciful a spirit, that he never beheld the miseries of mankind without pity and relief.

He was earnest and unwearied in the search of knowledge, with which his vigorous soul is now satisfied, and employed in a continual praise of that God that first breathed it into his active body: that body, which once was a temple of the Holy Ghost, and is now become a small quantity of Christian dust:—

But I shall see it re-animated.
Feb. 15, 1639.

Read the rest of this biography at the following web address:
http://www.bartleby.com/15/2/11.html

Notice Donne's relationship to King James and to the next poet you'll read, George Herbert.

Before you read *The Bait*, look back to Christopher Marlowe's poem that begins, "Come live with me and be my love." Compare ways in which each poet develops this theme. Use the usual set of inductive study skills to observe and interpret this poem.

The Bait

Come live with me, and be my love,
And we will some new pleasures prove
Of golden sands, and crystal brooks,
With silken lines, and silver hooks.

There will the river whispering run
Warm'd by thy eyes, more than the sun;
And there the 'enamour'd fish will stay,
Begging themselves they may betray.

When thou wilt swim in that live bath,
Each fish, which every channel hath,
Will amorously to thee swim,
Gladder to catch thee, than thou him.

If thou, to be so seen, be'st loth,
By sun or moon, thou dark'nest both,
And if myself have leave to see,
I need not their light having thee.

Let others freeze with angling reeds,
And cut their legs with shells and weeds,
Or treacherously poor fish beset,
With strangling snare, or windowy net.

Let coarse bold hands from slimy nest
The bedded fish in banks out-wrest;
Or curious traitors, sleeve-silk flies,
Bewitch poor fishes' wand'ring eyes.

For thee, thou need'st no such deceit,
For thou thyself art thine own bait:
That fish, that is not catch'd thereby,
Alas, is wiser far than I.

Read the next poem.

What can you tell about the speaker and the others mentioned in the poem. What metaphysical conceits do you find here?

What observations can you make about the form of the poem? about the sounds the poet uses?

The Flea

Mark but this flea, and mark in this,
How little that which thou deny'st me is;
It sucked me first, and now sucks thee,
And in this flea our two bloods mingled be;
Thou know'st that this cannot be said
A sin, nor shame, nor loss of maidenhead;
Yet this enjoys before it woo,
And pampered swells with one blood made of two,
And this, alas, is more than we would do.

Oh stay, three lives in one flea spare,
Where we almost, yea, more than married are.
This flea is you and I, and this
Our marriage bed, and marriage temple is;
Though parents grudge, and you, w'are met,
And cloistered in these living walls of jet.
Though use make you apt to kill me,
Let not to that, self-murder added be,
And sacrilege, three sins in killing three.

Cruel and sudden, hast thou since
Purpled thy nail in blood of innocence?
Wherein could this flea guilty be,
Except in that drop which it sucked from thee?

Yet thou triumph'st and say'st that thou
Find'st not thyself, nor me the weaker now;
'Tis true, then learn how false fears be:
Just so much honor, when thou yield'st to me,
Will waste, as this flea's death took life from thee.

The rest of the poems in this section were written by John Donne. The last piece is one of his prose mediations. Observe and interpret carefully. If you find examples of Metaphysical conceits, please note them and be prepared to explain them and tell how the conceits work within the poem.

Good Friday, 1613. Riding Westward

Let man's Soule be a Spheare, and then, in this,
The intelligence that moves, devotion is,
And as the other Spheares, by being growne
Subject to forraigne motion, lose their owne,
And being by others hurried every day,
Scarce in a yeare their naturall forme obey:
Pleasure or businesse, so, our Soules admit
For their first mover, and are whirld by it.
Hence is't, that I am carryed towards the West
This day, when my Soules forme bends toward the East.
There I should see a Sunne, by rising set,
And by that setting endlesse day beget;
But that Christ on this Crosse, did rise and fall,
Sinne had eternally benighted all.
Yet dare I'almost be glad, I do not see
That spectacle of too much weight for mee.
Who sees Gods face, that is selfe life, must dye;
What a death were it then to see God dye?
It made his owne Lieutenant Nature shrinke,
It made his footstoole crack, and the Sunne winke.
Could I behold those hands which span the Poles,
And tune all spheares at once peirc'd with those holes?
Could I behold that endlesse height which is
Zenith to us, and our Antipodes,
Humbled below us? or that blood which is
The seat of all our Soules, if not of his,
Made durt of dust, or that flesh which was worne
By God, for his apparell, rag'd, and torne?
If on these things I durst not looke, durst I
Upon his miserable mother cast mine eye,
Who was Gods partner here, and fu
Restore thine Image, so much, by thy grace,
That thou may'st know mee, and I'll turne my face. rnish'd thus
Halfe of that Sacrifice, which ransom'd us?
Though these things, as I ride, be from mine eye,
They'are present yet unto my memory,
For that looks towards them; and thou look'st towards mee,
O Saviour, as thou hang'st upon the tree;
I turne my backe to thee, but to receive
Corrections, till thy mercies bid thee leave.
O thinke mee worth thine anger, punish mee,
Burne off my rusts, and my deformity,

The Sun Rising

Busy old fool, unruly Sun,
Why dost thou thus,
Through windows, and through curtains, call on us?
Must to thy motions lovers' seasons run?
Saucy pedantic wretch, go chide
Late schoolboys, and sour prentices,
Go tell court-huntsmen that the king will ride,
Call country ants to harvest offices,
Love, all alike, no season knows, nor clime,
Nor hours, days, months, which are the rags of time.

Thy beams, so reverend and strong
Why shouldst thou think?
I could eclipse and cloud them with a wink,
But that I would not lose her sight so long:
If her eyes have not blinded thine,
Look, and tomorrow late, tell me
Whether both the'Indias of spice and mine
Be where thou leftst them, or lie here with me.
Ask for those kings whom thou saw'st yesterday,
And thou shalt hear: "All here in one bed lay."

She'is all states,and all princes I,
Nothing else is.
Princes do but play us; compar'd to this,
All honour's mimic, all wealth alchemy.
Thou, sun, art half as happy'as we,
In that the world's contracted thus;
Thine age asks ease, and since thy duties be
To warm the world, that's done in warming us.
Shine here to us, and thou art everywhere;
This bed thy centre is, these walls, thy sphere.

A Valediction: Forbidding Mourning

As virtuous men pass mildly away,
And whisper to their souls, to go,
Whilst some of their sad friends do say,
"The breath goes now," and some say, "No:"

So let us melt, and make no noise,
No tear-floods, nor sigh-tempests move;
'Twere profanation of our joys
To tell the laity our love.

Moving of th' earth brings harms and fears;
Men reckon what it did, and meant;
But trepidation of the spheres,
Though greater far, is innocent.

Dull sublunary lovers' love
(Whose soul is sense) cannot admit
Absence, because it doth remove
Those things which elemented it.

But we by a love so much refin'd,
That ourselves know not what it is,
Inter-assured of the mind,
Care less, eyes, lips, and hands to miss.

Our two souls therefore, which are one,
Though I must go, endure not yet
A breach, but an expansion,
Like gold to airy thinness beat.

If they be two, they are two so
As stiff twin compasses are two;
Thy soul, the fix'd foot, makes no show
To move, but doth, if the' other do.

And though it in the centre sit,
Yet when the other far doth roam,
It leans, and hearkens after it,
And grows erect, as that comes home.

Such wilt thou be to me, who must
Like th' other foot, obliquely run;
Thy firmness makes my circle just,
And makes me end, where I begun.

Izaak Walton's biography gives this background to the writing of Valediction Forbidding Mourning:

At this time of Mr. Donne's and his wife's living in Sir Robert's house, the Lord Hay was, by King James, sent upon a glorious embassy to the then French king, Henry the Fourth; and Sir Robert put on a sudden resolution to accompany him to the French court, and to be present at his audience there. And Sir Robert put on a sudden resolution to solicit Mr. Donne to be his companion in that journey. And this desire was suddenly made known to his wife, who was then with child, and otherwise under so dangerous a habit of body, as to her health, that she professed an unwillingness to allow him any absence from her; saying, "Her divining soul boded her some ill in his absence;" and therefore desired him not to leave her. This made Mr. Donne lay aside all thoughts of the journey, and really to resolve against it. But Sir Robert became restless in his persuasions for it, and Mr. Donne was so generous as to think he had sold his liberty, when he received so many charitable kindnesses from him; and told his wife so, who did therefore, with an unwilling-willingness, give a faint consent to the journey, which was proposed to be but for two months; for about that time they determined their return. Within a few days after this resolve, the Ambassador, Sir Robert, and Mr. Donne left London; and were the twelfth day got all safe to Paris. Two days after their arrival there, Mr. Donne was left alone in that room in which Sir Robert, and he, and some other friends had dined together. To this place Sir Robert returned within half-an-hour; and as he left, so he found, Mr. Donne alone, but in such an ecstasy, and so altered as to his looks, as amazed Sir Robert to behold him; insomuch that he earnestly desired Mr. Donne to declare what had befallen him in the short time of his absence. To which Mr. Donne was not able to make a present answer, but after a long and perplexed pause, did at last say, "I have seen a dreadful vision since I saw you: I have seen my dear wife pass twice by me through this room, with her hair hanging about her shoulders, and a dead child in her arms; this I have seen since I saw you." To which Sir Robert replied, "Sure, sir, you have slept since I saw you; and this is the result of some melancholy dream, which I desire you to forget, for you are now awake." To which Mr. Donne's reply was, "I cannot be surer that I now live than that I have not slept since I saw you; and am as sure that at her second appearing she stopped and looked me in the face, and vanished." Rest and sleep had not altered Mr. Donne's opinion the next day, for he then affirmed this opinion with a more deliberate, and so confirmed a confidence, that he inclined Sir Robert to a faint belief that the vision was true.—It is truly said that desire and doubt have no rest, and it proved so with Sir Robert; for he immediately sent a servant to Drewry House, with a charge to hasten back, and bring him word whether Mrs. Donne we alive; and, if alive, in what condition she was as to her health. The twelfth day, the messenger returned with this account: That he found and left Mrs. Donne very sad, and sick in her bed; and that, after a long and dangerous labour, she had been delivered of a dead child. And, upon examination, the abortion proved to be the same day, and about the very hour, that Mr. Donne affirmed he saw her pass by him in his chamber.

This is a relation that will beget some wonder, and it well many; for most of our world are at present possessed with an opinion that visions and miracles are ceased. And, though it is most certain that two lutes being both strung and tuned to an equal pitch, and then one played upon, the other, that is not touched, being laid upon a table at a fit distance, will—like an echo to a trumpet—warble a faint audible harmony in answer to the same tune; yet many will not believe there is any such thing as a sympathy of souls; and I am well pleased that every reader do enjoy his own opinion. But if the unbelieving will not allow the believing reader of this story a liberty to believe that it may be true, then I wish him to consider, many wise men have believed that the ghost of Julius Caesar did appear to Brutus, and that both St. Austin and Monica his mother had visions in order to his conversion. And though these, and many others—too many to name—have but the authority of human story, yet the incredible reader may find in the sacred story 3 that Samuel did appear to Saul even after his death—whether realy or not, I undertake not to determine.—And Bildad, in the Book of Job, says these words: “A spirit passed before my face; the hair of my head stood up; fear and trembling came upon me, and made all my bones to shake.” 4 Upon which words I will make no comment, but leave them to be considered by the incredulous reader; to whom I will also commend this following consideration: That there be many pious and learned men that believe our merciful God hath assigned to every man a particular guardian angel, to be his constant monitor, and to attend him in all his dangers, both of body and soul. And the opinion that every man hath his particular Angel may gain some authority by the relation of St. Peter’s miraculous deliverance out of prison, 5 not by many, but by one angel. And this belief may yet gain more credit by the reader’s considering, that when Peter after his enlargement knocked at the door of Mary the mother of John, and Rhode, the maidservant, being surprised with joy that Peter was there, did not let him in, but ran in haste and told the disciples—who were then and there met together—that Peter was at the door; and they, not believing it, said she was mad; yet, when she again affirmed it, though they then believed it not, yet. This is a relation that will beget some wonder, and it well many; for most of our world are at present possessed with an opinion that visions and miracles are ceased. And, though it is most certain that two lutes being both strung and tuned to an equal pitch, and then one played upon, the other, that is not touched, being laid upon a table at a fit distance, will—like an echo to a trumpet—warble a faint audible harmony in answer to the same tune; yet many will not believe there is any such thing as a sympathy of souls;

and I am well pleased that every reader do enjoy his own opinion. But if the unbelieving will not allow the believing reader of this story a liberty to believe that it may be true, then I wish him to consider, many wise men have believed that the ghost of Julius Caesar did appear to Brutus, and that both St. Austin and Monica his mother had visions in order to his conversion. And though these, and many others—too many to name—have but the authority of human story, yet the incredible reader may find in the sacred story [3] that Samuel did appear to Saul even after his death—whether realy or not, I undertake not to determine.—And Bildad, in the Book of Job, says these words: "A spirit passed before my face; the hair of my head stood up; fear and trembling came upon me, and made all my bones to shake." [4] Upon which words I will make no comment, but leave them to be considered by the incredulous reader; to whom I will also commend this following consideration: That there be many pious and learned men that believe our merciful God hath assigned to every man a particular guardian angel, to be his constant monitor, and to attend him in all his dangers, both of body and soul. And the opinion that every man hath his particular Angel may gain some authority by the relation of St. Peter's miraculous deliverance out of prison, [5] not by many, but by one angel. And this belief may yet gain more credit by the reader's considering, that when Peter after his enlargement knocked at the door of Mary the mother of John, and Rhode, the maidservant, being surprised with joy that Peter was there, did not let him in, but ran in haste and told the disciples—who were then and there met together—that Peter was at the door; and they, not believing it, said she was mad; yet, when she again affirmed it, though they then believed it not, yet they concluded, and said, "It is his angel." More observations of this nature, and inferences from them, might be made to gain the relation a firmer belief; but I forbear, lest I that intended to be but a relator, may be thought to be an engaged person for the proving what was related to me; and yet I think myself bound to declare, that though it was not told me by Mr. Donne himself, it was told me—now long since—by a person of honour, and of such intimacy with him, that he knew more of the secrets of his soul than any person then living: and I think he told me the truth; for it was told with such circumstances, and such asseverations, that—to say nothing of my own thoughts—I verily believe he that told it me did himself believe it to be true.

I forbear the reader's further wife at the time he then parted from trouble, as to the relation, and what concerns it; and will conclude mine with commending to his view a copy of verses given by Mr. Donne to her

From the *Holy Sonnets*:

Batter my heart, three-person'd God

Batter my heart, three-person'd God, for you
As yet but knock, breathe, shine, and seek to mend;
That I may rise and stand, o'erthrow me, and bend
Your force to break, blow, burn, and make me new.
I, like an usurp'd town to'another due,
Labor to'admit you, but oh, to no end;
Reason, your viceroy in me, me should defend,
But is captiv'd, and proves weak or untrue.
Yet dearly'I love you, and would be lov'd fain,
But am betroth'd unto your enemy;
Divorce me,'untie or break that knot again,
Take me to you, imprison me, for I,
Except you'enthrall me, never shall be free,
Nor ever chaste, except you ravish me.

Death, be not proud

Death, be not proud, though some have called thee
Mighty and dreadful, for thou art not so;
For those whom thou think'st thou dost overthrow,
Die not, poor Death, nor yet canst thou kill me.
From rest and sleep, which but thy pictures be,
Much pleasure; then from thee much more must flow,
And soonest our best men with thee do go,
Rest of their bones, and soul's delivery.
Thou art slave to fate, chance, kings, and desperate men,
And dost with poison, war, and sickness dwell;
And poppy or charms can make us sleep as well
And better than thy stroke; why swell'st thou then?
One short sleep past, we wake eternally,
And death shall be no more; Death, thou shalt die.

Meditation **XVII**

Nunc lento sonitu dicunt, Morieris

Now, this Bell tolling softly for another, saies to me, Thou must die.

PERCHANCE hee for whom this *Bell* tolls, may be so ill, as that he knowes not it tolls for him; And perchance I may thinke my selfe so much better than I am, as that they who are about mee, and see my state, may have caused it to toll for mee, and I know not that. The *Church* is *Catholike*, *universall*, so are all her *Actions; All* that she does, belongs to *all*. When she *baptizes a child*, that action concernes mee; for that child is thereby connected to that *Head* which is my *Head* too, and engraffed into that *body*, whereof I am a *member*. And when she *buries a Man*, that action concernes me: All *mankinde* is of one *Author*, and is one *volume;* when one Man dies, one *Chapter* is not *torne* out of the *booke*, but *translated* into a better *language;* and every *Chapter* must be so *translated; God* emploies several *translators;* some peeces are translated by *age*, some by *sicknesse*, some by warre, some by *justice;* but *Gods* hand is in every *translation;* and his hand shall binde up all our scattered leaves againe, for that *Librarie* where every *booke* shall lie open to one another: As therefore the *Bell* that rings to a *Sermon*, calls not upon the *Preacher* onely, but upon the *Congregation* to come; so this *Bell* calls us all: but how much more mee, who am brought so neere the *doore* by this sicknesse. There was a *contention* as farre as a *suite*, (in which both *pietie* and *dignitie*, *religion*, and *estimation*, were mingled) which of the religious *Orders* should ring to *praiers* first in the *Morning;* and it was that *they should ring first that rose earliest*. If we understand aright the *dignitie* of this *Belle* that tolls for our *evening prayer*, wee would bee glad to make it ours, by rising early, in that *application*, that it might bee ours, as wel as his, whose indeed it is. The *Bell* doth toll for him that *thinkes* it doth; and though it *intermit* againe, yet from that *minute*, that that occasion wrought upon him, hee is united to *God*. Who casts not up his *Eye* to the *Sunne* when it rises? but who takes off his *Eye* from a *Comet* when that breakes out? Who bends not his *eare* to any *bell*, which upon any occasion rings? but who can remove it from that *bell*, which is passing a *peece of himselfe* out of this *world?* No man is an *Iland*, intire of it selfe; every man is a peece of the *Continent*, a part of the *maine;* if a Clod bee washed away by the *Sea, Europe* is the lesse, as well as if a *Promontorie* were, as well as if a *Mannor* of thy *friends* or of *thine owne* were; any mans *death* diminishes *me*, because I am involved in *Mankinde;* And therefore never send to know for whom the *bell* tolls; It tolls for *thee*. Neither can we call this a *begging of Miserie* or a *borrowing of Miserie*, as though we were not miserable enough of our selves, but must fetch in more from the next house, in taking upon us the *Miserie* of our *Neighbours*. Truly it were an excusable *covetousnesse* if wee did; for *affliction* is a *treasure*, and scarce any man hath *enough* of it. No man hath *affliction* enough that is not matured, and ripened by it, and made fit for God by that *affliction*. If a man carry *treasure* in *bullion*, or in a *wedge* of *gold*, and have none coined into *currant Monies*, his *treasure* will not defray him as he travells. *Tribulation* is *Treasure* in the *nature* of it, but it is not *currant money* in the *use* of it, except wee get nearer and nearer our *home, Heaven*, by it. Another man may be sicke too, and sick to *death*, and this *affliction* may lie in his *bowels*, as *gold* in a *Mine*, and be of no use to him; but this *bell*, that tells me of his *affliction*, digs out, and applies that *gold* to *mee:* if by this consideration of anothers danger, I take mine owne into contemplation, and so secure my selfe, by making my recourse to my *God*, who is our onely securitie.

Comparing John Donne and Ben Jonson

Donne and Jonson were contemporaries. And both Donne and Jonson influenced other poets. Some literary critics feel that for the rest of the century it is possible to identify are two "schools" of poetry -- those who followed Donne and those who followed Ben Jonson.

Think back over the poems you have just read. What have you noticed about the styles of the two poets? Re-read the poems.

List the differences you observe between the two below.

Diction (casual or formal)

Allusions or references (Are they Biblical, classical, or scientific....?)

Imagery: (simple or complex)

Form: (structures of the line and stanza/rhyme schemes)

Audience (Are they writing to a public or private audience?)

Lesson 6

George Herbert (1593-1633)

George Herbert was a favorite of King James, serving as his Orator. His expectation was that he would eventually be appointed to serve as Secretary of State. However, things changed quickly for him: two of Herbert's most influential supporters died and shortly after that, King James also died.

Herbert had to decide whether he would return to the court and attempt to build his future in the court of King Charles I or return to the study of divinity and go into the ministry. Eventually, he chose the church over the court and entered the ministry in 1626. You can read the rest of his biography (a short one) at this site:

http://www.bartleby.com/15/2/21.html

Herbert, a contemporary of John Donne, wrote sacred verse (as opposed to secular). He is considered a Metaphysical Poet, though he has a much simpler style than Donne. A very devout follower of Jesus, his poetry is full of Biblical references. Therefore, the more familiar you are with the Old and New Testament, the better you will understand the allusions found in Herbert's poetry.

One of the things you will notice right off about Herbert's poetry will be the shapes of the poems.

In the poem, "Easter Wings,"the lines on the page look like wings. Often this type of poem is called, concrete poetry. In concrete poetry, the shape of the poem (the length of the line, the amount of white space around the line, even the shapes of the words, themselves) is used as imagery to reinforce the meaning of the poem. Herbert is one of the few poets to use this technique successfully. A successful Concrete (or Shape) poem, does not merely imitate or represent the shape the primary thing it describes. In good Concrete Poetry, (like all good poetry) the imagery, the sounds of the words, the rhythms, and the physical layout of the poem on the page all work together to reinforce the meaning.

Watch for the ways in which Herbert works with the images of decreasing and increasing though a varied use of short lines, long lines, and empty spaces.

Read Poetry for Dummies,"The Shape of the Poem: Visual Rhythm," pages 59-60. Then read the following poems.

The Altar

A broken ALTAR, Lord, thy servant rears,
Made of a heart and cemented with tears;
Whose parts are as thy hand did frame;
No workman's tool hath touch'd the same.
A HEART alone
Is such a stone,
As nothing but
Thy pow'r doth cut.
Wherefore each part
Of my hard heart
Meets in this frame
To praise thy name.
That if I chance to hold my peace,
These stones to praise thee may not cease.
Oh, let thy blessed SACRIFICE be mine,
And sanctify this ALTAR to be thine.

Background note: Refer to Exodus 20:22 to see how God commanded Israel to build altars. How does that apply to the poem?

The Collar*

I struck the board, and cried, "No more!
I will abroad.
What! shall I ever sigh and pine?
My lines and life are free; free as the road,
Loose as the wind, as large as store.
Shall I be still in suit?
Have I no harvest but a thorn
To let me blood, and not restore
What I have lost with cordial fruit?
Sure there was wine
Before my sighs did dry it; there was corn
Before my tears did drown it.
Is the year only lost to me?
Have I no bays to crown it?
No flowers, no garlands gay? all blasted?
All wasted?
Not so, my heart; but there is fruit,
And thou hast hands.
Recover all thy sigh-blown age
On double pleasures; leave thy cold dispute
Of what is fit and not; forsake thy cage,
Thy rope of sands,
Which petty thoughts have made, and made to thee
Good cable, to enforce and draw,
And be thy law,
While thou didst wink and wouldst not see.
Away! take heed;
I will abroad.
Call in thy death's-head there; tie up thy fears;
He that forbears
To suit and serve his need
Deserves his load."
But as I rav'd, and grew more fierce and wild
At every word,
Me thoughts I heard one calling, "Child";
And I replied, "My Lord."

***Notes: 1. Herbert likes to play with words that have multiple meanings. List the things a collar can refer to below. (Make sure you include a clerical collar in the list. That was a hint.) 2. You might also refer to Matthew 11:20-30 and notice what Jesus says about his "yoke. 3. *board* is a table, as in the phrase *room and board* (place to sleep and place to eat food)**

Easter Wings

Lord, who createdst man in wealth and store,
Though foolishly he lost the same,
Decaying more and more,
Till he became
Most poore:
With thee
O let me rise
As larks, harmoniously,
And sing this day thy victories:
Then shall the fall further the flight in me.

My tender age in sorrow did beginne
And still with sicknesses and shame.
Thou didst so punish sinne,
That I became
Most thinne.
With thee
Let me combine,
And feel thy victorie:
For, if I imp my wing on thine,
Affliction shall advance the flight in me.

Jordan (I)

Who says that fictions only and false hair
Become a verse? Is there in truth no beauty?
Is all good structure in a winding stair?
May no lines pass, except they do their duty
Not to a true, but painted chair?

Is it no verse, except enchanted groves
And sudden arbours shadow coarse-spun lines?
Must purling streams refresh a lover's loves?
Must all be veil'd, while he that reads, divines,
Catching the sense at two removes?

Shepherds are honest people; let them sing;
Riddle who list, for me, and pull for prime;
I envy no man's nightingale or spring;
Nor let them punish me with loss of rhyme,
Who plainly say, *my God, my King.*

The Pulley

When God at first made man,
Having a glass of blessings standing by,
"Let us," said he, "pour on him all we can;
Let the world's riches, which dispersed lie,
Contract into a span."

So strength first made a way;
Then beauty flow'd, then wisdom, honour, pleasure;
When almost all was out, God made a stay,
Perceiving that alone of all his treasure,
Rest in the bottom lay.

"For if I should," said he,
"Bestow this jewel also on my creature,
He would adore my gifts instead of me,
And rest in Nature, not the God of Nature:
So both should losers be.

"Yet let him keep the rest,
But keep them with repining restlessness;
Let him be rich and weary, that at least,
If goodness lead him not, yet weariness
May toss him to my breast."

Church Monuments.

While that my soul repairs to her devotion,
Here I intombe my flesh, that it betimes
May take acquaintance of this heap of dust;
To which the blast of deaths incessant motion,
Fed with the exhalation of our crimes,
Drives all at last. Therefore I gladly trust

My bodie to this school, that it may learn
To spell his elements, and finde his birth
Written in dustie heraldrie and lines;
Which dissolution sure doth best discern,
Comparing dust with dust, and earth with earth.
These laugh at Ieat, and Marble put for signes,

to sever the good fellowship of dust,
and spoil the meeting. What shall point out them,
when they shall bow, and kneel, and fall down flat
to kisse those heaps, which now they have in trust?
deare flesh, while I do pray, learn here thy stemme
and true descent; that when thou shalt grow fat,

and wanton in thy cravings, thou mayst know,
that flesh is but the glasse, which holds the dust
That measures all our time; which also shall
be crumbled into dust. Mark here below
how tame these ashes are, how free from lust,
That thou mayst fit thy self against thy fall.

Temper (I)

How should I praise thee, Lord! How should my rhymes
Gladly engrave thy love in steel,
If what my soul doth feel sometimes,
My soul might ever feel!

Although there were some forty heav'ns, or more,
Sometimes I peer above them all;
Sometimes I hardly reach a score;
Sometimes to hell I fall.

O rack me not to such a vast extent;
Those distances belong to thee:
The world's too little for thy tent,
A grave too big for me.

Wilt thou meet arms with man, that thou dost stretch
A crumb of dust from heav'n to hell?
Will great God measure with a wretch?
Shall he thy stature spell?

O let me, when thy roof my soul hath hid,
O let me roost and nestle there:
Then of a sinner thou art rid,
And I of hope and fear.

Yet take thy way; for sure thy way is best:
Stretch or contract me thy poor debtor:
This is but tuning of my breast,
To make the music better.

Whether I fly with angels, fall with dust,
Thy hands made both, and I am there;
Thy power and love, my love and trust,
Make one place ev'rywhere.

Love (III)

Love bade me welcome, yet my soul drew back,
Guilty of dust and sin.
But quick-ey'd Love, observing me grow slack
From my first entrance in,
Drew nearer to me, sweetly questioning
If I lack'd anything.
A guest," I answer'd, "worthy to be here";
Love said, "You shall be he."
"I, the unkind, the ungrateful? Ah my dear,
I cannot look on thee."
Love took my hand and smiling did reply,
"Who made the eyes but I?"

"Truth, Lord, but I have marr'd them; let my shame
Go where it doth deserve."
"And know you not," says Love, "who bore the blame?"
"My dear, then I will serve."
"You must sit down," says Love, "and taste my meat."
So I did sit and eat

Charley,(Cromwell, etc)*. . .*

Lesson 7: The English Civil War

BACKGROUND: From Henry VIII to the Restoration

From reading *Foxe's Book of Martyrs,* and from listening to our class discussions, you should have gathered that the religious "scene" has been full of disagreement, disputation and (shall we say?) decapitation. To recap briefly, let us begin with Henry VIII.

Henry VIII, you may recall, married his older brother's widow, Katherine of Aragon. Though Henry was not a particularly faithful husband, for eighteen years they did seem to have had a stable marriage. Henry was increasingly troubled, however, by the fact that Katherine had not been able to provide him with a male heir. After their marriate in 1509, Katherine gave birth to a stillborn daughter (1510), a son who lived only 52 days (1511), a stillborn daughter, and a son who died soon after birth. In 1516, Katherine bore a daughter, Mary – the only one of their children to survive to adulthood. After Mary's birth, Katherine had only one more daughter who was also stillborn (1518). After that she was unable to have any more children.

Up until this point in English history, only one woman had ruled as Monarch – Matilda, aka "Maud" aka, the "Empress Maud." Her right to the throne was not universally accepted, and when Stephen challenged her sovereignty, she had been unable to avoid civil war. Henry was adamant that he must have a male heir to secure the Tudor line, largely because he did not want to risk another civil war.

In addition to his concerns about who would rule after him, Henry claimed to have spiritual concerns. These repeated stillbirths and infant deaths had convinced him that he should never have married his brother's widow, and that her inability to produce an heir was evidence that God had cursed their union. Henry insisted that these were not convenient pangs of conscience, that it had nothing to do with any interest he might or might not have had in the young and lovely Anne Boleyn. We might take Henry's word for it that he was purely motivated by a grieved conscience and a desire to make things right with God.

The Pope, however, was not moved by Henry's need for a male heir nor for his troubled conscience. He repeatedly put Henry off, but eventually, he refused to grant Henry's request for an annulment. When the Pope did finally deny Henry's request he just happened, for all intents and purposes, to be imprisoned by Katherine's nephew, Holy Roman Emporer, Charles V. No pressure. Really.

In a huff, Henry separated himself and the English Church from the Roman Church. He declared himself the head of the Church of England and granted himself, not a divorce, but an annulment. A divorce would have dissolved the existing marriage. An annulment, however, declared to the world that no legal marriage had ever existed between Henry and Catherine.

Having publically declared that he and Catherine had never been married, Henry had essentially demoted Catherine from legitimate wife to skuzzy shack-up. Henry put their daughter Mary in a bit of a bind as well. In declaring that Mary's mother had never been married, he also publically announced that Mary was illegitimate. (This did not seem to embarrass Henry nearly so much as it embarrassed Mary. Catherine and Mary were packed off to some obscure corner of England while Henry married Anne Boleyn).

Henry was ecstatic when he and Anne conceived a child. Alas, all hopes were dashed when she delivered a girl, whom they named Elizabeth. From that point on, marital bliss – not so blissful. Anne was accused and convicted of adultery, then beheaded.

Henry soon married Jane Seymour, who produced young Edward. Edward was sickly but managed to live long enough to survive his father. Jane, however, died in childbirth. Henry was now the father of Mary, Elizabeth and (Huzzah! a male heir!!) Edward.

Following Jane's death, Henry went on to marry and divorce Anne of Cleves, then marry and behead Kathryn Howard, before marrying Katherine Parr. Katherine Parr actually survived Henry. Since none of the last three wives gave Henry any children, we will pass over them quickly and cut to the chase.

Henry died. **Young Edward VI** ascended the throne. Surrounded by Protestant advisors and ministers, young Edward initiated major reforms of the Church of England, making it more Protestant and less Catholic in form and practice. Unfortunately for his Protestant advisors, Edward didn't have the good sense to outlive his sister, Mary. He died at a very young age after an even shorter reign.

Mary reigned. Already in a bad mood (thanks to Henry) and enraged over Edward's reforms, she stomped onto the throne with a vengeance. First, she reversed all of Edward's reforms. Then, she started burning Protestants. She didn't just torch common garden variety laymen and humble country parsons. She began by burning bishops (including the one who annulled her parents' marriage, Thomas Cranmer). You have already read about her relish for roasting non-conformists in *Foxe's Book of Martyrs.* Had marshmallows been available in 1553, Mary would have brought them.

Eventually, Mary died.

England cheered. Mary's reign had been so bloody and so vicious that she has ever since been known as *Bloody Mary*. For many, many years after Mary's death, the English people were terrified at the thought of having another Catholic king or queen.

At Mary's death, Protestant **Elizabeth** took the throne. Though there was some grumbling about the lack of a male heir, the nation was so happy that she was *not* Mary, that Elizabeth's coronation was widely celebrated. Reform of the church continued. Not everyone was happy though. Some felt that Elizabeth's reforms were only superficial and did not go deeply enough. Indeed, Elizabeth did not seem to have the same enthusiasm for "pure religion" that her younger brother's advisors had had. So there continued to be murmurs of dissent here and there. But in general, Elizabethan England experienced something of a renaissance. (Which is why the period is referred to as the *English* Renaissance) Eventually, even Elizabeth died.

Because Elizabeth, the Virgin Queen, had neither husband nor children, Elizabeth had no heir (obvious, no?). The English went back up the family tree and brought **James I** from Scotland to rule.

As time passed, there was (on the part of some) a growing irritation with the state of the Church of England. Those who were dissatisfied generally felt that the reformation of the English Church had been half-hearted and incomplete. Some grumbled from within the church. These men felt that the Church needed to be purified of ALL its Roman Catholic trappings. Priestly vestments, celebrations of holidays like Easter and Christmas, all things ever remotely related to Catholic worship must go.

This group of people were called Puritans. Others threw up their hands and separated themselves from the Church of England altogether. This group is called, oddly enough, the Separatists. Eventually, many Separatists left England for Holland, and then for North America. (Mayflower passage, anyone?)

King James I, however, hated the Separatists. Although he agreed to allow translation work to go forward for a new, revised English translation of the Bible, he was no friend of the Puritans or the Separatists. Though most of the translation was taken from Tyndale's earlier work, we know this as the King James Version (AKA the *Authorized Version*), and not the Tyndale Translation. Kings trump martyrs.

James I died in 1625 and was replaced by his son, **Charles I.** Things went downhill rather quickly. Charles made Parliament and everyone else very nervous when he announced his intention to marry a French Catholic princess,

Henreitta Maria. But the major problem turned out to be over whether the King or the Parliament would lead the government. Charles saw Parliament as his temporarly advisor. When he wanted Parliament's advice, he would ask for it, and whenever he felt that he'd had enough advice, he expected to be able to send them home. The difficultly was that the Parliament did not like his attitude.The reality was that Parliament was the body that authorized the taxes that supported the King. If Parliament decided not to give the King money, the King had no money. And, the King needed money.

Charles and the Parliament quarreled constanty over money, over Charles participation in foreign wars, over what the citizen had and did not have a right to insist on, and primarily, over whether the King could send Parliament packing whenever he wanted to do so. Eventually, their quarrelling became a full-fledged civil war, The English Civil War, to be specific. Those who fought for the king were known as Royalists, or Cavaliers. Those who fought for Parliament were known as the Round Heads, after the bald heads of the Puritan majority that controlled Parliament.

Charles did not fare so well. His army was beaten by Parliament's army. Eventually, he was captured. He escaped, was recaptured, and imprisoned. Even from prison, Charles, unable to take a hint, stirred up yet another round of fighting with the Scots. His continued defiance was more than the Parliamentary leaders could bear, and finally Charles was charged, tried and convicted of treason. He was beheaded in January of 1649, and Puritan leader, Oliver Cromwell, became the leader of what was called The Commonwealth of England. For the first time in her history, England had no monarch.

Cromwell was not through fighting, however. Charles' son, **Charles II** continued his father's fight. Finally, in 1651 Charles was defeated by Cromwell in Scotland and was forced to flee to France.

Once settled into power in London, the Puritan government was free to focus its attention on further reform – both of matters of Church government and doctrine, as well as matters affecting what might otherwise have been thought of as secular activity. Now we have "Boo, the Pope!" "Boo, vestments!" "Boo, the Theater" and "Boo, Christmas."

Since the Church of England was reformed, and so cleansed of its previous errors, more pressure was put on non-conformists to conform. John Bunyan, a non-conformist pastor, spent much of his adult life in prison for his refusal to conform. All was not well in the Commonwealth. The powers that were in charge were perplexed and annoyed: Parliament had executed the King and reformed the English Church. Why should there be any reason left for non-conformists to continue their stubborn non-conformity? Cromwell and the Puritans felt everyone should just suck it up and re-join the local parish of the

Church of England. But the non-conformists continued to refuse to join up and new conflicts festered.

Ironically, Cromwell had almost as much trouble as Charles I getting along with Parliament. Eventually, he sent a troop of horses to force them to adjourn and go home. He governed England under a kind of martial law, with Generals whom he appointed in charge of Scotland, Ireland, Wales, Cornwall, and England.

When Oliver died, the torch was passed to his son Richard. Richard, however, did not have the army's support. One of the Generals marched his troops from Scotland to London and opened a correspondence with the exiled Charles II. Before long, Charles II was recalled from exile in France restored to the English throne. (The period between the monarchies of Charles I and Charles II is known, by the way, as the *inter-regnum.)* As it happened, Charles the II had had quite a pleasant time in France – as had his court. They returned with a special fondness for all things French – including French theater. English theaters, closed during the Inter-regnum, were re-opened. Celebrations forbidden during this time, like Christmas, were again celebrated.

So now, it was "Yea, Theater!" "Yea, Christmas!" AND "Yea, France"

The name given to this period of English history is *The Restoration* (as in, "The KING was restored to his throne).

In the next several weeks, you are going to read selections from various authors who wrote during the English Civil War, during the Inter-regnum, and during the Restoration.

We will begin with the writers of the English Civil War.

The Cavalier Poets

Read Chapter 5 in Poetry for Dummies, "Connecting with Poems of the Past," pages 79-90. The tools mentioned in the section, "Gathering Your Tools," are handy things to have, but not necessary for your work here.

Discovering the Historical Background:

For a good introduction to the events surrounding the English Civil War, you might go the following website:

3 Minute History -- English Civil War

In short, those who fought for the king were called, Cavaliers (giving you a mental image of a strong, dashing knight on horseback)! Those who fought against the king on behalf of the Puritans and Parliament were called the Roundheads (giving you the image of a bald, round-headed Puritan). For a rabbit trail moment, think a minute – sounds like which side picked the nicknames?

Though the supporters of Charles I were called the Cavaliers, the word also has other connotations. Look up *cavalier (check the adjectives as well), and summarize what you learn below*

What attitudes would you expect to find a "cavalier" poet to express in his poetry?

Now read each of the following poems aloud at least twice, and then read each one again, pencil in hand, and carefully noting your observations.

Richard Lovelace

To Lucasta, Going to the Wars

Tell me not (Sweet) I am unkind,
That from the nunnery
Of thy chaste breast and quiet mind
To war and arms I fly.

True, a new mistress now I chase,
The first foe in the field;
And with a stronger faith embrace
A sword, a horse, a shield.

Yet this inconstancy is such
As you too shall adore;
I could not love thee (Dear) so much,
Lov'd I not Honour more.

Robert Herrick (1591-1674)

His Prayer for Absolution

For those my unbaptized rhymes,
Writ in my wild unhallowed times,
For every sentence, clause, and word,
That's not inlaid with Thee, my Lord,
Forgive me, God, and blot each line
Out of my book, that is not Thine.
But if, 'mongst all, Thou find'st here one
Worthy thy benediction,
That one of all the rest shall be
The glory of my work, and me.

His Prayer to Ben Jonson

When I a verse shall make,
Know I have pray'd thee,
For old religion's sake,
Saint Ben to aid me.

Make the way smooth for me,
When I, thy Herrick,
Honouring thee, on my knee
Offer my lyric.

Candles I'll give to thee,
And a new altar,
And thou, Saint Ben, shalt be
Writ in my psalter.

Upon Julia's Clothes

Whenas in silks my Julia goes,
Then, then (methinks) how sweetly flows
That liquefaction of her clothes.

Next, when I cast mine eyes, and see
That brave vibration each way free,
O how that glittering taketh me!

To His Conscience

Can I not sin, but thou wilt be
My private protonotary?
Can I not woo thee to pass by
A short and sweet iniquity?
I'll cast a mist and cloud upon
My delicate transgression,
So utter dark as that no eye
Shall see the hugg'd impiety.
Gifts blind the wise, and bribes do please,
And wind all other witnesses;
And wilt not thou with gold be tied
To lay thy pen and ink aside,
That in the murk and tongueless night
Wanton I may, and thou not write?
It will not be; and therefore, now,
For times to come I'll make this vow,
From aberrations to live free,
So I'll not fear the Judge, or thee.

To Virgins, to Make Much of Time

Gather ye rosebuds while ye may,
Old Time is still a-flying;
And this same flower that smiles today,
To-morrow will be dying.

The glorious lamp of heaven, the Sun,
The higher he's a-getting;
The sooner will his race be run,
And nearer he's to setting.

That age is best, which is the first,
When youth and blood are warmer;
But being spent, the worse, and worst
Times still succeed the former.

Then be not coy, but use your time,
And while ye may, go marry;
For having lost but once your prime,
You may for ever tarry.

Delight in Disorder

A sweet disorder in the dress
Kindles in clothes a wantonness;
A lawn about the shoulders thrown
Into a fine distraction;
An erring lace, which here and there
Enthrals the crimson stomacher;
A cuff neglectful, and thereby
Ribands to flow confusedly;
A winning wave, deserving note,
In the tempestuous petticoat;
A careless shoe-string, in whose tie
I see a wild civility:
Do more bewitch me, than when art
Is too precise in every part.

To Althea, from Prison

When Love with unconfined wings
Hovers within my gates,
And my divine Althea brings
To whisper at the grates;
When I lie tangled in her hair,
And fetter'd to her eye,
The gods, that wanton in the air,
Know no such liberty.

When flowing cups run swiftly round
With no allaying Thames,
Our careless heads with roses bound,
Our hearts with loyal flames;
When thirsty grief in wine we steep,
When healths and draughts go free,
Fishes, that tipple in the deep,
Know no such liberty.

When (like committed linnets) I
With shriller throat shall sing
The sweetness, mercy, majesty,
And glories of my king;
When I shall voice aloud how good
He is, how great should be,
Enlarged winds, that curl the flood,
Know no such liberty.

Stone walls do not a prison make,
Nor iron bars a cage;
Minds innocent and quiet take
That for an hermitage;
If I have freedom in my love,
And in my soul am free,
Angels alone that soar above,
Enjoy such liberty.

Would you say that the Cavalier poets are more influenced by Donne or Jonson or a combination of the two? Prepare to defend your answer with specific examples!!

Charley, (The Cromwells), Charley. . .

Lesson 8: The English Civil War

John Milton (1608-1674)

John Milton is considered by many to be one of the greatest English poets. He is best known for his epic poem, Paradise Lost, which recounts the story of the Fall of Man. (We will only read a short exerpt from PL. My apologies in advance for any distress that may cause you!)

Milton sympathies during the English Civil War were never in doubt, a fact that caused him much trouble after Charles II came to the throne.

On a personal note, Milton lost his sight toward the end of his life, and that is the subject of the first poem below.

Sonnet XIX: When I Consider How my Light is Spent

When I consider how my light is spent
Ere half my days in this dark world and wide,
And that one talent which is death to hide
Lodg'd with me useless, though my soul more bent
To serve therewith my Maker, and present
My true account, lest he returning chide,
"Doth God exact day-labour, light denied?"
I fondly ask. But Patience, to prevent
That murmur, soon replies: "God doth not need
Either man's work or his own gifts: who best

Bear his mild yoke, they serve him best. His state
Is kingly; thousands at his bidding speed
And post o'er land and ocean without rest:
They also serve who only stand and wait."

Paradise Lost: Book I (excerpt)

Of Man's first disobedience, and the fruit
Of that forbidden tree whose mortal taste
Brought death into the world and all our woe,
With loss of Eden, till one greater Man
Restore us and regain the blissful seat,
Sing, Heav'nly Muse, that on the secret top
Of Oreb, or of Sinai, didst inspire
That shepherd who first taught the chosen seed
In the beginning how the heav'ns and earth
Rose out of Chaos; or if Sion hill
Delight thee more, and Siloa's brook that flow'd
Fast by the oracle of God, I thence
Invoke thy aid to my advent'rous song,
That with no middle flight intends to soar
Above th' Aonian mount, while it pursues
Things unattempted yet in prose or rhyme.
And chiefly thou, O Spirit, that dost prefer
Before all temples th' upright heart and pure,
Instruct me, for thou know'st; thou from the first
Wast present, and, with mighty wings outspread,
Dove-like sat'st brooding on the vast Abyss
And mad'st it pregnant: what in me is dark
Illumine, what is low raise and support,
That to the highth of this great argument
I may assert Eternal Providence
And justify the ways of God to men.

Say first--for Heav'n hides nothing from thy view,
Nor the deep tract of Hell--say first what cause
Mov'd our grand parents in that happy state,
Favour'd of Heav'n so highly, to fall off
From their Creator and transgress his will
For one restraint, lords of the world besides?
Who first seduc'd them to that foul revolt?
Th' infernal Serpent; he it was, whose guile,
Stirr'd up with envy and revenge, deceiv'd
The Mother of Mankind, what time his pride
Had cast him out from Heav'n, with all his host

Of rebel Angels, by whose aid, aspiring
To set himself in glory above his peers,
He trusted to have equall'd the Most High,
If he oppos'd; and with ambitious aim
Against the throne and monarchy of God
Rais'd impious war in Heav'n and battle proud,
With vain attempt. Him the Almighty Power
Hurl'd headlong flaming from th' ethereal sky,
With hideous ruin and combustion, down
To bottomless perdition, there to dwell
In adamantine chains and penal fire,
Who durst defy th' Omnipotent to arms.
Nine times the space that measures day and night
To mortal men, he with his horrid crew
Lay vanquish'd, rolling in the fiery gulf,
Confounded though immortal. But his doom
Reserv'd him to more wrath; for now the thought
Both of lost happiness and lasting pain
Torments him; round he throws his baleful eyes,
That witness'd huge affliction and dismay
Mix'd with obdurate pride and steadfast hate.
At once, as far as Angels ken, he views
The dismal situation waste and wild:
A dungeon horrible on all sides round
As one great furnace flam'd; yet from those flames
No light, but rather darkness visible
Serv'd only to discover sights of woe,
Regions of sorrow, doleful shades, where peace
And rest can never dwell, hope never comes
That comes to all, but torture without end
Still urges, and a fiery deluge, fed
With ever-burning sulphur unconsum'd.
Such place Eternal Justice had prepar'd
For those rebellious; here their prison ordain'd
In utter darkness, and their portion set,
As far remov'd from God and light of Heav'n
As from the centre thrice to th' utmost pole.
Oh how unlike the place from whence they fell!
There the companions of his fall, o'erwhelm'd
With floods and whirlwinds of tempestuous fire,
He soon discerns; and welt'ring by his side
One next himself in power and next in crime,
Long after known in Palestine and nam'd
Beëlzebub. To whom th' Arch-Enemy,
And thence in Heav'n call'd Satan, with bold words
Breaking the horrid silence, thus began:

"If thou beest he--but oh how fall'n! how chang'd
From him who, in the happy realms of light,
Cloth'd with transcendent brightness didst outshine
Myriads though bright!--if he whom mutual league,
United thoughts and counsels, equal hope
And hazard in the glorious enterprise,
Join'd with me once, now misery hath join'd
In equal ruin, into what pit thou seest
From what highth fall'n. So much the stronger prov'd
He with his thunder--and till then who knew
The force of those dire arms? Yet not for those,
Nor what the potent victor in his rage
Can else inflict, do I repent or change,
Though chang'd in outward lustre, that fix'd mind,
And high disdain from sense of injur'd merit,
That with the mightiest rais'd me to contend,
And to the fierce contention brought along
Innumerable force of Spirits arm'd,
That durst dislike his reign and, me preferring,
His utmost power with adverse power oppos'd
In dubious battle on the plains of Heav'n,
And shook his throne. What though the field be lost?
All is not lost--the unconquerable will,
And study of revenge, immortal hate,
And courage never to submit or yield:
And what is else not to be overcome?
That glory never shall his wrath or might
Extort from me. To bow and sue for grace
With suppliant knee, and deify his power
Who from the terror of this arm so late
Doubted his empire, that were low indeed;
That were an ignominy and shame beneath
This downfall: since by fate the strength of Gods
And this empyreal substance cannot fail,
Since through experience of this great event
In arms not worse, in foresight much advanc'd,
We may with more successful hope resolve
To wage by force or guile eternal war,
Irreconcilable to our grand foe,
Who now triumphs and, in th' excess of joy
Sole reigning, holds the tyranny of Heav'n."

So spake th' apostate Angel, though in pain,
Vaunting aloud, but rack'd with deep despair.
And him thus answer'd soon his bold compeer:

"O Prince, O Chief of many throned Powers,
That led th' embattl'd Seraphim to war
Under thy conduct and, in dreadful deeds
Fearless, endanger'd Heav'n's perpetual King,
And put to proof his high supremacy,
Whether upheld by strength, or chance, or fate,
Too well I see and rue the dire event
That with sad overthrow and foul defeat
Hath lost us Heav'n, and all this mighty host
In horrible destruction laid thus low,
As far as Gods and heav'nly essences
Can perish: for the mind and spirit remains
Invincible, and vigour soon returns,
Though all our glory extinct, and happy state
Here swallow'd up in endless misery.
But what if he our conqueror (whom I now
Of force believe almighty, since no less
Than such could have o'erpow'r'd such force as ours)
Have left us this our spirit and strength entire,
Strongly to suffer and support our pains,
That we may so suffice his vengeful ire,
Or do him mightier service as his thralls
By right of war, whate'er his business be,
Here in the heart of Hell to work in fire,
Or do his errands in the gloomy deep:
What can it then avail though yet we feel
Strength undiminish'd, or eternal being
To undergo eternal punishment?"
Whereto with speedy words th' Arch-Fiend replied:
"Fall'n Cherub, to be weak is miserable,
Doing or suffering: but of this be sure,
To do aught good never will be our task,
But ever to do ill our sole delight,
As being the contrary to his high will
Whom we resist. If then his providence
Out of our evil seek to bring forth good,
Our labour must be to pervert that end,
And out of good still to find means of evil;
Which ofttimes may succeed so as perhaps
Shall grieve him, if I fail not, and disturb
His inmost counsels from their destin'd aim.
But see! the angry victor hath recall'd
His ministers of vengeance and pursuit
Back to the gates of Heav'n: the sulphurous hail,
Shot after us in storm, o'erblown hath laid
The fiery surge that from the precipice

Of Heav'n receiv'd us falling, and the thunder,
Wing'd with red lightning and impetuous rage,
Perhaps hath spent his shafts, and ceases now
To bellow through the vast and boundless deep.
Let us not slip th' occasion, whether scorn
Or satiate fury yield it from our foe.
Seest thou yon dreary plain, forlorn and wild,
The seat of desolation, void of light,
Save what the glimmering of these livid flames
Casts pale and dreadful? Thither let us tend
From off the tossing of these fiery waves;
There rest, if any rest can harbour there,
And, re-assembling our afflicted powers,
Consult how we may henceforth most offend
Our enemy, our own loss how repair,
How overcome this dire calamity,
What reinforcement we may gain from hope,
If not, what resolution from despair."

Excerpt from Book Three

Now had the Almighty Father from above,
From the pure **Empyrean** where he sits
High Thron'd above all highth, bent down his eye,
His own works and their works at once to view:
About him all the **Sanctities** of Heaven
Stood thick as Starrs, and from his sight receiv'd
Beatitude past utterance; on his right
The **radiant image of his Glory** sat,
His onely Son; On Earth he first beheld
Our two first Parents, yet the onely two
Of mankind, in the happie Garden plac't,
Reaping immortal fruits of joy and love,
Uninterrupted joy, unrivald love
In blissful solitude; he then survey'd
Hell and the Gulf between, and *Satan* there
Coasting the wall of Heav'n on **this side Night**
In the dun Air sublime, and ready now
To **stoop** with wearied wings, and willing feet
On the bare outside of this **World**, that seem'd
Firm land imbosom'd without Firmament,
Uncertain which, in Ocean or in Air.
Him God beholding from his prospect high,

Wherein past, present, future he beholds,
Thus to his onely Son foreseeing spake.

Onely begotten Son, seest thou what rage
Transports our adversarie, whom no bounds
Prescrib'd, no barrs of Hell, nor all the chains
Heapt on him there, nor yet the main Abyss
Wide interrupt can hold; so bent he seems
On desparate reveng, that shall redound
Upon his own rebellious head. And now
Through all restraint broke loose he wings his way
Not farr off Heav'n, in the Precincts of light,
Directly towards the new created World,
And Man there plac't, with purpose to **assay**
If him by force he can destroy, or worse,
By some false guile pervert; and shall pervert
For man will heark'n to his **glozing** lyes,
And easily transgress the **sole Command**,
Sole pledge of his obedience: So will fall,
Hee and his faithless Progenie: whose fault?
Whose but his own? ingrate, he had of mee
All he could have; I made him just and right,
Sufficient to have stood, though free to fall.
Such I created all th' **Ethereal** Powers
And Spirits, both them who stood and them who faild;
Freely they stood who stood, and fell who fell.
Not free, what proof could they have givn sincere
Of true allegiance, constant Faith or Love,
Where onely what they needs must do, appeard,
Not what they would? what praise could they receive?
What pleasure I from such obedience paid,
When Will and Reason (**Reason also is choice**)
Useless and vain, of freedom both despoild,
Made passive both, had servd necessitie,
Not mee. They therefore as to right belongd,
So were created, nor can justly accuse
Thir maker, or thir making, or thir Fate,
As if **predestination** over-rul'd
Thir will, dispos'd by absolute Decree
Or high foreknowledge; they themselves decreed
Thir own revolt, not I: if I foreknew,
Foreknowledge had no influence on their fault,
Which had no less prov'd certain unforeknown.
So without least impulse or shadow of Fate,
Or aught by me immutablie foreseen,
They trespass, Authors to themselves in all

Both what they judge and what they choose; for so
I formd them free, and free they must remain,
Till they enthrall themselves: I else must change
Thir nature, and revoke the high Decree
Unchangeable, Eternal, which ordain'd
Thir freedom, they themselves ordain'd thir fall.
The first sort by thir own suggestion fell,
Self-tempted, self-deprav'd: **Man falls deceiv'd**
By the other first: Man therefore shall find grace,
The other none: in Mercy and Justice both,
Through Heav'n and Earth, so shall my glorie excel,
But Mercy first and last shall brightest shine.

Thus while God spake, ambrosial fragrance fill'd
All Heav'n, and in the blessed **Spirits elect**
Sense of new joy ineffable diffus'd:
Beyond compare the Son of God was seen
Most glorious, in him all his Father shon
Substantially express'd, and in his face
Divine compassion visibly appeerd,
Love without end, and without measure Grace,
Which uttering thus he to his Father spake.

O Father, gracious was that word which clos'd
Thy sovran sentence, that Man should find grace;
For which both Heav'n and Earth shall high extoll
Thy praises, with th' innumerable sound
Of Hymns and sacred Songs, wherewith thy Throne
Encompass'd shall resound thee ever blest.
For should Man finally be lost, should Man
Thy creature late so lov'd, thy youngest Son
Fall circumvented thus by fraud, though joynd
With his own folly? that be from thee farr,
That farr be from thee, Father, who art Judg
Of all things made, and judgest onely right.
Or shall the **Adversarie** thus obtain
His end, and frustrate thine, shall he fulfill
His malice, and thy goodness bring to naught,
Or proud return though to his heavier doom,
Yet with revenge accomplish't and to Hell
Draw after him the whole Race of mankind,
By him corrupted? or wilt thou thy self
Abolish thy Creation, and unmake,
For him, what for thy glorie thou hast made?
So should thy goodness and thy greatness both
Be questiond and blaspheam'd without defence.

To whom the great Creatour thus reply'd.
O Son, in whom my Soul hath chief delight,
Son of my bosom, Son who art alone
My word, my wisdom, and effectual might,
All hast thou spok'n as my thoughts are, all
As my Eternal purpose hath decreed:
Man shall not quite be lost, but sav'd who will,
Yet not of will in him, but grace in me
Freely voutsaft; once more I will renew
His lapsed powers, though forfeit and enthrall'd
By sin to foul exorbitant desires;
Upheld by me, yet once more he shall stand
On even ground against his mortal foe,
By me upheld, that he may know how frail
His fall'n condition is, and to me ow
All his deliv'rance, and to none but me.
Some I have chosen of peculiar grace
Elect above the rest; so is my will:
The rest shall hear me call, and oft be warnd
Thir sinful state, and to appease betimes
Th' incensed Deitie while offerd grace
Invites; for I will cleer thir senses dark,
What may suffice, and soft'n stonie hearts
To **pray, repent, and bring obedience due**.
To Prayer, repentance, and obedience due,
Though but endevord with sincere intent,
Mine ear shall not be slow, mine eye not shut.
And I will place within them as a guide
My Umpire *Conscience,* whom if they will hear,
Light after light well us'd they shall attain,
And to the end persisting, safe arrive.
This my long sufferance and my day of grace
They who neglect and scorn, shall never taste;
But hard be hard'nd, blind be blinded more,
That they may stumble on, and deeper fall;
And none but such from mercy I exclude.
But yet all is not don; Man disobeying,
Disloyal breaks his fealtie, and sinns
Against the high Supremacie of Heav'n,
Affecting God-head, and so loosing all,
To expiate his Treason hath naught left,
But to destruction sacred and devote,
He with his whole posteritie must dye,
Dye hee or Justice must; unless for him
Som other able, and as willing, pay
The rigid satisfaction, death for death.

Say Heav'nly Powers, where shall we find such love,
Which of ye will be mortal to redeem
Mans mortal crime, and just th' unjust to save,
Dwels in all Heaven charitie so deare?

He ask'd, but all the **Heav'nly Quire stood mute**,
And silence was in Heav'n: on mans behalf
Patron or Intercessor none appeerd,
Much less that durst upon his own head draw
The deadly forfeiture, and ransom set.
And now without redemption all mankind
Must have bin lost, adjudg'd to Death and Hell
By doom severe, had not the Son of God,
In whom the fulness dwells of love divine,
His dearest mediation thus renewd.

Father, thy word is past, man shall find grace;
And shall grace not find means, that finds her way,
The speediest of thy winged messengers,
To visit all thy creatures, and to all
Comes **unprevented**, unimplor'd, unsought,
Happie for man, so coming; he her aide
Can never seek, once dead in sins and lost;
Attonement for himself or offering meet,
Indebted and undon, hath none to bring:
Behold mee then, mee for him, life for life
I offer, on mee let thine anger fall;
Account mee man; I for his sake will leave
Thy bosom, and this glorie next to thee
Freely put off, and for him lastly dye
Well pleas'd, on me let Death wreck all his rage;
Under his gloomie power I shall not long
Lie vanquisht; thou hast givn me to possess
Life in my self for ever, **by thee I live**,
Though now to **Death** I yield, and am his due
All that of me can die, yet that debt paid,
Thou wilt not leave me in the loathsom grave
His prey, nor suffer my unspotted Soule
For ever with corruption there to dwell;
But I shall rise Victorious, and subdue
My Vanquisher, spoild of his vanted spoile;
Death his deaths wound shall then receive, and stoop
Inglorious, of his **mortal sting** disarm'd.
I through the ample Air in Triumph high
Shall lead Hell Captive **maugre** Hell, and show
The powers of darkness bound. Thou at the sight

Pleas'd, out of Heaven shalt look down and smile,
While by thee rais'd I ruin all my Foes,
Death last, and with his Carcass glut the Grave:
Then with the multitude of my redeemd
Shall enter Heaven long absent, and returne,
Father, to see thy face, wherein no cloud
Of anger shall remain, but peace assur'd,
And reconcilement; wrauth shall be no more
Thenceforth, but in thy presence Joy entire.

His words here ended, but his meek aspect
Silent yet spake, and breath'd immortal love
To mortal men, above which only shon
Filial obedience: as a sacrifice
Glad to be offer'd, he attends the will
Of his great Father. Admiration seis'd
All Heav'n, what this might mean, and whither tend
Wondring; but soon th' Almighty thus reply'd:

O thou in Heav'n and Earth the only peace
Found out for mankind under wrauth, O thou
My sole **complacence**! well thou know'st how dear,
To me are all my works, nor Man the least
Though last created, that for him I spare
Thee from my bosom and **right hand**, to save,
By loosing thee a while, the whole Race lost.
Thou therefore whom thou only canst redeem,
Thir Nature also to thy Nature joyn;
And be thy self Man among men on Earth,
Made flesh, when time shall be, of **Virgin** seed,
By wondrous birth: Be thou in *Adams* **room**
The Head of all mankind, though ***Adams*** **Son**.
As **in him perish all** men, so in thee
As from a second root shall be restor'd,
As many as are restor'd, **without thee none**.
His crime makes guiltie all his Sons, thy merit
Imputed shall absolve them who renounce
Thir own both righteous and unrighteous deeds,
And live in thee transplanted, and from thee
Receive **new life**. So Man, as is most just,
Shall satisfie for Man, be judg'd and die,
And dying rise, and rising with him raise
His Brethren, ransomd with his own dear life.
So Heav'nly love shall outdoo Hellish hate,
Giving to death, and dying to redeeme,
So dearly to redeem what Hellish hate

So easily destroy'd, and still destroyes
In those who, when they may, accept not grace.
Nor shalt thou by descending to assume
Mans Nature, less'n or degrade thine owne.
Because thou hast, though Thron'd in highest bliss
Equal to God, and equally enjoying
God-like fruition, quitted all to save
A World from utter loss, and hast been found
By **Merit** more then Birthright Son of God,
Found worthiest to be so by being Good,
Farr more then Great or High; because in thee
Love hath abounded more then Glory abounds,
Therefore thy Humiliation shall exalt
With thee **thy Manhood also** to this Throne;
Here shalt thou sit incarnate, here shalt Reign
Both God and Man, Son both of God and Man,
Anointed universal King, all Power
I give thee, reign for ever, and assume
Thy Merits; **under thee as Head Supream**
Thrones, Princedoms, Powers, Dominions I reduce:
All knees to thee shall bow, of them that bide
In Heaven, or Earth, or under Earth in Hell;
When thou attended gloriously from Heav'n
Shalt in the Sky appeer, and from thee send
The summoning Arch-Angels to proclaime
Thy dread Tribunal: forthwith **from all Windes**
The living, and forthwith the **cited** dead
Of all past Ages to the general **Doom**
Shall hast'n, such a peal shall rouse thir sleep.
Then all thy Saints assembl'd, thou shalt judge
Bad men and Angels, they arraignd shall sink
Beneath thy Sentence; Hell her numbers full,
Thenceforth shall be for ever shut. Mean while
The World shall burn, and from her ashes spring
New Heav'n and Earth, wherein the just shall dwell
And after all thir tribulations long
See golden days, fruitful of golden deeds,
With Joy and Love triumphing, and fair Truth.
Then thou thy regal Scepter shalt lay by,
For regal Scepter then no more shall need,
God shall be **All in All**. But all ye Gods,
Adore him, who to compass all this dies,
Adore the Son, and honour him as mee.

No sooner had th' Almighty ceas't, but all
The multitude of Angels with a shout

Loud as from numbers without number, sweet
As from blest voices, uttering joy, Heav'n rung
With Jubilee, and loud Hosanna's filld
Th' eternal Regions: lowly reverent
Towards either Throne they bow, and to the ground
With solemn adoration down they cast
Thir Crowns inwove with Amarant and Gold,
Immortal Amarant, a Flour which once
In Paradise, fast by the Tree of Life
Began to bloom, but soon for mans offence
To Heav'n remov'd where first it grew, there grows,
And flours aloft shading the Fount of Life,
And where the river of Bliss through midst of Heavn
Rowls o're ***Elisian*** Flours her Amber stream;
With these that never fade the Spirits elect
Bind thir resplendent locks inwreath'd with beams,
Now in loose Garlands thick thrown off, the bright
Pavement that like a Sea of Jasper shon
Impurpl'd with Celestial Roses smil'd.
Then Crown'd again thir gold'n Harps they took,
Harps ever tun'd, that glittering by thir side
Like Quivers hung, and with Præamble sweet
Of charming symphonie they introduce
Thir sacred Song, and waken raptures high;
No voice exempt, no voice but well could joine
Melodious part, such concord is in Heav'n.

Now that you have read this excerpt once, I would like you to go back through it and make some notes.

1. Draw a circle around every reference to Satan (and all names/synonyms used for Satan).

2. Draw a triangle over all references to God the Father, a cross over all references to God the Son, a box around all references to the Holy Spirit.

3. Go back now and make a list of everything you found out about Satan here below.

4. Make a list of everything you find about the Father, Son, and Holy Spirit.

5. What are you impressions of Satan?

6. What are your impressions of each of the Members of the Godhead (Father, Son, Holy Spirit).

7. As you read again, tell which characters in the poem capture your interest and/or your sympathy?

8. How does Milton lead you to sympathize for one character or another? What was it about any particular character that made him more sympathetic than another?

Lesson 9: English Civil War, (yet again)

Andrew Marvell (1621-1678)

It is not entirely clear whether Marvell supported the Royalists or the Puritan Parlimentarians in the English Civil War. It seems he was out of the country for the worst of it. He does seem to have had connections with people from both sidesof the conflict, having been tutor for children of the Oliver Cromwell household and the Lord Fairfax household. He served as a member of parliament after the Restoration where he was critical of the more oppressive policies of the government of Charles II.

He became Milton's secretary, fortunately for Milton. When Milton was imprisoned, Marvell's actions on his behalf may have saved the poet's life. Most of Marvell's poetry was published after his death. By the time it was published, much of his work was "out of fashion." There is much debate over how to categorize his work. Some call him a Metaphysical poet, and some say he has more in common with the Cavalier poets. (He was friends with both.) Read and see what you think.

The Mower

Luxurious man, to bring his vice in use,
    Did after him the world seduce;
And from the fields the flow'rs and plants allure,
    Where nature was most plain and pure.
He first enclos'd within the garden's square
    A dead and standing pool of air;
And a more luscious earth for them did knead,
    Which stupefied them while it fed.
The pink grew then as double as his mind;
    The nutriment did change the kind.
With strange perfumes he did the roses taint,
    And flow'rs themselves were taught to paint.
The tulip, white, did for complexion seek,
    And learn'd to interline its cheek;
Its onion root they then so high did hold,
    That one was for a meadow sold.
Another world was search'd, through oceans new,
    To find the Marvel of Peru.
And yet these rarities might be allow'd,
    To man, that sov'reign thing and proud;
Had he not dealt between the bark and tree,
    Forbidden mixtures there to see.
No plant now knew the stock from which it came,
    He grafts upon the wild the tame;
That the uncertain and adult'rate fruit
    Might put the palate in dispute.
His green seraglio has its eunuchs too,
    Lest any tyrant him out-do;
And in the cherry he does nature vex,
    To procreate without a sex.
'Tis all enforc'd, the fountain and the grot,
    While the sweet fields do lie forgot;
Where willing nature does to all dispense
    A wild and fragrant innocence;
And fauns and fairies do the meadows till,
    More by their presence than their skill.
Their statues polish'd by some ancient hand,
    May to adorn the gardens stand;
But howso'ere the figures do excel,
    The gods themselves with us do dwell.

To his Coy Mistress

Had we but world enough, and time,
This coyness, lady, were no crime.
We would sit down and think which way
To walk, and pass our long love's day;
Thou by the Indian Ganges' side
Shouldst rubies find; I by the tide
Of Humber would complain. I would
Love you ten years before the Flood;
And you should, if you please, refuse
Till the conversion of the Jews.
My vegetable love should grow
Vaster than empires, and more slow.
An hundred years should go to praise
Thine eyes, and on thy forehead gaze;
Two hundred to adore each breast,
But thirty thousand to the rest;
An age at least to every part,
And the last age should show your heart.
For, lady, you deserve this state,
Nor would I love at lower rate.

But at my back I always hear
Time's winged chariot hurrying near;
And yonder all before us lie
Deserts of vast eternity.
Thy beauty shall no more be found,
Nor, in thy marble vault, shall sound
My echoing song; then worms shall try
That long preserv'd virginity,
And your quaint honour turn to dust,
And into ashes all my lust.
The grave's a fine and private place,
But none I think do there embrace.
Now therefore, while the youthful hue
Sits on thy skin like morning dew,
And while thy willing soul transpires
At every pore with instant fires,
Now let us sport us while we may;
And now, like am'rous birds of prey,
Rather at once our time devour,
Than languish in his slow-chapp'd power.
Let us roll all our strength, and all

Our sweetness, up into one ball;
And tear our pleasures with rough strife
Thorough the iron gates of life.
Thus, though we cannot make our sun
Stand still, yet we will make him run.

The Garden

How vainly men themselves amaze
To win the palm, the oak, or bays ;
And their uncessant labors see
Crowned from some single herb or tree,
Whose short and narrow-vergèd shade
Does prudently their toils upbraid ;
While all the flowers and trees do close
To weave the garlands of repose.

Fair Quiet, have I found thee here,
And Innocence, thy sister dear!
Mistaken long, I sought you then
In busy companies of men :
Your sacred plants, if here below,
Only among the plants will grow ;
Society is all but rude,
To this delicious solitude.

No white nor red was ever seen
So amorous as this lovely green ;
Fond lovers, cruel as their flame,
Cut in these trees their mistress' name.
Little, alas, they know or heed,
How far these beauties hers exceed!
Fair trees! wheresoe'er your barks I wound
No name shall but your own be found.

When we have run our passion's heat,
Love hither makes his best retreat :
The gods who mortal beauty chase,
Still in a tree did end their race.
Apollo hunted Daphne so,
Only that she might laurel grow,
And Pan did after Syrinx speed,
Not as a nymph, but for a reed.

What wondrous life is this I lead!
Ripe apples drop about my head ;
The luscious clusters of the vine
Upon my mouth do crush their wine ;
The nectarine and curious peach
Into my hands themselves do reach ;

Stumbling on melons as I pass,
Insnared with flowers, I fall on grass.

Meanwhile the mind, from pleasure less,
Withdraws into its happiness :
The mind, that ocean where each kind
Does straight its own resemblance find ;
Yet it creates, transcending these,
Far other worlds, and other seas ;
Annihilating all that's made
To a green thought in a green shade.

Here at the fountain's sliding foot,
Or at some fruit-tree's mossy root,
Casting the body's vest aside,
My soul into the boughs does glide :
There like a bird it sits and sings,
Then whets and combs its silver wings ;
And, till prepared for longer flight,
Waves in its plumes the various light.

Such was that happy garden-state,
While man there walked without a mate :
After a place so pure and sweet,
What other help could yet be meet!
But 'twas beyond a mortal's share
To wander solitary there :
Two paradises 'twere in one
To live in Paradise alone.

How well the skillful gard'ner drew
Of flowers and herbs this dial new ;
Where from above the milder sun
Does through a fragrant zodiac run ;
And, as it works, th' industrious bee
Computes its time as well as we.
How could such sweet and wholesome hours
Be reckoned but with herbs and flowers!

Horatian Ode upon Cromwell's Return from Ireland

THE forward youth that would appear,
Must now forsake his Muses dear,
   Nor in the shadows sing
   His numbers languishing.

'Tis time to leave the books in dust,
And oil the unused armour's rust,
   Removing from the wall
   The corslet of the hall.

So restless Cromwell could not cease
In the inglorious arts of peace,
   But through adventurous war
   Urgèd his active star:

And like the three-fork'd lightning, first
Breaking the clouds where it was nurst,
   Did thorough his own Side
   His fiery way divide:

For 'tis all one to courage high,
The emulous, or enemy;
   And with such, to enclose
   Is more than to oppose;

Then burning through the air he went,
And palaces and temples rent;
   And Cæsar's head at last
   Did through his laurels blast.

'Tis madness to resist or blame
The face of angry heaven's flame;
   And if we would speak true,
   Much to the Man is due

Who, from his private gardens, where
He lived reservèd and austere,
   (As if his highest plot
   To plant the bergamot),

Could by industrious valour climb

To ruin the great work of time,
   And cast the Kingdoms old
   Into another mould;

Though Justice against Fate complain,
And plead the ancient Rights in vain—
   But those do hold or break
   As men are strong or weak;

Nature, that hateth emptiness,
Allows of penetration less,
   And therefore must make room
   Where greater spirits come.

What field of all the civil war
Where his were not the deepest scar?
   And Hampton shows what part
   He had of wiser art,

Where, twining subtle fears with hope,
He wove a net of such a scope
   That Charles himself might chase
   To Carisbrook's narrow case,

That thence the Royal actor borne
The tragic scaffold might adorn:
   While round the armèd bands
   Did clap their bloody hands.

He nothing common did or mean
Upon that memorable scene,
   But with his keener eye
   The axe's edge did try;

Nor call'd the Gods, with vulgar spite,
To vindicate his helpless right;
   But bow'd his comely head
   Down, as upon a bed.

—This was that memorable hour
Which first assured the forcèd power:
   So when they did design
   The Capitol's first line,

A Bleeding Head, where they begun,

Did fright the architects to run;
  And yet in that the State
  Foresaw its happy fate!

And now the Irish are ashamed
To see themselves in one year tamed:
  So much one man can do
  That does both act and know.

They can affirm his praises best,
And have, though overcome, confest
  How good he is, how just
  And fit for highest trust.

Nor yet grown stiffer with command,
But still in the Republic's hand—
  How fit he is to sway
  That can so well obey!

He to the Commons' feet presents
A Kingdom for his first year's rents,
  And (what he may) forbears
  His fame, to make it theirs:

And has his sword and spoils ungirt
To lay them at the Public's skirt;
  So when the falcon high
  Falls heavy from the sky,

She, having kill'd, no more doth search
But on the next green bough to perch,
  Where, when he first does lure
  The falconer has her sure.

—What may not then our Isle presume
While victory his crest does plume?
  What may not others fear
  If thus he crowns each year?

As Cæsar he, ere long, to Gaul,
To Italy an Hannibal,
  And to all States not free
  Shall climacteric be.

The Pict no shelter now shall find

Within his parti-colour'd mind,
   But from this valour sad
   Shrink underneath the plaid—

Happy, if in the tufted brake
The English hunter him mistake,
   Nor lay his hounds in near
   The Caledonian deer.

But Thou, the War's and Fortune's son,
March indefatigably on;
   And for the last effect
   Still keep the sword erect:

Besides the force it has to fright
The spirits of the shady night,
   The same arts that did gain
   A power, must it maintain.

Lesson 10:

Meanwhile in America:

Anne Bradstreet (ca. 1612-1672)

Anne Bradstreet left England for America at age 18, two years after marrying Simon Bradstreet. Though schools of the time were not open to women, Anne had the benefit of a father who seems to have had an enthusiastic interest in his daughter's education. In addition to her father's instruction, Anne had several tutors and access to the large library of the Earl of Lincoln (her father's employer).

Bradstreet is considered to be the first American poet, and in addition, the first published American woman poet.

The Author to her Book

Thou ill-form'd offspring of my feeble brain,
Who after birth did'st by my side remain,
Till snatcht from thence by friends, less wise than true,
Who thee abroad expos'd to public view,
Made thee in rags, halting to th' press to trudge,
Where errors were not lessened (all may judge).
At thy return my blushing was not small,
My rambling brat (in print) should mother call.
I cast thee by as one unfit for light,
Thy Visage was so irksome in my sight,
Yet being mine own, at length affection would
Thy blemishes amend, if so I could.
I wash'd thy face, but more defects I saw,
And rubbing off a spot, still made a flaw.
I stretcht thy joints to make thee even feet,

Yet still thou run'st more hobbling than is meet.
In better dress to trim thee was my mind,
But nought save home-spun Cloth, i' th' house I find.
In this array, 'mongst Vulgars mayst thou roam.
In Critics' hands, beware thou dost not come,
And take thy way where yet thou art not known.
If for thy Father askt, say, thou hadst none;
And for thy Mother, she alas is poor,
Which caus'd her thus to send thee out of door.

By Night when Others Soundly Slept

1

By night when others soundly slept
And hath at once both ease and Rest,
My waking eyes were open kept
And so to lie I found it best.

2

I sought him whom my Soul did Love,
With tears I sought him earnestly.
He bow'd his ear down from Above.
In vain I did not seek or cry.

3

My hungry Soul he fill'd with Good;
He in his Bottle put my tears,
My smarting wounds washt in his blood,
And banisht thence my Doubts and fears.

4

What to my Saviour shall I give
Who freely hath done this for me?
I'll serve him here whilst I shall live
And Loue him to Eternity.

Deliverance from Another Sore Fit

In my distress I sought the Lord
When naught on earth could comfort give,
And when my soul these things abhorred,
Then, Lord, Thou said'st unto me, "Live."

Thou knowest the sorrows that I felt;
My plaints and groans were heard of Thee,
And how in sweat I seemed to melt
Thou help'st and Thou regardest me.

My wasted flesh Thou didst restore,
My feeble loins didst gird with strength,
Yea, when I was most low and poor,
I said I shall praise Thee at length.

What shall I render to my God
For all His bounty showed to me?
Even for His mercies in His rod,
Where pity most of all I see.

My heart I wholly give to Thee;
O make it fruitful, faithful Lord.
My life shall dedicated be
To praise in thought, in deed, in word.

Thou know'st no life I did require
Longer than still Thy name to praise,
Nor ought on earth worthy desire,
In drawing out these wretched days.

Thy name and praise to celebrate,
O Lord, for aye is my request.
O grant I do it in this state,
And then with Thee, which is the best.

The Prologue

To sing of wars, of captains, and of kings,
Of cities founded, commonwealths begun,
For my mean pen are too superior things:
Or how they all, or each, their dates have run;
Let poets and historians set these forth,
My obscure lines shall not so dim their work.

But when my wondering eyes and envious heart
Great Bartas' sugared lines do but read o'er,
Fool I do grudge the Muses did not part
'Twixt him and me that overfluent store;--
A Bartas can do what a Bartas will,
But simple I according to my skill.

From school-boys tongues no rhetoric we expect,
Nor yet a sweet consort from broken strings,
Nor perfect beauty where's a main defect:
My foolish, broken, blemished Muse so sings;
And this to mend, alas, no art is able,
'Cause nature made is so, irreparable.

Nor can I, like that fluent, sweet-tongued Greek
Who lisped at first, in future times speak plain;
By art he gladly found what he did seek--
A full requital of his striving pain.
Art can do much, but this maxim's most sure:
A weak or wounded brain admits no cure.

I am obnoxious to each carping tongue
Who says my hand a needle better fits.
A poet's pen all scorn I should thus wrong;
For such despite they cast on female wits,
If what I do prove well, it won't advance--
They'll say it was stolen, or else it was by chance.

But shure the ancient Greeks were far more mild,
Else of our sex why feignéd they those Nine,
And Posey made Calliope's own child?
So 'mongst the rest they placed the Arts Divine.
But this weak knot they will full soon untie--
The Greeks did naught but play the fools and lie.

Let Greeks be Greeks, and women what they are.
Men have precenency, and still excell.

It is but vain unjustly to wage war,
Men can do best, and women know it well.
Preëminence in all and each is yours--
Yet grant some small acknowledgement of ours.

And oh, ye high flownquills that soar the skies,
And ever with your prey still catch your praise,
If e'er you deign these lowly lines your eyes,
Give thyme or parsley wreath; I ask no bays.
This mean and unrefinéd ore of mine
Will make your glistening gold but more to shine.

Lesson 11

Meanwhile on the Continent –

Moliere's (Jean Baptiste Poquelin) 1622-

Tartuffe

Also writing during this period was French playwright, Moliere. Moliere's plays were written between 1645 and 1673. Moliere is known for his comedies. His favorite theme involves the exposure of hypocrisy and fraud.

Born Jean-Baptiste Poquelin, Moliere's father was one of the king's valets de chamber tapissiers whose duties were to care for the royal furniture and upholstery. Because this job gave Poquelin some status, Moliere attended the finest schools. His father wanted him to attend law school, but his heart drew him to the theater. Though no one knows for certain why he took up a stage name, it is generally assumed that he did it out of respect for his family's position. Fathers at that time did not brag about "my son the actor," any more than fathers of our time would brag about "my son the homeless guy."

Moliere formed his own dramatic troupe, called *The Illustrious Theater, and* though they opened in Paris initially, they were by all accounts, spectacular failures. Failing to impress the city folk, *The Illustirous Theater* spent twelve years touring the French countryside.

Moliere's did not perform for the king until 1658. The troupe's performance of a tragedy was something of a flop. Alfred Bates describes this period of Moliere's life in *The Drama: Its History, Literature and Influence on Civilization,*

> Molière's first performance before the king took place in the guard hall of the old Louvre, and the players may well have been unnerved as they peeped through the little hole in the curtain at the audience. No such gathering had ever assembled to watch them. The court of France--the most splendid in history--was present in all its strength. Here was Louis XIV, now twenty years of age, an ardent votary of pleasure, yet stately and reserved, with strength of character plainly written in his face; here was his brother, dressed more like a girl than a boy; here was Anne of Austria, still regent of France, and though grown somewhat stout, retaining much of her celebrated beauty; here, conspicuous by his red robe, his finely-cut features and long, white hair, was Cardinal Mazarin, who for many years had guided the vessel of the State. To the rear was a host of the butterflies belonging to the court, together with a few actors of the Hôtel de Bourgogne, all anxious to see of what stuff these favored rivals were made. The play bespoken for the evening was Corneille's *Nicoméde*. We may suspect that, as the performance went on, a feeling of disappointment stole over the audience, the actors from the Bourgogne excepted. Molière and his companions were, of course, far less at home in the stately lines of Corneille than in the quick and vivacious dialogue of Molière, and the trepidation incident to the occasion must have rendered them unable to do anything like justice to themselves. *Nicoméde* finished, Molière, sensible to their shortcomings, took a very unusual step. He made a speech from the stage; he thanked his majesty for his goodness in bearing the defects of the troupe, who had naturally felt some agitation on finding themselves before so august an assembly, and who, in their eagerness to have the honor of playing before the greatest king in the world, had forgotten that he had already much better actors in his service. "As," continued Molière, "his majesty has so far endured our country manners, I venture, very humbly, to hope that I may be permitted to give one of the little pieces which have procured me some reputation, and with which I have been fortunate enough to amuse the provinces." The king assented by retaining his seat, and the audience, who but a moment before had been preparing to disperse, resumed an attitude of attention. The piece referred to was *Le Docteur Amoureux*, one of Molière's earliest farces. The result must have more than equalled his anticipations. He quickly converted failure into triumph, and everybody present had much ado to restrain his loudest laughter. The actors from the Bourgogne must have felt that in Molière they had a dangerous rival in comedy--an impression considerably deepened when, an hour or two later, it was found that the

king had requested him and his comrades to establish themselves in Paris under the style and title of the "Troupe de Monsieur."

And now the goal was won. After a probation of twelve years, representing the best period of his life, Molière had fully justified his abandonment of the career once prepared for him. His self-imposed exile from Paris, an exile which, as might have been expected of a Frenchman born and bred there, he had felt very deeply, was at an end. He had appeared before the king, had won his favor and had received from him a substantial guarantee of future support. No longer was it necessary for him and those who had cast in their lot with his to trudge from one provincial town to another, to bow low for permission to regale the populace with the choicest productions of French dramatic genius, and then, as was often the case, to be received with apathy by a throng incapable of appreciating the value of what he set before them. Nor was his exultation materially dampened by a want of cordial recognition from his family. Even after he had become famous, his brother omitted his name from a genealogy which, in the pride of their mother's descent, they caused to be drawn up; but old M. Poquelin, actuated by an almost superstitious faith in the judgement of kings, to say nothing of his paternal affection, welcomed him with open arms. Next came social recognition; the doors of many exclusive houses were open to the man on whom the sun of Court favor had begun to shine. If only his mother, the devout Marie Cresse of thirty years before, who had been pious enough to thrash him for mimicking a priest, could have lived to join in the welcome! As for the troupe, he had endeared himself to them by his good-will and generosity, and a sense of the fact that they owed their present position to his gifts served to strengthen the ties which bound them to him. No leader was ever regarded with more affectionate loyalty by his followers than Molière.

The theatre assigned to him was the Hôtel du Petit Bourbon, where, by the influence of Mazarin, a new troupe of Italian players had begun to appear three times a week in farce. The rivalry of these foreigners was not to be despised, especially as they showed a very strong tendency to use French, in preference to their own language. From one point of view, no doubt, their entertainment had a rather monotonous aspect. Its personages, as in bygone times, were nearly always the same--harlequin, pantaloon, columbine and the rest--but to the delight of the cardinal, who probably supported it as a means of establishing opera in France, the more it was shown the better it seemed to be liked. Frequently novel in plot, it was animated throughout by a joyous spirit, to which ample effect was given on the stage.

Molière took the off-days of the Italian comedians--Tuesdays, Thursdays and Sundays. Before his campaign opened he was joined by L'Epi, of

> the Marais, and an actor of great excellence in both tragedy and comedy, Guillaume Marcoureau, Sieur de Brécourt, formerly an officer in the army. Unfortunately, the latter had an ungovernable temper, and his engagement in the troupe had hardly been signed when, having run an insolent coachmen through the body on the Fontainbleau road, he sought refuge in Holland from the vengeance of the law. Molière began with *Héraclius* and other tragedies by Corneille, but it was not until *L'Etourdi* and *Le Dépit Amoureaux* were played that his troupe won the town they were permitted to woo. The charms of these pieces, set forth by clever and disciplined acting, were acknowledged with enthusiasm, and nothing was wanting to the triumph of the dramatist but the presence of the king. Alive to the mistake he had made in giving, at the outset, a succession of tragedies, Molière instantly proceeded to confirm the advantage he had gained. He would write another comedy, and it occurred to him that by importing into his work some genial, yet incisive ridicule, of a popular folly, he would do himself no harm. (www.theatrehistory.com/french/moliere005.html, June 18, 2007)

In his final play, The Malade Imagninaire (or *The Imaginary Invalid*), Tartuffe played, as he often did, the lead role. Bates describes this last performance:

> It was the last effort of the dying dramatist. Early in the day fixed for the fourth performance, he was so weak that his wife and Baron united in urging him not to play. But, as usual, he thought of others before himself. "How," he asked, "can I refuse to go on when so many persons' bread depends upon it? I should reproach myself for the distress I might cause them, having sufficient strength to prevent it." Nor was he to be diverted from his resolution. Soon after four o'clock, by which time an audience well disposed to appreciate the new satire on the physicians had filled the theatre to repletion, he again appeared in the high-backed arm-chair of the malade imaginaire. His acting showed no falling off in subtlety or humor, but to those who anxiously watched him from the side of the stage it was painfully evident that the comparatively slight exertion it entailed told heavily upon him. How curious it must have seemed to some of them that a man in such a state should be employed in giving expression to the fancies of a mere hypochondriac!
>
> In the closing interlude, where Argan takes his oath as a new doctor, swearing to adhere to the remedies approved by antiquity, be they right or wrong, and to ignore modern discovery, there occurred something which had not been set down for him in the play. The last "juro" had hardly passed his lips when he was seized with a convulsion. He sought to disguise it by forcing a laugh, but its ring was so hard and harsh that many among that

> hilarious assembly felt a shiver pass through their frames. The curtain was lowered, and the stricken dramatist, now fainting and speechless, was tenderly conveyed to his home. Soon he was able to speak. "My course," he said, "is run. My wife promised me a drugged pillow to make me sleep; let me have it. The only remedies I shrink from are those which have to be swallowed; they are enough to rob me of the little life that remains." While being put to bed he was seized with a fit of coughing; blood streamed from his mouth, and he faintly asked that the consolations of religion might not be denied him. Baron and Armande immediately sought out two ecclesiastics of the parish of St. Eustache, who, however, told them that the author of *Tartuffe* was not a fit person to receive the last consolations. The next priest applied to had a better sense of his duties, but he arrived only in time to see Molière die in the arms of two Sisters of Mercy, to whom he had long given shelter during their Lenten visits to Paris, and who, by a suggestive coincidence, had chanced to knock at his door as the ecclesiastics of St. Eustache were refusing to soothe his last moments. (http://www.theatrehistory.com/french/moliere003.html, June 18, 2007)

Because many of the supporters of the English monarchy were exiled in France during Moliere's early career, Moliere's influence was felt well into the Restoration period when Charles II returned to the throne and Puritan prohibitions against the Theater were lifted. (Felix E. Schelling, *Cambridge History of British and American Literature,* http://www.bartleby.com/218/0517.html, June 18, 2007).

As you read:

As always, begin with the basic observation questions: Who, What, When, Where, Why, How.

Who are the characters in the play? (List them)

What do you learn about each of them?

Where does the play happen?
1. Geographically?
2. As far as the number of places depicted within the play, how many different sets would you expect to see during a performance?

When does the play happen?
1. Historically?
2. How much time elapses from the beginning to the end of the play?

What would you say is the major point or theme of the play?

Though somethings about a writer's technique will be somewhat obscured when you are reading a translation of a work, what observations can you make about the technique and style? How do those technical and stylistic details add to the meaning of the play?

Charley, Charley, James again,
William and Mary, Anne Gloria. . .

Lesson 12
THE NEO-CLASSICAL PERIOD (1660-1785)
THE AGE OF DRYDEN (1660-1700)

This period of time begins with the restoration of Charles II to the throne and ends with the Glorious Revolution in which Catholic James II abdicates and protestant King William and Queen Mary rule. It continues through the reigns of George I, George II, AND George III.

As a literary period, Neo-Classicism begins with the restoration of Charles II to the throne and ends in 1785 with the publication of Wordsworth's *Preludes.*

The writers of the "Victorian Web" website describe the period as follows:

> To a certain extent Neoclassicism represented a reaction against the optimistic, exuberant, and enthusiastic Renaissance view of man as a being fundamentally good and possessed of an infinite potential for spiritual and intellectual growth. Neoclassical theorists, by contrast, saw man as an imperfect being, inherently sinful, whose potential was limited. They replaced the Renaissance emphasis on the imagination, on invention and experimentation, and on mysticism with an emphasis on order and reason, on restraint, on common sense, and on religious, political, economic and philosophical conservatism. They maintained that man himself was the most appropriate subject of art, and saw art itself as essentially pragmatic--as valuable because it was somehow useful--and as something which was properly intellectual rather than emotional.
>
> Hence their emphasis on proper subject matter; and hence their attempts to subordinate details to an overall design, to employ in their work concepts like symmetry, proportion, unity, harmony, and grace, which would facilitate the process of delighting, instructing, educating, and correcting the social animal which they believed man to be. Their favorite prose literary forms were the essay, the letter, the satire, the parody, the burlesque, and the moral fable; in poetry, the favorite verse form was the rhymed couplet, which reached its greatest sophistication in heroic couplet of Pope; while the theatre saw the development of the heroic drama, the melodrama, the sentimental comedy, and the comedy of manners.

(http://www.victorianweb.org/previctorian/nc/ncintro.html
ACCESSED June 21, 2007)

WORLDVIEW BACKGROUND

THE RISE OF RATIONALISM:

As a philosophy, Rationalism believes that knowledge comes though *rational* anaylsis of the world around us. The Rationalist demands objective evidence and will not accept an argument based solely on human experience, divine revelation, or expert opinion. The only *authority* the Rationalist accepts is Reason. "Because I said so," would not motivate a good Rationalist.

Historically, Rationalism "reacted against Renaissance enthusiasm for man's potential (and against religious strife) and sought to impose reason, order, and a decent sense of limits on man. . . Wit was praised rather than feeling. Nature was seen as a source of natural law, and liked best when it had been reduced to order."

(*Late 17th, 18th & 19th Centuries: Neoclassicism & Romanticism, http://www.whs.babienko.net/AP12/Assignments/Poetry/18th_19thCPoets.pdf)*

Now, think about this for a minute. Previously, to what final authority did previous generations look for support when they wanted to make a pronouncement about truth or error, good or evil?

The answer: The Bible, The Church, (or the King....but even in this case the King would often claim that since God obviously put *him* in charge, what he had to say was obviously what *God* wanted!)

It is also important to keep the turmoil of the events surround the English Civil war – and all the discord brought on because of religious wrangling in mind. And while most deists would say that the Bible is still o.k. *in it's place*, there is such a reaction against the discord and disharmony and decapitation, that the intellectuals of the time (called, *philosophes*) are predisposed to completely reject its authority.

French philosopher and writer Voltaire's summary of Enlightenment ideals:

1. autonomy of reason
2. perfectibility and progress
3. confidence in the ability to discover causality
4. principles governing nature, man and society
5. assault on authority
6. cosmopolitan solidarity of enlightened intellectuals
7. disgust with nationalism (*Age of the Enlightenment*).

Gerhard Rempel, lecture notes originally found at (**http://mars.wnec.edu/~grempel/courses/wc2/lectures/enlightenment.html**). Website no longer available.

Compare this list of Enlightenment values with comparable Renaissance ideals:

CONTRASTS
BETWEEN ENLIGHTENMENT AND RENAISSANCE WORLD VIEWS

Enlightenment values*	Renaissance Worldview
autonomy of reason*	autonomy of the Church (medieval) autonomy of the Scriptures (reformation)
confidence in the ability to discover causality [what actually causing a thing to happen]^	God is the cause of many things. Outside of revelation, cause is not usually possible to know
principles governing nature, man and society (impersonal)*	a personal God governs nature, man and society
assault on authority*	belief in the "Great Chain of Being" in which God is the ultimate authority over a hierarchy of lesser authorities. Since God has established all authority, to disobey any authority is ultimately to disobey God
cosmopolitan solidarity of enlightened intellectuals* [*Another way to say it: The philosophers KNOW stuff the ignorant, rural people don't. Exclusive club for "Us-guys" that only admits "Us-guys" Oh, and by the way, Us-guys all live in the city – in solidarity with all the other "Us-guys." [My own addition c.s].*	Community was perceived largely as national or spiritual or family.
disgust with nationalism" *	Loyalty to king assumed. Anything else was treasonous and fatal.

Now having read this material, make 2 lists:

What were the most common *prose* literary forms used during this period?

What were the most common *poetic* literary forms used during this time?

Literary critics have many opinions about how these 125 years of literature might be subdivided and labeled. As a whole the period is referred to as The Neo-Classical period, after a renewed interest in Ancient Greek and Roman culture.

During the Renaissance, the cry had been, Back to the Sources. Since the fall of the Roman Empire, copies of Ancient texts had been available only in Latin Translation. During the Renaissance, scholars began to recover use of Greek and Hebrew. In some ways you could say that the the writers of this period could be seen as heirs of the Renaissance scholarly return to study of ancient Greek languages and culture. Earlier writers had alluded to Biblical people and Biblical stories. The Neo-classical writers of made references to the heroes and stories of Greek and Roman history and mythology.

Because of this renewed interest in the Classics, this 125-time period is often refered to as the *Neo*-Classical period.

With the return of monarchy, the sense was that England had cast off the chains of the Interregnum and weathered the upheaval preceding the Glorious Revolution's disposition of yet another English monarch when James II abdicates. With the ascention of George I, the sense was that England was about to enter its own "golden age," ruled by a king whose glories would rival those of Augustus Caesar. After the upheaval of civil war and the austere rule of the Puritan Protectorate, many hoped to see a literary "golden age" as well. Thus, the period is sometimes called "The Augustine Age."

Sometime you will see the period divided into three sub-sections. These sub-sections bear the names of the men whose work dominated the writing of that time:

The Age of Dryden (1660-1700)
The Age of Pope (1700-1745)
The Age of Johnson (1745-1785)

The poets of this period did not tend to write personal, introspective verse. They wrote for a very public audience, and their subject matter was usually in

someway connected to contemporary events and personalities. Those events are often obscure
That is why it is extremely important for you to read slowly and carefully. Use the basic Observation questions (WWWWWH), and find the answers to these questions in the text of the poem. You may not know WHO a character in the poem is supposed to represent historically, since that will not be clearly stated, but you should be able discern something about the relationship of one individual to another. You should also be able to tell something about the quality of an individual's character.

Because the poems were generally written to address some contemporary event, the more background information you have before you read, the more sense the poem will make to you. THEREFORE, read the following background information carefully. Read it as if you were going to be quizzed on it. You never know. It COULD happen.

(Oh, and be sure and answer the questions that follow the poem IN WRITING ON THE PAPER (not just in your lovely head). Bring your written answers with you to class. You never know when someone will want to look at them. That has been known to happen, too.

John Dryden (1631-1700)

Up until the 1680s Dryden wrote mostly plays and essays on drama. In 1663, he was named Poet Laureat of England. He was known for his mastery of the rhymed couplet. Dryden's poems often satirized political figures and playwrights that displeased him. In the mid-1880s Dryden converted to Catholicism, a move which did not serve him well politically. After the unpopular, and incidentally, Catholic King James II abdicated the throne there was quite a renewal of hostility to all things Catholic. As a result of his identification with James II and because of his Catholicism, Dryden fell out of favor at Court and lost his title as Poet Laureate. After 1688, Dryden supported himself and his family by writing plays and translating Latin and Greek poetry into English.

Ruth Nestvold, in her summary of the Augustan Age, points out that "Dryden forms the link between Restoration and Augustan literature; although he wrote ribald comedies in the Restoration vein, his verse satires were highly admired by the generation of poets who followed him, and his writings on literature were very much in a neoclassical spirit." (Nestvold, Ruth. "The Augustan Age." Ruth Nesvold. 2001. 20 Jun 2007 <http://www.ruthnestvold.com/Augustan.htm.>.

The following poem by Dryden grew out of a bitter quarrel between Dryden and a poet and playwright named Thomas Shadwell. Though Shadwell and Dryden appear to have been on friendly terms at one point, they seemed to have had a falling out after Dryden support for James II over his protestant opposition. identified himself with the court of James II. The short history of their quarrel follows: Charles II was outwardly a member of the Church of England, but had the political reality been different, Charles would have been quite happy to identify himself with the Catholic Church. The fact that Charles had no heir, opened the door to quarrels and maneuverings on behalf of those who had some potential claim to the throne.

There were at least two candidates: The Duke of York (later James II, and a known Catholic) and the Duke of Monmouth (one of Charles II many illegitimate sons and a Protestant). The Earl of Shaftesbury attempted to have Parliament pass a law excluding York from the line of succession in favor of Monmouth. King Charles responded by accusing Shafesbury of treason. Dryden responded by writing the poem, *Absalom and Achitophel* , drawing the connection between Shaftesbury's treason against Charles II and Achitophel's treason against King David.

When Shaftesbury was aquitted of the charge, his friends celebrated by presenting him with a medal of honor. Dryden responded by writing a satire titled, *The Medal*. Thomas Shadwell responded by writing a satire against Dryden titled *The Medal of John Bayes: A Satire against Folly and Knavery.* Dryden responded by writing *MacFlecknoe* in which Shadwell was identified as the heir of a odd little Irish (and Protestant) poet, Richard Flecknoe. In 1688, James II abdicated and left England. The same year Dryden converted to Catholicism and was removed from his office as poet laureate. Shadwell was appointed to serve in his place.

Shadwell was a prolific playwright, producing a new play nearly every year.

To get a feel for the verse Shadwell produced, read the following short poems:

Dear Pretty Youth

Dear pretty youth, unveil your eyes,
How can you sleep when I am by?
Were I with you all night to be,
Methinks I could from sleep be free.
Alas, my dear, you're cold as stone:
You must no longer lie alone.
But be with me my dear, and I in each arm
Will hug you close and keep you warm.

Halcyon Days

Halcyon days, now wars are ending.
You shall find where-e'er you sail
Tritons all the while attending
With a kind and gentle gale.

Shadwell

Love In Their Little Veins Inspires

Love in their little veins inspires
their cheerful notes, their soft desires.
While heat makes buds and blossoms spring,
those pretty couples love and sing.
But winter puts out their desire,
and half the year they want love's fire.

Nymphs And Shepherds

Nymphs and shepherds, come away.
In the groves let's sport and play,
For this is Flora's holiday,
Sacred to ease and happy love,
To dancing, to music and to poetry;
Your flocks may now securely rove
Whilst you express your jollity.
Nymphs and shepherds, come away.

Before you read *MacFlecknoe*, you need to know two more things:

1. The prefix *Mac* means "legitimate son of." The prefix, *Fitz*, means illegitimate son of."

2. The story of MacFlecknoe specifically alludes to the biblical story of Elijah and Elisha found in 2 Kings 2:1-16.

2 Kings 2

1 And it came to pass, when the LORD would take up Elijah into heaven by a
whirlwind, that Elijah went with Elisha from Gilgal. 2 And Elijah said unto Elisha,
Tarry here, I pray thee; for the LORD hath sent me to Bethel. And Elisha said
unto him, As the LORD liveth, and as thy soul liveth, I will not leave thee. So
they went down to Bethel. 3 And the sons of the prophets that were at Bethel
came forth to Elisha, and said unto him, Knowest thou that the LORD will take
away thy master from thy head to day? And he said, Yea, I know it; hold ye
your peace. 4 And Elijah said unto him, Elisha, tarry here, I pray thee; for the
LORD hath sent me to Jericho. And he said, As the LORD liveth, and as thy
soul liveth, I will not leave thee. So they came to Jericho. 5 And the sons of the
prophets that were at Jericho came to Elisha, and said unto him, Knowest thou
that the LORD will take away thy master from thy head to day? And he
answered, Yea, I know it; hold ye your peace. 6 And Elijah said unto him, Tarry,
I pray thee, here; for the LORD hath sent me to Jordan. And he said, As the
LORD liveth, and as thy soul liveth, I will not leave thee. And they two went on.
7 And fifty men of the sons of the prophets went, and stood to viewa afar off:
and they two stood by Jordan. 8 And Elijah took his mantle, and wrapped it
together, and smote the waters, and they were divided hither and thither, so
that they two went over on dry ground.
9 And it came to pass, when they were gone over, that Elijah said unto Elisha,
Ask what I shall do for thee, before I be taken away from thee. And Elisha said,
I pray thee, let a double portion of thy spirit be upon me. 10 And he said, Thou
hast asked a hard thing: nevertheless, if thou see me when I am taken from
thee, it shall be so unto thee; but if not, it shall not be so. 11 And it came to
pass, as they still went on, and talked, that, behold, there appeared a chariot of
fire, and horses of fire, and parted them both asunder; and Elijah went up by a
whirlwind into heaven. 12 And Elisha saw it, and he cried, My father, my father,
the chariot of Israel, and the horsemen thereof. And he saw him no more: and
he took hold of his own clothes, and rent them in two pieces.
13 He took up also the mantle of Elijah that fell from him, and went back, and
stood by the bankb of Jordan; 14 And he took the mantle of Elijah that fell from
him, and smote the waters, and said, Where is the LORD God of Elijah? and
when he also had smitten the waters, they parted hither and thither: and Elisha
went over. 15 And when the sons of the prophets which were to view at Jericho
saw him, they said, The spirit of Elijah doth rest on Elisha. And they came to
meet him, and bowed themselves to the ground before him.

Finally, the satire of this period is so rooted in the political events and personalitys of the time. A full understanding of the references and commentary in the poem will be very obscure if you are not very familiar with the history of that period.

There is help! Go to this site to help in understanding some of the more obscure contemporary references made in *Mac Flecknoe* – it will really help you to do this!

http://andromeda.rutgers.edu/~jlynch/Texts/macflecknoe.html#1

Mac Flecknoe: A Satire upon the True-blue Protestant Poet T.S.

All human things are subject to decay,
And, when Fate summons, monarchs must obey:
This Flecknoe found, who, like Augustus, young
Was call'd to empire, and had govern'd long:
In prose and verse, was own'd, without dispute
Through all the realms of Non-sense, absolute.
This aged prince now flourishing in peace,
And blest with issue of a large increase,
Worn out with business, did at length debate
To settle the succession of the State:
And pond'ring which of all his sons was fit
To reign, and wage immortal war with wit;
Cry'd, 'tis resolv'd; for nature pleads that he
Should only rule, who most resembles me:
Sh--- alone my perfect image bears,
Mature in dullness from his tender years.
Imy sons, is he
Who stands confirm'd in full stupidity.
The rest to some faint meaning make pretence,
But Sh--- never deviates into sense.
Some beams of wit on other souls may fall,
Strike through and make a lucid interval;
But Sh---'s genuine night admits no ray,
His rising fogs prevail upon the day:
Besides his goodly fabric fills the eye,
And seems design'd for thoughtl
Thou last great prophet of tautology:
Even I, a dunce of more renown than they,
Was sent before but to prepare thy way;
And coarsely clad in Norwich drugget came
To teach the nations in thy greater name.
My warbling lute, the lute I whilom strung
When to King John of Portugal I sung,

Was but the prelude to that glorious day,
When thou on silver Thames did'st cut thy way,
With well tim'd oars before the royal barge,
Swell'd with the pride of thy celestial charge;
And big with hymn, commander of an host,
The like was ne'er in Epsom blankets toss'd.
Methinks I see the new Arion sail,

The lute still trembling underneath thy nail.
At thy well sharpen'd thumb from shore to shore
The treble squeaks for fear, the basses roar:
Echoes from Pissing-Alley, Sh--- call,
And Sh--- they resound from Aston Hall.
About thy boat the little fishes throng,
As at the morning toast, that floats along.
Sometimes as prince of thy harmonious band
Thou wield'st thy papers in thy threshing hand.
St. Andre's feet ne'er kept more equal time,
Not ev'n the feet of thy own Psyche's rhyme:
Though they in number as in sense excel;
So just, so like tautology they fell,
That, pale with envy, Singleton forswore
The lute and sword which he in triumph bore
And vow'd he ne'er would act Villerius more.
Here stopt the good old sire; and wept for joy
In silent raptures of the hopeful boy.
All arguments, but most his plays, persuade,
That for anointed dullness he was made.

Close to the walls which fair Augusta bind,
(The fair Augusta much to fears inclin'd)
An ancient fabric, rais'd t'inform the sight,

There stood of yore, and Barbican it hight:
A watch tower once; but now, so fate ordains,
Of all the pile an empty name remains.
From its old ruins brothel-houses rise,
Scenes of lewd loves, and of polluted joys.
Where their vast courts, the mother-strumpets keep,
And, undisturb'd by watch, in silence sleep.
Near these a nursery erects its head,
Where queens are form'd, and future heroes bred;
Where unfledg'd actors learn to laugh and cry,
Where infant punks their tender voices try,
And little Maximins the gods defy.
Great Fletcher never treads in buskins here,
Nor greater Jonson dares in socks appear;

But gentle Simkin just reception finds
Amidst this monument of vanish'd minds:
Pure clinches, the suburbian muse affords;
And Panton waging harmless war with words.
Here Flecknoe, as a place to fame well known,
Ambitiously design'd his Sh---'s throne.
For ancient Decker prophesi'd long since,
That in this pile should reign a mighty prince,
Born for a scourge of wit, and flail of sense:
To whom true dullness should some Psyches owe,
But worlds of Misers from his pen should flow;
Humorists and hypocrites it should produce,
Whole Raymond families, and tribes of Bruce.
Now Empress Fame had publisht the renown,
Of Sh---'s coronation through the town.
Rous'd by report of fame, the nations meet,
From near Bun-Hill, and distant Watling-street.
No Persian carpets spread th'imperial way,
But scatter'd limbs of mangled poets lay:
From dusty shops neglected authors come,
Martyrs of pies, and reliques of the bum.
Much Heywood, Shirley, Ogleby there lay,
But loads of Sh--- almost chok'd the way.
Bilk'd stationers for yeoman stood prepar'd,
And Herringman was Captain of the Guard.
The hoary prince in majesty appear'd,
High on a throne of his own labours rear'd.
At his right hand our young Ascanius sat
Rome's other hope, and pillar of the state.
His brows thick fogs, instead of glories, grace,
And lambent dullness play'd around his face.
As Hannibal did to the altars come,
Sworn by his sire a mortal foe to Rome;
So Sh--- swore, nor should his vow be vain,
That he till death true dullness would maintain;
And in his father's right, and realm's defence,
Ne'er to have peace with wit, nor truce with sense.
The king himself the sacred unction made,
As king by office, and as priest by trade:
In his sinister hand, instead of ball,
He plac'd a mighty mug of potent ale;
Love's kingdom to his right he did convey,
At once his sceptre and his rule of sway;
Whose righteous lore the prince had practis'd young,
And from whose loins recorded Psyche sprung,
His temples last with poppies were o'er spread,

That nodding seem'd to consecrate his head:
Just at that point of time, if fame not lie,
On his left hand twelve reverend owls did fly.
So Romulus, 'tis sung, by Tiber's brook,
Presage of sway from twice six vultures took.
Th'admiring throng loud acclamations make,
And omens of his future empire take.
The sire then shook the honours of his head,
And from his brows damps of oblivion shed
Full on the filial dullness: long he stood,
Repelling from his breast the raging god;
At length burst out in this prophetic mood:

Heavens bless my son, from Ireland let him reign
To far Barbadoes on the Western main;
Of his dominion may no end be known,
And greater than his father's be his throne.
Beyond love's kingdom let him stretch his pen;
He paus'd, and all the people cry'd Amen.
Then thus, continu'd he, my son advance
Still in new impudence, new ignorance.
Success let other teach, learn thou from me
Pangs without birth, and fruitless industry.
Let Virtuosos in five years be writ;
Yet not one thought accuse thy toil of wit.
Let gentle George in triumph tread the stage,
Make Dorimant betray, and Loveit rage;
Let Cully, Cockwood, Fopling, charm the pit,
And in their folly show the writer's wit.
Yet still thy fools shall stand in thy defence,
And justify their author's want of sense.
Let 'em be all by thy own model made
Of dullness, and desire no foreign aid:
That they to future ages may be known,
Not copies drawn, but issue of thy own.
Nay let thy men of wit too be the same,
All full of thee, and differing but in name;
But let no alien Sedley interpose
To lard with wit thy hungry Epsom prose.
And when false flowers of rhetoric thou would'st cull,
Trust Nature, do not labour to be dull;
But write thy best, and top; and in each line,
Sir Formal's oratory will be thine.
Sir Formal, though unsought, attends thy quill,
And does thy Northern Dedications fill.
Nor let false friends seduce thy mind to fame,

By arrogating Jonson's hostile name.
Let Father Flecknoe fire thy mind with praise,
And Uncle Ogleby thy envy raise.
Thou art my blood, where Jonson has no part;
What share have we in Nature or in Art?
Where did his wit on learning fix a brand,
And rail at arts he did not understand?
Where made he love in Prince Nicander's vein,
Or swept the dust in Psyche's humble strain?
Where sold he bargains, whip-stitch, kiss my arse,
Promis'd a play and dwindled to a farce?
When did his muse from Fletcher scenes purloin,
As thou whole Eth'ridge dost transfuse to thine?
But so transfus'd as oil on waters flow,
His always floats above, thine sinks below.
This is thy province, this thy wondrous way,
New humours to invent for each new play:
This is that boasted bias of thy mind,
By which one way, to dullness, 'tis inclin'd,
Which makes thy writings lean on one side still,
And in all changes that way bends thy will.
Nor let thy mountain belly make pretence
Of likeness; thine's a tympany of sense.
A tun of man in thy large bulk is writ,
But sure thou 'rt but a kilderkin of wit.
Like mine thy gentle numbers feebly creep,
Thy Tragic Muse gives smiles, thy Comic sleep.
With whate'er gall thou sett'st thy self to write,
Thy inoffensive satires never bite.
In thy felonious heart, though venom lies,
It does but touch thy Irish pen, and dies.
Thy genius calls thee not to purchase fame
In keen iambics, but mild anagram:
Leave writing plays, and choose for thy command
Some peaceful province in acrostic land.
There thou may'st wings display and altars raise,
And torture one poor word ten thousand ways.
Or if thou would'st thy diff'rent talents suit,
Set thy own songs, and sing them to thy lute.
He said, but his last words were scarcely heard,
For Bruce and Longvil had a trap prepar'd,
And down they sent the yet declaiming bard.
Sinking he left his drugget robe behind,
Born upwards by a subterranean wind.
The mantle fell to the young prophet's part,
With double portion of his father's art.

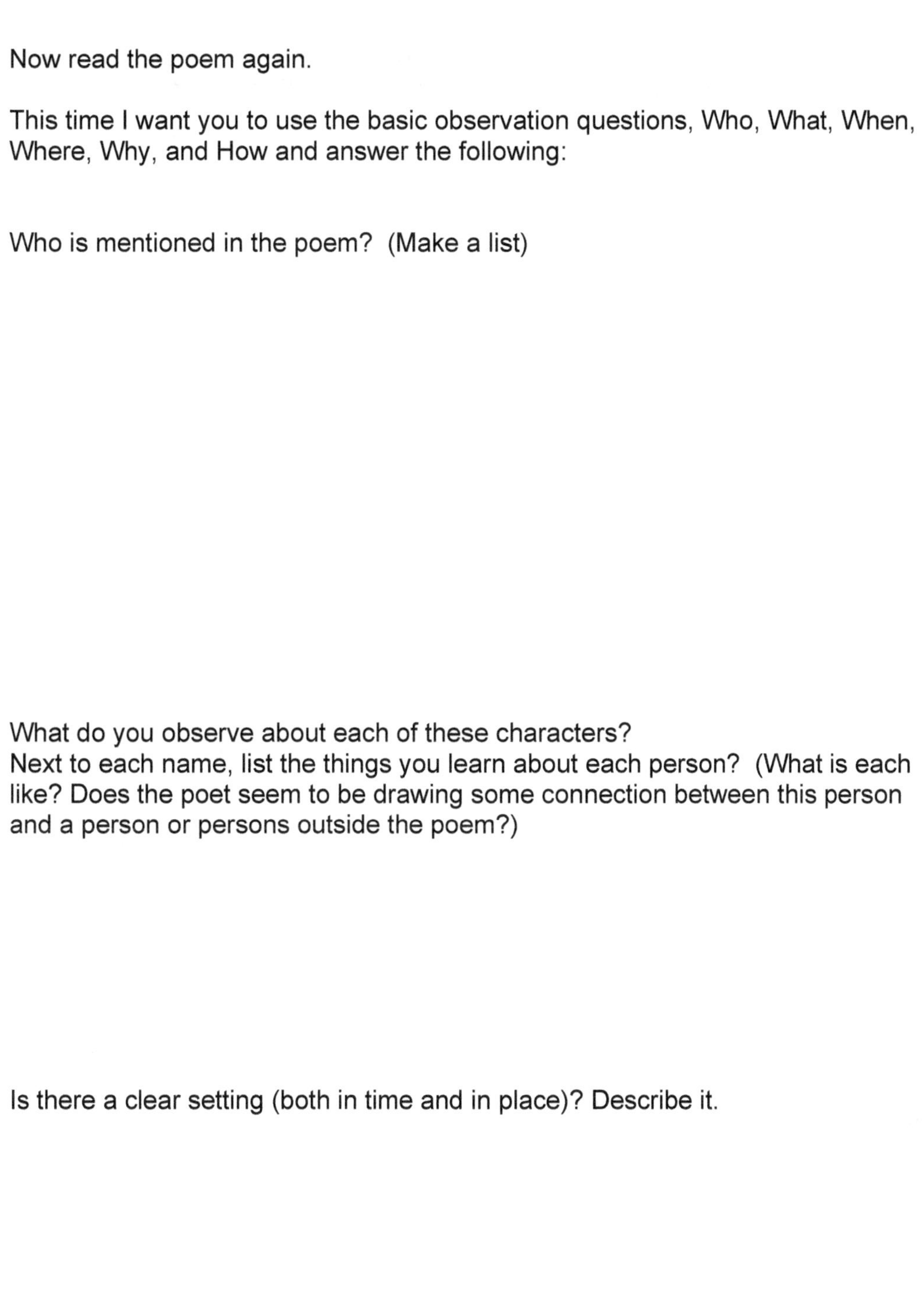

Now read the poem again.

This time I want you to use the basic observation questions, Who, What, When, Where, Why, and How and answer the following:

Who is mentioned in the poem? (Make a list)

What do you observe about each of these characters?
Next to each name, list the things you learn about each person? (What is each like? Does the poet seem to be drawing some connection between this person and a person or persons outside the poem?)

Is there a clear setting (both in time and in place)? Describe it.

What is the basic action of the poem? What do the character do? (PLOT) Briefly describe it below (Summarize briefly in list form using bullets below. Use as many as you need.)

-
-
-
-
-
-
-
-
-

How does Dryden use the story of Elijah's exit? How is Elijah's exit similar to or different from Flecknoe's exit?

In the same way, how is Elisha's appointment similar to or different from MacFlecknoe's appointment?

How does Dryden's use of this allusion work? (Did you laugh?)

If you didn't laugh, read the poem again. (I'm not kidding!)

Look up the definition of satire, and write it out below.

Is *MacFlecknoe* satirical?

Mark all uses of the word, *wit*. Write its definition below.

Charlie, <u>Charlie James Again</u>
<u>William & Mary, Anne Gloria</u>
<u>4 Georges</u> (George 1, actually)

LESSON 13

Jonathan Swift (1667-1745)

Though Jonathan Swift may have expected his fellow human creatures to behave noblely, he had no illusions about human nature. "I never wonder to see men wicked," said Swift, "but I often wonder to see them not ashamed." Man is prideful and his pride often makes him ridiculous. More than that, pride often blinds us to our own faults.

Swift, himself noted, "Satire is a sort of glass, wherein beholders do generally discover everybody's face but their own; which is the chief reason for that kind of reception it meets in the world, and that so very few are offended with it." (*The Battle of the Books, Preface. 1697)*

In fact, the advantage of Satire is its ability to play with the reader, taking advantage of our human tendancy to hold everyone else to the standards we ourselves, happily ignore.

In *A Modest Proposal*, Swift turns his attention to the English oppression of his Irish homeland. You could, I suppose, say that it is the most "biting" of his satirical works. (That was a joke. You can explain it after you have read the essay.)

In *Gulliver's Travels*, probably his best-known work, Swift's Gulliver journeys to four exotic cultures. As he records the practices and culture of each society, he lampoons elements of contemporary English culture.

It will be your job, gentle reader, to sort out the intent of his many observations. He will not do that for you.

Go to the following website for a good biography of Swift:
http://www.victorianweb.org/previctorian/swift/swiftov.html

You might also enjoy reading a few short Swift quotations:

> **"Ambition often puts Men upon doing the meanest offices; so climbing is performed in the same position with creeping."**
>
> **"Better belly burst than good liquor be lost."**
>
> **"I never knew a man come to greatness or eminence who lay abed late in the morning."**
>
> **"I said there was a society of men among us, bred up from their youth in the art of proving by words multiplied for that purpose, that white is black, and black is white, according as they are paid."**
>
> **"To this society all the rest of the people are as slaves."**
>
> **"I wonder what fool it was that first invented kissing."**
>
> **"No wise man ever wished to be younger."**
>
> **"She wears clothes as if they were thrown on with a pitch fork."**
>
> **"When a true genius appears in this world, you may know him by this sign, that the dunces are all in a confederacy against him."**

Advice to the Grub Street Verse-writers

Ye poets ragged and forlorn
  Down from your garrets haste,
Ye rhymers, dead as soon as born,
  Not yet consign'd to paste;

I know a trick to make you thrive;
  O, 'tis a quaint device:
Your still-born poems shall revive,
  And scorn to wrap up spice.

Get all your verses printed fair,

    Then let them well be dried;
And Curll must have a special care
    To leave the margin wide.

Lend these to paper-sparing Pope;
    And when he sets to write,
No letter with an envelope
    Could give him more delight.

When Pope has fill'd the margins round,
    Why then recall your loan;
Sell them to Curll for fifty pound,
    And swear they are your own.

A Modest Proposal

A MODEST PROPOSAL FOR PREVENTING THE CHILDREN OF POOR PEOPLE IN IRELAND FROM BEING A BURDEN TO THEIR PARENTS OR COUNTRY, AND FOR MAKING THEM BENEFICIAL TO THE PUBLIC

It is a melancholy object to those who walk through this great town or travel in the country, when they see the streets, the roads, and cabin doors, crowded with beggars of the female sex, followed by three, four, or six children, all in rags and importuning every passenger for an alms. These mothers, instead of being able to work for their honest livelihood, are forced to employ all their time in strolling to beg sustenance for their helpless infants: who as they grow up either turn thieves for want of work, or leave their dear native country to fight for the Pretender in Spain, or sell themselves to the Barbadoes.

I think it is agreed by all parties that this prodigious number of children in the arms, or on the backs, or at the heels of their mothers, and frequently of their fathers, is in the present deplorable state of the kingdom a very great additional grievance; and, therefore, whoever could find out a fair, cheap, and easy method of making these children sound, useful members of the commonwealth, would deserve so well of the public as to have his statue set up for a preserver of the nation.

But my intention is very far from being confined to provide only for the children of professed beggars; it is of a much greater extent, and shall take in the whole number of infants at a certain age who are born of parents in effect as little able to support them as those who demand our charity in the streets.

As to my own part, having turned my thoughts for many years upon this important subject, and maturely weighed the several schemes of other projectors, I have always found them grossly mistaken in the computation. It is true, a child just dropped from its dam may be supported by her milk for a solar year, with little other nourishment; at most not above the value of 2s., which the mother may certainly get, or the value in scraps, by her lawful occupation of begging; and it is exactly at one year old that I propose to provide for them in such a manner as instead of being a charge upon their parents or the parish, or wanting food and raiment for the rest of their lives, they shall on the contrary contribute to the feeding, and partly to the clothing, of many thousands.

There is likewise another great advantage in my scheme, that it will prevent those voluntary abortions, and that horrid practice of women murdering their bastard children, alas! too frequent among us! sacrificing the poor innocent babes I doubt more to avoid the expense than the shame, which would move tears and pity in the most savage and inhuman breast.

The number of souls in this kingdom being usually reckoned one million and a half, of these I calculate there may be about two hundred thousand couple whose wives are breeders; from which number I subtract thirty thousand couples who are able to maintain their own children, although I apprehend there cannot be so many, under the present distresses of the kingdom; but this being granted, there will remain an hundred and seventy thousand breeders. I again subtract fifty thousand for those women who miscarry, or whose children die by accident or disease within the year. There only remains one hundred and twenty thousand children of poor parents annually born: the question therefore is, how this number shall be reared and provided for, which, as I have already said, under the present situation of affairs, is utterly impossible by all the methods hitherto proposed. For we can neither employ them in handicraft or agriculture; we neither build houses (I mean in the country) nor cultivate land: they can very seldom pick up a livelihood by stealing, till they arrive at six years old, except where they are of towardly parts, although I confess they learn the rudiments much earlier, during which time, they can however be properly looked upon only as probationers, as I have been informed by a principal gentleman in the county of Cavan, who protested to me that he never knew above one or two instances under the age of six, even in a part of the kingdom so renowned for the quickest proficiency in that art.

I am assured by our merchants, that a boy or a girl before twelve years old is no salable commodity; and even when they come to this age they will not yield above three pounds, or three pounds and half-a-crown at most on the exchange; which cannot turn to account either to the parents or kingdom, the charge of nutriment and rags having been at least four times that value.

I shall now therefore humbly propose my own thoughts, which I hope will not be liable to the least objection.

I have been assured by a very knowing American of my acquaintance in London, that a young healthy child well nursed is at a year old a most delicious, nourishing, and wholesome food, whether stewed, roasted, baked, or boiled; and I make no doubt that it will equally serve in a fricassee or a ragout.

I do therefore humbly offer it to public consideration that of the hundred and twenty thousand children already computed, twenty thousand may be reserved for breed, whereof only one-fourth part to be males; which is more than we allow to sheep, black cattle or swine; and my reason is, that these children are seldom the fruits of marriage, a circumstance not much regarded by our savages, therefore one male will be sufficient to serve four females. That the remaining hundred thousand may, at a year old, be offered in the sale to the persons of quality and fortune through the kingdom; always advising the mother to let them suck plentifully in the last month, so as to render them plump and fat for a good table. A child will make two dishes at an entertainment for friends; and when the family dines alone, the fore or hind quarter will make a reasonable dish, and seasoned with a little pepper or salt will be very good boiled on the fourth day, especially in winter.

I have reckoned upon a medium that a child just born will weigh 12 pounds, and in a solar year, if tolerably nursed, increaseth to 28 pounds.

I grant this food will be somewhat dear, and therefore very proper for landlords, who, as they have already devoured most of the parents, seem to have the best title to the children.

Infant's flesh will be in season throughout the year, but more plentiful in March, and a little before and after; for we are told by a grave author, an eminent French physician, that fish being a prolific diet, there are more children born in Roman Catholic countries about nine months after Lent than at any other season; therefore, reckoning a year after Lent, the markets will be more glutted than usual, because the number of popish infants is at least three to one in this kingdom: and therefore it will have one other collateral advantage, by lessening the number of papists among us.

I have already computed the charge of nursing a beggar's child (in which list I reckon all cottagers, laborers, and four-fifths of the farmers) to be about two shillings per annum, rags included; and I believe no gentleman would repine to give ten shillings for the carcass of a good fat child, which, as I have said, will make four dishes of excellent nutritive meat, when he hath only some particular friend or his own family to dine with him. Thus the squire will learn to be a good landlord, and grow popular among his tenants; the mother will have eight shillings net profit, and be fit for work till she produces another child.

Those who are more thrifty (as I must confess the times require) may flay the carcass; the skin of which artificially dressed will make admirable gloves for ladies, and summer boots for fine gentlemen.

As to our city of Dublin, shambles may be appointed for this purpose in the most convenient parts of it, and butchers we may be assured will not be wanting; although I rather recommend buying the children alive, and dressing them hot from the knife, as we do roasting pigs.

A very worthy person, a true lover of his country, and whose virtues I highly esteem, was lately pleased in discoursing on this matter to offer a refinement upon my scheme. He said that many gentlemen of this kingdom, having of late destroyed their deer, he conceived that the want of venison might be well supplied by the bodies of young lads and maidens, not exceeding fourteen years of age nor under twelve; so great a number of both sexes in every country being now ready to starve for want of work and service; and these to be disposed of by their parents, if alive, or otherwise by their nearest relations. But with due deference to so excellent a friend and so deserving a patriot, I cannot be altogether in his sentiments; for as to the males, my American acquaintance assured me, from frequent experience, that their flesh was generally tough and lean, like that of our schoolboys by continual exercise, and their taste disagreeable; and to fatten them would not answer the charge. Then as to the females, it would, I think, with humble submission be a loss to the public, because they soon would become breeders themselves; and besides, it is not improbable that some scrupulous people might be apt to censure such a practice (although indeed very unjustly), as a little bordering upon cruelty; which, I confess, hath always been with me the strongest objection against any project, however so well intended.

But in order to justify my friend, he confessed that this expedient was put into his head by the famous Psalmanazar, a native of the island Formosa, who came from thence to London above twenty years ago, and in conversation told my friend, that in his country when any young person happened to be put to death, the executioner sold the carcass to persons of quality as a prime dainty; and that in his time the body of a plump girl of fifteen, who was crucified for an attempt to poison the emperor, was sold to his imperial majesty's prime minister of state, and other great mandarins of the court, in joints from the gibbet, at four hundred crowns. Neither indeed can I deny, that if the same use were made of several plump young girls in this town, who without one single groat to their fortunes cannot stir abroad without a chair, and appear at playhouse and assemblies in foreign fineries which they never will pay for, the kingdom would not be the worse.

Some persons of a desponding spirit are in great concern about that vast number of poor people, who are aged, diseased, or maimed, and I have been desired to employ my thoughts what course may be taken to ease the nation of so grievous an encumbrance. But I am not in the least pain upon that matter, because it is very well known that they are every day dying and rotting by cold and famine, and filth and vermin, as fast as can be reasonably expected. And as to the young laborers, they are now in as hopeful a condition; they cannot get work, and consequently pine away for want of nourishment, to a degree that if at any time they are accidentally hired to common labor, they have not strength to perform it; and thus the country and themselves are happily delivered from the evils to come.

I have too long digressed, and therefore shall return to my subject. I think the advantages by the proposal which I have made are obvious and many, as well as of the highest importance.

For first, as I have already observed, it would greatly lessen the number of papists, with whom we are yearly overrun, being the principal breeders of the nation as well as our most dangerous enemies; and who stay at home on purpose with a design to deliver the kingdom to the Pretender, hoping to take their advantage by the absence of so many good protestants, who have chosen rather to leave their country than stay at home and pay tithes against their conscience to an Episcopal curate.

Secondly, the poorer tenants will have something valuable of their own, which by law may be made liable to distress and help to pay their landlord's rent, their corn and cattle being already seized, and money a thing unknown.

Thirdly, Whereas the maintenance of an hundred thousand children, from two years old and upward, cannot be computed at less than ten shillings a-piece per annum, the nation's stock will be thereby increased fifty thousand pounds per annum, beside the profit of a new dish introduced to the tables of all gentlemen of fortune in the kingdom who have any refinement in taste. And the money will circulate among ourselves, the goods being entirely of our own growth and manufacture.

Fourthly, The constant breeders, beside the gain of eight shillings sterling per annum by the sale of their children, will be rid of the charge of maintaining them after the first year. Fifthly, This food would likewise bring great custom to taverns; where the vintners will certainly be so prudent as to procure the best receipts for dressing it to perfection, and consequently have their houses frequented by all the fine gentlemen, who justly value themselves upon their knowledge in good eating: and a skilful cook, who understands how to oblige his guests, will contrive to make it as expensive as they please.

Sixthly, This would be a great inducement to marriage, which all wise nations have either encouraged by rewards or enforced by laws and penalties. It would increase the care and tenderness of mothers toward their children, when they were sure of a settlement for life to the poor babes, provided in some sort by the public, to their annual profit instead of expense. We should see an honest emulation among the married women, which of them could bring the fattest child to the market. Men would become as fond of their wives during the time of their pregnancy as they are now of their mares in foal, their cows in calf, their sows when they are ready to farrow; nor offer to beat or kick them (as is too frequent a practice) for fear of a miscarriage.

Many other advantages might be enumerated. For instance, the addition of some thousand carcasses in our exportation of barreled beef, the propagation of swine's flesh, and improvement in the art of making good bacon, so much wanted among us by the great destruction of pigs, too frequent at our tables; which are no way comparable in taste or magnificence to a well-grown, fat, yearling child, which roasted whole will make a considerable figure at a lord mayor's feast or any other public entertainment. But this and many others I omit, being studious of brevity.

Supposing that one thousand families in this city would be constant customers for infants flesh, besides others who might have it at merry meetings, particularly weddings and christenings: I compute that Dublin would take off annually about twenty thousand carcasses, and the rest of the kingdom (where probably they will be sold somewhat cheaper) the remaining eighty thousand.

I can think of no one that will possibly be raised against this proposal, unless it should be urged that the number of people will be thereby much lessened in the kingdom. This I freely own, and it was indeed one principal design in offering it to the world. I desire the reader will observe, that I calculated my remedy for this one individual Kingdom of Ireland, and for no other that ever was, is, or, I think, ever can be upon earth. Therefore let no man talk to me of other expedients: Of taxing our absentees at five shillings a pound: Of using neither clothes, nor household furniture, except what is our own growth and manufacture: Of utterly rejecting the materials and instruments that promote foreign luxury: Of curing the expensiveness of pride, vanity, idleness, and gaming in our women: Of introducing a vein of parsimony, prudence, and temperance: Of learning to love our country, wherein we differ even from Laplanders, and the inhabitants of Tompinamboo: Of quitting our animosities and factions, nor act any longer like the Jews, who were murdering one another at the very moment their city was taken: Of being a little cautious not to sell our country and consciences for nothing: Of teaching landlords to have at least one degree of mercy towards their tenants. Lastly, of putting a spirit of honesty, industry, into our shopkeepers, who, if a resolution could now be taken to buy only our native goods, would immediately unite to cheat and exact upon us in the price, the measure and goodness, nor could ever yet be brought to make one fair proposal of just dealing, though often and earnestly invited to it.

Therefore I repeat, let no man talk to me of these and the likes expedients, till he hath at least a glimpse of hope that there will ever be some hearty and sincere attempt to put them in practice. But as to myself, having been wearied out for many years with offering vain, idle, visionary thoughts, and at length utterly despairing of success, I fortunately fell upon this proposal, which as it is wholly new, so it hath something solid and real, of no expense and little trouble, full in our own power, and whereby we can incur no danger in disobliging England. For this kind of commodity will not bear exportation, the flesh being of too tender a consistence to admit a long continuance in salt, although perhaps I could name a country that would be glad to eat up our whole nation without it.

After all, I am not so violently bent upon my own opinion as to reject any offer proposed by wise men, which shall be found equally innocent, cheap, easy, and effectual. But before something of that kind shall be advanced in contradiction to my scheme, and offering a better, I desire the author or authors will be pleased maturely to consider two points. First, as things now stand, how they will be able to find food and raiment for an hundred thousand useless mouths and backs. And secondly, there being a round million of creatures in human figure throughout this kingdom, whose whole subsistence put into a common stock would leave them in debt two millions of pounds sterling, adding those who are beggars by profession to the bulk of farmers, cottagers, and laborers, with their wives and children who are beggars in effect: I desire those politicians who dislike my overture, and may perhaps be so bold as to attempt an answer, that they will first ask the parents of these mortals, whether they would not at this day think it a great happiness to have been sold for food, at a year old in the manner I prescribe, and thereby have avoided such a perpetual scene of misfortunes as they have since gone through by the oppression of landlords, the impossibility of paying rent without money or trade, the want of common sustenance, with neither house nor clothes to cover them from the inclemencies of the weather, and the most inevitable prospect of entailing the like or greater miseries upon their breed forever.

I profess, in the sincerity of my heart, that I have not the least personal interest in endeavoring to promote this necessary work, having no other motive than the public good of my country, by advancing our trade, providing for infants, relieving the poor, and giving some pleasure to the rich. I have no children by which I can propose to get a single penny; the youngest being nine years old, and my wife past child-bearing.

(1729)

Gulliver's Travels into Several Remote Nations of the World

by Jonathan Swift

THE PUBLISHER TO THE READER.

[As given in the original edition.]

The author of these Travels, Mr. Lemuel Gulliver, is my ancient and intimate friend; there is likewise some relation between us on the mother's side. About three years ago, Mr. Gulliver growing weary of the concourse of curious people coming to him at his house in Redriff, made a small purchase of land, with a convenient house, near Newark, in Nottinghamshire, his native country; where he now lives retired, yet in good esteem among his neighbours.

Although Mr. Gulliver was born in Nottinghamshire, where his father dwelt, yet I have heard him say his family came from Oxfordshire; to confirm which, I have observed in the churchyard at Banbury in that county, several tombs and monuments of the Gullivers.

Before he quitted Redriff, he left the custody of the following papers in my hands, with the liberty to dispose of them as I should think fit. I have carefully perused them three times. The style is very plain and simple; and the only fault I find is, that the author, after the manner of travelers, is a little too circumstantial. There is an air of truth apparent through the whole; and indeed the author was so distinguished for his veracity, that it became a sort of proverb among his neighbours at Redriff, when any one affirmed a thing, to say, it was as true as if Mr. Gulliver had spoken it.

By the advice of several worthy persons, to whom, with the author's permission, I communicated these papers, I now venture to send them into the world, hoping they may be, at least for some time, a better entertainment to our young noblemen, than the common scribbles of politics and party.

This volume would have been at least twice as large, if I had not made bold to strike out innumerable passages relating to the winds and tides, as well as to the variations and bearings in the several voyages, together with the minute descriptions of the management of the ship in storms, in the style of sailors; likewise the account of longitudes and latitudes; wherein I have reason to apprehend, that Mr. Gulliver may be a little dissatisfied. But I was resolved to fit the work as much as possible to the general capacity of readers. However, if my own ignorance in sea affairs shall have led me to commit some mistakes, I alone am answerable for them. And if any traveler hath a curiosity to see the whole work at large, as it came from the hands of the author, I will be ready to gratify him.

As for any further particulars relating to the author, the reader will receive satisfaction from the first pages of the book.

RICHARD SYMPSON.

A LETTER FROM CAPTAIN GULLIVER TO HIS COUSIN SYMPSON.

(WRITTEN IN THE YEAR 1727)

I hope you will be ready to own publicly, whenever you shall be called to it, that by your great and frequent urgency you prevailed on me to publish a very loose and uncorrect account of my travels, with directions to hire some young gentleman of either university to put them in order, and correct the style, as my cousin Dampier did, by my advice, in his book called "A Voyage round the world." But I do not remember I gave you power to consent that anything should be omitted, and much less that anything should be inserted; therefore, as to the latter, I do here renounce everything of that kind; particularly a paragraph about her majesty Queen Anne, of most pious and glorious memory; although I did reverence and esteem her more than any of human species. But you, or your interpolator, ought to have considered, that it was not my inclination, so was it not decent to praise any animal of our composition before my master Houyhnhnm: And besides, the fact was altogether false; for to my knowledge, being in England during some part of her majesty's reign, she did govern by a chief minister; nay even by two successively, the first whereof was the lord of Godolphin, and the second the lord of Oxford; so that you have made me say the thing that was not. Likewise in the account of the academy of projectors, and several passages of my discourse to my master Houyhnhnm, you have either omitted some material circumstances, or minced or changed them in such a manner, that I do hardly know my own work. When I formerly hinted to you something of this in a letter, you were pleased to answer that you were afraid of giving offence; that people in power were very watchful over the press, and apt not only to interpret, but to punish everything which looked like an innuendo (as I think you call it). But, pray how could that which I spoke so many years ago, and at about five thousand leagues distance, in another reign, be applied to any of the Yahoos, who now are said to govern the herd; especially at a time when I little thought, or feared, the unhappiness of living under them? Have not I the most reason to complain, when I seethes very Yahoos carried by Houyhnhnms in a vehicle, as if they were brutes, and those the rational creatures? And indeed to avoid so monstrous and detestable a sight was one principal motive of my retirement hither.

Thus much I thought proper to tell you in relation to yourself, and to the trust I reposed in you.

I do, in the next place, complain of my own great want of judgment, in being prevailed upon by the entreaties and false reasoning of you and some others, very much against my own opinion, to suffer my travels to be published. Pray bring to your mind how often I desired you to consider, when you insisted on the motive of public good, that the Yahoos were a species of animals utterly incapable of amendment by precept or example: and so it has proved; for, instead of seeing a full stop put to all abuses and corruptions, at least in this little island, as I had reason to expect; behold, after above six months warning, I cannot learn that my book has produced one single effect according to my intentions. I desired you would let me know, by a letter, when party and faction were extinguished; judges learned and upright; pleaders honest and modest, with some tincture of common sense, and Smithfield blazing with pyramids of law books; the young nobility's education entirely changed; the physicians banished; the female Yahoos abounding in virtue, honor, truth, and good sense; courts and levees of great ministers thoroughly weeded and swept; wit, merit, and learning rewarded; all disgracers of the press in prose and verse condemned to eat nothing but their own cotton, and quench their thirst with their own ink. These, and a thousand other reformations, I firmly counted upon by your encouragement; as indeed they were plainly deducible from the precepts delivered in my book. And it must browned, that seven months were a sufficient time to correct every vice and folly to which Yahoos are subject, if their natures had been capable of the least disposition to virtue or wisdom. Yet, so far have you been from answering my expectation in any of your letters; that on the contrary you are loading our carrier every week with libels, and keys, and reflections, and memoirs, and second parts; wherein I see myself accused of reflecting upon great state folk; of degrading human nature (for so they have still the confidence to style it), and of abusing the female sex. I find likewise that the writers of those bundles are not agreed among themselves; for some of them will not allow me to be the author of my own travels; and others make me author of books to which I am wholly a stranger.

I find likewise that your printer has been so careless as to confound the times, and mistake the dates, of my several voyages and returns; neither assigning the true year, nor the true month, nor day of the month: and I hear the original manuscript is all destroyed since the publication of my book; neither have I any copy left: however, I have sent you some corrections, which you may insert, if ever there should be a second edition: and yet I cannot stand to them; but shall leave that matter to my judicious and candid readers to adjust it as they please.

I hear some of our sea Yahoos find fault with my sea-language, as not proper in many parts, nor now in use. I cannot help it. In my first voyages, while I was young, I was instructed by the oldest mariners, and learned to speak as they did. But I have since found that the sea Yahoos are apt, like the land ones, to become new-fangled in their words, which the latter change every year; insomuch, as I remember upon each return to my own country their old dialect was so altered, that I could hardly understand the new. And I observe, when any Yahoo comes from London out of curiosity to visit me at my house, we neither of us are able to deliver our conceptions in a manner intelligible to the other.

If the censure of the Yahoos could any way affect me, I should have great reason to complain, that some of them are so bold as to think my book of travels a mere fiction out of mine own brain, and have gone so far as to drop hints, that the Houyhnhnms and Yahoos have no more existence than the inhabitants of Utopia.

Indeed I must confess, that as to the people of Lilliput, Brobdingrag (for so the word should have been spelt, and not erroneously Brobdingnag), and Laputa, I have never yet heard of any Yahoo so presumptuous as to dispute their being, or the facts I have related concerning them; because the truth immediately strikes every reader with conviction. And is there less probability in my account of the Houyhnhnms or Yahoos, when it is manifest as to the latter, there are so many thousands even in this country, who only differ from their brother brutes in Houyhnhnmland, because they use a sort of jabber, and do not go naked? I wrote for their amendment, and not their approbation. The united praise of the whole race would be of less consequence to me, than the neighing of those two degenerate Houyhnhnms I keep in my stable; because from these, degenerate as they are, I still improve in some virtues without any mixture of vice.

Do these miserable animals presume to think, that I am so degenerated as to defend my veracity? Yahoo as I am, it is well-known through all Houyhnhnmland, that, by the instructions and example of my illustrious master, I was able in the compass of two years (although I confess with the utmost difficulty) to remove that infernal habit of lying, shuffling, deceiving, and equivocating, so deeply rooted in the very souls of all my species; especially the Europeans.

I have other complaints to make upon this vexatious occasion; but I forbear troubling myself or you any further. I must freely confess, that since my last return, some corruptions of my Yahoo nature have revived in me by conversing with a few of your species, and particularly those of my own family, by an unavoidable necessity; else I should never have attempted so absurd a project as that of reforming the Yahoo race in this kingdom: But I have now done with all such visionary schemes for ever.

April 2, 1727

PART I--A VOYAGE TO LILLIPUT.

CHAPTER I

[The author gives some account of himself and family. His first inducements to travel. He is shipwrecked, and swims for his life. Gets safe on shore in the country of Lilliput; is made a prisoner, and carried up the country.]

My father had a small estate in Nottinghamshire: I was the third of five sons. He sent me to Emanuel College in Cambridge at fourteen years old, where I resided three years, and applied myself close to my studies; but the charge of maintaining me, although I had a very scanty allowance, being too great for a narrow fortune, I was bound apprentice to Mr. James Bates, an eminent surgeon in London, with whom I continued four years. My father now and then sending me small sums of money, I laid them out in learning navigation, and other parts of the mathematics, useful to those who intend to travel, as I always believed it would be, some time or other, my fortune to do. When I left Mr. Bates, I went down to my father: where, by the assistance of him and my uncle John, and some other relations, I got forty pounds, and a promise of thirty pounds a year to maintain me at Leyden: there I studied physic two years and seven months, knowing it would be useful in long voyages.

Soon after my return from Leyden, I was recommended by my good master, Mr. Bates, to be surgeon to the Swallow, Captain Abraham Pannel, commander; with whom I continued three years and a half, making a voyage or two into the Levant, and some other parts. When I came back I resolved to settle in London; to which Mr. Bates, my master, encouraged me, and by him I was recommended to several patients. I took part of a small house in the Old Jewry; and being advised to alter my condition, I married Mrs. Mary Burton, second daughter to Mr. Edmund Burton, hosier, in Newgate-street, with whom I received four hundred pounds for a portion.

But my good master Bates dying in two years after, and I having few friends, my business began to fail; for my conscience would not suffer me to imitate the bad practice of too many among my brethren. Having therefore consulted with my wife, and some of my acquaintance, I determined to go again to sea. I was surgeon successively in two ships, and made several voyages, for six years, to the East and West Indies, by which I got some addition to my fortune. My hours of leisure I spent in reading the best authors, ancient and modern, being always provided with a good number of books; and when I was ashore, in observing the manners and dispositions of the people, as well as learning their language; wherein I had a great facility, by the strength of my memory.

The last of these voyages not proving very fortunate, I grew weary of the sea, and intended to stay at home with my wife and family. I removed from the Old Jewry to Fetter Lane, and from thence to Wapping, hoping to get business among the sailors; but it would not turn to account. After three years expectation that things would mend, I accepted an advantageous offer from

Captain William Prichard, master of the Antelope, who was making a voyage to the South Sea. We set sail from Bristol, May 4, 1699, and our voyage was at first very prosperous.

It would not be proper, for some reasons, to trouble the reader with the particulars of our adventures in those seas; let it suffice to inform him, that in our passage from thence to the East Indies, we were driven by a violent storm to the north-west of Van Diemen's Land. By an observation, we found ourselves in the latitude of 30 degrees 2 minutes south. Twelve of our crew were dead by immoderate labour and ill food; the rest were in a very weak condition. On the 5th of November, which was the beginning of summer in those parts, the weather being very hazy, the seamen spied a rock within half a cable's length of the ship; but the wind was so strong, that we were driven directly upon it, and immediately split. Six of the crew, of whom I was one, having let down the boat into the sea, made a shift to get clear of the ship and the rock. We rowed, by my computation, about three leagues, till we were able to work no longer, being already spent with labour while we were in the ship. We therefore trusted ourselves to the mercy of the waves, and in about half an hour the boat was overset by a sudden flurry from the north. What became of my companions in the boat, as well as of those who escaped on the rock, or were left in the vessel, I cannot tell; but conclude they were all lost. For my own part, I swam as fortune directed me, and was pushed forward by wind and tide. I often let my legs drop, and could feel no bottom; but when I was almost gone, and able to struggle no longer, I found myself within my depth; and by this time the storm was much abated. The declivity was so small, that I walked near a mile before I got to the shore, which I conjectured was about eight o'clock in the evening. I then advanced forward near half a mile, but could not discover any sign of houses or inhabitants; at least I was in so weak a condition, that I did not observe them. I was extremely tired, and with that, and the heat of the weather, and about half a pint of brandy that I drank as I left the ship, I found myself much inclined to sleep. I lay down on the grass, which was very short and soft, where I slept sounder than ever I remembered to have done in my life, and, as I reckoned, about nine hours; for when I awaked, it was just day-light. I attempted to rise, but was not able to stir: for, as I happened to lie on my back, I found my arms and legs were strongly fastened on each side to the ground; and my hair, which was long and thick, tied down in the same manner. I likewise felt several slender ligatures across my body, from my arm-pits to my thighs. I could only look upwards; the sun began to grow hot, and the light offended my eyes. I heard a confused noise about me; but in the posture I lay, could see nothing except the sky. In a little time I felt something alive moving on my left leg, which advancing gently forward over my breast, came almost up to my chin; when, bending my eyes downwards as much as I could, I perceived it to be a human creature not six inches high, with a bow and arrow in his hands, and a quiver at his back. In the mean time, I felt at least forty more of the same kind (as I conjectured) following the first. I was in the utmost astonishment, and roared so loud, that they all ran back in a fright; and some of them, as I was afterwards told, were hurt with the falls they got by leaping from my sides upon the ground. However, they soon returned, and one of them, who ventured so far as to get a full sight of my face, lifting up his hands and eyes by way of admiration, cried out in a shrill but distinct voice, Hekinah degul: the others repeated the same words several times, but then I knew not what they meant. I lay all this while, as the reader may believe, in great uneasiness. At length, struggling to get loose, I had the fortune to break the strings, and wrench out the pegs that fastened my left arm to the ground; for, by lifting it up to my face, I discovered the methods they had taken to bind me, and at the same time with a violent pull, which gave me excessive pain, I a little loosened the strings that tied down my hair on the left side, so that I was just able to turn my head about two inches. But the creatures ran off a second time, before I could seize them; whereupon there was a great shout in a very shrill accent, and after it ceased I heard one of them cry aloud Tolgo phonac; when in an instant I felt above a hundred arrows discharged on my left hand, which, pricked me like so many needles; and besides, they shot another flight into the air, as we do bombs in Europe, whereof many, I suppose, fell on my body, (though I felt them not), and some on my face, which I immediately covered with my left hand. When this shower of arrows was over, I fell a groaning with grief and pain; and then striving again to get loose, they discharged another volley larger than the first, and some of them attempted with spears to stick me in the sides; but by good luck I had on a buff jerkin, which they could not pierce. I thought it the most prudent method to lie still, and my design was to continue so till night, when, my left hand being already loose, I could easily free myself: and as for the inhabitants, I had reason to believe I might be a match for the greatest army they could bring against me, if they were all of the same size with him that I saw. But fortune disposed otherwise of me. When the people observed I was quiet, they discharged no more arrows; but, by the noise I heard, I knew their numbers increased; and about four yards from me, over against my right ear, I heard a knocking for above an hour, like that of people at work; when turning my head that way, as well as the pegs and strings would permit me, I saw a stage erected about a foot and a half from the ground, capable of holding four of the inhabitants, with two or three ladders to mount it: from whence one of them, who seemed to be a person of quality, made me a long speech, whereof I understood not one syllable. But I should have mentioned, that before the principal person began his oration, he cried out three times, Langro dehul san (these words and the former were afterwards repeated and explained to me); whereupon, immediately, about fifty of the inhabitants came and cut the strings that fastened the left side of my head, which gave me the liberty of turning it to the right, and of observing the person and gesture of him that was to speak. He appeared to be of a middle age, and taller than any of the other three who attended him, whereof one was a page that held up his train, and seemed to be somewhat longer than my middle finger; the other two stood one on each side to support him. He acted every part of an orator, and I could observe many periods of threatenings, and others of promises, pity, and kindness. I answered in a few words, but in the most submissive manner, lifting up my left hand, and both my eyes to the sun, as calling him for a witness; and being almost famished with hunger, having not eaten a morsel for some hours before I left the ship, I found the demands of nature so strong upon me, that I could not forbear showing my impatience (perhaps against the strict rules of decency) by putting my finger frequently to my mouth, to signify that I wanted food. The hurgo (for so they call a great lord, as I afterwards learnt) understood me very well. He descended from the stage, and commanded that several ladders should be applied to my sides, on which above a hundred of the inhabitants mounted and walked towards my mouth, laden with baskets full of meat, which had been provided and sent thither by the king's orders, upon the first intelligence he received of me. I observed there was the flesh of several animals, but could not distinguish them by the taste. There were shoulders, legs, and loins, shaped like those of mutton, and very well dressed, but smaller than the wings of a lark. I ate them by two or three at a mouthful, and took three loaves at a time, about the bigness of musket bullets. They supplied me as fast as they could, showing a thousand marks of wonder and astonishment at my bulk and appetite. I then made another sign, that I wanted drink. They found by my eating that a small quantity would not suffice me; and being a most ingenious people, they slung up, with great dexterity, one of their largest hogsheads, then rolled it towards my hand, and beat out the top; I drank it off at a draught, which I might well do, for it did not hold half a pint, and tasted like a small wine of Burgundy, but much more delicious. They brought me a second hogshead, which I drank in the same manner, and made signs for more; but they had none to give me. When I had performed these wonders, they shouted for joy, and danced upon my breast, repeating several times as they did at first, Hekinah degul. They made me a sign that I should throw down the two hogsheads, but first warning the people below to stand out of the way, crying aloud, Borach mevolah; and when they saw the vessels in the air, there was a universal shout of Hekinah degul. I confess I was often tempted, while they were passing backwards and forwards on my body, to seize forty or fifty of the first that came in my reach, and dash them against the ground. But the remembrance of what I had felt, which probably might not be the worst they could do, and the promise of honour I made them--for so I interpreted my submissive behaviour-- soon drove out these imaginations. Besides, I now considered myself as bound by the laws of hospitality, to a people who had treated me with so much expense and magnificence. However, in my thoughts I could not sufficiently wonder at the intrepidity of these diminutive mortals, who durst venture to mount and walk upon my body, while one of my hands was at liberty, without trembling at the very sight of so prodigious a creature as I must appear to them. After some time, when they observed that I made no more demands for meat, there appeared before me a person of high rank from his imperial majesty. His excellency, having mounted on the small of my right leg, advanced forwards up to my face, with about a dozen of his retinue; and producing his credentials under the signet royal, which he applied close to my eyes, spoke about ten minutes without any signs of anger, but with a kind of determinate resolution, often pointing forwards, which, as I afterwards found, was towards the capital city, about half a mile distant; whither it was agreed by his majesty in council that I must be conveyed. I answered in few words, but to no purpose, and made a sign with my hand that was loose, putting it to the other (but over his excellency's head for fear of hurting him or his train) and then to my own head and body, to signify that I desired my liberty. It appeared that he understood me well enough, for he shook his head by way of disapprobation, and held his hand in a posture to show that I must be carried as a prisoner. However, he made other signs to let me understand that I should have meat and drink enough, and very good treatment. Whereupon I once more thought of attempting to break my bonds; but again, when I felt the smart of their arrows upon my face and hands, which were all in blisters, and many of the darts still sticking in them, and observing likewise that the number of my enemies increased, I gave tokens to let them know that they might do with me what they pleased. Upon this, the hurgo and his train withdrew, with much civility and cheerful countenances. Soon after I heard a general shout, with frequent repetitions of the words Peplom selan; and I felt great numbers of people on my left side relaxing the cords to such a degree, that I was able to turn upon my right, and to ease myself with making water; which I very plentifully did, to the great astonishment of the people; who, conjecturing by my motion what I was going to do, immediately opened to the right and left on that side, to avoid the torrent, which fell with such noise and violence from me. But before this, they had daubed my face and both my hands with a sort of ointment, very pleasant to the smell, which, in a few minutes, removed all the smart of their arrows. These circumstances, added to the refreshment I had received by their victuals and drink, which were very nourishing, disposed me to sleep. I slept about eight hours, as I was afterwards assured; and it was no wonder, for the physicians, by the emperor's order, had mingled a sleepy potion in the hogsheads of wine.

It seems, that upon the first moment I was discovered sleeping on the ground, after my landing, the emperor had early notice of it by an express; and determined in council, that I should be tied in the manner I have related, (which was done in the night while I slept;) that plenty of meat and drink should be sent to me, and a machine prepared to carry me to the capital city.

This resolution perhaps may appear very bold and dangerous, and I am confident would not be imitated by any prince in Europe on the like occasion. However, in my opinion, it was extremely prudent, as well as generous: for, supposing these people had endeavoured to kill me with their spears and arrows, while I was asleep, I should certainly have awaked with the first sense of smart, which might so far have roused my rage and strength, as to have enabled me to break the strings wherewith I was tied; after which, as they were not able to make resistance, so they could expect no mercy. These people are most excellent mathematicians, and arrived to a great perfection in mechanics, by the countenance and encouragement of the emperor, who is a renowned patron of learning. This prince has several machines fixed on wheels, for the carriage of trees and other great weights. He often builds his largest men of war, whereof some are nine feet long, in the woods where the timber grows, and has them carried on these engines three or four hundred yards to the sea. Five hundred carpenters and engineers were immediately set at work to prepare the greatest engine they had. It was a frame of wood raised three inches from the ground, about seven feet long, and four wide, moving upon twenty-two wheels. The shout I heard was upon the arrival of this engine, which, it seems, set out in four hours after my landing. It was brought parallel to me, as I lay. But the principal difficulty was to raise and place me in this vehicle. Eighty poles, each of one foot high, were erected for this purpose, and very strong cords, of the bigness of packthread, were fastened by hooks to many bandages, which the workmen had girt round my neck, my hands, my body, and my legs. Nine hundred of the strongest men were employed to draw up these cords, by many pulleys fastened on the poles; and thus, in less than three hours, I was raised and slung into the engine, and there tied fast. All this I was told; for, while the operation was performing, I lay in a profound sleep, by the force of that soporiferous medicine infused into my liquor. Fifteen hundred of the emperor's largest horses, each about four inches and a half high, were employed to draw me towards the metropolis, which, as I said, was half a mile distant.

About four hours after we began our journey, I awaked by a very ridiculous accident; for the carriage being stopped a while, to adjust something that was out of order, two or three of the young natives had the curiosity to see how I looked when I was asleep; they climbed up into the engine, and advancing very softly to my face, one of them, an officer in the guards, put the sharp end of his half-pike a good way up into my left nostril, which tickled my nose like a straw, and made me sneeze violently; whereupon they stole off unperceived, and it was three weeks before I knew the cause of my waking so suddenly. We made a long march the remaining part of the day, and, rested at night with five hundred guards on each side of me, half with torches, and half with bows and arrows, ready to shoot me if I should offer to stir. The next morning at sun-rise we continued our march, and arrived within two hundred yards of the city gates about noon. The emperor, and all his court, came out to meet us; but his great officers would by no means suffer his majesty to endanger his person by mounting on my body.

At the place where the carriage stopped there stood an ancient temple, esteemed to be the largest in the whole kingdom; which, having been polluted some years before by an unnatural murder, was, according to the zeal of those people, looked upon as profane, and therefore had been applied to common use, and all the ornaments and furniture carried away. In this edifice it was determined I should lodge. The great gate fronting to the north was about four feet high, and almost two feet wide, through which I could easily creep. On each side of the gate was a small window, not above six inches from the ground: into that on the left side, the king's smith conveyed fourscore and eleven chains, like those that hang to a lady's watch in Europe, and almost as large, which were locked to my left leg with six-and-thirty padlocks. Over against this temple, on the other side of the great highway, at twenty feet distance, there was a turret at least five feet high. Here the emperor ascended, with many principal lords of his court, to have an opportunity of viewing me, as I was told, for I could not see them. It was reckoned that above a hundred thousand inhabitants came out of the town upon the same errand; and, in spite of my guards, I believe there could not be fewer than ten thousand at several times, who mounted my body by the help of ladders. But a proclamation was soon issued, to forbid it upon pain of death. When the workmen found it was impossible for me to break loose, they cut all the strings that bound me; whereupon I rose up, with as melancholy a disposition as ever I had in my life. But the noise and astonishment of the people, at seeing me rise and walk, are not to be expressed. The chains that held my left leg were about two yards long, and gave me not only the liberty of walking backwards and forwards in a semicircle, but, being fixed within four inches of the gate, allowed me to creep in, and lie at my full length in the temple.

CHAPTER II

[The emperor of Lilliput, attended by several of the nobility, comes to see the author in his confinement. The emperor's person and habit described. Learned men appointed to teach the author their language. He gains favour by his mild disposition. His pockets are searched, and his sword and pistols taken from him.]

When I found myself on my feet, I looked about me, and must confess I never beheld a more entertaining prospect. The country around appeared like a continued garden, and the enclosed fields, which were generally forty feet square, resembled so many beds of flowers. These fields were intermingled with woods of half a stang, {1} and the tallest trees, as I could judge, appeared to be seven feet high. I viewed the town on my left hand, which looked like the painted scene of a city in a theatre.

I had been for some hours extremely pressed by the necessities of nature; which was no wonder, it being almost two days since I had last disburdened myself. I was under great difficulties between urgency and shame. The best expedient I could think of, was to creep into my house, which I accordingly did; and shutting the gate after me, I went as far as the length of my chain would suffer, and discharged my body of that uneasy load. But this was the only time I was ever guilty of so uncleanly an action; for which I cannot but hope the candid reader will give some allowance, after he has maturely and impartially considered my case, and the distress I was in. From this time my constant practice was, as soon as I rose, to perform that business in open air, at the full extent of my chain; and due care was taken every morning before company came, that the offensive matter should be carried off in wheel-barrows, by two servants appointed for that purpose. I would not have dwelt so long upon a circumstance that, perhaps, at first sight, may appear not very momentous, if I had not thought it necessary to justify my character, in point of cleanliness, to the world; which, I am told, some of my maligners have been pleased, upon this and other occasions, to call in question.

When this adventure was at an end, I came back out of my house, having occasion for fresh air. The emperor was already descended from the tower, and advancing on horseback towards me, which had like to have cost him dear; for the beast, though very well trained, yet wholly unused to such a sight, which appeared as if a mountain moved before him, reared up on its hinder feet: but that prince, who is an excellent horseman, kept his seat, till his attendants ran in, and held the bridle, while his majesty had time to dismount. When he alighted, he surveyed me round with great admiration; but kept beyond the length of my chain. He ordered his cooks and butlers, who were already prepared, to give me victuals and drink, which they pushed forward in a sort of vehicles upon wheels, till I could reach them. I took these vehicles and soon emptied them all; twenty of them were filled with meat, and ten with liquor; each of the former afforded me two or three good mouthfuls; and I emptied the liquor of ten vessels, which was contained in earthen vials, into one vehicle, drinking it off at a draught; and so I did with the rest. The empress, and young princes of the blood of both sexes, attended by many ladies, sat at some distance in their chairs; but upon the accident that happened to the emperor's horse, they alighted, and came near his person, which I am now going to describe. He is taller by almost the breadth of my nail, than any of his court; which alone is enough to strike an awe into the beholders. His features are strong and masculine, with an Austrian lip and arched nose, his complexion olive, his countenance erect, his body and limbs well proportioned, all his motions graceful, and his deportment majestic. He was then past his prime, being twenty-eight years and three quarters old, of which he had reigned about seven in great felicity, and generally victorious. For the better convenience of beholding him, I lay on my side, so that my face was parallel to his, and he stood but three yards off: however, I have had him since many times in my hand, and therefore cannot be deceived in the description. His dress was very plain and simple, and the fashion of it between the Asiatic and the European; but he had on his head a light helmet of gold, adorned with jewels, and a plume on the crest. He held his sword drawn in his hand to defend himself, if I should happen to break loose; it was almost three inches long; the hilt and scabbard were gold enriched with diamonds. His voice was shrill, but very clear and articulate; and I could distinctly hear it when I stood up. The ladies and courtiers were all most magnificently clad; so that the spot they stood upon seemed to resemble a petticoat spread upon the ground, embroidered with figures of gold and silver. His imperial majesty spoke often to me, and I returned answers: but neither of us could understand a syllable. There were several of his priests and lawyers present (as I conjectured by their habits), who were commanded to address themselves to me; and I spoke to them in as many languages as I had the least smattering of, which were High and Low Dutch, Latin, French, Spanish, Italian, and Lingua Franca, but all to no purpose. After about two hours the court retired, and I was left with a strong guard, to prevent the impertinence, and probably the malice of the rabble, who were very impatient to crowd about me as near as they durst; and some of them had the impudence to shoot their arrows at me, as I sat on the ground by the door of my house, whereof one very narrowly missed my left eye. But the colonel ordered six of the ringleaders to be seized, and thought no punishment so proper as to deliver them bound into my hands; which some of his soldiers accordingly did, pushing them forward with the butt-ends of their pikes into my reach. I took them all in my right hand, put five of them into my coat-pocket; and as to the sixth, I made a countenance as if I would eat him alive. The poor man squalled terribly, and the colonel and his officers were in much pain, especially when they saw me take out my penknife: but I soon put them out of fear; for, looking mildly, and immediately cutting the strings he was bound with, I set him gently on the ground, and away he ran. I treated the rest in the same manner, taking them one by one out of my pocket; and I observed both the soldiers and people were highly delighted at this mark of my clemency, which was represented very much to my advantage at court.

Towards night I got with some difficulty into my house, where I lay on the ground, and continued to do so about a fortnight; during which time, the emperor gave orders to have a bed prepared for me. Six hundred beds of the common measure were brought in carriages, and worked up in my house; a hundred and fifty of their beds, sewn together, made up the breadth and length; and these were four double: which, however, kept me but very indifferently from the hardness of the floor, that was of smooth stone. By the same computation, they provided me with sheets, blankets, and coverlets, tolerable enough for one who had been so long inured to hardships.

As the news of my arrival spread through the kingdom, it brought prodigious numbers of rich, idle, and curious people to see me; so that the villages were almost emptied; and great neglect of tillage and household affairs must have ensued, if his imperial majesty had not provided, by several proclamations and orders of state, against this inconveniency. He directed that those who had already beheld me should return home, and not presume to come within fifty yards of my house, without license from the court; whereby the secretaries of state got considerable fees.

In the mean time the emperor held frequent councils, to debate what course should be taken with me; and I was afterwards assured by a particular friend, a person of great quality, who was as much in the secret as any, that the court was under many difficulties concerning me. They apprehended my breaking loose; that my diet would be very expensive, and might cause a famine. Sometimes they determined to starve me; or at least to shoot me in the face and hands with poisoned arrows, which would soon despatch me; but again they considered, that the stench of so large a carcass might produce a plague in the metropolis, and probably spread through the whole kingdom. In the midst of these consultations, several officers of the army went to the door of the great council-chamber, and two of them being admitted, gave an account of my behaviour to the six criminals above-mentioned; which made so favourable an impression in the breast of his majesty and the whole board, in my behalf, that an imperial commission was issued out, obliging all the villages, nine hundred yards round the city, to deliver in every morning six beeves, forty sheep, and other victuals for my sustenance; together with a proportionable quantity of bread, and wine, and other liquors; for the due payment of which, his majesty gave assignments upon his treasury:- for this prince lives chiefly upon his own demesnes; seldom, except upon great occasions, raising any subsidies upon his subjects, who are bound to attend him in his wars at their own expense. An establishment was also made of six hundred persons to be my domestics, who had board-wages allowed for their maintenance, and tents built for them very conveniently on each side of my door. It was likewise ordered, that three hundred tailors should make me a suit of clothes, after the fashion of the country; that six of his majesty's greatest scholars should be employed to instruct me in their language; and lastly, that the emperor's horses, and those of the nobility and troops of guards, should be frequently exercised in my sight, to accustom themselves to me. All these orders were duly put in execution; and in about three weeks I made a great progress in learning their language; during which time the emperor frequently honoured me with his visits, and was pleased to assist my masters in teaching me. We began already to converse together in some sort; and the first words I learnt, were to express my desire "that he would please give me my liberty;" which I every day repeated on my knees. His answer, as I could comprehend it, was, "that this must be a work of time, not to be thought on without the advice of his council, and that first I must lumos kelmin pesso desmar lon emposo;" that is, swear a peace with him and his kingdom. However, that I should be used with all kindness. And he advised me to "acquire, by my patience and discreet behaviour, the good opinion of himself and his subjects." He desired "I would not take it ill, if he gave orders to certain proper officers to search me; for probably I might carry about me several weapons, which must needs be dangerous things, if they answered the bulk of so prodigious a person." I said, "His majesty should be satisfied; for I was ready to strip myself, and turn up my pockets before him." This I delivered part in words, and part in signs. He replied, "that, by the laws of the kingdom, I must be searched by two of his officers; that he knew this could not be done without my consent and assistance; and he had so good an opinion of my generosity and justice, as to trust their persons in my hands; that whatever they took from me, should be returned when I left the country, or paid for at the rate which I would set upon them." I took up the two officers in my hands, put them first into my coat-pockets, and then into every other pocket about me, except my two fobs, and another secret pocket, which I had no mind should be searched, wherein I had some little necessaries that were of no consequence to any but myself. In one of my fobs there was a silver watch, and in the other a small quantity of gold in a purse. These gentlemen, having pen, ink, and paper, about them, made an exact inventory of every thing they saw; and when they had done, desired I would set them down, that they might deliver it to the emperor. This inventory I afterwards translated into English, and is, word for word, as follows:

"Imprimis: In the right coat-pocket of the great man-mountain" (for so I interpret the words quinbus flestrin,) "after the strictest search, we found only one great piece of coarse-cloth, large enough to be a foot-cloth for your majesty's chief room of state. In the left pocket we saw a huge silver chest, with a cover of the same metal, which we, the searchers, were not able to lift. We desired it should be opened, and one of us stepping into it, found himself up to the mid leg in a sort of dust, some part whereof flying up to our faces set us both a sneezing for several times together. In his right waistcoat-pocket we found a prodigious bundle of white thin substances, folded one over another, about the bigness of three men, tied with a strong cable, and marked with black figures; which we humbly conceive to be writings, every letter almost half as large as the palm of our hands. In the left there was a sort of engine, from the back of which were extended twenty long poles, resembling the pallisados before your majesty's court: wherewith we conjecture the man- mountain combs his head; for we did not always trouble him with questions, because we found it a great difficulty to make him understand us. In the large pocket, on the right side of his middle cover" (so I translate the word ranfulo, by which they meant my breeches,) "we saw a hollow pillar of iron, about the length of a man, fastened to a strong piece of timber larger than the pillar; and upon one side of the pillar, were huge pieces of iron sticking out, cut into strange figures, which we know not what to make of. In the left pocket, another engine of the same kind. In the smaller pocket on the right side, were several round flat pieces of white and red metal, of different bulk; some of the white, which seemed to be silver, were so large and heavy, that my comrade and I could hardly lift them. In the left pocket were two black pillars irregularly shaped: we could not, without difficulty, reach the top of them, as we stood at the bottom of his pocket. One of them was covered, and seemed all of a piece: but at the upper end of the other there appeared a white round substance, about twice the bigness of our heads. Within each of these was enclosed a prodigious plate of steel; which, by our orders, we obliged him to show us, because we apprehended they might be dangerous engines. He took them out of their cases, and told us, that in his own country his practice was to shave his beard with one of these, and cut his meat with the other. There were two pockets which we could not enter: these he called his fobs; they were two large slits cut into the top of his middle cover, but squeezed close by the pressure of his belly. Out of the right fob hung a great silver chain, with a wonderful kind of engine at the bottom. We directed him to draw out whatever was at the end of that chain; which appeared to be a globe, half silver, and half of some transparent metal; for, on the transparent side, we saw certain strange figures circularly drawn, and thought we could touch them, till we found our fingers stopped by the lucid substance. He put this engine into our ears, which made an incessant noise, like that of a water-mill: and we conjecture it is either some unknown animal, or the god that he worships; but we are more inclined to the latter opinion, because he assured us, (if we understood him right, for he expressed himself very imperfectly) that he seldom did any thing without consulting it. He called it his oracle, and said, it pointed out the time for every action of his life. From the left fob he took out a net almost large enough for a fisherman, but contrived to open and shut like a purse, and served him for the same use: we found therein several massy pieces of yellow metal, which, if they be real gold, must be of immense value.

"Having thus, in obedience to your majesty's commands, diligently searched all his pockets, we observed a girdle about his waist made of the hide of some prodigious animal, from which, on the left side, hung a sword of the length of five men; and on the right, a bag or pouch divided into two cells, each cell capable of holding three of your majesty's subjects. In one of these cells were several globes, or balls, of a most ponderous metal, about the bigness of our heads, and requiring a strong hand to lift them: the other cell contained a heap of certain black grains, but of no great bulk or weight, for we could hold above fifty of them in the palms of our hands.

"This is an exact inventory of what we found about the body of the man-mountain, who used us with great civility, and due respect to your majesty's commission. Signed and sealed on the fourth day of the eighty-ninth moon of your majesty's auspicious reign.

CLEFRIN FRELOCK, MARSI FRELOCK."

When this inventory was read over to the emperor, he directed me, although in very gentle terms, to deliver up the several particulars. He first called for my scimitar, which I took out, scabbard and all. In the mean time he ordered three thousand of his choicest troops (who then attended him) to surround me at a distance, with their bows and arrows just ready to discharge; but I did not observe it, for mine eyes were wholly fixed upon his majesty. He then desired me to draw my scimitar, which, although it had got some rust by the sea water, was, in most parts, exceeding bright. I did so, and immediately all the troops gave a shout between terror and surprise; for the sun shone clear, and the reflection dazzled their eyes, as I waved the scimitar to and fro in my hand. His majesty, who is a most magnanimous prince, was less daunted than I could expect: he ordered me to return it into the scabbard, and cast it on the ground as gently as I could, about six feet from the end of my chain. The next thing he demanded was one of the hollow iron pillars; by which he meant my pocket pistols. I drew it out, and at his desire, as well as I could, expressed to him the use of it; and charging it only with powder, which, by the closeness of my pouch, happened to escape wetting in the sea (an inconvenience against which all prudent mariners take special care to provide,) I first cautioned the emperor not to be afraid, and then I let it off in the air. The astonishment here was much greater than at the sight of my scimitar. Hundreds fell down as if they had been struck dead; and even the emperor, although he stood his ground, could not recover himself for some time. I delivered up both my pistols in the same manner as I had done my scimitar, and then my pouch of powder and bullets; begging him that the former might be kept from fire, for it would kindle with the smallest spark, and blow up his imperial palace into the air. I likewise delivered up my watch, which the emperor was very curious to see, and commanded two of his tallest yeomen of the guards to bear it on a pole upon their shoulders, as draymen in England do a barrel of ale. He was amazed at the continual noise it made, and the motion of the minute-hand, which he could easily discern; for their sight is much more acute than ours: he asked the opinions of his learned men about it, which were various and remote, as the reader may well imagine without my repeating; although indeed I could not very perfectly understand them. I then gave up my silver and copper money, my purse, with nine large pieces of gold, and some smaller ones; my knife and razor, my comb and silver snuff-box, my handkerchief and journal-book. My scimitar, pistols, and pouch, were conveyed in carriages to his majesty's stores; but the rest of my goods were returned me.

I had as I before observed, one private pocket, which escaped their search, wherein there was a pair of spectacles (which I sometimes use for the weakness of mine eyes,) a pocket perspective, and some other little conveniences; which, being of no consequence to the emperor, I did not think myself bound in honour to discover, and I apprehended they might be lost or spoiled if I ventured them out of my possession.

CHAPTER III

[The author diverts the emperor, and his nobility of both sexes, in a very uncommon manner. The diversions of the court of Lilliput described. The author has his liberty granted him upon certain conditions.]

My gentleness and good behaviour had gained so far on the emperor and his court, and indeed upon the army and people in general, that I began to conceive hopes of getting my liberty in a short time. I took all possible methods to cultivate this favourable disposition. The natives came, by degrees, to be less apprehensive of any danger from me. I would sometimes lie down, and let five or six of them dance on my hand; and at last the boys and girls would venture to come and play at hide-and-seek in my hair. I had now made a good progress in understanding and speaking the language. The emperor had a mind one day to entertain me with several of the country shows, wherein they exceed all nations I have known, both for dexterity and magnificence. I was diverted with none so much as that of the rope-dancers, performed upon a slender white thread, extended about two feet, and twelve inches from the ground. Upon which I shall desire liberty, with the reader's patience, to enlarge a little.

This diversion is only practised by those persons who are candidates for great employments, and high favour at court. They are trained in this art from their youth, and are not always of noble birth, or liberal education. When a great office is vacant, either by death or disgrace (which often happens,) five or six of those candidates petition the emperor to entertain his majesty and the court with a dance on the rope; and whoever jumps the highest, without falling, succeeds in the office. Very often the chief ministers themselves are commanded to show their skill, and to convince the emperor that they have not lost their faculty. Flimnap, the treasurer, is allowed to cut a caper on the straight rope, at least an inch higher than any other lord in the whole empire. I have seen him do the summerset several times together, upon a trencher fixed on a rope which is no thicker than a common packthread in England. My friend

Reldresal, principal secretary for private affairs, is, in my opinion, if I am not partial, the second after the treasurer; the rest of the great officers are much upon a par.

These diversions are often attended with fatal accidents, whereof great numbers are on record. I myself have seen two or three candidates break a limb. But the danger is much greater, when the ministers themselves are commanded to show their dexterity; for, by contending to excel themselves and their fellows, they strain so far that there is hardly one of them who has not received a fall, and some of them two or three. I was assured that, a year or two before my arrival, Flimnap would infallibly have broke his neck, if one of the king's cushions, that accidentally lay on the ground, had not weakened the force of his fall.

There is likewise another diversion, which is only shown before the emperor and empress, and first minister, upon particular occasions. The emperor lays on the table three fine silken threads of six inches long; one is blue, the other red, and the third green. These threads are proposed as prizes for those persons whom the emperor has a mind to distinguish by a peculiar mark of his favour. The ceremony is performed in his majesty's great chamber of state, where the candidates are to undergo a trial of dexterity very different from the former, and such as I have not observed the least resemblance of in any other country of the new or old world. The emperor holds a stick in his hands, both ends parallel to the horizon, while the candidates advancing, one by one, sometimes leap over the stick, sometimes creep under it, backward and forward, several times, according as the stick is advanced or depressed. Sometimes the emperor holds one end of the stick, and his first minister the other; sometimes the minister has it entirely to himself. Whoever performs his part with most agility, and holds out the longest in leaping and creeping, is rewarded with the blue- coloured silk; the red is given to the next, and the green to the third, which they all wear girt twice round about the middle; and you see few great persons about this court who are not adorned with one of these girdles.

The horses of the army, and those of the royal stables, having been daily led before me, were no longer shy, but would come up to my very feet without starting. The riders would leap them over my hand, as I held it on the ground; and one of the emperor's huntsmen, upon a large courser, took my foot, shoe and all; which was indeed a prodigious leap. I had the good fortune to divert the emperor one day after a very extraordinary manner. I desired he would order several sticks of two feet high, and the thickness of an ordinary cane, to be brought me; whereupon his majesty commanded the master of his woods to give directions accordingly; and the next morning six woodmen arrived with as many carriages, drawn by eight horses to each. I took nine of these sticks, and fixing them firmly in the ground in a quadrangular figure, two feet and a half square, I took four other sticks, and tied them parallel at each corner, about two feet from the ground; then I fastened my handkerchief to the nine sticks that stood erect; and extended it on all sides, till it was tight as the top of a drum;

and the four parallel sticks, rising about five inches higher than the handkerchief, served as ledges on each side. When I had finished my work, I desired the emperor to let a troop of his best horses twenty-four in number, come and exercise upon this plain. His majesty approved of the proposal, and I took them up, one by one, in my hands, ready mounted and armed, with the proper officers to exercise them. As soon as they got into order they divided into two parties, performed mock skirmishes, discharged blunt arrows, drew their swords, fled and pursued, attacked and retired, and in short discovered the best military discipline I ever beheld. The parallel sticks secured them and their horses from falling over the stage; and the emperor was so much delighted, that he ordered this entertainment to be repeated several days, and once was pleased to be lifted up and give the word of command; and with great difficulty persuaded even the empress herself to let me hold her in her close chair within two yards of the stage, when she was able to take a full view of the whole performance. It was my good fortune, that no ill accident happened in these entertainments; only once a fiery horse, that belonged to one of the captains, pawing with his hoof, struck a hole in my handkerchief, and his foot slipping, he overthrew his rider and himself; but I immediately relieved them both, and covering the hole with one hand, I set down the troop with the other, in the same manner as I took them up. The horse that fell was strained in the left shoulder, but the rider got no hurt; and I repaired my handkerchief as well as I could: however, I would not trust to the strength of it any more, in such dangerous enterprises.

About two or three days before I was set at liberty, as I was entertaining the court with this kind of feat, there arrived an express to inform his majesty, that some of his subjects, riding near the place where I was first taken up, had seen a great black substance lying on the around, very oddly shaped, extending its edges round, as wide as his majesty's bedchamber, and rising up in the middle as high as a man; that it was no living creature, as they at first apprehended, for it lay on the grass without motion; and some of them had walked round it several times; that, by mounting upon each other's shoulders, they had got to the top, which was flat and even, and, stamping upon it, they found that it was hollow within; that they humbly conceived it might be something belonging to the man-mountain; and if his majesty pleased, they would undertake to bring it with only five horses. I presently knew what they meant, and was glad at heart to receive this intelligence. It seems, upon my first reaching the shore after our shipwreck, I was in such confusion, that before I came to the place where I went to sleep, my hat, which I had fastened with a string to my head while I was rowing, and had stuck on all the time I was swimming, fell off after I came to land; the string, as I conjecture, breaking by some accident, which I never observed, but thought my hat had been lost at sea. I entreated his imperial majesty to give orders it might be brought to me as soon as possible, describing to him the use and the nature of it: and the next day the waggoners arrived with it, but not in a very good condition; they had bored two holes in the brim, within an inch and half of the edge, and fastened two hooks in the holes; these hooks were tied by a long cord to the harness, and thus my hat was dragged along for above half an English mile; but, the ground in that country being extremely smooth and level, it received less damage than I expected.

Two days after this adventure, the emperor, having ordered that part of his army which quarters in and about his metropolis, to be in readiness, took a fancy of diverting himself in a very singular manner. He desired I would stand like a Colossus, with my legs as far asunder as I conveniently could. He then commanded his general (who was an old experienced leader, and a great patron of mine) to draw up the troops in close order, and march them under me; the foot by twenty-four abreast, and the horse by sixteen, with drums beating, colours flying, and pikes advanced. This body consisted of three thousand foot, and a thousand horse. His majesty gave orders, upon pain of death, that every soldier in his march should observe the strictest decency with regard to my person; which however could not prevent some of the younger officers from turning up their eyes as they passed under me: and, to confess the truth, my breeches were at that time in so ill a condition, that they afforded some opportunities for laughter and admiration.

I had sent so many memorials and petitions for my liberty, that his majesty at length mentioned the matter, first in the cabinet, and then in a full council; where it was opposed by none, except Skyresh Bolgolam, who was pleased, without any provocation, to be my mortal enemy. But it was carried against him by the whole board, and confirmed by the emperor. That minister was galbet, or admiral of the realm, very much in his master's confidence, and a person well versed in affairs, but of a morose and sour complexion. However, he was at length persuaded to comply; but prevailed that the articles and conditions upon which I should be set free, and to which I must swear, should be drawn up by himself. These articles were brought to me by Skyresh Bolgolam in person attended by two under-secretaries, and several persons of distinction. After they were read, I was demanded to swear to the performance of them; first in the manner of my own country, and afterwards in the method prescribed by their laws; which was, to hold my right foot in my left hand, and to place the middle finger of my right hand on the crown of my head, and my thumb on the tip of my right ear. But because the reader may be curious to have some idea of the style and manner of expression peculiar to that people, as well as to know the article upon which I recovered my liberty, I have made a translation of the whole instrument, word for word, as near as I was able, which I here offer to the public.

"Golbasto Momarem Evlame Gurdilo Shefin Mully Ully Gue, most mighty Emperor of Lilliput, delight and terror of the universe, whose dominions extend five thousand blustrugs (about twelve miles in circumference) to the extremities of the globe; monarch of all monarchs, taller than the sons of men; whose feet press down to the centre, and whose head strikes against the sun; at whose nod the princes of the earth shake their knees; pleasant as the spring, comfortable as the summer, fruitful as autumn, dreadful as winter: his most sublime majesty proposes to the man-mountain, lately arrived at our celestial dominions, the following articles, which, by a solemn oath, he shall be obliged to perform:-

"1st, The man-mountain shall not depart from our dominions, without our license under our great seal.

"2d, He shall not presume to come into our metropolis, without our express order; at which time, the inhabitants shall have two hours warning to keep within doors.

"3d, The said man-mountain shall confine his walks to our principal high roads, and not offer to walk, or lie down, in a meadow or field of corn.

"4th, As he walks the said roads, he shall take the utmost care not to trample upon the bodies of any of our loving subjects, their horses, or carriages, nor take any of our subjects into his hands without their own consent.

"5th, If an express requires extraordinary despatch, the man- mountain shall be obliged to carry, in his pocket, the messenger and horse a six days journey, once in every moon, and return the said messenger back (if so required) safe to our imperial presence.

"6th, He shall be our ally against our enemies in the island of Blefuscu, and do his utmost to destroy their fleet, which is now preparing to invade us.

"7th, That the said man-mountain shall, at his times of leisure, be aiding and assisting to our workmen, in helping to raise certain great stones, towards covering the wall of the principal park, and other our royal buildings.

"8th, That the said man-mountain shall, in two moons' time, deliver in an exact survey of the circumference of our dominions, by a computation of his own paces round the coast.

"Lastly, That, upon his solemn oath to observe all the above articles, the said man-mountain shall have a daily allowance of meat and drink sufficient for the support of 1724 of our subjects, with free access to our royal person, and other marks of our favour. Given at our palace at Belfaborac, the twelfth day of the ninety-first moon of our reign."

I swore and subscribed to these articles with great cheerfulness and content, although some of them were not so honourable as I could have wished; which proceeded wholly from the malice of Skyresh Bolgolam, the high-admiral: whereupon my chains were immediately unlocked, and I was at full liberty. The emperor himself, in person, did me the honour to be by at the whole ceremony. I made my acknowledgements by prostrating myself at his majesty's feet: but he commanded me to rise; and after many gracious expressions, which, to avoid the censure of vanity, I shall not repeat, he added, "that he hoped I should prove a useful servant, and well deserve all the favours he had already conferred upon me, or might do for the future."

The reader may please to observe, that, in the last article of the recovery of my liberty, the emperor stipulates to allow me a quantity of meat and drink sufficient for the support of 1724 Lilliputians. Some time after, asking a friend at court how they came to fix on that determinate number, he told me that his majesty's mathematicians, having taken the height of my body by the help of a quadrant, and finding it to exceed theirs in the proportion of twelve to one, they concluded from the similarity of their bodies, that mine must contain at least 1724 of theirs, and consequently would require as much food as was necessary to support that number of Lilliputians. By which the reader may conceive an idea of the ingenuity of that people, as well as the prudent and exact economy of so great a prince.

CHAPTER IV

[Mildendo, the metropolis of Lilliput, described, together with the emperor's palace. A conversation between the author and a principal secretary, concerning the affairs of that empire. The author's offers to serve the emperor in his wars.]

The first request I made, after I had obtained my liberty, was, that I might have license to see Mildendo, the metropolis; which the emperor easily granted me, but with a special charge to do no hurt either to the inhabitants or their houses. The people had notice, by proclamation, of my design to visit the town. The wall which encompassed it is two feet and a half high, and at least eleven inches broad, so that a coach and horses may be driven very safely round it; and it is flanked with strong towers at ten feet distance. I stepped over the great western gate, and passed very gently, and sidling, through the two principal streets, only in my short waistcoat, for fear of damaging the roofs and eaves of the houses with the skirts of my coat. I walked with the utmost circumspection, to avoid treading on any stragglers who might remain in the streets, although the orders were very strict, that all people should keep in their houses, at their own peril. The garret windows and tops of houses were so crowded with spectators, that I thought in all my travels I had not seen a more populous place. The city is an exact square, each side of the wall being five hundred feet long. The two great streets, which run across and divide it into four quarters, are five feet wide. The lanes and alleys, which I could not enter, but only view them as I passed, are from twelve to eighteen inches. The town is capable of holding five hundred thousand souls: the houses are from three to five stories: the shops and markets well provided.

The emperor's palace is in the centre of the city where the two great streets meet. It is enclosed by a wall of two feet high, and twenty feet distance from the buildings. I had his majesty's permission to step over this wall; and, the space being so wide between that and the palace, I could easily view it on every side. The outward court is a square of forty feet, and includes two other courts: in the inmost are the royal apartments, which I was very desirous to see, but found it extremely difficult; for the great gates, from one square into another, were but eighteen inches high, and seven inches wide. Now the buildings of the outer court were at least five feet high, and it was impossible for me to stride over them without infinite damage to the pile, though the walls were strongly built of hewn stone, and four inches thick. At the same time the emperor had a great desire that I should see the magnificence of his palace; but this I was not able to do till three days after, which I spent in cutting down with my knife some of the largest trees in the royal park, about a hundred yards distant from the city. Of these trees I made two stools, each about three feet high, and strong enough to bear my weight. The people having received notice a second time, I went again through the city to the palace with my two stools in my hands. When I came to the side of the outer court, I stood upon one stool, and took the other in my hand; this I lifted over the roof, and gently set it down on the space between the first and second court, which was eight feet wide. I then stept over the building very conveniently from one stool to the other, and drew up the first after me with a hooked stick. By this contrivance I got into the inmost court; and, lying down upon my side, I applied my face to the windows of the middle stories, which were left open on purpose, and discovered the most splendid apartments that can be imagined. There I saw the empress and the young princes, in their several lodgings, with their chief attendants about them. Her imperial majesty was pleased to smile very graciously upon me, and gave me out of the window her hand to kiss.

But I shall not anticipate the reader with further descriptions of this kind, because I reserve them for a greater work, which is now almost ready for the press; containing a general description of this empire, from its first erection, through along series of princes; with a particular account of their wars and politics, laws, learning, and religion; their plants and animals; their peculiar manners and customs, with other matters very curious and useful; my chief design at present being only to relate such events and transactions as happened to the public or to myself during a residence of about nine months in that empire.

One morning, about a fortnight after I had obtained my liberty, Reldresal, principal secretary (as they style him) for private affairs, came to my house attended only by one servant. He ordered his coach to wait at a distance, and desired I would give him an hours audience; which I readily consented to, on account of his quality and personal merits, as well as of the many good offices he had done me during my solicitations at court. I offered to lie down that he might the more conveniently reach my ear, but he chose rather to let me hold him in my hand during our conversation. He began with compliments on my liberty; said "he might pretend to some merit in it;" but, however, added, "that if it had not been for the present situation of things at court, perhaps I might not have obtained it so soon. For," said he, "as flourishing a condition as we may appear to be in to foreigners, we labour under two mighty evils: a violent faction at home, and the danger of an invasion, by a most potent enemy, from abroad. As to the first, you are to understand, that for about seventy moons past there have been two struggling parties in this empire, under the names of Tramecksan and Slamecksan, from the high and low heels of their shoes, by which they distinguish themselves. It is alleged, indeed, that the high heels are most agreeable to our ancient constitution; but, however this be, his majesty has determined to make use only of low heels in the administration of the government, and all offices in the gift of the crown, as you cannot but observe; and particularly that his majesty's imperial heels are lower at least by a drurr than any of his court (drurr is a measure about the fourteenth part of an inch). The animosities between these two parties run so high, that they will neither eat, nor drink, nor talk with each other. We compute the Tramecksan, or high heels, to exceed us in number; but the power is wholly on our side. We apprehend his imperial highness, the heir to the crown, to have some tendency towards the high heels; at least we can plainly discover that one of his heels is higher than the other, which gives him a hobble in his gait. Now, in the midst of these intestine disquiets, we are threatened with an invasion from the island of Blefuscu, which is the other great empire of the universe, almost as large and powerful as this of his majesty. For as to what we have heard you affirm, that there are other kingdoms and states in the world inhabited by human creatures as large as yourself, our philosophers are in much doubt, and would rather conjecture that you dropped from the moon, or one of the stars; because it is certain, that a hundred mortals of your bulk would in a short time destroy all the fruits and cattle of his majesty's dominions: besides, our histories of six thousand moons make no mention of any other regions than the two great empires of Lilliput and Blefuscu. Which two mighty powers have, as I was going to tell you, been engaged in a most obstinate war for six-and-thirty moons past. It began upon the following occasion. It is allowed on all hands, that the primitive way of breaking eggs, before we eat them, was upon the larger end; but his present majesty's grandfather, while he was a boy, going to eat an egg, and breaking it according to the ancient practice, happened to cut one of his fingers. Whereupon the emperor his father published an edict, commanding all his subjects, upon great penalties, to break the smaller end of their eggs. The people so highly resented this law, that our histories tell us, there have been six rebellions raised on that account; wherein one emperor lost his life, and another his crown. These civil commotions were constantly fomented by the monarchs of Blefuscu; and when they were quelled, the exiles always fled for refuge to that empire. It is computed that eleven thousand persons have at several times suffered death, rather than submit to break their eggs at the smaller end. Many hundred large volumes have been published upon this controversy: but the books of the Big- endians have been long forbidden, and the whole party rendered incapable by law of holding employments. During the course of these troubles, the emperors of Blefusca did frequently expostulate by their ambassadors, accusing us of making a schism in religion, by offending against a fundamental doctrine of our great prophet Lustrog, in the fifty-fourth chapter of the Blundecral (which is their Alcoran). This, however, is thought to be a mere strain upon the text; for the words are these: 'that all true believers break their eggs at the convenient end.' And which is the convenient end, seems, in my humble opinion to be left to every man's conscience, or at least in the power of the chief magistrate to determine. Now, the Big-endian exiles have found so much credit in the emperor of Blefuscu's court, and so much private assistance and encouragement from their party here at home, that a bloody war has been carried on between the two empires for six-and-thirty moons, with various success; during which time we have lost forty capital ships, and a much a greater number of smaller vessels, together with thirty thousand of our best seamen and soldiers; and the damage received by the enemy is reckoned to be somewhat greater than ours. However, they have now equipped a numerous fleet, and are just preparing to make a descent upon us; and his imperial majesty, placing great confidence in your valour and strength, has commanded me to lay this account of his affairs before you."

I desired the secretary to present my humble duty to the emperor; and to let him know, "that I thought it would not become me, who was a foreigner, to interfere with parties; but I was ready, with the hazard of my life, to defend his person and state against all invaders."

CHAPTER V

[The author, by an extraordinary stratagem, prevents an invasion. A high title of honour is conferred upon him. Ambassadors arrive from the emperor of Blefuscu, and sue for peace. The empress's apartment on fire by an accident; the author instrumental in saving the rest of the palace.]

The empire of Blefuscu is an island situated to the north-east of Lilliput, from which it is parted only by a channel of eight hundred yards wide. I had not yet seen it, and upon this notice of an intended invasion, I avoided appearing on that side of the coast, for fear of being discovered, by some of the enemy's ships, who had received no intelligence of me; all intercourse between the two empires having been strictly forbidden during the war, upon pain of death, and an embargo laid by our emperor upon all vessels whatsoever. I communicated to his majesty a project I had formed of seizing the enemy's whole fleet; which, as our scouts assured us, lay at anchor in the harbour, ready to sail with the first fair wind. I consulted the most experienced seamen upon the depth of the channel, which they had often plumbed; who told me, that in the middle, at high-water, it was seventy glumgluffs deep, which is about six feet of European measure; and the rest of it fifty glumgluffs at most. I walked towards the north-east coast, over against Blefuscu, where, lying down behind a hillock, I took out my small perspective glass, and viewed the enemy's fleet at anchor, consisting of about fifty men of war, and a great number of transports: I then came back to my house, and gave orders (for which I had a warrant) for a great quantity of the strongest cable and bars of iron. The cable was about as thick as packthread and the bars of the length and size of a knitting-needle. I trebled the cable to make it stronger, and for the same reason I twisted three of the iron bars together, bending the extremities into a hook. Having thus fixed fifty hooks to as many cables, I went back to the north-east coast, and putting off my coat, shoes, and stockings, walked into the sea, in my leathern jerkin, about half an hour before high water. I waded with what haste I could, and swam in the middle about thirty yards, till I felt ground. I arrived at the fleet in less than half an hour. The enemy was so frightened when they saw me, that they leaped out of their ships, and swam to shore, where there could not be fewer than thirty thousand souls. I then took my tackling, and, fastening a hook to the hole at the prow of each, I tied all the cords together at the end. While I was thus employed, the enemy discharged several thousand arrows, many of which stuck in my hands and face, and, beside the excessive smart, gave me much disturbance in my work. My greatest apprehension was for mine eyes, which I should have infallibly lost, if I had not suddenly thought of an expedient. I kept, among other little necessaries, a pair of spectacles in a private pocket, which, as I observed before, had escaped the emperor's searchers. These I took out and fastened as strongly as I could upon my nose, and thus armed, went on boldly with my work, in spite of the enemy's arrows, many of which struck against the glasses of my spectacles, but without any other effect, further than a little to discompose them. I had now fastened all the hooks, and, taking the knot in my hand, began to pull; but not a ship would stir, for they were all too fast held by their anchors, so that the boldest part of my enterprise remained. I therefore let go the cord, and leaving the looks fixed to the ships, I resolutely cut with my knife the cables that fastened the anchors, receiving about two hundred shots in my face and hands; then I took up the knotted end of the cables, to which my hooks were tied, and with great ease drew fifty of the enemy's largest men of war after me.

The Blefuscudians, who had not the least imagination of what I intended, were at first confounded with astonishment. They had seen me cut the cables, and thought my design was only to let the ships run adrift or fall foul on each other: but when they perceived the whole fleet moving in order, and saw me pulling at the end, they set up such a scream of grief and despair as it is almost impossible to describe or conceive. When I had got out of danger, I stopped awhile to pick out the arrows that stuck in my hands and face; and rubbed on some of the same ointment that was given me at my first arrival, as I have formerly mentioned. I then took off my spectacles, and waiting about an hour, till the tide was a little fallen, I waded through the middle with my cargo, and arrived safe at the royal port of Lilliput.

The emperor and his whole court stood on the shore, expecting the issue of this great adventure. They saw the ships move forward in a large half-moon, but could not discern me, who was up to my breast in water. When I advanced to the middle of the channel, they were yet more in pain, because I was under water to my neck. The emperor concluded me to be drowned, and that the enemy's fleet was approaching in a hostile manner: but he was soon eased of his fears; for the channel growing shallower every step I made, I came in a short time within hearing, and holding up the end of the cable, by which the fleet was fastened, I cried in a loud voice, "Long live the most puissant king of Lilliput!" This great prince received me at my landing with all possible encomiums, and created me a nardac upon the spot, which is the highest title of honour among them.

His majesty desired I would take some other opportunity of bringing all the rest of his enemy's ships into his ports. And so unmeasureable is the ambition of princes, that he seemed to think of nothing less than reducing the whole empire of Blefuscu into a province, and governing it, by a viceroy; of destroying the Big- endian exiles, and compelling that people to break the smaller end of their eggs, by which he would remain the sole monarch of the whole world. But I endeavoured to divert him from this design, by many arguments drawn from the topics of policy as well as justice; and I plainly protested, "that I would never be an instrument of bringing a free and brave people into slavery." And, when the matter was debated in council, the wisest part of the ministry were of my opinion.

This open bold declaration of mine was so opposite to the schemes and politics of his imperial majesty, that he could never forgive me. He mentioned it in a very artful manner at council, where I was told that some of the wisest appeared, at least by their silence, to be of my opinion; but others, who were my secret enemies, could not forbear some expressions which, by a side-wind, reflected on me. And from this time began an intrigue between his majesty and a junto of ministers, maliciously bent against me, which broke out in less than two months, and had like to have ended in my utter destruction. Of so little weight are the greatest services to princes, when put into the balance with a refusal to gratify their passions.

About three weeks after this exploit, there arrived a solemn embassy from Blefuscu, with humble offers of a peace, which was soon concluded, upon conditions very advantageous to our emperor, wherewith I shall not trouble the reader. There were six ambassadors, with a train of about five hundred persons, and their entry was very magnificent, suitable to the grandeur of their master, and the importance of their business. When their treaty was finished, wherein I did them several good offices by the credit I now had, or at least appeared to have, at court, their excellencies, who were privately told how much I had been their friend, made me a visit in form. They began with many compliments upon my valour and generosity, invited me to that kingdom in the emperor their master's name, and desired me to show them some proofs of my prodigious strength, of which they had heard so many wonders; wherein I readily obliged them, but shall not trouble the reader with the particulars.

When I had for some time entertained their excellencies, to their infinite satisfaction and surprise, I desired they would do me the honour to present my most humble respects to the emperor their master, the renown of whose virtues had so justly filled the whole world with admiration, and whose royal person I resolved to attend, before I returned to my own country. Accordingly, the next time I had the honour to see our emperor, I desired his general license to wait on the Blefuscudian monarch, which he was pleased to grant me, as I could perceive, in a very cold manner; but could not guess the reason, till I had a whisper from a certain person, "that Flimnap and Bolgolam had represented my intercourse with those ambassadors as a mark of disaffection;" from which I am sure my heart was wholly free. And this was the first time I began to conceive some imperfect idea of courts and ministers.

It is to be observed, that these ambassadors spoke to me, by an interpreter, the languages of both empires differing as much from each other as any two in

Europe, and each nation priding itself upon the antiquity, beauty, and energy of their own tongue, with an avowed contempt for that of their neighbour; yet our emperor, standing upon the advantage he had got by the seizure of their fleet, obliged them to deliver their credentials, and make their speech, in the Lilliputian tongue. And it must be confessed, that from the great intercourse of trade and commerce between both realms, from the continual reception of exiles which is mutual among them, and from the custom, in each empire, to send their young nobility and richer gentry to the other, in order to polish themselves by seeing the world, and understanding men and manners; there are few persons of distinction, or merchants, or seamen, who dwell in the maritime parts, but what can hold conversation in both tongues; as I found some weeks after, when I went to pay my respects to the emperor of Blefuscu, which, in the midst of great misfortunes, through the malice of my enemies, proved a very happy adventure to me, as I shall relate in its proper place.

The reader may remember, that when I signed those articles upon which I recovered my liberty, there were some which I disliked, upon account of their being too servile; neither could anything but an extreme necessity have forced me to submit. But being now a nardac of the highest rank in that empire, such offices were looked upon as below my dignity, and the emperor (to do him justice), never once mentioned them to me. However, it was not long before I had an opportunity of doing his majesty, at least as I then thought, a most signal service. I was alarmed at midnight with the cries of many hundred people at my door; by which, being suddenly awaked, I was in some kind of terror. I heard the word Burglum repeated incessantly: several of the emperor's court, making their way through the crowd, entreated me to come immediately to the palace, where her imperial majesty's apartment was on fire, by the carelessness of a maid of honour, who fell asleep while she was reading a romance. I got up in an instant; and orders being given to clear the way before me, and it being likewise a moonshine night, I made a shift to get to the palace without trampling on any of the people. I found they had already applied ladders to the walls of the apartment, and were well provided with buckets, but the water was at some distance. These buckets were about the size of large thimbles, and the poor people supplied me with them as fast as they could: but the flame was so violent that they did little good. I might easily have stifled it with my coat, which I unfortunately left behind me for haste, and came away only in my leathern jerkin. The case seemed wholly desperate and deplorable; and this magnificent palace would have infallibly been burnt down to the ground, if, by a presence of mind unusual to me, I had not suddenly thought of an expedient. I had, the evening before, drunk plentifully of a most delicious wine called glimigrim, (the Blefuscudians call it flunec, but ours is esteemed the better sort,) which is very diuretic. By the luckiest chance in the world, I had not discharged myself of any part of it. The heat I had contracted by coming very near the flames, and by labouring to quench them, made the wine begin to operate by urine; which I voided in such a quantity, and applied so well to the proper places, that in three minutes the fire was wholly extinguished, and the rest of that noble pile, which had cost so many ages in erecting, preserved from destruction.

It was now day-light, and I returned to my house without waiting to congratulate with the emperor: because, although I had done a very eminent piece of service, yet I could not tell how his majesty might resent the manner by which I had performed it: for, by the fundamental laws of the realm, it is capital in any person, of what quality soever, to make water within the precincts of the palace. But I was a little comforted by a message from his majesty, "that he would give orders to the grand justiciary for passing my pardon in form:" which, however, I could not obtain; and I was privately assured, "that the empress, conceiving the greatest abhorrence of what I had done, removed to the most distant side of the court, firmly resolved that those buildings should never be repaired for her use: and, in the presence of her chief confidents could not forbear vowing revenge."

CHAPTER VI

[Of the inhabitants of Lilliput; their learning, laws, and customs; the manner of educating their children. The author's way of living in that country. His vindication of a great lady.]

Although I intend to leave the description of this empire to a particular treatise, yet, in the mean time, I am content to gratify the curious reader with some general ideas. As the common size of the natives is somewhat under six inches high, so there is an exact proportion in all other animals, as well as plants and trees: for instance, the tallest horses and oxen are between four and five inches in height, the sheep an inch and half, more or less: their geese about the bigness of a sparrow, and so the several gradations downwards till you come to the smallest, which to my sight, were almost invisible; but nature has adapted the eyes of the Lilliputians to all objects proper for their view: they see with great exactness, but at no great distance. And, to show the sharpness of their sight towards objects that are near, I have been much pleased with observing a cook pulling a lark, which was not so large as a common fly; and a young girl threading an invisible needle with invisible silk. Their tallest trees are about seven feet high: I mean some of those in the great royal park, the tops whereof I could but just reach with my fist clenched. The other vegetables are in the same proportion; but this I leave to the reader's imagination.

I shall say but little at present of their learning, which, for many ages, has flourished in all its branches among them: but their manner of writing is very peculiar, being neither from the left to the right, like the Europeans, nor from the right to the left, like the Arabians, nor from up to down, like the Chinese, but aslant, from one corner of the paper to the other, like ladies in England.

They bury their dead with their heads directly downward, because they hold an opinion, that in eleven thousand moons they are all to rise again; in which period the earth (which they conceive to be flat) will turn upside down, and by this means they shall, at their resurrection, be found ready standing on their feet. The learned among them confess the absurdity of this doctrine; but the practice still continues, in compliance to the vulgar.

There are some laws and customs in this empire very peculiar; and if they were not so directly contrary to those of my own dear country, I should be tempted to say a little in their justification. It is only to be wished they were as well executed. The first I shall mention, relates to informers. All crimes against the state, are punished here with the utmost severity; but, if the person accused makes his innocence plainly to appear upon his trial, the accuser is immediately put to an ignominious death; and out of his goods or lands the innocent person is quadruply recompensed for the loss of his time, for the danger he underwent, for the hardship of his imprisonment, and for all the charges he has been at in making his defence; or, if that fund be deficient, it is largely supplied by the crown. The emperor also confers on him some public mark of his favour, and proclamation is made of his innocence through the whole city.

They look upon fraud as a greater crime than theft, and therefore seldom fail to punish it with death; for they allege, that care and vigilance, with a very common understanding, may preserve a man's goods from thieves, but honesty has no defence against superior cunning; and, since it is necessary that there should be a perpetual intercourse of buying and selling, and dealing upon credit, where fraud is permitted and connived at, or has no law to punish it, the honest dealer is always undone, and the knave gets the advantage. I remember, when I was once interceding with the emperor for a criminal who had wronged his master of a great sum of money, which he had received by order and ran away with; and happening to tell his majesty, by way of extenuation, that it was only a breach of trust, the emperor thought it monstrous in me to offer as a defence the greatest aggravation of the crime; and truly I had little to say in return, farther than the common answer, that different nations had different customs; for, I confess, I was heartily ashamed. {2}

Although we usually call reward and punishment the two hinges upon which all government turns, yet I could never observe this maxim to be put in practice by any nation except that of Lilliput. Whoever can there bring sufficient proof, that he has strictly observed the laws of his country for seventy-three moons, has a claim to certain privileges, according to his quality or condition of life, with a proportionable sum of money out of a fund appropriated for that use: he likewise acquires the title of snilpall, or legal, which is added to his name, but does not descend to his posterity. And these people thought it a prodigious defect of policy among us, when I told them that our laws were enforced only by penalties, without any mention of reward. It is upon this account that the image of Justice, in their courts of judicature, is formed with six eyes, two before, as many behind, and on each side one, to signify circumspection; with a bag of gold open in her right hand, and a sword sheathed in her left, to show she is more disposed to reward than to punish.

In choosing persons for all employments, they have more regard to good morals than to great abilities; for, since government is necessary to mankind, they believe, that the common size of human understanding is fitted to some station or other; and that Providence never intended to make the management of public affairs a mystery to be comprehended only by a few persons of sublime genius, of which there seldom are three born in an age: but they suppose truth, justice, temperance, and the like, to be in every man's power; the practice of which virtues, assisted by experience and a good intention, would qualify any man for the service of his country, except where a course of study is required. But they thought the want of moral virtues was so far from being supplied by superior endowments of the mind, that employments could never be put into such dangerous hands as those of persons so qualified; and, at least, that the mistakes committed by ignorance, in a virtuous disposition, would never be of such fatal consequence to the public weal, as the practices of a man, whose inclinations led him to be corrupt, and who had great abilities to manage, to multiply, and defend his corruptions.

In like manner, the disbelief of a Divine Providence renders a man incapable of holding any public station; for, since kings avow themselves to be the deputies of Providence, the Lilliputians think nothing can be more absurd than for a prince to employ such men as disown the authority under which he acts.

In relating these and the following laws, I would only be understood to mean the original institutions, and not the most scandalous corruptions, into which these people are fallen by the degenerate nature of man. For, as to that infamous practice of acquiring great employments by dancing on the ropes, or badges of favour and distinction by leaping over sticks and creeping under them, the reader is to observe, that they were first introduced by the grandfather of the emperor now reigning, and grew to the present height by the gradual increase of party and faction.

Ingratitude is among them a capital crime, as we read it to have been in some other countries: for they reason thus; that whoever makes ill returns to his benefactor, must needs be a common enemy to the rest of mankind, from whom he has received no obligation, and therefore such a man is not fit to live.

Their notions relating to the duties of parents and children differ extremely from ours. For, since the conjunction of male and female is founded upon the great law of nature, in order to propagate and continue the species, the Lilliputians will needs have it, that men and women are joined together, like other animals, by the motives of concupiscence; and that their tenderness towards their young proceeds from the like natural principle: for which reason they will never allow that a child is under any obligation to his father for begetting him, or to his mother for bringing him into the world; which, considering the miseries of human life, was neither a benefit in itself, nor intended so by his parents, whose thoughts, in their love encounters, were otherwise employed. Upon these, and the like reasonings, their opinion is, that parents are the last of all others to be trusted with the education of their own children; and therefore they have in every town public nurseries, where all parents, except cottagers and labourers, are obliged to send their infants of both sexes to be reared and educated, when they come to the age of twenty moons, at which time they are supposed to have some rudiments of docility. These schools are of several kinds, suited to different qualities, and both sexes. They have certain professors well skilled in preparing children for such a condition of life as befits the rank of their parents, and their own capacities, as well as inclinations. I shall first say something of the male nurseries, and then of the female.

The nurseries for males of noble or eminent birth, are provided with grave and learned professors, and their several deputies. The clothes and food of the children are plain and simple. They are bred up in the principles of honour, justice, courage, modesty, clemency, religion, and love of their country; they are always employed in some business, except in the times of eating and sleeping, which are very short, and two hours for diversions consisting of bodily exercises. They are dressed by men till four years of age, and then are obliged to dress themselves, although their quality be ever so great; and the women attendant, who are aged proportionably to ours at fifty, perform only the most menial offices. They are never suffered to converse with servants, but go together in smaller or greater numbers to take their diversions, and always in the presence of a professor, or one of his deputies; whereby they avoid those early bad impressions of folly and vice, to which our children are subject. Their parents are suffered to see them only twice a year; the visit is to last but an hour; they are allowed to kiss the child at meeting and parting; but a professor, who always stands by on those occasions, will not suffer them to whisper, or use any fondling expressions, or bring any presents of toys, sweetmeats, and the like.

The pension from each family for the education and entertainment of a child, upon failure of due payment, is levied by the emperor's officers.

The nurseries for children of ordinary gentlemen, merchants, traders, and handicrafts, are managed proportionably after the same manner; only those designed for trades are put out apprentices at eleven years old, whereas those of persons of quality continue in their exercises till fifteen, which answers to twenty-one with us: but the confinement is gradually lessened for the last three years.

In the female nurseries, the young girls of quality are educated much like the males, only they are dressed by orderly servants of their own sex; but always in the presence of a professor or deputy, till they come to dress themselves, which is at five years old. And if it be found that these nurses ever presume to entertain the girls with frightful or foolish stories, or the common follies practised by chambermaids among us, they are publicly whipped thrice about the city, imprisoned for a year, and banished for life to the most desolate part of the country. Thus the young ladies are as much ashamed of being cowards and fools as the men, and despise all personal ornaments, beyond decency and cleanliness: neither did I perceive any difference in their education made by their difference of sex, only that the exercises of the females were not altogether so robust; and that some rules were given them relating to domestic life, and a smaller compass of learning was enjoined them: for their maxim is, that among peoples of quality, a wife should be always a reasonable and agreeable companion, because she cannot always be young. When the girls are twelve years old, which among them is the marriageable age, their parents or guardians take them home, with great expressions of gratitude to the professors, and seldom without tears of the young lady and her companions.

In the nurseries of females of the meaner sort, the children are instructed in all kinds of works proper for their sex, and their several degrees: those intended for apprentices are dismissed at seven years old, the rest are kept to eleven.

The meaner families who have children at these nurseries, are obliged, besides their annual pension, which is as low as possible, to return to the steward of the nursery a small monthly share of their gettings, to be a portion for the child; and therefore all parents are limited in their expenses by the law. For the Lilliputians think nothing can be more unjust, than for people, in subservience to their own appetites, to bring children into the world, and leave the burthen of supporting them on the public. As to persons of quality, they give security to appropriate a certain sum for each child, suitable to their condition; and these funds are always managed with good husbandry and the most exact justice.

The cottagers and labourers keep their children at home, their business being only to till and cultivate the earth, and therefore their education is of little consequence to the public: but the old and diseased among them, are supported by hospitals; for begging is a trade unknown in this empire.

And here it may, perhaps, divert the curious reader, to give some account of my domestics, and my manner of living in this country, during a residence of nine months, and thirteen days. Having a head mechanically turned, and being likewise forced by necessity, I had made for myself a table and chair convenient enough, out of the largest trees in the royal park. Two hundred sempstresses were employed to make me shirts, and linen for my bed and table, all of the strongest and coarsest kind they could get; which, however, they were forced to quilt together in several folds, for the thickest was some degrees finer than lawn. Their linen is usually three inches wide, and three feet make a piece. The sempstresses took my measure as I lay on the ground, one standing at my neck, and another at my mid-leg, with a strong cord extended, that each held by the end, while a third measured the length of the cord with a rule of an inch long. Then they measured my right thumb, and desired no more; for by a mathematical computation, that twice round the thumb is once round the wrist, and so on to the neck and the waist, and by the help of my old shirt, which I displayed on the ground before them for a pattern, they fitted me exactly. Three hundred tailors were employed in the same manner to make me clothes; but they had another contrivance for taking my measure. I kneeled down, and they raised a ladder from the ground to my neck; upon this ladder one of them mounted, and let fall a plumb-line from my collar to the floor, which just answered the length of my coat: but my waist and arms I measured myself. When my clothes were finished, which was done in my house (for the largest of theirs would not have been able to hold them), they looked like the patch-work made by the ladies in England, only that mine were all of a colour.

I had three hundred cooks to dress my victuals, in little convenient huts built about my house, where they and their families lived, and prepared me two dishes a-piece. I took up twenty waiters in my hand, and placed them on the table: a hundred more attended below on the ground, some with dishes of meat, and some with barrels of wine and other liquors slung on their shoulders; all which the waiters above drew up, as I wanted, in a very ingenious manner, by certain cords, as we draw the bucket up a well in Europe. A dish of their meat was a good mouthful, and a barrel of their liquor a reasonable draught. Their mutton yields to ours, but their beef is excellent. I have had a sirloin so large, that I have been forced to make three bites of it; but this is rare. My servants were astonished to see me eat it, bones and all, as in our country we do the leg of a lark. Their geese and turkeys I usually ate at a mouthful, and I confess they far exceed ours. Of their smaller fowl I could take up twenty or thirty at the end of my knife.

One day his imperial majesty, being informed of my way of living, desired "that himself and his royal consort, with the young princes of the blood of both sexes, might have the happiness," as he was pleased to call it, "of dining with me." They came accordingly, and I placed them in chairs of state, upon my table, just over against me, with their guards about them. Flimnap, the lord high treasurer, attended there likewise with his white staff; and I observed he often looked on me with a sour countenance, which I would not seem to regard, but ate more than usual, in honour to my dear country, as well as to fill the court with admiration. I have some private reasons to believe, that this visit from his majesty gave Flimnap an opportunity of doing me ill offices to his master. That minister had always been my secret enemy, though he outwardly caressed me more than was usual to the moroseness of his nature. He represented to the emperor "the low condition of his treasury; that he was forced to take up money at a great discount; that exchequer bills would not circulate under nine per cent. below par; that I had cost his majesty above a million and a half of sprugs" (their greatest gold coin, about the bigness of a spangle) "and, upon the whole, that it would be advisable in the emperor to take the first fair occasion of dismissing me."

I am here obliged to vindicate the reputation of an excellent lady, who was an innocent sufferer upon my account. The treasurer took a fancy to be jealous of his wife, from the malice of some evil tongues, who informed him that her grace had taken a violent affection for my person; and the court scandal ran for some time, that she once came privately to my lodging. This I solemnly declare to be a most infamous falsehood, without any grounds, further than that her grace was pleased to treat me with all innocent marks of freedom and friendship. I own she came often to my house, but always publicly, nor ever without three more in the coach, who were usually her sister and young daughter, and some particular acquaintance; but this was common to many other ladies of the court. And I still appeal to my servants round, whether they at any time saw a coach at my door, without knowing what persons were in it. On those occasions, when a servant had given me notice, my custom was to go immediately to the door, and, after paying my respects, to take up the coach and two horses very carefully in my hands (for, if there were six horses, the postillion always unharnessed four,) and place them on a table, where I had fixed a movable rim quite round, of five inches high, to prevent accidents. And I have often had four coaches and horses at once on my table, full of company, while I sat in my chair, leaning my face towards them; and when I was engaged with one set, the coachmen would gently drive the others round my table. I have passed many an afternoon very agreeably in these conversations. But I defy the treasurer, or his two informers (I will name them, and let them make the best of it) Clustril and Drunlo, to prove that any person ever came to me incognito, except the secretary Reldresal, who was sent by express command of his imperial majesty, as I have before related. I should not have dwelt so long upon this particular, if it had not been a point wherein the reputation of a great lady is so nearly concerned, to say nothing of my own; though I then had the honour to be a nardac, which the treasurer himself is not; for all the world knows, that he is only a glumglum, a title inferior by one degree, as that of a marquis is to a duke in England; yet I allow he preceded me in right of his post. These false informations, which I afterwards came to the knowledge of by an accident not proper to mention, made the treasurer show his lady for some time an ill countenance, and me a worse; and although he was at last undeceived and reconciled to her, yet I lost all credit with him, and found my interest decline very fast with the emperor himself, who was, indeed, too much governed by that favourite.

CHAPTER VII

[The author, being informed of a design to accuse him of high- treason, makes his escape to Blefuscu. His reception there.]

Before I proceed to give an account of my leaving this kingdom, it may be proper to inform the reader of a private intrigue which had been for two months forming against me.

I had been hitherto, all my life, a stranger to courts, for which I was unqualified by the meanness of my condition. I had indeed heard and read enough of the dispositions of great princes and ministers, but never expected to have found such terrible effects of them, in so remote a country, governed, as I thought, by very different maxims from those in Europe.

When I was just preparing to pay my attendance on the emperor of Blefuscu, a considerable person at court (to whom I had been very serviceable, at a time when he lay under the highest displeasure of his imperial majesty) came to my house very privately at night, in a close chair, and, without sending his name, desired admittance. The chairmen were dismissed; I put the chair, with his lordship in it, into my coat-pocket: and, giving orders to a trusty servant, to say I was indisposed and gone to sleep, I fastened the door of my house, placed the chair on the table, according to my usual custom, and sat down by it. After the common salutations were over, observing his lordship's countenance full of concern, and inquiring into the reason, he desired "I would hear him with patience, in a matter that highly concerned my honour and my life." His speech was to the following effect, for I took notes of it as soon as he left me:-

"You are to know," said he, "that several committees of council have been lately called, in the most private manner, on your account; and it is but two days since his majesty came to a full resolution.

"You are very sensible that Skyresh Bolgolam" (galbet, or high- admiral) "has been your mortal enemy, almost ever since your arrival. His original reasons I know not; but his hatred is increased since your great success against Blefuscu, by which his glory as admiral is much obscured. This lord, in conjunction with Flimnap the high-treasurer, whose enmity against you is notorious on account of his lady, Limtoc the general, Lalcon the chamberlain, and Balmuff the grand justiciary, have prepared articles of impeachment against you, for treason and other capital crimes."

This preface made me so impatient, being conscious of my own merits and innocence, that I was going to interrupt him; when he entreated me to be silent, and thus proceeded:-

"Out of gratitude for the favours you have done me, I procured information of the whole proceedings, and a copy of the articles; wherein I venture my head for your service.

"'Articles of Impeachment against QUINBUS FLESTRIN, (the Man-Mountain.)

ARTICLE I.

"'Whereas, by a statute made in the reign of his imperial majesty Calin Deffar Plune, it is enacted, that, whoever shall make water within the precincts of the royal palace, shall be liable to the pains and penalties of high-treason; notwithstanding, the said Quinbus Flestrin, in open breach of the said law, under colour of extinguishing the fire kindled in the apartment of his majesty's most dear imperial consort, did maliciously, traitorously, and devilishly, by discharge of his urine, put out the said fire kindled in the said apartment, lying and being within the precincts of the said royal palace, against the statute in that case provided, etc. against the duty, etc.

ARTICLE II.

"'That the said Quinbus Flestrin, having brought the imperial fleet of Blefuscu into the royal port, and being afterwards commanded by his imperial majesty to seize all the other ships of the said empire of Blefuscu, and reduce that empire to a province, to be governed by a viceroy from hence, and to destroy and put to death, not only all the Big-endian exiles, but likewise all the people of that empire who would not immediately forsake the Big-endian heresy, he, the said Flestrin, like a false traitor against his most auspicious, serene, imperial majesty, did petition to be excused from the said service, upon pretence of unwillingness to force the consciences, or destroy the liberties and lives of an innocent people.

ARTICLE III.

"'That, whereas certain ambassadors arrived from the Court of Blefuscu, to sue for peace in his majesty's court, he, the said Flestrin, did, like a false traitor, aid, abet, comfort, and divert, the said ambassadors, although he knew them to be servants to a prince who was lately an open enemy to his imperial majesty, and in an open war against his said majesty.

ARTICLE IV.

"'That the said Quinbus Flestrin, contrary to the duty of a faithful subject, is now preparing to make a voyage to the court and empire of Blefuscu, for which he has received only verbal license from his imperial majesty; and, under colour of the said license, does falsely and traitorously intend to take the said voyage, and thereby to aid, comfort, and abet the emperor of Blefuscu, so lately an enemy, and in open war with his imperial majesty aforesaid.'

"There are some other articles; but these are the most important, of which I have read you an abstract.

"In the several debates upon this impeachment, it must be confessed that his majesty gave many marks of his great lenity; often urging the services you had done him, and endeavouring to extenuate your crimes. The treasurer and admiral insisted that you should be put to the most painful and ignominious death, by setting fire to your house at night, and the general was to attend with twenty thousand men, armed with poisoned arrows, to shoot you on the face and hands. Some of your servants were to have private orders to strew a poisonous juice on your shirts and sheets, which would soon make you tear your own flesh, and die in the utmost torture. The general came into the same opinion; so that for a long time there was a majority against you; but his majesty resolving, if possible, to spare your life, at last brought off the chamberlain.

"Upon this incident, Reldresal, principal secretary for private affairs, who always approved himself your true friend, was commanded by the emperor to deliver his opinion, which he accordingly did; and therein justified the good thoughts you have of him. He allowed your crimes to be great, but that still there was room for mercy, the most commendable virtue in a prince, and for which his majesty was so justly celebrated. He said, the friendship between you and him was so well known to the world, that perhaps the most honourable board might think him partial; however, in obedience to the command he had received, he would freely offer his sentiments. That if his majesty, in consideration of your services, and pursuant to his own merciful disposition, would please to spare your life, and only give orders to put out both your eyes, he humbly conceived, that by this expedient justice might in some measure be satisfied, and all the world would applaud the lenity of the emperor, as well as the fair and generous proceedings of those who have the honour to be his counsellors. That the loss of your eyes would be no impediment to your bodily strength, by which you might still be useful to his majesty; that blindness is an addition to courage, by concealing dangers from us; that the fear you had for your eyes, was the greatest difficulty in bringing over the enemy's fleet, and it would be sufficient for you to see by the eyes of the ministers, since the greatest princes do no more.

"This proposal was received with the utmost disapprobation by the whole board. Bolgolam, the admiral, could not preserve his temper, but, rising up in fury, said, he wondered how the secretary durst presume to give his opinion for preserving the life of a traitor; that the services you had performed were, by all true reasons of state, the great aggravation of your crimes; that you, who were able to extinguish the fire by discharge of urine in her majesty's apartment (which he mentioned with horror), might, at another time, raise an inundation by the same means, to drown the whole palace; and the same strength which enabled you to bring over the enemy's fleet, might serve, upon the first discontent, to carry it back; that he had good reasons to think you were a Big-endian in your heart; and, as treason begins in the heart, before it appears in overt-acts, so he accused you as a traitor on that account, and therefore insisted you should be put to death.

"The treasurer was of the same opinion: he showed to what straits his majesty's revenue was reduced, by the charge of maintaining you, which would soon grow insupportable; that the secretary's expedient of putting out your eyes, was so far from being a remedy against this evil, that it would probably increase it, as is manifest from the common practice of blinding some kind of fowls, after which they fed the faster, and grew sooner fat; that his sacred majesty and the council, who are your judges, were, in their own consciences, fully convinced of your guilt, which was a sufficient argument to condemn you to death, without the formal proofs required by the strict letter of the law.

"But his imperial majesty, fully determined against capital punishment, was graciously pleased to say, that since the council thought the loss of your eyes too easy a censure, some other way may be inflicted hereafter. And your friend the secretary, humbly desiring to be heard again, in answer to what the treasurer had objected, concerning the great charge his majesty was at in maintaining you, said, that his excellency, who had the sole disposal of the emperor's revenue, might easily provide against that evil, by gradually lessening your establishment; by which, for want of sufficient for you would grow weak and faint, and lose your appetite, and consequently, decay, and consume in a few months; neither would the stench of your carcass be then so dangerous, when it should become more than half diminished; and immediately upon your death five or six thousand of his majesty's subjects might, in two or three days, cut your flesh from your bones, take it away by cart-loads, and bury it in distant parts, to prevent infection, leaving the skeleton as a monument of admiration to posterity.

"Thus, by the great friendship of the secretary, the whole affair was compromised. It was strictly enjoined, that the project of starving you by degrees should be kept a secret; but the sentence of putting out your eyes was entered on the books; none dissenting, except Bolgolam the admiral, who, being a creature of the empress, was perpetually instigated by her majesty to insist upon your death, she having borne perpetual malice against you, on account of that infamous and illegal method you took to extinguish the fire in her apartment.

"In three days your friend the secretary will be directed to come to your house, and read before you the articles of impeachment; and then to signify the great lenity and favour of his majesty and council, whereby you are only condemned to the loss of your eyes, which his majesty does not question you will gratefully and humbly submit to; and twenty of his majesty's surgeons will attend, in order to see the operation well performed, by discharging very sharp-pointed arrows into the balls of your eyes, as you lie on the ground.

"I leave to your prudence what measures you will take; and to avoid suspicion, I must immediately return in as private a manner as I came."

His lordship did so; and I remained alone, under many doubts and perplexities of mind.

It was a custom introduced by this prince and his ministry (very different, as I have been assured, from the practice of former times,) that after the court had decreed any cruel execution, either to gratify the monarch's resentment, or the malice of a favourite, the emperor always made a speech to his whole council, expressing his great lenity and tenderness, as qualities known and confessed by all the world. This speech was immediately published throughout the kingdom; nor did any thing terrify the people so much as those encomiums on his majesty's mercy; because it was observed, that the more these praises were enlarged and insisted on, the more inhuman was the punishment, and the sufferer more innocent. Yet, as to myself, I must confess, having never been designed for a courtier, either by my birth or education, I was so ill a judge of things, that I could not discover the lenity and favour of this sentence, but conceived it (perhaps erroneously) rather to be rigorous than gentle. I sometimes thought of standing my trial, for, although I could not deny the facts alleged in the several articles, yet I hoped they would admit of some extenuation. But having in my life perused many state-trials, which I ever observed to terminate as the judges thought fit to direct, I durst not rely on so dangerous a decision, in so critical a juncture, and against such powerful enemies. Once I was strongly bent upon resistance, for, while I had liberty the whole strength of that empire could hardly subdue me, and I might easily with stones pelt the metropolis to pieces; but I soon rejected that project with horror, by remembering the oath I had made to the emperor, the favours I received from him, and the high title of nardac he conferred upon me. Neither had I so soon learned the gratitude of courtiers, to persuade myself, that his majesty's present seventies acquitted me of all past obligations.

At last, I fixed upon a resolution, for which it is probable I may incur some censure, and not unjustly; for I confess I owe the preserving of mine eyes, and consequently my liberty, to my own great rashness and want of experience;

because, if I had then known the nature of princes and ministers, which I have since observed in many other courts, and their methods of treating criminals less obnoxious than myself, I should, with great alacrity and readiness, have submitted to so easy a punishment. But hurried on by the precipitancy of youth, and having his imperial majesty's license to pay my attendance upon the emperor of Blefuscu, I took this opportunity, before the three days were elapsed, to send a letter to my friend the secretary, signifying my resolution of setting out that morning for Blefuscu, pursuant to the leave I had got; and, without waiting for an answer, I went to that side of the island where our fleet lay. I seized a large man of war, tied a cable to the prow, and, lifting up the anchors, I stripped myself, put my clothes (together with my coverlet, which I carried under my arm) into the vessel, and, drawing it after me, between wading and swimming arrived at the royal port of Blefuscu, where the people had long expected me: they lent me two guides to direct me to the capital city, which is of the same name. I held them in my hands, till I came within two hundred yards of the gate, and desired them "to signify my arrival to one of the secretaries, and let him know, I there waited his majesty's command." I had an answer in about an hour, "that his majesty, attended by the royal family, and great officers of the court, was coming out to receive me." I advanced a hundred yards. The emperor and his train alighted from their horses, the empress and ladies from their coaches, and I did not perceive they were in any fright or concern. I lay on the ground to kiss his majesty's and the empress's hands. I told his majesty, "that I was come according to my promise, and with the license of the emperor my master, to have the honour of seeing so mighty a monarch, and to offer him any service in my power, consistent with my duty to my own prince;" not mentioning a word of my disgrace, because I had hitherto no regular information of it, and might suppose myself wholly ignorant of any such design; neither could I reasonably conceive that the emperor would discover the secret, while I was out of his power; wherein, however, it soon appeared I was deceived.

I shall not trouble the reader with the particular account of my reception at this court, which was suitable to the generosity of so great a prince; nor of the difficulties I was in for want of a house and bed, being forced to lie on the ground, wrapped up in my coverlet.

CHAPTER VIII

[The author, by a lucky accident, finds means to leave Blefuscu; and, after some difficulties, returns safe to his native country.]

Three days after my arrival, walking out of curiosity to the north- east coast of the island, I observed, about half a league off in the sea, somewhat that looked like a boat overturned. I pulled off my shoes and stockings, and, wailing two or three hundred yards, I found the object to approach nearer by force of the tide; and then plainly saw it to be a real boat, which I supposed might by some tempest have been driven from a ship. Whereupon, I returned immediately towards the city, and desired his imperial majesty to lend me twenty of the tallest vessels he had left, after the loss of his fleet, and three thousand seamen, under the command of his vice-admiral. This fleet sailed round, while I went back the shortest way to the coast, where I first discovered the boat. I found the tide had driven it still nearer. The seamen were all provided with cordage, which I had beforehand twisted to a sufficient strength. When the ships came up, I stripped myself, and waded till I came within a hundred yards off the boat, after which I was forced to swim till I got up to it. The seamen threw me the end of the cord, which I fastened to a hole in the fore-part of the boat, and the other end to a man of war; but I found all my labour to little purpose; for, being out of my depth, I was not able to work. In this necessity I was forced to swim behind, and push the boat forward, as often as I could, with one of my hands; and the tide favouring me, I advanced so far that I could just hold up my chin and feel the ground. I rested two or three minutes, and then gave the boat another shove, and so on, till the sea was no higher than my arm-pits; and now, the most laborious part being over, I took out my other cables, which were stowed in one of the ships, and fastened them first to the boat, and then to nine of the vessels which attended me; the wind being favourable, the seamen towed, and I shoved, until we arrived within forty yards of the shore; and, waiting till the tide was out, I got dry to the boat, and by the assistance of two thousand men, with ropes and engines, I made a shift to turn it on its bottom, and found it was but little damaged.

I shall not trouble the reader with the difficulties I was under, by the help of certain paddles, which cost me ten days making, to get my boat to the royal port of Blefuscu, where a mighty concourse of people appeared upon my arrival, full of wonder at the sight of so prodigious a vessel. I told the emperor "that my good fortune had thrown this boat in my way, to carry me to some place whence I might return into my native country; and begged his majesty's orders for getting materials to fit it up, together with his license to depart;" which, after some kind expostulations, he was pleased to grant.

I did very much wonder, in all this time, not to have heard of any express relating to me from our emperor to the court of Blefuscu. But I was afterward given privately to understand, that his imperial majesty, never imagining I had the least notice of his designs, believed I was only gone to Blefuscu in performance of my promise, according to the license he had given me, which was well known at our court, and would return in a few days, when the ceremony was ended. But he was at last in pain at my long absence; and after consulting with the treasurer and the rest of that cabal, a person of quality was dispatched with the copy of the articles against me. This envoy had instructions to represent to the monarch of Blefuscu, "the great lenity of his master, who was content to punish me no farther than with the loss of mine eyes; that I had fled from justice; and if I did not return in two hours, I should be deprived of my title of nardac, and declared a traitor." The envoy further added, "that in order to maintain the peace and amity between both empires, his master expected that his brother of Blefuscu would give orders to have me sent back to Lilliput, bound hand and foot, to be punished as a traitor."

The emperor of Blefuscu, having taken three days to consult, returned an answer consisting of many civilities and excuses. He said, "that as for sending me bound, his brother knew it was impossible; that, although I had deprived him of his fleet, yet he owed great obligations to me for many good offices I had done him in making the peace. That, however, both their majesties would soon be made easy; for I had found a prodigious vessel on the shore, able to carry me on the sea, which he had given orders to fit up, with my own assistance and direction; and he hoped, in a few weeks, both empires would be freed from so insupportable an encumbrance."

With this answer the envoy returned to Lilliput; and the monarch of Blefuscu related to me all that had passed; offering me at the same time (but under the strictest confidence) his gracious protection, if I would continue in his service; wherein, although I believed him sincere, yet I resolved never more to put any confidence in princes or ministers, where I could possibly avoid it; and therefore, with all due acknowledgments for his favourable intentions, I humbly begged to be excused. I told him, "that since fortune, whether good or evil, had thrown a vessel in my way, I was resolved to venture myself on the ocean, rather than be an occasion of difference between two such mighty monarchs." Neither did I find the emperor at all displeased; and I discovered, by a certain accident, that he was very glad of my resolution, and so were most of his ministers.

These considerations moved me to hasten my departure somewhat sooner than I intended; to which the court, impatient to have me gone, very readily contributed. Five hundred workmen were employed to make two sails to my boat, according to my directions, by quilting thirteen folds of their strongest linen together. I was at the pains of making ropes and cables, by twisting ten, twenty, or thirty of the thickest and strongest of theirs. A great stone that I happened to find, after a long search, by the sea-shore, served me for an anchor. I had the tallow of three hundred cows, for greasing my boat, and other uses. I was at incredible pains in cutting down some of the largest timber-trees, for oars and masts, wherein I was, however, much assisted by his majesty's ship- carpenters, who helped me in smoothing them, after I had done the rough work.

In about a month, when all was prepared, I sent to receive his majesty's commands, and to take my leave. The emperor and royal family came out of the palace; I lay down on my face to kiss his hand, which he very graciously gave me: so did the empress and young princes of the blood. His majesty presented me with fifty purses of two hundred sprugs a-piece, together with his picture at full length, which I put immediately into one of my gloves, to keep it from being hurt. The ceremonies at my departure were too many to trouble the reader with at this time.

I stored the boat with the carcases of a hundred oxen, and three hundred sheep, with bread and drink proportionable, and as much meat ready dressed as four hundred cooks could provide. I took with me six cows and two bulls alive, with as many ewes and rams, intending to carry them into my own country, and propagate the breed. And to feed them on board, I had a good bundle of hay, and a bag of corn. I would gladly have taken a dozen of the natives, but this was a thing the emperor would by no means permit; and, besides a diligent search into my pockets, his majesty engaged my honour "not to carry away any of his subjects, although with their own consent and desire."

Having thus prepared all things as well as I was able, I set sail on the twenty-fourth day of September 1701, at six in the morning; and when I had gone about four-leagues to the northward, the wind being at south-east, at six in the evening I descried a small island, about half a league to the north-west. I advanced forward, and cast anchor on the lee-side of the island, which seemed to be uninhabited. I then took some refreshment, and went to my rest. I slept well, and as I conjectured at least six hours, for I found the day broke in two hours after I awaked. It was a clear night. I ate my breakfast before the sun was up; and heaving anchor, the wind being favourable, I steered the same course that I had done the day before, wherein I was directed by my pocket compass. My intention was to reach, if possible, one of those islands. which I had reason to believe lay to the north-east of Van Diemen's Land. I discovered nothing all that day; but upon the next, about three in the afternoon, when I had by my computation made twenty-four leagues from Blefuscu, I descried a sail steering to the south- east; my course was due east. I hailed her, but could get no answer; yet I found I gained upon her, for the wind slackened. I made all the sail I could, and in half an hour she spied me, then hung out her ancient, and discharged a gun. It is not easy to express the joy I was in, upon the unexpected hope of once more seeing my beloved country, and the dear pledges I left in it. The ship slackened her sails, and I came up with her between five and six in the evening, September 26th; but my heart leaped within me to see her English colours. I put my cows and sheep into my coat-pockets, and got on board with all my little cargo of provisions. The vessel was an English merchantman, returning from Japan by the North and South seas; the captain, Mr. John Biddel, of Deptford, a very civil man, and a excellent sailor.

We were now in the latitude of 30 degrees south; there were about fifty men in the ship; and here I met an old comrade of mine, one Peter Williams, who gave me a good character to the captain. This gentleman treated me with kindness, and desired I would let him know what place I came from last, and whither I was bound; which I did in a few words, but he thought I was raving, and that the dangers I underwent had disturbed my head; whereupon I took my black cattle and sheep out of my pocket, which, after great astonishment, clearly convinced him of my veracity. I then showed him the gold given me by the emperor of Blefuscu, together with his majesty's picture at full length, and some other rarities of that country. I gave him two purses of two hundreds sprugs each, and promised, when we arrived in England, to make him a present of a cow and a sheep big with young.

I shall not trouble the reader with a particular account of this voyage, which was very prosperous for the most part. We arrived in the Downs on the 13th of

April, 1702. I had only one misfortune, that the rats on board carried away one of my sheep; I found her bones in a hole, picked clean from the flesh. The rest of my cattle I got safe ashore, and set them a-grazing in a bowling-green at Greenwich, where the fineness of the grass made them feed very heartily, though I had always feared the contrary: neither could I possibly have preserved them in so long a voyage, if the captain had not allowed me some of his best biscuit, which, rubbed to powder, and mingled with water, was their constant food. The short time I continued in England, I made a considerable profit by showing my cattle to many persons of quality and others: and before I began my second voyage, I sold them for six hundred pounds. Since my last return I find the breed is considerably increased, especially the sheep, which I hope will prove much to the advantage of the woollen manufacture, by the fineness of the fleeces.

I stayed but two months with my wife and family, for my insatiable desire of seeing foreign countries, would suffer me to continue no longer. I left fifteen hundred pounds with my wife, and fixed her in a good house at Redriff. My remaining stock I carried with me, part in money and part in goods, in hopes to improve my fortunes. My eldest uncle John had left me an estate in land, near Epping, of about thirty pounds a-year; and I had a long lease of the Black Bull in Fetter-Lane, which yielded me as much more; so that I was not in any danger of leaving my family upon the parish. My son Johnny, named so after his uncle, was at the grammar-school, and a towardly child. My daughter Betty (who is now well married, and has children) was then at her needle-work. I took leave of my wife, and boy and girl, with tears on both sides, and went on board the Adventure, a merchant ship of three hundred tons, bound for Surat, captain John Nicholas, of Liverpool, commander. But my account of this voyage must be referred to the Second Part of my Travels.

Lesson 14: The Age of Pope

John Gay (1685-1732)

John Gay's most famous work was *The Beggar's Opera, set to music and* performed in 1728. Though it is not included in your reading list, it would be a good one to pick up on your own and read. With some help from Jonathan Swift, Gay was appointed British ambassador to Hanover. Queen Anne's death ended his diplomatic career, however. Gay maintained a long-standing friendship with Alexander Pope and Swift, and was supported by many patrons. These friendships stood him in good stead when bad investments bankrupted him.

The Beggar's Opera, a satire which charicatured several court figures, was very successful – but did nothing to win the affection of those who had been charicatured. And Gay, himself, was quite clear about the fact that he had intended his audience to interpret the play as a political attack on Prime Minister Robert Walpole by portraying him as a highwayman. Walpole was not pleased. In fact, when Gay attempted to produce a sequel to the Beggar's Opera the Lord Chamberlain blocked it. Eventually, Gay was able to publish the play by selling subscriptions, many of which were bought by members of the court.

At his death, Gay was buried in Westinster Abbey. Alexander Pope wrote his epitaph.

An Elegy on a Lap-dog

Shock's fate I mourn; poor Shock is now no more,
Ye Muses mourn, ye chamber-maids deplore.
Unhappy Shock! yet more unhappy fair,
Doom'd to survive thy joy and only care!
Thy wretched fingers now no more shall deck,
And tie the fav'rite ribbon round his neck;
No more thy hand shall smooth his glossy hair,
And comb the wavings of his pendent ear.
Yet cease thy flowing grief, forsaken maid;
All mortal pleasures in a moment fade:
Our surest hope is in an hour destroy'd,
And love, best gift of heav'n, not long enjoy'd.

Methinks I see her frantic with despair,
Her streaming eyes, wrung hands, and flowing hair
Her Mechlen pinners rent the floor bestrow,
And her torn fan gives real signs of woe.
Hence Superstition, that tormenting guest,
That haunts with fancied fears the coward breast;
No dread events upon his fate attend,
Stream eyes no more, no more thy tresses rend.
Tho' certain omens oft forewarn a state,
And dying lions show the monarch's fate;
Why should such fears bid Celia's sorrow rise?
For when a lap-dog falls no lover dies.

Cease, Celia, cease; restrain thy flowing tears,
Some warmer passion will dispel thy cares.
In man you'll find a more substantial bliss,
More grateful toying, and a sweeter kiss.

He's dead. Oh, lay him gently in the ground!
And may his tomb be by this verse renown'd.
Here Shock, the pride of all his kind, is laid;
Who fawn'd like man, but ne'er like man betray'd.

Gray's Epitaph

Life is a jest, and all things show it,
I thought so once, and now I know it.

Alexander Pope (1688-1744)

(from http://www.island-of-freedom.com/POPE.HTM):

Alexander Pope was an English poet who, modeling himself after the great poets of classical antiquity, wrote highly polished verse, often in a didactic or satirical vein. In verse translations, moral and critical essays, and satires that made him the foremost poet of his age, he brought the heroic couplet, which had been refined by John Dryden, to ultimate perfection. Pope was the son of a London cloth merchant. His parents were Roman Catholics, which automatically barred him from England's Protestant universities. Until he was 12 years old, he was educated largely by priests; primarily self-taught afterward, he read widely in English letters, as well as in French, Italian, Latin, and Greek. A devastating illness, probably tuberculosis of the spine, struck him in childhood, leaving him deformed. He never grew taller than 4 ft 6 in and was subject to violent headaches. Perhaps as a result of this condition, he was hypersensitive and exceptionally irritable all his life.

In 1717 Pope moved to a villa in Twickenham, west of London on the Thames River, where he lived for the rest of his life. The most celebrated personages of the day came to visit him there. He was a bitterly quarrelsome man and attacked his literary contemporaries viciously and often without provocation. To some, however, he was warm and affectionate; he had a long and close friendship with the English writers Jonathan Swift and John Gay.

Pope's literary career began in 1704, when the playwright William Wycherley, pleased by Pope's verse, introduced him into the circle of fashionable London wits and writers, who welcomed him as a prodigy. He first attracted public attention in 1709 with his Pastorals. In 1711 his Essay on Criticism, a brilliant exposition of the canons of taste, was published. His most famous poem, The Rape of the Lock (first published 1712; revised edition published 1714), a fanciful and ingenious mock-heroic work based on a true story, established his reputation securely. In 1713 Pope published Windsor Forest, which endeared him to the Tories by referring to the Peace of Utrecht. In 1714 his work The Wife of Bath appeared, which, like his The Temple of Fame (1715), was imitative of the works of the same title by the 14th-century English poet Geoffrey Chaucer. In 1717 a collection of Pope's works containing the most noteworthy of his lyrics was published. Pope's translation of Homer's Iliad was published in six volumes from 1715 to 1720; a translation of the Odyssey followed (1725-1726). He also published an edition of Shakespeare's plays (1725).

Pope and his friend Swift had for years written scornful and very successful critical reviews of those whom they considered poor writers; in 1727 they began a series of parodies of the same writers. The adversaries hurled insults at Swift and Pope in return, and in 1728 Pope lampooned them in one of his best-known works, The Dunciad, a satire celebrating dullness. He later enlarged the work to four volumes, the final one appearing in 1743. In 1734 he completed his Essay on Man. Pope's last works, Imitations of Horace (1733-1739), were attacks on political enemies of his friends.

Pope used the heroic couplet with exceptional brilliance, giving it a witty, occasionally biting quality. His success made it the dominant poetic form of his century, and his poetry was translated into many languages.

References:

Microsoft Encarta 98 Encyclopedia, Copyright 1993-1997 Microsoft ***Corporation.***

Historical background – What is *L'Hombre*?

L'Hombre was developed in Spain in the early 17th century, as a variation of an earlier four player game, also called *Hombre*. The three player version, which in Spain was originally called *Hombre Renegado* spread rapidly across Europe and during the 17th and 18th centuries became the premier card game, occupying a position of prestige similar to Bridge today. It was variously known as *Hombre*, *Ombre* or *L'Hombre*, and over the years it acquired many variations, of increasing complexity. Its popularity was eclipsed in the late 18th century by a new four player variant *Quadrille*, which was in turn displaced by **Whist**, *Boston* and eventually **Bridge**.

Although L'Hombre died out in other parts of Europe, it remained popular in Denmark right up to the 21st century. It is played mostly in Jutland and on the island of Funen, and is organised by the **L'Hombre union**. Versions of the game have also survived in Spain itself, where it is known as **El Tresillo**, in the Faroes and in Iceland, and in Peru and Bolivia, where it is known as *Rocambor*.

L'Hombre was one of the first games to introduce bidding, through which one player becomes the declarer, trying to make a contract, with the other players cooperating to prevent him. The declarer was originally called *Hombre* (i.e. the man). It was from L'Hombre that the idea of bidding was adopted into other card games such as **Tarot**, **Skat** and Boston.

An excellent account of the early history of L'Hombre (from which some of the above information is taken) can be found in a series of three articles by *Thierry Depaulis* in *The Playing-Card (Journal of the International Playing-Card Society)*. They are entitled *"Ombre et Lumière. Un Peu de Lumière sur L'Hombre"* and appeared in *Vol XV, No 4, pp 101-110*, *Vol XVI, No 1, pp 10-18*, and *Vol XVI, No 2, pp 44-53*.

from: **http://www.pagat.com/lhombre/lhombre.html#history**

General Description of the Game:

L'Hombre is a three-handed trick taking game. It is also quite often played by four people, but there are still only 3 active players in each hand; the player opposite the dealer sits out. A deck of 40 cards is used. Each active player is dealt 9 cards and the remaining 13 form the talon. Each hand begins with an auction. The winner of the bidding becomes the declarer, and plays alone against the other two players (defenders) in partnership.

The final bid by declarer determines the contract. Declarer plays either a game contract, where his objective is to take more tricks than either defender, or a nolo contract, where his objective is not to take any tricks at all.

When the contract is known, the players take turns exchanging cards with the talon, subject to restrictions particular to each contract.

Afterwards, nine tricks are played. However, as soon as the outcome of the contract is clear, declarer will face his hand and make a statement to that effect.

After the play, immediate payment is made in the form of tokens. In general, the amount of payment increases with the rank of the contract. When declarer makes his contract, the defenders each pay declarer; when the contract fails, declarer pays each defender.

The general direction of rotation in the game is counter-clockwise.

Now that you have the gist of the game, on to the poem, itself . . .

The Rape of the Lock

Canto I

WHAT dire Offence from am'rous Causes springs,
What mighty Contests rise from trivial Things,
I sing--This Verse to Caryll, Muse! is due;
This, ev'n Belinda may vouchfafe to view:
Slight is the Subject, but not so the Praise,
If She inspire, and He approve my Lays.

Say what strange Motive, Goddess! cou'd compel
A well-bred Lord t'assault a gentle Belle?
Oh say what stranger Cause, yet unexplor'd,
Cou'd make a gentle Belle reject a Lord?
And dwells such Rage in softest Bosoms then?
And lodge such daring Souls in Little Men?

Sol thro' white Curtains shot a tim'rous Ray,
And op'd those Eyes that must eclipse the Day;
Now Lapdogs give themselves the rowzing Shake,
And sleepless Lovers, just at Twelve, awake:
Thrice rung the Bell, the Slipper knock'd the Ground,
And the press'd Watch return'd a silver Sound.
Belinda still her downy Pillow prest,
Her Guardian Sylph prolong'd the balmy Rest.
'Twas he had summon'd to her silent Bed
The Morning-Dream that hover'd o'er her Head.
A Youth more glitt'ring than a Birth-night Beau,
(That ev'n in Slumber caus'd her Cheek to glow)

Seem'd to her Ear his winning Lips to lay,
And thus in Whispers said, or seem'd to say.

Fairest of Mortals, thou distinguish'd Care
Of thousand bright Inhabitants of Air!
If e'er one Vision touch'd thy infant Thought,
Of all the Nurse and all the Priest have taught,
Of airy Elves by Moonlight Shadows seen,
The silver Token, and the circled Green,
Or Virgins visited by Angel-Pow'rs,
With Golden Crowns and Wreaths of heav'nly Flowers,
Hear and believe! thy own Importance know,
Nor bound thy narrow Views to Things below.
Some secret Truths from Learned Pride conceal'd,
To Maids alone and Children are reveal'd:

What tho' no Credit doubting Wits may give?
The Fair and Innocent shall still believe.
Know then, unnumbered Spirits round thee fly,
The light Militia of the lower Sky;

These, tho' unseen, are ever on the Wing,
Hang o'er the Box, and hover round the Ring.
Think what an Equipage thou hast in Air,
And view with scorn Two Pages and a Chair.
As now your own, our Beings were of old,
And once inclos'd in Woman's beauteous Mold;
Thence, by a soft Transition, we repair
From earthly Vehicles to these of Air.
Think not, when Woman's transient Breath is fled,
That all her Vanities at once are dead:
Succeeding Vanities she still regards,
And tho' she plays no more, o'erlooks the Cards.
Her Joy in gilded Chariots, when alive,
And Love of Ombre, after Death survive.
For when the Fair in all their Pride expire,
To their first Elements the Souls retire:
The Sprights of fiery Termagants in Flame
Mount up, and take a Salamander's Name.
Soft yielding Minds to Water glide away,
And sip with Nymphs, their Elemental Tea.

The graver Prude sinks downward to a Gnome,
In search of Mischief still on Earth to roam.
The light Coquettes in Sylphs aloft repair,
And sport and flutter in the Fields of Air.

Know farther yet; Whoever fair and chaste
Rejects Mankind, is by some Sylph embrac'd:
For Spirits, freed from mortal Laws, with ease
Assume what Sexes and what Shapes they please.
What guards the Purity of melting Maids,
In Courtly Balls, and Midnight Masquerades,
Safe from the treach'rous Friend, and daring Spark,
The Glance by Day, the Whisper in the Dark;
When kind Occasion prompts their warm Desires,
When Musick softens, and when Dancing fires?
'Tis but their Sylph, the wise Celestials know,
Tho' Honour is the Word with Men below.

Some Nymphs there are, too conscious of their Face,
For Life predestin'd to the Gnomes' Embrace.

These swell their Prospects and exalt their Pride,
When Offers are disdain'd, and Love deny'd.
Then gay Ideas crowd the vacant Brain;
While Peers and Dukes, and all their sweeping Train,
And Garters, Stars, and Coronets appear,
And in soft Sounds, Your Grace salutes their Ear.
'Tis these that early taint the Female Soul,
Instruct the Eyes of young Coquettes to roll,
Teach Infants Cheeks a bidden Blush to know,
And little Hearts to flutter at a Beau.

Oft when the World imagine Women stray,
The Sylphs thro' mystick Mazes guide their Way,
Thro' all the giddy Circle they pursue,
And old Impertinence expel by new.
What tender Maid but must a Victim fall
To one Man's Treat, but for another's Ball?
When Florio speaks, what Virgin could withstand,
If gentle Damon did not squeeze her Hand?

With varying Vanities, from ev'ry Part,
They shift the moving Toyshop of their Heart;
Where Wigs with Wigs, with Sword-knots Sword-knots strive,
Beaus banish Beaus, and Coaches Coaches drive.
This erring Mortals Levity may call,
Oh blind to Truth! the Sylphs contrive it all.

Of these am I, who thy Protection claim,
A watchful Sprite, and Ariel is my Name.
Late, as I rang'd the Crystal Wilds of Air,
In the clear Mirror of thy ruling Star
I saw, alas! some dread Event impend,
E're to the Main this Morning Sun descend.
But Heav'n reveals not what, or how, or where:
Warn'd by thy Sylph, oh Pious Maid beware!
This to disclose is all thy Guardian can.
Beware of all, but most beware of Man!

He said; when Shock, who thought she slept too long,
Leapt up, and wak'd his Mistress with his Tongue.

'Twas then Belinda! if Report say true,
Thy Eyes first open'd on a Billet-doux;
Wounds, Charms, and Ardors, were no sooner read,
But all the Vision vanish'd from thy Head.

And now, unveil'd, the Toilet stands display'd,
Each Silver Vase in mystic Order laid.
First, rob'd in White, the Nymph intent adores
With Head uncover'd, the cosmetic Pow'rs.
A heav'nly Image in the Glass appears,
To that she bends, to that her Eyes she rears;
Th' inferior Priestess, at her Altar's side,
Trembling, begins the sacred Rites of Pride.
Unnumber'd Treasures ope at once, and here
The various Off'rings of the World appear;
From each she nicely culls with curious Toil,
And decks the Goddess with the glitt'ring Spoil.
This Casket India's glowing Gems unlocks,
And all Arabia breathes from yonder Box.

The Tortoise here and Elephant unite,
Transform'd to Combs, the speckled and the white.
Here Files of Pins extend their shining Rows,
Puffs, Powders, Patches, Bibles, Billet-doux.
Now awful Beauty puts on all its Arms;
The Fair each moment rises in her Charms,
Repairs her Smiles, awakens ev'ry Grace,
And calls forth all the Wonders of her Face;
Sees by Degrees a purer Blush arise,
And keener Lightnings quicken in her Eyes.
The busy Sylphs surround their darling Care;
These set the Head, and those divide the Hair,
Some fold the Sleeve, while others plait the Gown;
And Betty's prais'd for Labours not her own.

Canto II

NOT with more Glories, in th' Etherial Plain,
The Sun first rises o'er the purpled Main,
Than issuing forth, the Rival of his Beams
Lanch'd on the Bosom of the Silver Thames.
Fair Nymphs, and well-drest Youths around her shone,
But ev'ry Eye was fix'd on her alone.
On her white Breast a sparkling Cross she wore,
Which Jews might kiss, and Infidels adore.

Her lively Looks a sprightly Mind disclose,
Quick as her Eyes, and as unfix'd as those:
Favours to none, to all she Smiles extends,

Oft she rejects, but never once offends.
Bright as the Sun, her Eyes the Gazers strike,
And, like the sun, they shine on all alike.
Yet graceful Ease, and Sweetness void of Pride,
Might hide her Faults, if Belles had faults to hide:
If to her share some Female Errors fall,
Look on her Face, and you'll forget 'em all.

This Nymph, to the Destruction of Mankind,
Nourish'd two Locks, which graceful hung behind
In equal Curls, and well conspir'd to deck
With shining Ringlets her smooth Iv'ry Neck.
Love in these Labyrinths his Slaves detains,
And mighty Hearts are held in slender Chains.
With hairy Sprindges we the Birds betray,
Slight Lines of Hair surprize the Finny Prey,

Fair Tresses Man's Imperial Race insnare,
And Beauty draws us with a single Hair.

Th' Adventrous Baron the bright Locks admir'd,
He saw, he wish'd, and to the Prize aspir'd:
Resolv'd to win, he meditates the way,
By Force to ravish, or by Fraud betray;
For when Success a Lover's Toil attends,
Few ask, if Fraud or Force attain'd his Ends.

For this, e're Phoebus rose, he had implor'd
Propitious Heav'n, and ev'ry Pow'r ador'd,
But chiefly Love---to Love an Altar built,
Of twelve vast French Romances, neatly gilt.
There lay three Garters, half a Pair of Gloves;
And all the Trophies of his former Loves.
With tender Billet-doux he lights the Pyre,
And breathes three am'rous Sighs to raise the Fire.
Then prostrate falls, and begs with ardent Eyes
Soon to obtain, and long possess the Prize:
The Pow'rs gave Ear, and granted half his Pray'r,
The rest, the Winds dispers'd in empty Air.

But now secure the painted Vessel glides,
The Sun-beams trembling on the floating Tydes,
While melting Musick steals upon the Sky,
And soften'd Sounds along the Waters die.
Smooth flow the Waves, the Zephyrs gently play
Belinda smil'd, and all the World was gay.

All but the Sylph----With careful Thoughts opprest,
Th' impending Woe sate heavy on his Breast.
He summons strait his Denizens of Air;
The lucid Squadrons round the Sails repair:
Soft o'er the Shrouds Aerial Whispers breathe,
That seem'd but Zephyrs to the Train beneath.
Some to the Sun their Insect-Wings unfold,
Waft on the Breeze, or sink in Clouds of Gold.
Transparent Forms, too fine for mortal Sight,
Their fluid Bodies half dissolv'd in Light.
Loose to the Wind their airy Garments flew,
Thin glitt'ring Textures of the filmy Dew;
Dipt in the richest Tincture of the Skies,
Where Light disports in ever-mingling Dies,
While ev'ry Beam new transient Colours flings,
Colours that change whene'er they wave their Wings.
Amid the Circle, on the gilded Mast,
Superior by the Head, was Ariel plac'd;
His Purple Pinions opening to the Sun,
He rais'd his Azure Wand, and thus begun.

Ye Sylphs and Sylphids, to your Chief give Ear,
Fays, Fairies, Genii, Elves, and Daemons hear!
Ye know the Spheres and various Tasks assign'd,
By Laws Eternal, to th' Aerial Kind.
Some in the Fields of purest AEther play,
And bask and whiten in the Blaze of Day.
Some guide the Course of wandring Orbs on high,
Or roll the Planets thro' the boundless Sky.
Some less refin'd, beneath the Moon's pale Light
Hover, and catch the shooting stars by Night;
Or suck the Mists in grosser Air below,
Or dip their Pinions in the painted Bow,
Or brew fierce Tempests on the wintry Main,
Or o'er the Glebe distill the kindly Rain.
Others on Earth o'er human Race preside,
Watch all their Ways, and all their Actions guide:
Of these the Chief the Care of Nations own,
And guard with Arms Divine the British Throne.

Our humbler Province is to tend the Fair,
Not a less pleasing, tho' less glorious Care.
To save the Powder from too rude a Gale,
Nor let th' imprison'd Essences exhale,
To draw fresh Colours from the vernal Flow'rs,
To steal from Rainbows ere they drop in Show'rs

A brighter Wash; to curl their waving Hairs,
Assist their Blushes, and inspire their Airs;
Nay oft, in Dreams, Invention we bestow,
To change a Flounce, or add a Furbelo.

This Day, black Omens threat the brightest Fair
That e'er deserv'd a watchful Spirit's Care;
Some dire Disaster, or by Force, or Slight,
But what, or where, the Fates have wrapt in Night.
Whether the Nymph shall break Diana's Law,
Or some frail China Jar receive a Flaw,
Or stain her Honour, or her new Brocade,
Forget her Pray'rs, or miss a Masquerade,
Or lose her Heart, or Necklace, at a Ball;
Or whether Heav'n has doom'd that Shock must fall.
Haste then ye Spirits! to your Charge repair;
The flutt'ring Fan be Zephyretta's Care;
The Drops to thee, Brillante, we consign;
And Momentilla, let the Watch be thine;
Do thou, Crispissa, tend her fav'rite Lock;
Ariel himself shall be the Guard of Shock.

To Fifty chosen Sylphs, of special Note,
We trust th' important Charge, the Petticoat:
Oft have we known that sev'nfold Fence to fail;
Tho' stiff with Hoops, and arm'd with Ribs of Whale.
Form a strong Line about the Silver Bound,
And guard the wide Circumference around.

Whatever spirit, careless of his Charge,
His Post neglects, or leaves the Fair at large,
Shall feel sharp Vengeance soon o'ertake his Sins,
Be stopt in Vials, or transfixt with Pins;
Or plung'd in Lakes of bitter Washes lie,
Or wedg'd whole Ages in a Bodkin's Eye:
Gums and Pomatums shall his Flight restrain,
While clog'd he beats his silken Wings in vain;
Or Alom-Stypticks with contracting Power
Shrink his thin Essence like a rivell'd Flower.
Or as Ixion fix'd, the Wretch shall feel
The giddy Motion of the whirling Mill,
In Fumes of burning Chocolate shall glow,
And tremble at the Sea that froaths below!

He spoke; the Spirits from the Sails descend;

Some, Orb in Orb, around the Nymph extend,
Some thrid the mazy Ringlets of her Hair,
Some hang upon the Pendants of her Ear;
With beating Hearts the dire Event they wait,
Anxious, and trembling for the Birth of Fate.

Canto III

CLOSE by those Meads for ever crown'd with Flow'rs,
Where Thames with Pride surveys his rising Tow'rs,
There stands a Structure of Majestick Frame,
Which from the neighb'ring Hampton takes its Name.
Here Britain's Statesmen oft the Fall foredoom
Of Foreign Tyrants, and of Nymphs at home;
Here Thou, great Anna!* whom three Realms obey,
Dost sometimes Counsel take--and sometimes Tea.
Hither the Heroes and the Nymphs resort,
To taste awhile the Pleasures of a Court;
In various Talk th' instructive hours they past,
Who gave the Ball, or paid the Visit last:
One speaks the Glory of the British Queen,
And one describes a charming Indian Screen;
A third interprets Motions, Looks, and Eyes;
At ev'ry Word a Reputation dies.
Snuff, or the Fan, supply each Pause of Chat,
With singing, laughing, ogling, and all that.

Mean while declining from the Noon of Day,
The Sun obliquely shoots his burning Ray;
The hungry Judges soon the Sentence sign,
And Wretches hang that Jury-men may Dine;
The Merchant from th'Exchange returns in Peace,
And the long Labours of the Toilette cease----
Belinda now, whom Thirst of Fame invites,
Burns to encounter two adventrous Knights,
At Ombre singly to decide their Doom;
And swells her Breast with Conquests yet to come.
Strait the three Bands prepare in Arms to join,
Each Band the number of the Sacred Nine.
Soon as she spreads her Hand, th' Aerial Guard
Descend, and sit on each important Card,
First Ariel perch'd upon a Matadore,
Then each, according to the Rank they bore;
For Sylphs, yet mindful of their ancient Race,

Are, as when Women, wondrous fond of place.

Behold, four Kings in Majesty rever'd,
With hoary Whiskers and a forky Beard;
And four fair Queens whose hands sustain a Flow'r,
Th' expressive Emblem of their softer Pow'r;
Four Knaves in Garbs succinct, a trusty Band,
Caps on their heads, and Halberds in their hand;
And Particolour'd Troops, a shining Train,
Draw forth to Combat on the Velvet Plain.
The skilful Nymph reviews her Force with Care;
Let Spades be Trumps, she said, and Trumps they were.
Now move to War her Sable Matadores,
In Show like Leaders of the swarthy Moors.
Spadillio first, unconquerable Lord!
Led off two captive Trumps, and swept the Board.
As many more Manillio forc'd to yield,
And march'd a Victor from the verdant Field.
Him Basto follow'd, but his Fate more hard
Gain'd but one Trump and one Plebeian Card.
With his broad Sabre next, a Chief in Years,
The hoary Majesty of Spades appears;
Puts forth one manly Leg, to sight reveal'd;
The rest his many-colour'd Robe conceal'd.
The Rebel-Knave, who dares his Prince engage,
Proves the just Victim of his Royal Rage.
Ev'n mighty Pam that Kings and Queens o'erthrow,
And mow'd down Armies in the Fights of Lu,
Sad Chance of War! now, destitute of Aid,
Falls undistinguish'd by the Victor Spade!
Thus far both Armies to Belinda yield;
Now to the Baron Fate inclines the Field.
His warlike Amazon her Host invades,
Th' Imperial Consort of the Crown of Spades.
The Club's black Tyrant first her Victim dy'd,
Spite of his haughty Mien, and barb'rous Pride:
What boots the Regal Circle on his Head,
His Giant Limbs in State unwieldy spread?
That long behind he trails his pompous Robe,
And of all Monarchs only grasps the Globe?

The Baron now his Diamonds pours apace;
Th' embroider'd King who shows but half his Face,
And his refulgent Queen, with Pow'rs combin'd,
Of broken Troops an easie Conquest find.
Clubs, Diamonds, Hearts, in wild Disorder seen,

With Throngs promiscuous strow the level Green.
Thus when dispers'd a routed Army runs,
Of Asia's Troops, and Africk's Sable Sons,
With like Confusion different Nations fly,
In various habits and of various Dye,
The pierc'd Battalions dis-united fall,
In Heaps on Heaps; one Fate o'erwhelms them all.

The Knave of Diamonds now tries his wily Arts,
And wins (oh shameful Chance!) the Queen of Hearts.
At this, the Blood the Virgin's Cheek forsook,
A livid Paleness spreads o'er all her Look;
She sees, and trembles at th' approaching Ill,
Just in the Jaws of Ruin, and Codille*.
And now, (as oft in some distemper'd State)
On one nice Trick depends the gen'ral Fate.
An Ace of Hearts steps forth: The King unseen
Lurk'd in her Hand, and mourn'd his captive Queen.
He springs to Vengeance with an eager pace,
And falls like Thunder on the prostrate Ace.
The Nymph exulting fills with Shouts the Sky,
The Walls, the Woods, and long Canals reply.
Oh thoughtless Mortals! ever blind to Fate,
Too soon dejected, and too soon elate!
Sudden these Honours shall be snatch'd away,
And curs'd for ever this Victorious Day.

For lo! the Board with Cups and Spoons is crown'd,
The Berries crackle, and the Mill turns round.
On shining Altars of Japan they raise
The silver Lamp; the fiery Spirits blaze.
From silver Spouts the grateful Liquors glide,
And China's Earth receives the smoking Tyde.
At once they gratify their Scent and Taste,
While frequent Cups prolong the rich Repast.
Strait hover round the Fair her Airy Band;
Some, as she sip'd, the fuming Liquor fann'd,
Some o'er her Lap their careful Plumes display'd,
Trembling, and conscious of the rich Brocade.
Coffee, (which makes the Politician wise,
And see thro' all things with his half shut Eyes)
Sent up in Vapours to the Baron's Brain
New Stratagems, the radiant Lock to gain.
Ah cease rash Youth! desist e'er 'tis too late,
Fear the just Gods, and think of Scylla's Fate!
Chang'd to a Bird, and sent to flit in Air,

She dearly pays for Nisus' injur'd Hair!*

But when to Mischief Mortals bend their Will,
How soon they find fit Instruments of Ill!
Just then, Clarissa drew with tempting Grace
A two-edg'd Weapon from her shining Case;
So Ladies in Romance assist their Knight,
Present the Spear, and arm him for the Fight.
He takes the Gift with rev'rence, and extends
The little Engine on his Finger's Ends:
This just behind Belinda's Neck he spread,
As o'er the fragrant Steams she bends her Head:
Swift to the Lock a thousand Sprights repair,
A thousand Wings, by turns, blow back the Hair,
And thrice they twitch'd the Diamond in her Ear,
Thrice she look'd back, and thrice the Foe drew near.
Just in that instant, anxious Ariel sought
The close Recesses of the Virgin's Thought;
As on the Nosegay in her Breast reclin'd,
He watch'd th' Ideas rising in her Mind,
Sudden he view'd, in spite of all her Art,
An Earthly Lover lurking at her Heart.
Amaz'd, confus'd, he found his Pow'r expir'd,
Resign'd to Fate, and with a Sigh retir'd.

The Peer now spreads the glitt'ring Forfex wide,
T'inclose the Lock; now joins it, to divide.
Ev'n then, before the fatal Engine clos'd,
A wretched Sylph too fondly interpos'd;
Fate urg'd the Sheers, and cut the Sylph in twain,
(But Airy Substance soon unites again)
The meeting Points that sacred Hair dissever
From the fair Head, for ever and for ever!
Then flash'd the living Lightnings from her Eyes,
And Screams of Horror rend th' affrighted Skies.
Not louder Shrieks to pitying Heav'n are cast,
When Husbands or when Lap-dogs breath their last,
Or when rich China Vessels, fal'n from high,
In glittring Dust and painted Fragments lie!

Let Wreaths of Triumph now my Temples twine,
(The Victor cry'd) the glorious Prize is mine!
While Fish in Streams, or Birds delight in Air,
Or in a Coach and Six the British Fair,
As long as Atalantis* shall be read,
Or the small Pillow grace a Lady's Bed,

While Visits shall be paid on solemn Days,
When numerous Wax-lights in bright Order blaze,
While Nymphs take Treats, or Assignations give,
So long my Honour, Name, and Praise shall live!

What Time wou'd spare, from Steel receives its date,
And Monuments, like Men, submit to Fate!
Steel cou'd the Labour of the Gods destroy,
And strike to Dust th' Imperial Tow'rs of Troy;
Steel cou'd the Works of mortal Pride confound,
And hew Triumphal Arches to the Ground.
What Wonder then, fair Nymph! thy Hairs shou'd feel
The conqu'ring Force of unresisted Steel?

Notes:
*line 7. Queen of England, 1702-14
*line 92. the loss of a card game
*lines 122-4 When Scylla cut off her father's hair, he lost both his kingdom and his life
*line 165165. A scandalous novel by Delarivier Manley (1709)

Canto IV

BUT anxious Cares the pensive Nymph opprest,
And secret Passions labour'd in her Breast.
Not youthful Kings in Battel seiz'd alive,
Not scornful Virgins who their Charms survive,
Not ardent Lovers robb'd of all their Bliss,
Not ancient Ladies when refus'd a Kiss,
Not Tyrants fierce that unrepenting die,
Not Cynthia when her Manteau's pinn'd awry,
E'er felt such Rage, Resentment and Despair,
As Thou, sad Virgin! for thy ravish'd Hair.

For, that sad moment, when the Sylphs withdrew,
And Ariel weeping from Belinda flew,
Umbriel, a dusky melancholy Spright,
As ever sully'd the fair face of Light,
Down to the Central Earth, his proper Scene,
Repairs to search the gloomy Cave of Spleen.

Swift on his sooty Pinions flitts the Gnome,
And in a Vapour reach'd the dismal Dome.
No cheerful Breeze this sullen Region knows,

The dreaded East is all the Wind that blows.
Here, in a Grotto, sheltred close from Air,
And screen'd in Shades from Day's detested Glare,
She sighs for ever on her pensive Bed,
Pain at her side, and Megrim* at her Head.

Two Handmaids wait the Throne: Alike in Place,
But diff'ring far in Figure and in Face.
Here stood Ill-nature like an ancient Maid,
Her wrinkled Form in Black and White array'd;
With store of Pray'rs, for Mornings, Nights, and Noons,
Her Hand is fill'd; her Bosom with Lampoons.

There Affectation with a sickly Mien
Shows in her Cheek the Roses of Eighteen,
Practis'd to Lisp, and hang the Head aside,
Faints into Airs, and languishes with Pride;
On the rich Quilt sinks with becoming Woe,
Wrapt in a Gown, for Sickness, and for Show.
The Fair ones feel such Maladies as these,
When each new Night-Dress gives a new Disease.

A constant Vapour o'er the Palace flies;
Strange Phantoms rising as the Mists arise;
Dreadful, as Hermit's Dreams in haunted Shades,
Or bright as Visions of expiring Maids.
Now glaring Fiends, and Snakes on rolling Spires,
Pale Spectres, gaping Tombs, and Purple Fires:
Now Lakes of liquid Gold, Elysian Scenes,
And Crystal Domes, and Angels in Machines.

Unnumber'd Throngs on ev'ry side are seen
Of Bodies chang'd to various Forms by Spleen.
Here living Teapots stand, one Arm held out,
One bent; the Handle this, and that the Spout:
A Pipkin there like Homer's Tripod walks;
Here sighs a Jar, and there a Goose Pie talks;
Men prove with Child, as pow'rful Fancy works,
And Maids turn'd Bottels, call aloud for Corks.

Safe past the Gnome thro' this fantastick Band,
A Branch of healing Spleenwort in his hand.
Then thus addrest the Pow'r--Hail wayward Queen!
Who rule the Sex to Fifty from Fifteen,
Parent of Vapors and of Female Wit,
Who give th' Hysteric or Poetic Fit,

On various Tempers act by various ways,
Make some take Physick, others scribble Plays;
Who cause the Proud their Visits to delay,
And send the Godly in a Pett, to pray.
A Nymph there is, that all thy Pow'r disdains,
And thousands more in equal Mirth maintains.
But oh! if e'er thy Gnome could spoil a Grace,
Or raise a Pimple on a beauteous Face,
Like Citron-Waters Matron's Cheeks inflame,
Or change Complexions at a losing Game;
If e'er with airy Horns I planted Heads,
Or rumpled Petticoats, or tumbled Beds,
Or caus'd Suspicion when no Soul was rude,
Or discompos'd the Head-dress of a Prude,
Or e'er to costive Lap-Dog gave Disease,
Which not the Tears of brightest Eyes could ease:
Hear me, and touch Belinda with Chagrin;
That single Act gives half the World the Spleen.

The Goddess with a discontented Air
Seems to reject him, tho' she grants his Pray'r.
A wondrous Bag with both her Hands she binds,
Like that where once Ulysses held the Winds;
There she collects the Force of Female Lungs,
Sighs, Sobs, and Passions, and the War of Tongues.
A Vial next she fills with fainting Fears,
Soft Sorrows, melting Griefs, and flowing Tears.
The Gnome rejoicing bears her Gift away,
Spreads his black Wings, and slowly mounts to Day.

Sunk in Thalestris' Arms the Nymph he found,
Her Eyes dejected and her Hair unbound.
Full o'er their Heads the swelling Bag he rent,
And all the Furies issued at the Vent.
Belinda burns with more than mortal Ire,
And fierce Thalestris fans the rising Fire.
O wretched Maid! she spread her hands, and cry'd,
(While Hampton's Ecchos, wretched Maid reply'd)
Was it for this you took such constant Care
The Bodkin, Comb, and Essence to prepare;
For this your Locks in Paper-Durance bound,
For this with tort'ring Irons wreath'd around?
For this with Fillets strain'd your tender Head,
And bravely bore the double Loads of Lead?
Gods! shall the Ravisher display your Hair,
While the Fops envy, and the Ladies stare!

Honour forbid! at whose unrival'd Shrine
Ease, Pleasure, Virtue, All, our Sex resign.
Methinks already I your Tears survey,
Already hear the horrid things they say,
Already see you a degraded Toast,
And all your Honour in a Whisper lost!
How shall I, then, your helpless Fame defend?
'Twill then be Infamy to seem your Friend!
And shall this Prize, th' inestimable Prize,
Expos'd thro' Crystal to the gazing Eyes,
And heighten'd by the Diamond's circling Rays,
On that Rapacious Hand for ever blaze?
Sooner shall Grass in Hide-Park Circus* grow,
And Wits take Lodgings in the Sound of Bow*;
Sooner let Earth, Air, Sea, to Chaos fall,
Men, Monkies, Lap-dogs, Parrots, perish all!

She said; then raging to Sir Plume repairs,
And bids her Beau demand the precious Hairs:
(Sir Plume, of Amber Snuff-box justly vain,
And the nice Conduct of a clouded Cane)
With earnest Eyes, and round unthinking Face,
He first the Snuff-box open'd, then the Case,
And thus broke out---"My Lord, why, what the Devil?
"Zounds! damn the Lock! 'fore Gad, you must be civil!
"Plague on't! 'tis past a Jest---nay prithee, Pox!
"Give her the Hair---he spoke, and rapp'd his Box.

It grieves me much (reply'd the Peer again)
Who speaks so well shou'd ever speak in vain.
But by this Lock, this sacred Lock I swear,
(Which never more shall join its parted Hair,
Which never more its Honours shall renew,
Clipt from the lovely Head where late it grew)
That while my Nostrils draw the vital Air,
This Hand, which won it, shall for ever wear.
He spoke, and speaking, in proud Triumph spread
The long-contended Honours of her Head.

But Umbriel, hateful Gnome! forbears not so;
He breaks the Vial whence the Sorrows flow.
Then see! the Nymph in beauteous Grief appears,
Her Eyes half languishing, half drown'd in Tears;
On her heav'd Bosom hung her drooping Head,
Which, with a Sigh, she rais'd; and thus she said.

For ever curs'd be this detested Day,
Which snatch'd my best, my fav'rite Curl away!
Happy! ah ten times happy, had I been,
If Hampton-Court these Eyes had never seen!
Yet am not I the first mistaken Maid,
By Love of Courts to num'rous Ills betray'd.
Oh had I rather un-admir'd remain'd
In some lone Isle, or distant Northern Land;
Where the gilt Chariot never marks the way,
Where none learn Ombre, none e'er taste Bohea*!
There kept my Charms conceal'd from mortal Eye,
Like Roses that in Desarts bloom and die.
What mov'd my Mind with youthful Lords to rome?
O had I stay'd, and said my Pray'rs at home!
'Twas this, the Morning Omens seem'd to tell;
Thrice from my trembling hand the Patch-box fell;
The tott'ring China shook without a Wind,
Nay, Poll sate mute, and Shock was most Unkind!
A Sylph too warn'd me of the Threats of Fate,
In mystic Visions, now believ'd too late!
See the poor Remnants of these slighted Hairs!
My hands shall rend what ev'n thy Rapine spares:
These, in two sable Ringlets taught to break,
Once gave new Beauties to the snowie Neck.
The Sister-Lock now sits uncouth, alone,
And in its Fellow's Fate foresees its own;
Uncurl'd it hangs, the fatal Sheers demands;
And tempts once more thy sacrilegious Hands.
Oh hadst thou, Cruel! been content to seize
Hairs less in sight, or any Hairs but these!

Notes:
24 Migraine
117. where the fashionable drove their carriages
118. Bow Church in Cheapside, the mercantile section of London
156. A kind of tea

Canto V

She said: the pitying Audience melt in Tears,
But Fate and Jove had stopp'd the Baron's Ears.
In vain Thalestris with Reproach assails,
For who can move when fair Belinda fails?
Not half to fixt the Trojan* cou'd remain,

While Anna begg'd and Dido rag'd in vain.
Then grave Clarissa graceful wav'd her Fan;
Silence ensu'd, and thus the Nymph began.
Say, why are Beauties prais'd and honour'd most,
The wise Man's Passion, and the vain Man's Toast?
Why deck'd with all that Land and Sea afford,
Why Angels call'd, and Angel-like ador'd?
Why round our Coaches crowd the white-glov'd Beaus,
Why bows the Side-box from its inmost Rows?
How vain are all these Glories, all our Pains,
Unless good Sense preserve what Beauty gains:
That Men may say, when we the Front-box grace,
Behold the first in Virtue, as in Face!
Oh! if to dance all Night, and dress all Day,
Charm'd the Small-pox, or chas'd old Age away;
Who would not scorn what Huswife's Cares produce,
Or who would learn one earthly Thing of Use?
To patch, nay ogle, might become a Saint,
Nor could it sure be such a Sin to paint.
But since, alas! frail Beauty must decay,
Curl'd or uncurl'd, since Locks will turn to grey,
Since paint'd, or not paint'd, all shall fade,
And she who scorns a Man, must die a Maid;
What then remains, but well our Pow'r to use,
And keep good Humour still whate'er we lose?
And trust me, Dear! good Humour can prevail,
When Airs, and Flights, and Screams, and Scolding fail.
Beauties in vain their pretty Eyes may roll;
Charms strike the Sight, but Merit wins the Soul.
So spake the Dame, but no Applause ensu'd;
Belinda frown'd, Thalestris call'd her Prude.
To Arms, to Arms! the fierce Virago cries,
And swift as Lightning to the Combate flies.
All side in Parties, and begin th' Attack;
Fans clap, Silks russle, and tough Whalebones crack;
Heroes and Heroins Shouts confus'dly rise,
And base, and treble Voices strike the Skies.
No common Weapons in their Hands are found,
Like Gods they fight, nor dread a mortal Wound.

So when bold Homer makes the Gods engage,
And heav'nly Breasts with human Passions rage;
'Gainst Pallas, Mars; Latona, Hermes arms;
And all Olympus rings with loud Alarms.
Jove's Thunder roars, Heav'n trembles all around;
Blue Neptune storms, the bellowing Deeps resound;

Earth shakes her nodding Tow'rs, the Ground gives way;
And the pale Ghosts start at the Flash of Day!

Triumphant Umbriel on a Sconce's Height
Clapt his glad Wings, and sate to view the Fight,
Propt on their Bodkin Spears, the Sprights survey
The growing Combat, or assist the Fray.
While thro' the Press enrag'd Thalestries flies,
And scatters Deaths around from both her Eyes,
A Beau and Witling perish'd in the Throng,
One dy'd in Metaphor, and one in Song.
O cruel Nymph! a living Death I bear,
Cry'd Dapperwit, and sunk beside his Chair.
A mournful Glance Sir Fopling upwards cast,
Those Eyes are made so killing---was his last:
Thus on Meander's flow'ry Margin lies
Th' expiring Swan, and as he sings he dies.

When bold Sir Plume had drawn Clarissa down,
Chloe stept in, and kill'd him with a Frown;
She smil'd to see the doughty Hero slain,
But at her Smile, the Beau reviv'd again.

Now Jove suspends his golden Scales in Air,
Weighs the Mens Wits against the Lady's Hair;
The doubtful Beam long nods from side to side;
At length the Wits mount up, the Hairs subside.

See fierce Belinda on the Baron flies,
With more than usual Lightning in her Eyes;
Nor fear'd the Chief th' unequal Fight to try,
Who sought no more than on his Foe to die.
But this bold Lord, with manly Strength indu'd,
She with one Finger and a Thumb subdu'd,
Just where the Breath of Life his Nostrils drew,
A Charge of Snuff the wily Virgin threw;
The Gnomes direct, to ev'ry Atome just,
The pungent Grains of titillating Dust.
Sudden, with starting Tears each Eye o'erflows,
And the high Dome re-ecchoes to his Nose.

Now meet thy Fate, incens'd Belinda cry'd,
And drew a deadly Bodkin from her Side.
(The same, his ancient Personage to deck,
Her great great Grandsire wore about his Neck
In three Seal-Rings; which after, melted down,

Form'd a vast Buckle for his Widow's Gown:
Her infant Grandame's Whistle next it grew,
The Bells she gingled, and the Whistle blew;
Then in a Bodkin grac'd her Mother's Hairs,
Which long she wore, and now Belinda wears.)

Boast not my Fall (he cry'd) insulting Foe!
Thou by some other shalt be laid as low.
Nor think, to die dejects my lofty Mind;
All that I dread, is leaving you behind!
Rather than so, ah let me still survive,
And burn in Cupid's Flames,---but burn alive.

Restore the Lock! she cries; and all around
Restore the Lock! the vaulted Roofs rebound.
Not fierce Othello in so loud a Strain
Roar'd for the Handkerchief that caus'd his Pain.
But see how oft Ambitious Aims are cross'd,
And Chiefs contend 'till all the Prize is lost!
The Lock, obtain'd with Guilt, and kept with Pain,
In ev'ry place is sought, but sought in vain:
With such a Prize no Mortal must be blest,
So Heav'n decrees! with Heav'n who can contest?

Some thought it mounted to the Lunar Sphere,
Since all things lost on Earth, are treasur'd there.
There Heroe's Wits are kept in pondrous Vases,
And Beau's in Snuff-boxes and Tweezer-Cases.
There broken Vows, and Death-bed Alms are found,
And Lovers Hearts with Ends of Riband bound;
The Courtiers Promises, and Sick Man's Pray'rs,
The Smiles of Harlots, and the Tears of Heirs,
Cages for Gnats, and Chains to Yoak a Flea;
Dry'd Butterflies, and Tomes of Casuistry.

But trust the Muse---she saw it upward rise,
Tho' mark'd by none but quick Poetic Eyes:
(So Rome's great Founder* to the Heav'ns withdrew,
To Proculus alone confess'd in view.)
A sudden Star, it shot thro' liquid Air,
And drew behind a radiant Trail of Hair.
Not Berenice's Locks* first rose so bright,
The heav'ns bespangling with dishevel'd light.
The Sylphs behold it kindling as it flies,
And pleas'd pursue its Progress thro' the Skies.

This the Beau-monde shall from the Mall* survey,
And hail with Musick its propitious Ray.
This, the blest Lover shall for Venus take,
And send up Vows from Rosamonda's Lake*.
This Partridge* soon shall view in cloudless Skies,
When next he looks thro' Galilaeo's Eyes;
And hence th' Egregious Wizard shall foredoom
The Fate of Louis, and the Fall of Rome.

Then cease, bright Nymph! to mourn the ravish'd Hair
Which adds new Glory to the shining Sphere!
Not all the Tresses that fair Head can boast
Shall draw such Envy as the Lock you lost.
For, after all the Murders of your Eye,
When, after Millions slain, your self shall die;
When those fair Suns shall sett, as sett they must,
And all those Tresses shall be laid in Dust;
This Lock, the Muse shall consecrate to Fame,
And mid'st the Stars inscribe Belinda's Name!

Notes:
5. Aeneas.
125. Romulus, according to the report of Livy .
129. A lock of Berenice's hair was transformed into a constellation.
133. Pall Mall.
134. a pond in St. James's Park, London.
137. a popular astrologer.

(1712-1714)

LESSON 15

<u>Phillis Wheatley (1753?-1784)</u>

Phillis Wheatley began writing poetry at age 13, and modeled her work on the styles of English poets, John Milton, Thomas Grey, and Alexander Pope. Her book, *Poems on Various Subjects, Religious and Moral* identified the author as, "by Phillis Wheatley, Negro Servant to Mr. John Wheatley, of Boston, in New England" (This, of course, makes her one of the earliest American poets.)

Here are the titles of the poems contained in this volume. Can you identify a theme? If you would like to read more, you can find the full text at **http://www.uoregon.edu/~rbear/wheatley.html#38**.

- **To Mæcenas**
- **On Virtue**
- **To the University of Cambridge**, in New England
- **To the King's Most Excellent Majesty**
- **On being brought from Africa**
- **On the Rev. Dr. Sewell**
- **On the Rev. Mr. George Whitefield**

- **On the Death of a young Lady** of five Years of Age
- **On the Death of a young Gentleman**
- **To a Lady on the Death of her Husband**
- **Goliath of Gath**
- **Thoughts on the Works of Providence**
- **To a Lady on the Death of three Relations**
- **To a Clergyman** on the Death of his Lady
- **An Hymn to the Morning**
- **An Hymn to the Evening**
- **On Isaiah lxiii. 1------8**
- **On Recollection**
- **On Imagination**
- **A Funeral Poem** on the Death of an Infant aged twelve Months
- **To Captain H. D.** of the 65th Regiment
- **To the Right Hon. William,** Earl of Dartmouth
- **Ode to Neptune**
- **To a Lady on her coming to North America** with her Son, for the Recovery of her Health
- **To a Lady on her remarkable Preservation** in a Hurricane in North Carolina
- **To a Lady and her Children,** on the Death of her Son and their Brother.
- **To a Gentleman and Lady** on the Death of the Lady's Brother and Sister, and a
  Child of the Name of *Avis,* aged one Year.
- **On the Death of Dr. Samuel Marshall**
- **To a Gentleman** on his Voyage to Great-Britain, for the Recovery of his Health
- **To the Rev. Dr. Thomas Amory** on reading his Sermons on Daily Devotion, in which that Duty is recommended and assisted
- **On the Death of J. C. an Infant**
- **An Hymn to Humanity**
- **To the Hon. T. H. Esq;** on the Death of his Daughter
- **Niobe in Distress for her Children** slain by Apollo, from *Ovid's* Metamorphoses, Book VI, and from a View of the Painting of Mr. *Richard Wilson*
- **To S. M. a young African Painter,** on seeing his Works
- **To his Honour the Lieutenant-Governor,** on the Death of his Lady
- **A Farewel to America**
- **A Rebus by I. B.**
- **An Answer to ditto,** by *Phillis Wheatley*

On Being Brought from Africa to America

'Twas mercy brought me from my *Pagan* land,
Taught my benighted soul to understand
That there's a God, that there's a *Saviour* too:
Once I redemption neither sought nor knew.
Some view our sable race with scornful eye,
"Their colour is a diabolic die."
Remember, *Christians*, *Negros*, black as *Cain*,
May be refin'd, and join th' angelic train.

Thoughts on the Works of Providence (excerpt)

Arise, my soul, on wings enraptur'd rise
To praise the monarch of the earth and skies,
Whose goodness and beneficence appear
As round its center moves the rolling year,
Or when the morning lgows with rosy charms,
Or the sun slumbers in the ocean's arms:
Of light divine be a rich portion lent
To guide my soul, and favour my intend.
Celestial muse, my arduous flight sustain,
And raise my mind to a seraphic strain!

4 Georges, WIlliam

THOMAS GRAY (1716-1771)

Now, back to England. Thomas Gray is sometimes seen as a transitional poet, a bridge between the Neoclassical and Romantic periods. How is his like the other Neoclassical writers you have read so far? How not so like them? (You can make the connections between Gray and the Romantic writers later.)

Ode on the Death of a Favourite Cat Drowned in a Tub of Goldfishes

'Twas on a lofty vase's side,
Where China's gayest art had dy'd
The azure flow'rs that blow;
Demurest of the tabby kind,
The pensive Selima, reclin'd,
Gazed on the lake below.

Her conscious tail her joy declar'd;
The fair round face, the snowy beard,
The velvet of her paws,
Her coat, that with the tortoise vies,
Her ears of jet, and emerald eyes,
She saw: and purr'd applause.

Still had she gaz'd; but 'midst the tide
Two angel forms were seen to glide,

The Genii of the stream;
Their scaly armour's Tyrian hue
Thro' richest purple to the view
Betray'd a golden gleam.

The hapless Nymph with wonder saw:
A whisker first and then a claw,
With many an ardent wish,
She stretch'd in vain to reach the prize.
What female heart can gold despise?
What cat's averse to fish?

Presumptuous Maid! with looks intent
Again she stretch'd, again she bent,
Nor knew the gulf between.
(Malignant Fate sat by, and smil'd)
The slipp'ry verge her feet beguil'd,
She tumbled headlong in.

Eight times emerging from the flood
She mew'd to ev'ry wat'ry god,
Some speedy aid to send.
No Dolphin came, no Nereid stirr'd;
Nor cruel Tom, nor Susan heard.
A Fav'rite has no friend!

From hence, ye Beauties, undeceiv'd,
Know, one false step is ne'er retriev'd,
And be with caution bold.
Not all that tempts your wand'ring eyes
And heedless hearts is lawful prize,
Nor all, that glisters, gold.

Read the poem aloud to yourself at least once. Then read again and make your own annotations.

Elegy Written in a Country Churchyard

The curfew tolls the knell of parting day,
The lowing herd wind slowly o'er the lea,
The plowman homeward plods his weary way,
And leaves the world to darkness and to me.

Now fades the glimm'ring landscape on the sight,
And all the air a solemn stillness holds,
Save where the beetle wheels his droning flight,
And drowsy tinklings lull the distant folds;

Save that from yonder ivy-mantled tow'r
The moping owl does to the moon complain
Of such, as wand'ring near her secret bow'r,
Molest her ancient solitary reign.

Beneath those rugged elms, that yew-tree's shade,
Where heaves the turf in many a mould'ring heap,
Each in his narrow cell for ever laid,
The rude forefathers of the hamlet sleep.

The breezy call of incense-breathing Morn,
The swallow twitt'ring from the straw-built shed,
The cock's shrill clarion, or the echoing horn,
No more shall rouse them from their lowly bed.

For them no more the blazing hearth shall burn,
Or busy housewife ply her evening care:
No children run to lisp their sire's return,
Or climb his knees the envied kiss to share.

Oft did the harvest to their sickle yield,
Their furrow oft the stubborn glebe has broke;
How jocund did they drive their team afield!
How bow'd the woods beneath their sturdy stroke!

Let not Ambition mock their useful toil,
Their homely joys, and destiny obscure;
Nor Grandeur hear with a disdainful smile
The short and simple annals of the poor.

The boast of heraldry, the pomp of pow'r,
  And all that beauty, all that wealth e'er gave,
Awaits alike th' inevitable hour.
  The paths of glory lead but to the grave.

Nor you, ye proud, impute to these the fault,
  If Mem'ry o'er their tomb no trophies raise,
Where thro' the long-drawn aisle and fretted vault
  The pealing anthem swells the note of praise.

Can storied urn or animated bust
  Back to its mansion call the fleeting breath?
Can Honour's voice provoke the silent dust,
  Or Flatt'ry soothe the dull cold ear of Death?

Perhaps in this neglected spot is laid
  Some heart once pregnant with celestial fire;
Hands, that the rod of empire might have sway'd,
  Or wak'd to ecstasy the living lyre.

But Knowledge to their eyes her ample page
  Rich with the spoils of time did ne'er unroll;
Chill Penury repress'd their noble rage,
  And froze the genial current of the soul.

Full many a gem of purest ray serene,
  The dark unfathom'd caves of ocean bear:
Full many a flow'r is born to blush unseen,
  And waste its sweetness on the desert air.

Some village-Hampden, that with dauntless breast
  The little tyrant of his fields withstood;
Some mute inglorious Milton here may rest,
  Some Cromwell guiltless of his country's blood.

Th' applause of list'ning senates to command,
  The threats of pain and ruin to despise,
To scatter plenty o'er a smiling land,
  And read their hist'ry in a nation's eyes,

Their lot forbade: nor circumscrib'd alone
  Their growing virtues, but their crimes confin'd;
Forbade to wade through slaughter to a throne,
  And shut the gates of mercy on mankind,

The struggling pangs of conscious truth to hide,
  To quench the blushes of ingenuous shame,

Or heap the shrine of Luxury and Pride
With incense kindled at the Muse's flame.

Far from the madding crowd's ignoble strife,
Their sober wishes never learn'd to stray;
Along the cool sequester'd vale of life
They kept the noiseless tenor of their way.

Yet ev'n these bones from insult to protect,
Some frail memorial still erected nigh,
With uncouth rhymes and shapeless sculpture deck'd,
Implores the passing tribute of a sigh.

]

Their name, their years, spelt by th' unletter'd muse,
The place of fame and elegy supply:
And many a holy text around she strews,
That teach the rustic moralist to die.

For who to dumb Forgetfulness a prey,
This pleasing anxious being e'er resign'd,
Left the warm precincts of the cheerful day,
Nor cast one longing, ling'ring look behind?

On some fond breast the parting soul relies,
Some pious drops the closing eye requires;
Ev'n from the tomb the voice of Nature cries,
Ev'n in our ashes live their wonted fires.

For thee, who mindful of th' unhonour'd Dead
Dost in these lines their artless tale relate;
If chance, by lonely contemplation led,
Some kindred spirit shall inquire thy fate,

Haply some hoary-headed swain may say,
"Oft have we seen him at the peep of dawn
Brushing with hasty steps the dews away
To meet the sun upon the upland lawn.

"There at the foot of yonder nodding beech
That wreathes its old fantastic roots so high,
His listless length at noontide would he stretch,
And pore upon the brook that babbles by.

"Hard by yon wood, now smiling as in scorn,
Mutt'ring his wayward fancies he would rove,

Now drooping, woeful wan, like one forlorn,
Or craz'd with care, or cross'd in hopeless love.

"One morn I miss'd him on the custom'd hill,
Along the heath and near his fav'rite tree;
Another came; nor yet beside the rill,
Nor up the lawn, nor at the wood was he;

"The next with dirges due in sad array
Slow thro' the church-way path we saw him borne.
Approach and read (for thou canst read) the lay,
Grav'd on the stone beneath yon aged thorn."

THE EPITAPH

Here rests his head upon the lap of Earth
A youth to Fortune and to Fame unknown.
Fair Science frown'd not on his humble birth,
And Melancholy mark'd him for her own.

Large was his bounty, and his soul sincere,
Heav'n did a recompense as largely send:
He gave to Mis'ry all he had, a tear,
He gain'd from Heav'n ('twas all he wish'd) a friend.

No farther seek his merits to disclose,
Or draw his frailties from their dread abode,
(There they alike in trembling hope repose)
The bosom of his Father and his God.

IF YOU DIDN'T READ IT ALOUD TO YOURSELF, GO BACK AND READ IT AGAIN OUT LOUD.

Lesson 16

OLIVER GOLDSMITH (1728-1774)

She Stoops to Conquer

Oliver Goldsmith was born in Ireland, the son of a poor country pastor. Abused by the teachers and tormented by the students, Oliver's educational experience was, by all accounts, horrible. He unsuccessfully studied medicine and law. Hoping to have better success in America, he bought passage to America, but missed the ship. After this, he wandered through Europe for several years, supporting himself in a variety of ways (sometimes by playing his flute).

When he finally did return to London, he supported himself by taking a variety of writing jobs which produced a mix of mediocre and brilliant work. But as he was given to gambling, drunkenness, and general foolishness, Goldsmith was constantly in debt, and frequently in trouble.

Among the most remarkable of his literary works were his "laughing comedies" which did, in fact, change the direction of English theater. The English theater of Goldsmith's time was dominated by "sentimental comedies. In his essay: *An Essay on the Theatre; Or, a Comparison Between Laughing and Sentimental Comedy,* Goldsmith describes "Sentimental Comedy" this way:

> a new species of dramatic composition has been introduced, under the name of *sentimental comedy*, in which the virtues of private life are exhibited, rather than the vices exposed; and the distresses rather than the faults of mankind make our interest in the piece. These comedies have had of late great success, perhaps from their novelty, and also from their flattering everyman in his favorite foible. In these plays almost all the characters are good, and exceedingly generous; they are lavish

> enough of their *tin* money on the stage; and though they want humor, have abundance of sentiment and feeling. If they happen to have faults or foibles, the spectator is taught, not only to pardon, but to applaud them, in consideration of the goodness of their hearts; so that folly, instead of being ridiculed, is commended, and the comedy aims at touching our passions without the power of being truly pathetic. (Goldsmith)

While Goldsmith does grant "that these sentimental pieces do often amuse us," he goes on to ask "whether the true comedy would not amuse us more?" All that was necessary to produce such a play, says Goldsmith in the same essay, was to

> deck out the hero with a riband, or give the heroine a title, then to put an insipid dialogue, withough character or humor, into their mouths, give them mighty good hearts, very fine clothes, furnish a new set of scenes, make a pathetic scene or two with a sprinkling of tender melancholy converstation through the whole, and there is no doubt but all the ladies will cry and all the gentlemen applaud.

Finally, Goldsmith laments the effect of Sentimental Comedies on the stage as a whole:

> Humor at present seems to be departing from the stage, and it will soon happen that our comic players will have nothing left for it but a fine coat and a song. It depends upon the audience whether they will actually drive those poor merry creatures from the stage, or sit at a play as gloomy as at the Tabernacle. It is not easy to recover an art when once lost; and it will be but a just punishment, that when, by our being too fastidious, we have banished humor from the stage, we should ourselves be deprived of the art of laughing.

As you read *She Stoops to Conquer: or, The Mistakes of the Night,* look to see whether Goldsmith successfully writes in a "laughing comedy."

From reading just the short excerpts from Goldsmith's essay, you get a glimpse something of Goldsmith's character and can see why Dr. Johnson would write so affectionate a epitaph for Goldsmith's tomb:

A Poet, Naturalist, and Historian,
Who left scarcely any kinf of writing untouched,
And touched nothing that he did not adorn;
Whether smiles were to be stirred
Or tears,
Commanding our emotions, yet a gentle master;
In genius, lofty, lively, versatile,
In style, weighty, clear, en.gaging –
The memory of this monument is cherished
By love of Companions,
The faithfulness of Friends
The reverence of Readers.
He was born in Ireland,
At a place called Pallas,
(in the parish) of Forney, (and county) of Longford
On the 29th Nov. 1731.
Trained in letters at Dublin.
Died in London, 4th April, 1774 (Foster 428)

"Our greatest glory consists not in never failing, but in rising every time we fall."~ Oliver Goldsmith

Works Cited

Foster, John. "Life and Times of Oliver Goldsmith Volume II." Foster, John. The Life and Times of Oliver Goldsmith, volume II. London: Bickers & Sons, 1877. 428.

Goldsmith, Oliver. AN ESSAY ON THE THEATRE; OR, A COMPARISON BETWEEN LAUGHING AND SENTIMENTAL COMEDY. 2002. 25 July 2010 <http://www.theatredatabase.com/18th_century/essay_on_the_theatre_001.html>.

As you read the play, look for the ways in which Goldsmith critiques his society. Be able to speak about his attitude toward his characters – is he mean-spirited or fondly amused?

Make a list of the characters and write a brief description of each one. Be prepared to turn it in at the start of the next class.

4 Georges (George 3), William

Lesson 17

THE ROMANTIC PERIOD

(1785 – 1832)

Composers of this period:

Mozart
Gluck
K.P.E. Bach
Haydn
Rossini
Beethoven
Schubert
Berlioz

Mendelssohn
Chopin
Clementi
Liszt
(Bach's *St. Matthew Passion* rediscovered and revived by Mendelssohn)

Artists of this period:

Goya
David
Thomas Gainsborough
Delacroix

Benjamin West
Turner
Jean Baptiste Camille Corot

American Writers of this period:

Meriwether Lewis's journals
Washington Irving (1783-1859)

James Fenimore Cooper (1789-1851)
William Cullen Bryant (1794-1878)

The Romantic Period is considered to have begun with the publication of Wordsworth and Coleridge's *Lyrical Ballads* in 1798. Reprinted in 1800 and 1892.

Each of these events had significant influence on the Romantic writers:

- **The French Revolution** –they were initially drawn to the rhetoric, but later repulsed by the reality of it. 1775-1783 American Revolutionary War
- **Napoleon & the Napoleonic Wars** – Napoleon became a symbol of romantic individualism. Under the old rules, Napoleon would never have risen through the ranks as he did. Seen as the triumphant common man, and coming to power as he did out of the horror and chaos of the French Revolution, his rise to power seemed initially to promise that the ideals of the Revolution, -- Liberty, Equality and Brotherhood would indeed overcome the evils of repression and inequality. As long as Bonaparte wasn't besieging *their* homeland, people were captivated by his dynamic and often, narcissistic personality.
- **The Industrial Revolution** – move from agricultural to industry, a "new" oppression of workers, and a new base of wealth, pollution from early factories had an effect as well
- **The Peterloo Massacre** – English government's oppression and repression of free speech and an attack on peaceful protest

WORLDVIEW:

The Romantic movement could be said, in some ways, to be a product of the Enlightenment. The Neo-Classical/Deist world was a closed system. Once set in motion, it moved according to its (distant) Creator's design. Everything within that systems continued to operate according to the unbending dictates of Natural Law.

The kind folks at thefreedictionary.com define Natural Law as an "unwritten body of universal moral principles that underlie the ethical and legal norms by which human conduct is sometimes evaluated and governed" **(**http://legal-dictionary.thefreedictionary.com/Natural+Law**).**

The concept of Natural Law was not necessarily in conflict with the concept of Divine Law, if one believed that the universal moral principles were established by God. According the the Deists, God established the world to run according to these unwritten, universal, and unchanging principles The Deist worldview had no place for supernatural miraculous intervention or revelation as each of those things would disturb the established order. The assumption that God enters into the world of Man and reveals Truth, for the Deist, is unthinkable. For God to do such a thing, He would have to interfere with his Design. Man learns about God through accurate observation of His Creation.

Over time there was less interest in discovering more about the nature of the Creator and more interest in observing the natural world for its own sake At first, Nature personified. Eventually, this personified of Nature is supplanted by Deified Nature.

In contrast to the rationalists, who put all their trust in Reason, the romantics were believed that human reason was flawed. They believed in the power of the imagination. They preferred to follow intuition and emotion, to experience Nature rather than analyze and dissect it.

<u>CHARACTERISTICS OF ROMANTIC POETRY</u>:

Changes in the way poetry was viewed/approached with the Romantic poets:

1. Poetry expresses the poet's individual mind
2. Poetic spontaneity and freedom
3. Nature becomes a primary subject. Emotional and spiritual qualities are attributed to the natural landscape, as opposed to an earlier assumption that the natural world is essentially a machine which merely moves according to unalterable, physical laws of motion. Nature is frequently personified.
4. Glorification of the common places
5. Interest in the supernatural – "Strangeness in beauty" dark side, mesmerism, occult, esoteric doctrines.

William Blake 1757-1827

William Blake was both a poet and an artist. His poetry, engravings, and his watercolors contain similar images and vision – where spiritual and physical realities intersect. The art work does not merely illustrate the text, but is in its own media, an expression of the same ideas.

Born in Soho, London to a hosier, Blake was apprenticed to an engraver and proved to have a talent for it. In 1782, he published his first compilation of poetry, *Poetical Sketches.*

It wasn't long before he opened his own engraving workshop, and in 1788 illustrated his poetry with relief etchings. Songs of Experience followed in 1794. Blake political view would have been radical for his time – equality of women, abolition of slavery, support for child labor laws, and he shared the French revolutionary passion for "Liberty, Equality, and Brotherhood."

William Blake was not born into an average middle-class family.The family's religious affiliation has been a widely discussed., They are generally said to have identified themselves with one of the groups catagorized as dissenters or non-conformists but that doesn't tell us much. At least 17 sects would have identified themselves as Dissenters. Although some Dissenters would by today's standards, be considered to be quite orthodox in their understanding of

Scripture and Christ's divinity (Anabaptists, Puritans, and men like John Bunyan, author of *Pilgrim's Progress*,), others were anything but mainstream.

The Adamists believed that folks fellowship together best naked (like Adam in Eden before the Fall). Many non-conformist sects believed that there was divinity in every man. That true spirituality came as believers follow the inner light, obedience religious doctrines. In most of these groups, experience always took precedence over Scriptures or religious traditions.

Many of these non-orthodox groups held similar beliefs:

Antinomianism :whose who deny that the Scriptures have any authority over the way they behave are called *antinomian.* –Anti means "against," and "nom" has to do with the Law. So one who is antinomian is "against the Law."

Pantheism The Old and New Testaments teach that God is Omnipresent, meaning that God is everywhere. But in his omnipresence, He is not a *part* of Creation anymore than a painter is a *part* of the painting he has created. Pantheism maintains that the deity is an actual part of all things and has no separate existence. The divine exists withinall of Nature and so a part of all people, all creatures, all rocks, everything.

Universal salvation: Because all men are indwelled by the Spirit, there is no need for a Savior to redeem anyone. There was quite a bit of variation in what these groups believed about the person of Jesus.

Non-Trinitarian: Trinitarianism is the belief that God though God is one, He exists in three persons: Father, Son, and Spirit. Non-Trinitarians believe that God is one.

There appears to be considerable evidence that Blake's mom side of the family were Muggletonianists.

What the Muggletonians believed:

> The movement was born in 1652 from "visions" and the "commission from God" of a tailor, John Reeve. Reeve believed that both he and his cousin, Lodowicke Muggleton, whom his followers considered the "Voice of the last Prophet of God" were the two witnesses spoken of in the third verse of the eleventh chapter of the Biblical book of Revelation. . .They emphasized the Millennium and the Second Coming of Christ and believed, among other things, that the soul was mortal, that Jesus was God (and not being Trinitarian, that when he died there was no God in heaven, Moses and Elijah [were left with the responsibility of] looking after heaven until the resurrection), that Heaven was six miles above earth, that God was between five and six feet tall and, like the Quakers,

> that any external religious ceremony was not necessary.
> (**http://en.academic.ru/dic.nsf/enwiki/548293)**

The Muggletonians were hostile to any emphasis on corporate worship, professional clergy, or any facit of church government – since all would end up deemphasizing the absolute work of the inner Spirit within every individual. Muggletonian meetings were reported to have consisted of a shared meal,followed by unmoderated discussion.

Beginning in early childhood, Blake frequently saw visions. Sometimes he saw angels filling trees with lights; sometimes he saw angels walking among haymakers, And sometimes he saw things that disturbed him. His wife Catherine reportedly reminded him, "You know the first time you saw God was when you were four years old [a]nd he put his head to the window and set you ascreaming" (Bently). Blake was not impressed by rational world of the Enlightenment. It was not the observable, quantifiable, and rational world of the Enlightenment, but the world of the imagination: feeling as he did that "The imagination is not a State: it is the Human existence itself."

As an adult, Blake was heavily influenced by the teachings of Emanuel Swedenborg. After experiencing a series of visions in 1743-45, Swendenborg came to belief that " God had called him to bring a new revelation to the world" (Synnestvedt, "Calling"). Over the next few years, Swedenborg devoted himself to study and to his visions, writing prolifically. His study of Genesis and Exodus was 7,000 pages long. He explained the book of Revelation in eight volumes, and published other single-volume titles as well " (Synnestvedt, Theolgical).

Believing that God had called him to travel the spiritual world, Swedenborg details his journeys thoughout the solar system and his visits to both heaven and hell and recorded his experiences in *Heaven and Its Wonders and Hell*, *Journal of Dreams*, and *Journal of Travel.* In his account of his visit to the moon, Swedenborg describes its inhabitants and the way in which their voices were

> sent forth from the abdomen like a belching forth, made this loud thundering noise. It was perceived that this arose from the fact that the inhabitants of the Moon do not speak from the lungs, like the inhabitants of other earths, but from the abdomen, thus from some air that has collected there", (Swedenborg).

Interest in Swedenborg and his writing grew only as word of Swedenborg's clairvoyant abilities began to spread. Swedenborg claimed to communicate with angel guides and with the spirits of the dead,he believing as he did that he had been called by God to move between them.

As Blake had a similar interest in the interaction between the physical and spiritual realms, it is not surprising that he would have been drawn to Swedenborg, who maintained that “man is a spirit clothed with a body” (James)

Blake had great hopes that the French Revolution would live up to it’s slogans, and, like many, was greatly distressed when it did not. He advocated racial and sexual equality, and viewed the Church of his time as an instrument of oppression. Blake rejected what he interpreted as the God of the Old Testament, seeing Jesus as the God of love and liberty, the advocate of social justice for all men and women.

Blake is not only known for his poetry, but also for his art. He intended to both the literary work and the relief etchings and illuminated paintings to be experienced together.

Works Cited

Bently, G. E. "William Blake." William Blake. London: Routledge, 1996. 36.

James, Leon. Swedenborg Glossary. August 2007. 15 July 2010 <http://www.soc.hawaii.edu/leonj/leonj/leonpsy/instructor/gloss/correspondences.html>.

Swedenborg, Emanuel. "Arcana Celestia." Swedenborg. Arcana Celestia. Vol. 9. New York: American Swedenborg Printing and Publication Society, 1854. 41.

Synnestvedt, Sig. Emmanuel Swedenborg: Theological Works Begin. May 1995. 15 July 2010 <http://newearth.org/frontier/estheo.html>.

—. Swedenborg's "calling". 1977. Swedenborg Foundation. 15 July 2010 <http://newearth.org/frontier/escall.html>.

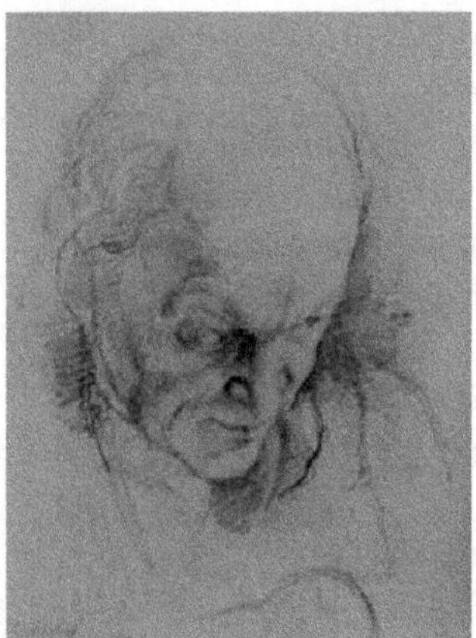

ALL RELIGIONS are ONE

The Voice of one crying in the Wilderness

The Argument As the true method of knowledge is experiment the true faculty of knowing must be the faculty which experiences. This faculty I treat of.

PRINCIPLE 1st That the Poetic Genius is the true Man. and that the body or outward form of Man is derived from the Poetic Genius. Likewise that the forms of all things are derived from their Genius. which by the Ancients was call'd an Angel & Spirit & Demon.

PRINCIPLE 2d As all men are alike in outward form, So (and with the same infinite variety) all are alike in the Poetic Genius

PRINCIPLE 3d No man can think write or speak from his heart, but he must intend truth. Thus all sects of Philosophy are from the Poetic Genius adapted to the weaknesses of every individual

PRINCIPLE 4. As none by traveling over known lands can find out the unknown. So from already acquired knowledge Man could not acquire more. therefore an universal Poetic Genius exists

PRINCIPLE. 5. The Religions of all Nations are derived from each Nations different reception of the Poetic Genius which is every where call'd the Spirit of Prophecy.

PRINCIPLE 6 The Jewish & Christian Testaments are An original derivation from the Poetic Genius. this is necessary from the confined nature of bodily sensation

PRINCIPLE 7th As all men are alike (tho' infinitely various) So all Religions & as all similars have one source

The true Man is the source he being the Poetic Genius

There Is No Natural Religion

The Argument: Man has no notion of moral fitness but from Education. Naturally he is only a natural organ subject to Sense

I. Man cannot naturally Percieve, but through his natural or bodily organs
II . Man by his reasoning power. can only compare & judge of what he has already perciev'd.
III. From a perception of only 3 senses or 3 elements none could deduce a fourth or fifth
IV. None could have other than natural or organic thoughts if he had none but organic perceptions
V . Mans desires are limited by his perceptions. none can desire what he has not perciev'd
VI . The desires & perceptions of man untaught by any thing but organs of sense, must be limited to objects of sense.

There Is No Natural Religion B

I Mans perceptions are not bounded by organs of perception. he perceives more than sense (tho' ever so acute) can discover.
II Reason or the ratio of all we have already known. is not the same that it shall be when we know more.
[III lacking]
IV The bounded is loathed by its possessor. The same dull round even of a univer[s]e would soon become a mill with complicated wheels.
V If the many become the same as the few, when possess'd, More! More! is the cry of a mistaken soul, less than All cannot satisfy Man.
VI If any could desire what he is incapable of possessing, despair must be his eternal lot

VII The desire of Man being Infinite the possession is Infinite & himself Infinite
Conclusion, If it were not for the Poetic or Prophetic character. the Philosophic & Experimental would soon be at the ratio of all things & stand still, unable to do other than repeat the same dull round over again
Application. He who sees the Infinite in all things sees God. He who sees the Ratio only sees himself only.

Therefore God becomes as we are, that we may be as he is.

The Lamb

Little lamb, who made thee?
Dost thou know who made thee?
Gave thee life, and bid thee feed
By the stream and o'er the mead;
Gave thee clothing of delight,
Softest clothing, woolly, bright;
Gave thee such a tender voice,
Making all the vales rejoice?
Little lamb, who made thee?
Dost thou know who made thee?

Little lamb, I'll tell thee,
Little lamb, I'll tell thee:
He is called by thy name,
For He calls Himself a Lamb.
He is meek, and He is mild;
He became a little child.
I a child, and thou a lamb,
We are called by His name.
Little lamb, God bless thee!
Little lamb, God bless thee!

The Tiger

Tiger! Tiger! burning bright
In the forests of the night,
What immortal hand or eye
Could frame thy fearful symmetry?

In what distant deeps or skies
Burnt the fire of thine eyes?
On what wings dare he aspire?
What the hand dare seize the fire?

And what shoulder, and what art,
Could twist the sinews of thy heart?
And when thy heart began to beat,
What dread hand? and what dread feet?

What the hammer? what the chain?
In what furnace was thy brain?
What the anvil? what dread grasp
Dare its deadly terrors clasp?

When the stars threw down their spears,
And watered heaven with their tears,
Did he smile his work to see?
Did he who made the Lamb make thee?

Tiger! Tiger! burning bright
In the forests of the night,
What immortal hand or eye
Dare frame thy fearful symmetry?

Songs of Innocence-The Chimney Sweeper

When my mother died I was very young,
And my father sold me while yet my tongue
Could scarcely cry 'weep! 'weep! 'weep! 'weep!
So your chimneys I sweep, and in soot I sleep.

There's little Tom Dacre, who cried when his head,
That curled like a lamb's back, was shaved: so I said,
"Hush, Tom! never mind it, for when your head's bare,
You know that the soot cannot spoil your white hair."

And so he was quiet; and that very night,
As Tom was a-sleeping, he had such a sight, -
That thousands of sweepers, Dick, Joe, Ned, and Jack,
Were all of them locked up in coffins of black.

And by came an angel who had a bright key,
And he opened the coffins and set them all free;
Then down a green plain leaping, laughing, they run,
And wash in a river, and shine in the sun.

Then naked and white, all their bags left behind,
They rise upon clouds and sport in the wind;
And the angel told Tom, if he'd be a good boy,
He'd have God for his father, and never want joy.

And so Tom awoke; and we rose in the dark,

And got with our bags and our brushes to work.
Though the morning was cold, Tom was happy and warm;
So if all do their duty they need not fear harm

The Chimney Sweeper-Songs of Experience

A little black thing among the snow,
Crying "'weep! 'weep!" in notes of woe!
"Where are thy father and mother, say?"
"They are both gone up to the church to pray.

"Because I was happy upon the heath,
And smiled among the winter's snow,
They clothed me in the clothes of death,
And taught me to sing the notes of woe.

"And because I am happy and dance and sing,
They think they have done me no injury,
And are gone to praise God and his Priest and King,
Who make up a heaven of our misery."

The Garden of Love

I went to the Garden of Love,
And saw what I never had seen:
A Chapel was built in the midst,
Where I used to play on the green.

And the gates of this Chapel were shut,
And "Thou shalt not" writ over the door;
So I turned to the Garden of Love,
That so many sweet flowers bore;

And I saw it was filled with graves,
And tombstones where flowers should be;
And Priests in black gowns were walking their rounds,
And binding with briers my joys and desires.

LONDON

I wander thro' each charter'd street,
Near where the charter'd Thames does flow.
And mark in every face I meet
Marks of weakness, marks of woe.

In every cry of every Man,
In every Infants cry of fear,
In every voice: in every ban,
The mind-forg'd manacles I hear

How the Chimney-sweepers cry
Every blackning Church appalls,
And the hapless Soldiers sigh
Runs in blood down Palace walls

But most thro' midnight streets I hear
How the youthful Harlots curse
Blasts the new-born Infants tear
And blights with plagues the Marriage hearse

SONGS 55: A DIVINE IMAGE

[An early Song of Experience included in one late copy]

Cruelty has a Human Heart
And Jealousy a Human Face
Terror, the Human Form Divine
And Secrecy, the Human Dress

The Human Dress, is forged Iron
The Human Form, a fiery Forge.
The Human Face, a Furnace seal'd
The Human Heart, its hungry Gorge

4 Georges, William, Victoria

Lesson 18

WILLIAM WORDSWORTH
(1770-1850)

The publication of William Wordsworth's and Sameul Taylor Coleridge's joint publication of poems, *Lyrical Ballads,* in 1798 marks the beginning of the Romantic Age in English Literature.

Like Blake, Wordsworth was an early supporter of the French Republican movement. He visited France in 1790 and fell in love with Annett Vallon. When his money ran out, Wordsworth was forced to return without her. Their child, Caroline, was born in 1792. Wordsworth supported them as he was able. Though he would later return to meet his daughter, Vallon and Wordsworth never married.

Unlike Blake, Wordsworth was horrified by the barbarity of the revolutionaries, and the more he learned about the Reign of Terror, the more disgusted Wordsworth became by it all.

Wordsworth maintained a close relationship with his sister Dorothy as long as she lived. When he married in 1802, she continued to live with Wordsworth and his wife, Mary.

The French Revolution

By 1792 word was beginning to get back to England of what was really going on in France. Horror replaced an enthusiasm as people realized that it was the bastion not of "Liberty, equality, fraternity!" many thought it was . Having returned to France in 1792 in order to improve his French, Wordsworth was increasingly disillusioned by what he saw.

(http://www.english.ucsb.edu/faculty/ayliu/research/around-1800/FR/times-9-10-1792.html)

London Times

Monday, Sept. 10, 1792

France. [page 1]

On Saturday morning Mr. Lindsay, Secretary to Lord Gower, arrived at the Secretary of State's Office from France, which place he left on Wednesday, though not without some difficulty, as there was much hesitation shewn in deliver him his passport. Mr. Lindsay may congratulate himself on having escaped with safety.

As the affairs of France very naturally engross the whole of the public attention, we have made it our business to collect the occurrences that have happened with as much precision as circumstances would admit. In the history of mankind, we have no precedent of such wanton and disgraceful excesses.

The GOTHS and VANDALS, when they levelled the gates of Rome, and triumphantly entered into the *capitol*, yet still retained those feelings which distinguished the mind of man from the ungovernable appetite of the brute creation. It is true, they commanded the Roman ladies to attend them with wine under the *Plantain Trees*, and insisted on the solders acting as slaves—but they neither violated the chastity of the one, nor deprived the others of life. Far otherwise has been the conduct of the French barbarians. They delight in that kind of murder, which is attended with cruelty, and rejoice in every occurrence which can debase and unsex the feelings of man.

We have very good authority for the detail that follows. Many of the facts have been related to us by a gentleman who was an eye-witness to them, and left Paris on Tuesday—and other channels of information furnish us with the news of Paris up to last Thursday noon—These facts stand not in need of exaggeration. It is impossible to add to a cup of iniquity already filled to the brim.

When Mr. Lindsay left Paris on Wednesday, the MASSACRE continued without abatement. The city had been a scene of bloodshed and violence without intermission since Sunday noon, and although it is difficult and indeed impossible to ascertain with any precision the number that had fallen victims to the fury of the mob during these three days, we believe the account will not be exaggerated when we state it at TWELVE THOUSAND PERSONS—(We state it as a fact, which we derive from the best information, that during the Massacre on the 2d instant, from SIX to EIGHT THOUSAND Persons perished).

To those whose situations do not lead them to enquiry, or who have not an opportunity to do so, this number will be considered as a gross exaggeration, and even an impossibility; but we are well warranted to believe the truth of this statement, after having been at very great pains to enquire into it. We rather think the calculation is *under* than *over* stated; and it will be more credible, when we assert on the authority of those whose business and duty it was to collect every information on the subject, that on the 19th of August last *only*, ELEVEN THOUSAND PERSONS were MASSACRED in Paris.[*] Those who were not on the spot, can have no idea of the slaughter or the cruelties that happened on that memorable day; and Sunday, Monday, Tuesday, and Wednesday last were merely a revival of them, though somewhat in a different shape. On the 10th of August, thousands died in defending their lives—but in this last massacre, there was no resistance; the unhappy victims were butchered like sheep at a slaughter house.

But if the mob were excited to arms on the first of these days on the supposition of treachery in the Court, they had no such pretext in this latter instance. There was no new circumstance to excite them to these excesses; they could spring only from a base, cruel and degenerate nature.

When the mob went to the prison *de la Force*, where the Royal attendants were chiefly confined, the Princess DE LAMBALLE went down on her knees to implore a suspension of her fate for 24 hours. This was at first granted, until a second mob more ferocious than the first, forced her apartments, and decapitated her. The circumstances which attended her death were such as makes humanity shudder, and which decency forbids us to repeat:—Previous to her death, the mob offered her every insult. Her thighs were cut across, and her bowels and heart torn from her, and for two days her mangled body was dragged through the streets.

It is said, though this report seems dubious, that every Lady and state prisoner was murdered, with only two exceptions—Madame de TOURZELLE, and Madame de SAINT BRICE, who were saved by the Commissioners of the National Assembly, the latter being pregnant. The heads and bodies of the Princess and other Ladies—those of the principal Clergy and Gentlemen—among whom we learn the names of the Cardinal de la ROCHEFAUCOULT, the Archbishop of ARLES, M. BOTIN, Vicar of St. Ferrol, &c. have been since particularly marked as trophies of *victory* and *justice!!!* Their trunkless heads and mangled bodies were carried about the streets on pikes in regular calvacade. At the *Palais Royal*, the procession stopped, and these lifeless victims were made the mockery of the mob.

Are these "the Rights of Man"? Is this the LIBERTY of Human Nature? The most savage four footed tyrants that range the unexplored desarts of Africa, in point of tenderness, rise superior to these two legged Parisian animals.—Common Brutes do not prey upon each other.

The number of Clergy found in the Carmelite Convent was about 220. They were handed out of the prison door two by two into the *Rue Vaugerard*, where their throats were cut. Their bodies were fixed on pikes and exhibited to the wretched victims who were next to suffer. The mangled bodies of others are piled against the houses in the streets; and in the quarters of Paris near to which the prisons are, the carcases lie scattered in hundreds, diffusing pestilence all around.

The streets of Paris, strewed with the carcases of the mangled victims, are become so familiar to the sight, that they are passed by and trod on without any particular notice. The mob think no more of killing a fellow-creature, who is not even an object of suspicion, than wanton boys would of killing a cat or a dog. We have it from a Gentleman who has been but too often an eye witness to the fact. In the massacre last week, every person who had the appearance of a gentleman, whether stranger or not, was run through the body with a pike. He was of course an *Aristocrate*, and that was a sufficient crime. A ring, a watch chain, a handsome pair of buckles, a new coat, or a good pair of boots in a word, every thing which marked the appearance of a gentleman, and which the mob fancied, was sure to cost the owner his life. EQUALITY was the pistol, and PLUNDER the object.

As every body the mob assassinates, is called an *Aristocrate*, it is highly dangerous for any one to express himself compassionately at what passes. He would then become himself an object of suspicion.

The army marching from Paris exhibits a very motley group. There are almost as many women as men, many without arms, and very little provision. A principal object with them is to destroy the corn and lay waste the country, so that the confederates may be cramped for want of supplies.

The following report of the massacre on Sunday, has been made by a Member of the National Assembly. Although we know that this report does not state the whole of the facts, which for obvious reasons are concealed, it is however, a very proper article to be here inserted; but it is to be remarked, that this report relates to the *prisons only*.

"The Commission assembled during the suspension of the night sitting, being informed by several citizens, that the people were continuing to rush in great numbers towards the different prisons, and were there exercising their vengeance, thought it necessary to write to the Council General of the Community, to learn officially the true state of things. The Community sent back word, that they had ordered a deputation to render an account to the commission of what had happened. At two o'clock the deputations, consisting of Mess. Tallion, Tronchon, and Cuiraté, was introduced in to the hall of the Assembly. M. Tronchon then said, that the greater part of the prisons were empty; that about four hundred prisoners were massacred; that he had thought it prudent to release all prisoners confined for debt at the prison *La Force*, and that he had done the same thing at *Saint Pelegíe*. That when he returned to the Community, he recollected that he had neglected to visit that part of *La Force*, where the women were confined; that he immediately returned, and set at liberty twenty-four. That he and his colleague had taken under their particular protection Madame *Tourzelle*, and

Madame *Saint Brice*, and that they had conducted these two ladies to the Section of the *Rights of Man*, to be kept there till they are tried.

"Mr. *Tallíen* added, that when he went to the Abbaye, the people were demanding the registers from the keeper; that the prisoners confined on account of crimes imputed to them on the 10th of August, and those confined for forging assignats, were almost all butchered, and that only eleven of them were saved. The Council of the Community had dispatched a deputation to endeavor to check the brutal fury of the mob: their Solicitor first addressed them, and employed every means to appease them. His efforts, however, were attended with no success, and multitudes around him fell victims to the barbarity of the populace.

"The mob next proceeded to the *Chatelet*, where they likewise sacrificed all the prisoners. About midnight, they were collected round *La Force*, to which the Commissioners instantly repaired, but were not able to prevail on the people to desist from their sanguinary proceedings. Several Deputations were successively sent to try if they could restore tranquility, and orders were given to the Commandant General to draw out detachments of the National Guards; but as the service of the barriers required such a great number of men, a sufficiency was not left to repress the audacity of the populace. The Commissioners once more attempted to bring back the ungovernable and infatuated multitude to a sense of justice and humanity; but they could not make the least impression on their minds, or check their ferocity or vengeance.

"M. Guiraud mentioned that the people were searching the bodies at the *Pont Neuf*, and collecting their money and pocket-books. He added, that he forgot to mention one fact—"In the different prisons, the mob formed a tribunal consisting of twelve persons; after examining the jailor's book, and asking different questions, the judges placed their hands upon the head of the prisoner, and said, 'Do you think that in our consciences we can release this gentleman?'—This word *release* was his condemnation. When they answered *yes*, the accused person, apparently set at liberty, was immediately dashed upon the pikes of the surrounding people. If they were judged innocent, they were released amidst the shouts of *Vive la Nation!*"

[Read this ye ENGLISHMEN, with attention, and ardently pray that your happy Constitution may never be outraged by the despotic tyranny of Equalization.] [. . .]

* Besides the bodies which were buried (the returns mention between 4 and 5000) and the carcasses that were thrown in the Seine and other places, it appears since, that hundreds of bodies have been thrown into storehouses and cellars, and to this moment lie unburied. It will be for future historians to ascertain these facts, which the circumstances of the times do not permit to be accurately identified.

Alan Liu, **English Dept.**, U. California, Santa Barbara (transcribed 2/17/00)

Preface to Lyrical Ballads 1802

By **William Wordsworth**

MAKE NOTES HERE

Characteristics of Poetry

The principal object, then, which I proposed to myself in these Poems was to chose incidents and situations from ***common life***, and to relate or describe them, throughout, as far as was possible, in a selection of ***language really used by men***; and, at the same time, to throw over them a certain colouring of imagination, whereby ***ordinary things should be presented to the mind in an unusual way***; and, further, and above all, to make these incidents and situations interesting by tracing in them, truly though not ostentatiously, the primary laws of our nature: chiefly, as far as regards the manner in which we associate ideas in a state of excitement. Low and rustic life was generally chosen, because in that condition, the essential passions of the heart find a better soil in which they can attain their maturity, are less under restraint, and speak a plainer and more emphatic language; because in that condition of life our elementary feelings co-exist in a state of greater simplicity, and, consequently, may be more accurately contemplated, and more forcibly communicated; because the manners of rural life germinate from those elementary feelings; and, from the necessary character of rural occupations, are more easily comprehended, and are more durable; and lastly, because in that condition the passions of men are incorporated with the beautiful and permanent forms of nature. The language, too, of these men is adopted (purified indeed from what appear to be its real defects, from all lasting and rational causes of dislike or disgust) because such men hourly communicate with the best objects from which the best part of language is originally derived; and because, from their rank in society and the sameness and narrow circle of their intercourse, being less under the influence of social vanity they convey their feelings and notions in **simple** and unelaborated expressions. Accordingly, such a language, arising out of repeated experience and regular feelings, is a more permanent, and a far more philosophical language, than that which is frequently substituted for it by Poets, who think that they are conferring honour upon themselves and their art, in proportion as they separate themselves from the sympathies of men, and indulge in arbitrary and capricious habits of expression, in order to furnish food for fickle tastes, and fickle appetites, of their own creation.

I cannot, however, be insensible of the present outcry against the triviality and meanness both of thought and language, which some of my contemporaries have occasionally introduced into their metrical compositions; and I acknowledge, that this defect, where it exists, is more dishonorable to the Writer's own character than false refinement or arbitrary innovation, though I should contend at the same time that it is far less pernicious in the sum of its consequences. From such verses the Poems in these volumes will be found distinguished at least by one mark of difference, that each of them bas a **worthy purpose**. Not that I mean to say, that I always began to write with a distinct purpose formally conceived; but I believe that my habits of meditation have so formed my feelings, as that my descriptions of such objects as strongly excite those feelings, will be found to carry along with them a purpose. If in this opinion I am mistaken, I can have little right to the name of a Poet. For all good poetry is the **spontaneous overflow of powerful feelings**: but though this be true, Poems to which any value can be attached, were never produced on any variety of subjects but by a man, who being possessed of more than usual organic sensibility, had also thought long and deeply. For our continued influxes of feeling are modified and directed by our thoughts, which are indeed the representatives of all our past feelings; and, as by contemplating the relation of these general representatives to each other we discover what is really important to men, so, by the repetition and continuance of this act, our feelings will be connected with important subjects, till at length, if we be originally possessed of much sensibility, such habits of mind will be produced, that, by obeying blindly and mechanically the impulses of those habits, we shall describe objects, and utter sentiments, of such a nature and in such connection with each other, that the understanding of the being to whom we address ourselves, if he be in a healthful state of association, must necessarily be in some degree enlightened, and his affections ameliorated.

I have said that each of these poems has a purpose. I have also informed my Reader what this purpose will be found principally to be: namely to illustrate the manner in which our feelings and ideas are associated in a state of excitement. But, speaking in language somewhat more appropriate, it is to follow the fluxes and refluxes of the mind when agitated by the great and simple affections of our nature.

I Wandered Lonely As a Cloud

I wandered lonely as a cloud
That floats on high o'er vales and hills,
When all at once I saw a crowd,
A host, of golden daffodils;
Beside the lake, beneath the trees,
Fluttering and dancing in the breeze.

Continuous as the stars that shine
And twinkle on the milky way,
They stretched in never-ending line
Along the margin of a bay:
Ten thousand saw I at a glance,
Tossing their heads in sprightly dance.

The waves beside them danced; but they
Out-did the sparkling waves in glee:
A poet could not but be gay,
In such a jocund company:
I gazed--and gazed--but little thought
What wealth the show to me had brought:

For oft, when on my couch I lie
In vacant or in pensive mood,
They flash upon that inward eye
Which is the bliss of solitude;
And then my heart with pleasure fills,
And dances with the daffodils.

1804.

Lines Composed a Few Miles Above Tintern Abbey, on Revisiting the Banks of the Wye During a Tour, July 13,

Five years have past; five summers, with the length
Of five long winters! and again I hear
These waters, rolling from their mountain-springs
With a soft inland murmur.--Once again
Do I behold these steep and lofty cliffs,
That on a wild secluded scene impress
Thoughts of more deep seclusion; and connect
The landscape with the quiet of the sky.
The day is come when I again repose
Here, under this dark sycamore, and view
These plots of cottage-ground, these orchard-tufts,
Which at this season, with their unripe fruits,
Are clad in one green hue, and lose themselves
'Mid groves and copses. Once again I see
These hedge-rows, hardly hedge-rows, little lines
Of sportive wood run wild: these pastoral farms,
Green to the very door; and wreaths of smoke
Sent up, in silence, from among the trees!
With some uncertain notice, as might seem
Of vagrant dwellers in the houseless woods,
Or of some Hermit's cave, where by his fire
The Hermit sits alone.
These beauteous forms,
Through a long absence, have not been to me
As is a landscape to a blind man's eye:
But oft, in lonely rooms, and 'mid the din
Of towns and cities, I have owed to them
In hours of weariness, sensations sweet,
Felt in the blood, and felt along the heart;
And passing even into my purer mind,
With tranquil restoration:--feelings too
Of unremembered pleasure: such, perhaps,
As have no slight or trivial influence
On that best portion of a good man's life,
His little, nameless, unremembered, acts
Of kindness and of love. Nor less, I trust,
To them I may have owed another gift,
Of aspect more sublime; that blessed mood,
In which the burthen of the mystery,
In which the heavy and the weary weight
Of all this unintelligible world,

Is lightened:--that serene and blessed mood,
In which the affections gently lead us on,--
Until, the breath of this corporeal frame
And even the motion of our human blood
Almost suspended, we are laid asleep
In body, and become a living soul:
While with an eye made quiet by the power
Of harmony, and the deep power of joy,
We see into the life of things.
                                        If this
Be but a vain belief, yet, oh! how oft--
In darkness and amid the many shapes
Of joyless daylight; when the fretful stir
Unprofitable, and the fever of the world,
Have hung upon the beatings of my heart--
How oft, in spirit, have I turned to thee,
O sylvan Wye! thou wanderer thro' the woods,
How often has my spirit turned to thee!
  And now, with gleams of half-extinguished thought,
With many recognitions dim and faint,
And somewhat of a sad perplexity,
The picture of the mind revives again:
While here I stand, not only with the sense
Of present pleasure, but with pleasing thoughts
That in this moment there is life and food
For future years. And so I dare to hope,
Though changed, no doubt, from what I was when first
I came among these hills; when like a roe
I bounded o'er the mountains, by the sides
Of the deep rivers, and the lonely streams,
Wherever nature led: more like a man
Flying from something that he dreads, than one
Who sought the thing he loved. For nature then
(The coarser pleasures of my boyish days,
And their glad animal movements all gone by)
To me was all in all.--I cannot paint
What then I was. The sounding cataract
Haunted me like a passion: the tall rock,
The mountain, and the deep and gloomy wood,
Their colours and their forms, were then to me
An appetite; a feeling and a love,
That had no need of a remoter charm,
By thought supplied, nor any interest
Unborrowed from the eye.--That time is past,
And all its aching joys are now no more,
And all its dizzy raptures. Not for this

Faint I, nor mourn nor murmur, other gifts
Have followed; for such loss, I would believe,
Abundant recompence. For I have learned
To look on nature, not as in the hour
Of thoughtless youth; but hearing oftentimes
The still, sad music of humanity,
Nor harsh nor grating, though of ample power
To chasten and subdue. And I have felt
A presence that disturbs me with the joy
Of elevated thoughts; a sense sublime
Of something far more deeply interfused,
Whose dwelling is the light of setting suns,
And the round ocean and the living air,
And the blue sky, and in the mind of man;
A motion and a spirit, that impels
All thinking things, all objects of all thought,
And rolls through all things. Therefore am I still
A lover of the meadows and the woods,
And mountains; and of all that we behold
From this green earth; of all the mighty world
Of eye, and ear,--both what they half create,
And what perceive; well pleased to recognise
In nature and the language of the sense,
The anchor of my purest thoughts, the nurse,
The guide, the guardian of my heart, and soul
Of all my moral being.
Nor perchance,
If I were not thus taught, should I the more
Suffer my genial spirits to decay:
For thou art with me here upon the banks
Of this fair river; thou my dearest Friend,
My dear, dear Friend; and in thy voice I catch
The language of my former heart, and read
My former pleasures in the shooting lights
Of thy wild eyes. Oh! yet a little while
May I behold in thee what I was once,
My dear, dear Sister! and this prayer I make,
Knowing that Nature never did betray
The heart that loved her; 'tis her privilege,
Through all the years of this our life, to lead
From joy to joy: for she can so inform
The mind that is within us, so impress
With quietness and beauty, and so feed
With lofty thoughts, that neither evil tongues,
Rash judgments, nor the sneers of selfish men,
Nor greetings where no kindness is, nor all

The dreary intercourse of daily life,
Shall e'er prevail against us, or disturb
Our cheerful faith, that all which we behold
Is full of blessings. Therefore let the moon
Shine on thee in thy solitary walk;
And let the misty mountain-winds be free
To blow against thee: and, in after years,
When these wild ecstasies shall be matured
Into a sober pleasure; when thy mind
Shall be a mansion for all lovely forms,
Thy memory be as a dwelling-place
For all sweet sounds and harmonies; oh! then,
If solitude, or fear, or pain, or grief,
Should be thy portion, with what healing thoughts
Of tender joy wilt thou remember me,
And these my exhortations! Nor, perchance--
If I should be where I no more can hear
Thy voice, nor catch from thy wild eyes these gleams
Of past existence--wilt thou then forget
That on the banks of this delightful stream
We stood together; and that I, so long
A worshipper of Nature, hither came
Unwearied in that service: rather say
With warmer love--oh! with far deeper zeal
Of holier love. Nor wilt thou then forget,
That after many wanderings, many years
Of absence, these steep woods and lofty cliffs,
And this green pastoral landscape, were to me
More dear, both for themselves and for thy sake!

1798.

LONDON, 1802

Milton! thou should'st be living at this hour:
England hath need of thee: she is a fen
Of stagnant waters: altar, sword, and pen,
Fireside, the heroic wealth of hall and bower,
Have forfeited their ancient English dower
Of inward happiness. We are selfish men;
Oh! raise us up, return to us again;
And give us manners, virtue, freedom, power.
Thy soul was like a Star, and dwelt apart:
Thou hadst a voice whose sound was like the sea:
Pure as the naked heavens, majestic, free,
So didst thou travel on life's common way,
In cheerful godliness; and yet thy heart
The lowliest duties on herself did lay.

ODE: INTIMATIONS OF IMMORTALITY FROM RECOLLECTIONS OF EARLY CHILDHOOD

I

THERE was a time when meadow, grove, and stream,
The earth, and every common sight,
To me did seem
Apparelled in celestial light,
The glory and the freshness of a dream.
It is not now as it hath been of yore;--
Turn wheresoe'er I may,
By night or day,
The things which I have seen I now can see no more.

II

The Rainbow comes and goes,
And lovely is the Rose,
The Moon doth with delight
Look round her when the heavens are bare,
Waters on a starry night
Are beautiful and fair;
The sunshine is a glorious birth;
But yet I know, where'er I go,
That there hath past away a glory from the earth.

III

Now, while the birds thus sing a joyous song,
   And while the young lambs bound
      As to the tabor's sound,
To me alone there came a thought of grief:
A timely utterance gave that thought relief,
      And I again am strong:
The cataracts blow their trumpets from the steep;
No more shall grief of mine the season wrong;
I hear the Echoes through the mountains throng,
The Winds come to me from the fields of sleep,
      And all the earth is gay;
         Land and sea
   Give themselves up to jollity,
      And with the heart of May
   Doth every Beast keep holiday;--
      Thou Child of Joy,
Shout round me, let me hear thy shouts, thou happy
      Shepherd-boy!

IV

Ye blessed Creatures, I have heard the call
   Ye to each other make; I see
The heavens laugh with you in your jubilee;
   My heart is at your festival,
   My head hath its coronal,
The fulness of your bliss, I feel--I feel it all.
   Oh evil day! if I were sullen
   While Earth herself is adorning,
      This sweet May-morning,
   And the Children are culling
      On every side,
   In a thousand valleys far and wide,
   Fresh flowers; while the sun shines warm,
And the Babe leaps up on his Mother's arm:--
   I hear, I hear, with joy I hear!
   --But there's a Tree, of many, one,
A single Field which I have looked upon,
Both of them speak of something that is gone:
   The Pansy at my feet
   Doth the same tale repeat:
Whither is fled the visionary gleam?
Where is it now, the glory and the dream?

V

Our birth is but a sleep and a forgetting:
The Soul that rises with us, our life's Star,
Hath had elsewhere its setting,
And cometh from afar:
Not in entire forgetfulness,
And not in utter nakedness,
But trailing clouds of glory do we come
From God, who is our home:
Heaven lies about us in our infancy!
Shades of the prison-house begin to close
Upon the growing Boy,
But He beholds the light, and whence it flows,
He sees it in his joy;
The Youth, who daily farther from the east
Must travel, still is Nature's Priest,
And by the vision splendid
Is on his way attended;
At length the Man perceives it die away,
And fade into the light of common day.

VI

Earth fills her lap with pleasures of her own;
Yearnings she hath in her own natural kind,
And, even with something of a Mother's mind,
And no unworthy aim,
The homely Nurse doth all she can
To make her Foster-child, her Inmate Man,
Forget the glories he hath known,
And that imperial palace whence he came.

VII

Behold the Child among his new-born blisses,
A six years' Darling of a pigmy size!
See, where 'mid work of his own hand he lies,
Fretted by sallies of his mother's kisses,
With light upon him from his father's eyes!
See, at his feet, some little plan or chart,
Some fragment from his dream of human life,
Shaped by himself with newly-learned art;
A wedding or a festival,
A mourning or a funeral;

And this hath now his heart,
And unto this he frames his song:
Then will he fit his tongue
To dialogues of business, love, or strife;
But it will not be long
Ere this be thrown aside,
And with new joy and pride
The little Actor cons another part;
Filling from time to time his "humorous stage"
With all the Persons, down to palsied Age,
That Life brings with her in her equipage;
As if his whole vocation
Were endless imitation.

VIII

Thou, whose exterior semblance doth belie
Thy Soul's immensity;
Thou best Philosopher, who yet dost keep
Thy heritage, thou Eye among the blind,
That, deaf and silent, read'st the eternal deep,
Haunted for ever by the eternal mind,--
Mighty Prophet! Seer blest!
On whom those truths do rest,
Which we are toiling all our lives to find,
In darkness lost, the darkness of the grave;
Thou, over whom thy Immortality
Broods like the Day, a Master o'er a Slave,
A Presence which is not to be put by;
Thou little Child, yet glorious in the might
Of heaven-born freedom on thy being's height,
Why with such earnest pains dost thou provoke
The years to bring the inevitable yoke,
Thus blindly with thy blessedness at strife?
Full soon thy Soul shall have her earthly freight,
And custom lie upon thee with a weight
Heavy as frost, and deep almost as life!

IX

O joy! that in our embers
Is something that doth live,
That nature yet remembers
What was so fugitive!
The thought of our past years in me doth breed
Perpetual benediction: not indeed

For that which is most worthy to be blest--
Delight and liberty, the simple creed
Of Childhood, whether busy or at rest,
With new-fledged hope still fluttering in his breast:--
Not for these I raise
The song of thanks and praise;
But for those obstinate questionings
Of sense and outward things,
Fallings from us, vanishings;
Blank misgivings of a Creature
Moving about in worlds not realised,
High instincts before which our mortal Nature
Did tremble like a guilty Thing surprised:
But for those first affections,
Those shadowy recollections,
Which, be they what they may,
Are yet the fountain light of all our day,
Are yet a master light of all our seeing;
Uphold us, cherish, and have power to make
Our noisy years seem moments in the being
Of the eternal Silence: truths that wake,
To perish never;
Which neither listlessness, nor mad endeavour,
Nor Man nor Boy,
Nor all that is at enmity with joy,
Can utterly abolish or destroy!
Hence in a season of calm weather
Though inland far we be,
Our Souls have sight of that immortal sea
Which brought us hither,
Can in a moment travel thither,
And see the Children sport upon the shore,
And hear the mighty waters rolling evermore.

X

Then sing, ye Birds, sing, sing a joyous song!
And let the young Lambs bound
As to the tabor's sound!
We in thought will join your throng,
Ye that pipe and ye that play,
Ye that through your hearts to-day
Feel the gladness of the May!
What though the radiance which was once so bright
Be now for ever taken from my sight,
Though nothing can bring back the hour

Of splendour in the grass, of glory in the flower;
We will grieve not, rather find
Strength in what remains behind;
In the primal sympathy
Which having been must ever be;
In the soothing thoughts that spring
Out of human suffering;
In the faith that looks through death,
In years that bring the philosophic mind.

XI

And O, ye Fountains, Meadows, Hills, and Groves,
Forebode not any severing of our loves!
Yet in my heart of hearts I feel your might;
I only have relinquished one delight
To live beneath your more habitual sway.
I love the Brooks which down their channels fret,
Even more than when I tripped lightly as they;
The innocent brightness of a new-born Day
Is lovely yet;
The Clouds that gather round the setting sun
Do take a sober colouring from an eye
That hath kept watch o'er man's mortality;
Another race hath been, and other palms are won.
Thanks to the human heart by which we live,
Thanks to its tenderness, its joys, and fears,
To me the meanest flower that blows can give
Thoughts that do often lie too deep for tears.
1803-6.

SURPRISED BY JOY

Surprised by joy--impatient as the Wind
I turned to share the transport--Oh! with whom
But Thee, deep buried in the silent tomb,
That spot which no vicissitude can find?
Love, faithful love, recalled thee to my mind--
But how could I forget thee? Through what power,
Even for the least division of an hour,
Have I been so beguiled as to be blind
To my most grievous loss?--That thought's return
Was the worst pang that sorrow ever bore,
Save one, one only, when I stood forlorn,
Knowing my heart's best treasure was no more;
That neither present time, nor years unborn
Could to my sight that heavenly face restore.

THE WORLD IS TOO MUCH WITH US

THE world is too much with us; late and soon,
Getting and spending, we lay waste our powers:
Little we see in Nature that is ours;
We have given our hearts away, a sordid boon!
The Sea that bares her bosom to the moon;
The winds that will be howling at all hours,
And are up-gathered now like sleeping flowers;
For this, for everything, we are out of tune;
It moves us not.--Great God! I'd rather be
A Pagan suckled in a creed outworn ,
So might I, standing on this pleasant lea,
Have glimpses that would make me less forlorn;
Have sight of Proteus rising from the sea;
Or hear old Triton blow his wreathed horn.

1806.

LESSON 19

THE BAD BOYS:
BYRON, KEATS, SHELLEY

(The following biographies of Byron, Keats and Shelly are brought to you by Mondragon, Brenda C. Neurotic Poets. 26 Jun. 2007 <http://www.neuroticpoets.com/>.)

Lord Byron (1788-1824)

Biographical sketch by Brenda C. Mondragon

George Gordon Byron was born with a lame foot, and his sensitivity to it haunted his life and his works. Overhearing a girl he was infatuated with refer to him as "that lame boy" certainly must have deepened his disappointment at being born with this deformity. A fragile self-esteem made Byron extremely sensitive to criticism, of himself or of his poetry, and he tended to make enemies rather quickly. His poetry, along with his lifestyle, was considered controversial in his time and often deemed "perverted" or even "satanic". The fact that he was often discontent and unhappy, combined with a constant desire for change meant that he created an unstable world for himself, though he never gave up his individual freedom to choose his own path and his own destiny.

He inherited the title of Lord Byron at the age of ten, giving him a rank in society, and a bit of wealth to go along with it. But by the time he was in college, Byron began to build up large debts due to an extravagant lifestyle. It is said that, at one point, he kept a pet bear in his rooms at Trinity College in Cambridge. Also while at Cambridge, he developed a great fondness for a choirboy named John Edleston.

Throughout his life, Byron fought a battle with obesity. He seemed obsessed with food, as well as being a picky eater. His letters to others, as well as his journals, indicate that he practiced starvation, often eating only one meal a day. Occasionally he would slide to the other extreme, drinking large amounts of soda-water or consuming great quantities of magnesia and Epsom salts in an effort to keep his weight down.

After college, he resided at various places, including the family home at Newstead Abbey. It was here that the alleged "wild parties" took place at which Byron would supposedly make toasts with and drink from a skull cup. Legend has it that the skull, which Byron had discovered at Newstead, was that of a monk. He polished it up and added silver plates. The cup was "secretly buried" by a later owner of the property.

In 1811 Byron embarked on a Grand Tour through the Mediterranean, and the experience was to influence him greatly. One attitude that he adopted from his travels was that he disliked sharing a meal with or watching a woman eat. After his return to England, his mother (with whom he had always had a tempestuous relationship) and several close friends died, throwing him into a state of deep grief.

Although he had published several books of poetry before, nothing produced quite the overnight success as the epic poem Childe Harold's Pilgrimage (1812), which allegedly caused Byron to remark later that "I awoke and found myself famous." The long poems that followed Childe Harold sold well and enhanced his reputation for being daring and dashing. But fame, as always, carried with it rewards as well as a price.

The young bachelor had romances and liaisons with several women, many of them married. One of the women aptly remarked that Byron was "mad, bad and dangerous to know." It is rumored that in 1813 he had an incestuous affair with his half-sister, Augusta Leigh. This idea is furthered by themes of incest and forbidden love that appear in several of Byron's poems. In the dramatic poem Manfred, he writes of the hero's love for a woman who is "like me in lineaments; her eyes / Her hair, her features, all, to the very tone / Even of her voice . . . were like to mine."

Byron married Annabella Milbanke in early 1815, and they had a daughter named Ada. But within a year the marriage had dissolved and they were separated. Byron felt hounded by the press, who covered every gossip about his personal and financial affairs. In 1816 he left England in a voluntary exile, never to return. His bitter outlook on life at this time is reflected in the poem Darkness, which he wrote in that same year.

In Geneva he met and began a lifelong relationship with the poet Shelley. Each had an admiration of and great respect for the other. Also with the Shelleys was Mary Godwin's stepsister Claire Clairmont, who was infatuated with Byron. In England she had written him letters, and had met with him. In Geneva she became pregnant by Byron, and had the baby, Allegra, in 1817.

Byron, meanwhile, had moved to Venice, reveling in its excesses. Friends have described his life at this time as somewhat licentious and depraved;

nonetheless, the flow of his poetical genius only increased. Shelley, who had informed Byron of his daughter's birth by letter, persuaded him to assume the care of Allegra's education and upbringing. A nurse brought the child to Byron in 1818, because he refused to have anything to do with Clare, and he sent her to a convent school.

Byron fell in love with the young Countess Teresa Guiccioli in Italy. He became involved in the Italian nationalism movement through her father and brother. Eventually Teresa's husband, who had allowed her affairs with Byron, applied for a separation. Shelley visited the couple in 1821 and commented on Byron's unusual lifestyle in a letter to a friend:

Lord Byron gets up at two. I get up, quite contrary to my usual custom . . . at 12. After breakfast we sit talking till six. From six to eight we gallop through the pine forest which divide Ravenna from the sea; we then come home and dine, and sit up gossiping till six in the morning. I don't suppose this will kill me in a week or fortnight, but I shall not try it longer. Lord B.'s establishment consists, besides servants, of ten horses, eight enormous dogs, three monkeys, five cats, an eagle, a crow, and a falcon; and all these, except the horses, walk about the house, which every now and then resounds with their unarbitrated quarrels, as if they were the masters of it. . . . [P.S.] I find that my enumeration of the animals in this Circean Palace was defective . . . . I have just met on the grand staircase five peacocks, two guinea hens, and an Egyptian crane. I wonder who all these animals were before they were changed into these shapes.

Shelley died in 1822, shortly after another visit to Byron. In 1823, Byron's daughter Allegra died of a fever in the convent school at the age of five. Facing the death of loved ones, and almost foreshadowing his own death, Byron wrote the following lines in On This Day I Complete My Thirty-Sixth Year (Jan 22, 1824):

'Tis time this heart should be unmoved,

  Since others hath it ceased to move:

Yet, though I cannot be beloved,

  Still let me love!

My days are in the yellow leaf;

  The flowers and fruits of love are gone;

The worm, the canker, and the grief

  Are mine alone!

He soon sailed for Greece to take part in the rebellion against the Turks. In February of 1824, he suffered a small stroke, probably brought on by a combination of drinking and stress. On April 9 he was caught in the rain while out riding and became ill. George Noel Gordon, Lord Byron, died of fever on April 19, 1824 at the age of thirty-six. While he was revered as a hero to the

Greeks, his reputation was still tarnished in England, even eight years after he had left. Both St. Paul's and Westminster Abbey refused him funeral services. He was eventually buried in the family tomb at Hucknall Torkard.

Brenda C. Mondragon (http://www.neuroticpoets.com)

Percy Bysshe Shelley

(1792-1822)

Biographical sketch by Brenda C. Mondragon

The spirit of revolution and the power of free thought were Percy Shelley's biggest passions in life. After being sent away to boarding school at the age of ten, he attended a lecture on science which piqued his interest in the properties of electricity, magnetism, chemistry and telescopes. On return trips home, he would try to cure his sisters' chilblains by passing electric currents through them. He also hinted of a mysterious "alchemist" living in a hidden room in the attic.

While attending the Eton school from 1804 to 1810, the quiet, odd and reflective boy was taunted relentlessly by schoolmates. This generated in him extremes of anger, once even driving him to stab another boy with a fork. Shelley detested the practice of younger boys buying protection (through doing menial tasks) from older bullies. He was ever the visionary and daydreamer, often forgetting to tie his shoelaces or to wear a hat. His odd behavior eventually earned him the nickname of "Mad Shelley".

At school, Shelley became intrigued with the revolutionary political and philosophical ideas of Thomas Paine and William Godwin. Throughout his life, he emphatically expressed his political and religious views in a struggle against social injustice, often to the point where it got him into trouble or mired in controversy. In Geneva later with Byron, he would often write "*democrat, great lover of mankind, and atheist*" in Greek after his signature in hotel ledgers. Upon finding one of these signatures, Lord Byron remarked: "Do you not think I shall do Shelley a service by scratching this out?" which he promptly did. Shelley detested the monarchy and aristocracy. He was a great believer in the idea of the power of the human mind to change circumstances for the better, in a non-violent way.

Shelley attended University College, Oxford in 1810. His friend, Thomas Jefferson Hogg describes Shelley's college rooms as such:

Books, boots, papers, shoes, philosophical instruments, clothes, pistols, linen, crockery, ammunition, and phials innumerable, with money, stockings, prints, crucibles, bags, and boxes were scattered on the floor and in every place. . . . The tables, and especially the carpet, were already stained with large spots of various hues, which frequently proclaimed the agency of fire. An electrical machine, an air pump, the galvanic trough, a solar microscope, and large glass jars and receivers, were conspicuous amidst the mass of matter.

The young Shelley was often seen indulging in his habit of sailing paper boats on the water of any nearby pond, lake or river, or reading with a book held right up to his eyes, lying very close to the fire.

In 1811 Shelley wrote and distributed to various bishops and heads of colleges a short pamphlet he wrote on *The Necessity of Atheism*. One of these he sent to a poetry professor with a letter signed with the name "Jeremiah Stukley". The professor then brought the letter and essay, which proposed free inquiry into religious belief and suggested that the existence of God remained unproven by physical evidence or reason, to the University College master. Shelley and his friend Hogg were both subsequently expelled from Oxford. This incident greatly upset Shelley's father and grandfather. His relationship with them and his closeness to the rest of his family was never completely mended.

Although he intellectually disliked the institution of marriage, stating that it was not necessary if two people loved each other, he eloped to Scotland in 1811 and married sixteen year-old Harriet Westbrook, the daughter of a London merchant and a school friend of his sister. Shelley's father immediately cut off his monetary allowance upon hearing the news, but was eventually persuaded to restart it. Meanwhile, Shelley continued to write political pamphlets, often sending them out in bottles or homemade paper boats over the water, or inside fire balloons into the sky.

At the beginning of 1812 Shelley started to suffer from "nervous attacks" for which he took doses of laudanum. He would start to sleepwalk when life became difficult or stressful. One evening he was either attacked, or imagined he was attacked, outside the door of his cottage. His wife and a neighbor found him lying senseless at the foot of the entryway. It was also in 1812 that he met and became friends with William Godwin and his family.

Harriet bore Shelley's first child, Elizabeth Ianthe, in June of 1813 and by the end of the year was pregnant again. But by 1814, Shelley had fallen in love with Mary Godwin, which upset both Harriet and Mary's father, William Godwin. When the two persuaded Mary to stop seeing Shelley for a little while, he showed up distraught and hysterical at her house with laudanum and a pistol, threatening to commit suicide. Soon reconciled, Shelley and Mary later traveled around Europe with Mary's sister Jane (later Claire) Clairmont. By the time they returned to London, Mary was pregnant. Harriet gave birth to Charles, Shelley's first-born son in November of 1814, but she was painfully aware that Shelley did not love her anymore.

Mary gave birth to a tiny girl in February of 1815, but it died within a few weeks. She was soon pregnant again, and gave birth to a son, William, in early 1816. Mary, Shelley and Claire spent the summer of 1816 at Lake Geneva near Byron. The famous "ghost story contest " which spawned Mary Shelley's *Frankenstein* took place during this period.

Tragedy struck twice at the end of 1816 after Mary and Shelley had returned to London. Depressed, Mary's sister Fanny committed suicide in October. Later, Harriet's body was found one November morning, drowned in Hyde Park's Serpentine. She had presumably killed herself. She was several months pregnant from an affair with a military officer who had later been sent abroad, and assumedly despondent about Shelley leaving her for Mary. Shelley had had no contact with Harriet since the spring. He soon proposed to Mary and they were married on December 30, 1816.

The newlyweds eventually moved to Great Marlow, where Mary finished her work on *Frankenstein* while pregnant, and Shelley provided help to the poor--a habit which made the local aristocrats call him "mad". In a bout of hypochondria, Shelley imagined for weeks that he was developing elephantiasis after sitting next to a woman with fat legs on a coach.

In 1817 daughter Clara was born, and in 1818 Shelley left England for good to seek warmer climes for his health, not to mention that he also wanted to escape his persecutors in the press and in his family. While in Italy, Claire Clairmont became pregnant again (after having had Byron's daughter Allegra in 1817), but the identity of the father remains uncertain. Many speculate that Shelley himself was the father, as it is obvious from letters and accounts that he felt a great love for both Claire and Mary; and after all, he was a great proponent of the completely radical idea of "free love" as put forth in his essay *On Love* and the poem *Epipsychidion*:

I never was attached to that great sect,
Whose doctrine is, that each one should select
Out of the crowd a mistress or a friend,
And all the rest, though fair and wise, commend
To cold oblivion, though it is in the code
Of modern morals. . . .

A baby (Elena Adelaide), born in late 1818 was listed as Shelley and Mary's, but scholars are convinced that it was most likely Claire's. Nonetheless, the baby was sent off to foster care, and died at the age of two.

Tragedy struck the Shelleys again and again in Italy. Baby Clara died in 1818 in Mary's arms while she waited in the hall of an inn for Shelley to find a doctor. Depressed and bitter in December of 1818, in failing health and with a marriage that was falling apart, Shelley composed his *Stanzas written in Dejection, near Naples*, where he writes:

Alas! I have nor hope nor health,
  Nor peace within nor calm around,

Nor that content surpassing wealth
  The sage in meditation found,
  And walked with inward glory crowned--
Nor fame, nor power, nor love, nor leisure.
  Others I see whom these surround--
Smiling they live, and call life pleasure;
To me that cup has been dealt in another measure.

Little William became ill in late May of 1819, and although watched over agonizingly by his loved ones, he died on June 7. This pain was mixed with the joy of the birth of son Percy Florence in November. Stress took its toll, as Shelley's cousin Medwin, during a visit in 1820, described the twenty-eight-year old poet as "tall, emaciated, stooping, with grey streaks in his hair."

Percy Shelley could not swim, and even though he had recently been involved in a boating accident in a canal one night in which he was nearly drowned, he and several friends decided to spend the summer of 1822 sailing on the Bay of Lerici. A boat was ordered and built for this purpose -- named *Don Juan* by Byron, but renamed *Ariel* by Shelley. Meanwhile, the pregnant Mary, who was expecting in December, suffered another miscarriage in June. Shelley himself suffered from disturbing recurring nightmares and hallucinations during the summer. One vision was of a naked child rising out of the sea and clapping its hands; another was an encounter with his own doppelganger on the terrace, who then asked him "How long do you mean to be content?"; and the most terrifying was of his good friends Jane and Edward Williams coming into his room one night, bloody and mangled, to tell him that the house was falling down--but when he went to Mary's room to warn her, he found himself strangling her. Shelley wrote to a friend and asked him to send a lethal dose of prussic acid, not to use immediately, but as comfort to hold "that golden key to the chamber of perpetual rest."

On July 7, after a long trip of sailing out to visit several different friends, a sudden afternoon storm sunk the *Ariel* ten miles from any land. The bodies of Shelley, Williams and the boat's sailor washed up ten days later and were treated and cremated on the beach because of quarantine laws to protect against the plague. Shelley's ashes were buried in the Protestant cemetery at Rome. His heart was first given to a friend, then to Mary, and eventually buried in Bournemouth. Shelley's final, unfinished poem was, perhaps ironically, titled *The Triumph of Life*.

Mondragon, Brenda C. Neurotic Poets. 25 Jul. 2017 <http://www.neuroticpoets.com/>.

JOHN KEATS
1795-1821

Biographical sketch by Brenda C. Mondragon

English lyric poet, the archetype of the Romantic writer. While still in good health, Keats was ambitious of doing the world some good, instead of focusing on his own sensitive soul. Keats felt that the deepest meaning of life lay in the apprehension of material beauty, although his mature poems reveal his fascination with a world of death and decay. Most of his best work appeared in one year.

Darkling I listen; and for many a time
I have been half in love with easeful Death
(from 'To a Nightingale')

John Keats was born in London as the son of a successful livery-stable manager. He was the oldest of four children, who remained deeply devoted to each other. Thomas, his father, was the chief hostler at the Swan and Hoop. After their father died in 1804 in a riding accident, Keats's mother, Frances Jennings Keats, remarried but the marriage was soon broken. She moved with the children, John and his sister Fanny and brothers George and Tom, to live with her mother at Edmonton, near London. She died of tuberculosis in 1810.

At school Keats read widely. He was educated at the progressive Clarke's School in Enfield, where he began a translation of the *Aeneid*. Keats, who was barely five feet tall, was not know at school for his enthusiasm for books, but his fighting. "My mind has been the most discontented and restless one that ever was put into a body too small for it," he wrote. 1811 Keats was apprenticed to a surgeon-apothecary. While studying for the licence, he completed his translation of *Aeneid*. Edmund Spenser's *Faerie Queene* impressed him deeply and his first poem, written in 1814, was 'Lines in Imitation of Spenser.' In that year he moved to London and resumed his surgical studies in 1815 as a student at Guy's hospital. Next year he became a Licentiate of the Society of Apothecaries and was allowed to practice surgery. Before devoting himself entirely to poetry, Keats worked as a dresser and junior house surgeon. In London he had met Leigh Hunt, the editor of the leading liberal magazine of the day, *The Examiner*. He introduced Keats to other young Romantics, including, and published in the magazine Keats's sonnet, 'O Solitude'.

Keats's first book, *Poems*, was published in 1817. Sales were poor. He spent the spring with his brother Tom and friends at Shankin. It was about this time Keats started to use his letters as the vehicle of his thoughts of poetry. They mixed the everyday events of his own life with comments with his correspondence. Among others T.S. Eliot considered the letters in *The Use of Poetry and the Use of Criticism* (1933) "certainly the most notable and most important ever written by any English poet," but also said about Keats's famous *Hyperion*: "it contains great lines, but I do not know whether it is a great poem." The first of his famous letters Keats wrote to Benjamin Bailey on November 22, 1817. "You perhaps at one time thought there was such thing as Worldly Happiness to be arrived at, at certain periods of time marked out - you have necessity from your disposition been thus led away - I scarcely remember counting upon any Happiness". *Endymion*, Keats's first long poem appeared, when he was 21. It told in 4000 lines of the love of the moon goddess Cynthia for the young shepherd Endymion. It was attacked among others by John Wilson Croker and John Gibson Lochard, who wrote in *Blackwood's Edinburgh Magazine*: '... it has just as much to do with Greece as it has with "old Tartary the fierce;" no man, whose mind has ever been imbued with the smallest knowledge or feeling of classical poetry or classical history, could have stooped to profane and vulgarize every association in the manner which has been adopted by this "son of promise."'

Although the critical reaction was lukewarm, Keats was not discouraged by it, but wrote to Richard Woodhouse: "I am ambitious of doing the world some good: if I should be spared that may be the work of mature years - in the interval I will assay to reach to as high a summit in Poetry as the nerve bestowed upon me will suffer." Keats's greatest works were written in the late 1810s, among them *Lamia*, *The Eve of St. Agnes*, the great odes and two versions of *Hyperion*. He worked briefly as a theatrical critic for *The Champion,* spent summer of 1818 touring the Lakes, Scotland and Northern Ireland. During his journey, which he made with his friend Charles Brown, a businessman, he vowed: "I shall learn poetry here and shall henceforth write more than ever." After returning to London he spent the next three months attending his brother Tom, who was seriously ill with tuberculosis.

After Tom's death in December, Keats moved to Hampstead to live with Charles Brown. Soon he fell in love with Fanny Brown, the daughter of a widowed neighbor, and they were betrothed. In the winter of 1818-19 he worked mainly on *Hyperion* and *The Eve of St Agnes*. The fragmentary *Eve of St Mark* were composed during a visit to his friend Charles Wentworth Dilke's parents and relatives in Sussex. In 1819

Keats finished *Lamia*, and wrote another version of *Hyperion*, called *The Fall of Hyperion*. His famous poem 'Ode on a Grecian Urn' was inspired by a Wedgwood copy of a Roman copy of a Greek vase. Josiah Wedgwood's copy was purchased by Sir William Hamilton, who sold it to the duchess of Portland. She denoted the vase to the British Museum in 1784.

'Beauty is truth, truth beauty,' - that is all
Ye know on earth and all ye need to know.
(from 'Ode on a Grecian Urn')

In 1820 appeared the second volume of Keats poems. It gained a huge critical success. However, Keats was suffering at that time from tuberculosis. His poems were marked with sadness partly because he was too poor to marry Fanny Brawne. Keats broke off his engagement and began what he called a "posthumous existence." In a letter from 1819 he had written. "I love you more in that I believe you have liked me for my own sake and nothing else. I have met with women whom I relay think would like to be married to a Poem and given away by a Novel." When his condition gradually worsened, he sailed for Italy in September with the painter Joseph Severn, to escape England's cold winter. Declining Shelley's invitation to join him at Pisa, Keats went to Rome, where he took up residence in rooms overlooking the Piazza di Spagna. He died in Rome at the age of 25, on February 23, 1821, and was buried in the Protestant Cemetery. Keats did not invent his own epitaph, but remembered words from the play Philaster, or Love Lies-Ableeding, written by Beaumont and Fletcher in 1611. "All your better deeds / Shall be in water writ," one of the characters says. Keats told his friend Joseph Severn that he wanted on his grave just the line, "Here lies one whose name was writ in water."

Bright star! would I were steadfast as thou art -
Not in lone splendour hung aloft the night
(from 'The Last Sonnet')

In spite of early harsh criticism, Keats's reputation grew after his death. The poet's letters were published in 1848 and 1878. . .Some later poets have attacked Keats and the Romantics: for T.S. Eliot Byron was "a disorderly mind, and an uninteresting one" and Keats and Shelley were "not nearly such great poets as they are supposed to be". Andrew Motion claims in his biography on Keats (1998) that the author was obsessed with sex and had venereal disease and these aspects of the poet’s life were hidden by early biographers, who underlined Keats's poverty, poor health, and misunderstanding criticism.

Mondragon, Brenda C. Neurotic Poets. 25 Jul. 2017 <http://www.neuroticpoets.com/>.

Lord George Gordon Byron

I can never get people to understand that poetry is the expression of excited passion, and that there is no such thing as a life of passion any more than a continuous earthquake, or an eternal fever. Besides, who would ever shave themselves in such a state? Lord Byron, in a letter to Thomas Moore, 5 July 1821

Prometheus

Titan! to whose immortal eyes
The sufferings of mortality,
Seen in their sad reality,
Were not as things that gods despise;
What was thy pity's recompense?
A silent suffering, and intense;
The rock, the vulture, and the chain,
All that the proud can feel of pain,
The agony they do not show,
The suffocating sense of woe,
Which speaks but in its loneliness,
And then is jealous lest the sky
Should have a listener, nor will sigh
Until its voice is echoless.

Titan! to thee the strife was given
Between the suffering and the will,
Which torture where they cannot kill;
And the inexorable Heaven,
And the deaf tyranny of Fate,
The ruling principle of Hate,
Which for its pleasure doth create
The things it may annihilate,
Refus'd thee even the boon to die:
The wretched gift Eternity
Was thine--and thou hast borne it well.
All that the Thunderer wrung from thee
Was but the menace which flung back
On him the torments of thy rack;
The fate thou didst so well foresee,
But would not to appease him tell;

And in thy Silence was his Sentence,
And in his Soul a vain repentance,
And evil dread so ill dissembled,
That in his hand the lightnings trembled.

Thy Godlike crime was to be kind,
To render with thy precepts less
The sum of human wretchedness,
And strengthen Man with his own mind;
But baffled as thou wert from high,
Still in thy patient energy,
In the endurance, and repulse
Of thine impenetrable Spirit,
Which Earth and Heaven could not convulse,
A mighty lesson we inherit:
Thou art a symbol and a sign
To Mortals of their fate and force;
Like thee, Man is in part divine,
A troubled stream from a pure source;
And Man in portions can foresee
His own funereal destiny;
His wretchedness, and his resistance,
And his sad unallied existence:
To which his Spirit may oppose
Itself--and equal to all woes,
And a firm will, and a deep sense,
Which even in torture can descry
Its own concenter'd recompense,
Triumphant where it dares defy,
And making Death a Victory.

She Walks in Beauty

She walks in beauty, like the night
Of cloudless climes and starry skies;
And all that's best of dark and bright
Meet in her aspect and her eyes:
Thus mellowed to that tender light
Which heaven to gaudy day denies.

One shade the more, one ray the less,
Had half impaired the nameless grace
Which waves in every raven tress,
Or softly lightens o'er her face;
Where thoughts serenely sweet express
How pure, how dear their dwelling-place.

And on that cheek, and o'er that brow,
So soft, so calm, yet eloquent,
The smiles that win, the tints that glow,
But tell of days in goodness spent,
A mind at peace with all below,
A heart whose love is innocent!

John Keats

Who killed John Keats?
  'I,' says the Quarterly,
So savage and Tartarly;
  "Twas one of my feats.'

Who shot the arrow?
  'The poet-priest Milman
(So ready to kill man),
  Or Southey or Barrow.'

1821

Percy Bysshe Shelly (1792-1822)

Song-To the Men of England

Men of England, wherefore plough
For the lords who lay ye low?
Wherefore weave with toil and care
The rich robes your tyrants wear?

Wherefore feed and clothe and save,
From the cradle to the grave,
Those ungrateful drones who would
Drain your sweat -nay, drink your blood?

Wherefore, Bees of England, forge
Many a weapon, chain, and scourge,
That these stingless drones may spoil
The forced produce of your toil?

Have ye leisure, comfort, calm,
Shelter, food, love's gentle balm?
Or what is it ye buy so dear
With your pain and with your fear?

The seed ye sow another reaps;
The wealth ye find another keeps;
The robes ye weave another wears;
The arms ye forge another bears.

Sow seed, -but let no tyrant reap;
Find wealth, -let no imposter heap;
Weave robes, -let not the idle wear;
Forge arms, in your defence to bear.

Shrink to your cellars, holes, and cells;
In halls ye deck another dwells.
Why shake the chains ye wrought? Ye see
The steel ye tempered glance on ye.

With plough and spade and hoe and loom,
Trace your grave, and build your tomb,
And weave your winding-sheet, till fair
England be your sepulchre!

Ode to the West Wind

O wild West Wind, thou breath of Autumn's being,
Thou, from whose unseen presence the leaves dead
Are driven, like ghosts from an enchanter fleeing,
Yellow, and black, and pale, and hectic red,
Pestilence-stricken multitudes: O thou,
Who chariotest to their dark wintry bed
The winged seeds, where they lie cold and low,
Each like a corpse within its grave, until
Thine azure sister of the Spring shall blow
Her clarion o'er the dreaming earth, and fill
(Driving sweet buds like flocks to feed in air)
With living hues and odours plain and hill:
Wild Spirit, which art moving everywhere;
Destroyer and preserver; hear, O hear!

Thou on whose stream, 'mid the steep sky's commotion,
Loose clouds like earth's decaying leaves are shed,
Shook from the tangled boughs of heaven and ocean,
Angels of rain and lightning; there are spread
On the blue surface of thine airy surge,
Like the bright hair uplifted from the head
Of some fierce Maenad, even from the dim verge
Of the horizon to the zenith's height -
The locks of the approaching storm. Thou dirge
Of the dying year, to which this closing night
Will be the dome of a vast sepulchre,
Vaulted with all thy congregated might
Of vapours, from whose solid atmosphere
Black rain, and fire, and hail, will burst: O hear!

Thou who didst waken from his summer dreams,
The blue Mediterranean, where he lay,
Lulled by the coil of his crystalline streams,
Beside a pumice isle in Baiae's bay,
And saw in sleep old palaces and towers
Quivering within the wave's intenser day,
All overgrown with azure moss and flowers
So sweet, the sense faints picturing them! Thou
For whose path the Atlantic's level powers
Cleave themselves into chasms, while far below
The sea-blooms and the oozy woods which wear

The sapless foliage of the ocean, know
Thy voice, and suddenly grow grey with fear,
And tremble and despoil themselves: O hear!
If I were a dead leaf thou mightest bear;
If I were a swift cloud to fly with thee;
A wave to pant beneath thy power, and share
The impulse of thy strength, only less free
Than thou, O uncontrollable! If even
I were as in my boyhood, and could be
The comrade of thy wanderings over heaven,
As then, when to outstrip the skiey speed
Scarce seemed a vision, I would ne'er have striven
As thus with thee in prayer in my sore need.
O, lift me as a wave, a leaf, a cloud!
I fall upon the thorns of life! I bleed!
A heavy weight of hours has chained and bowed
One too like thee: tameless, and swift, and proud.

Make me thy lyre, even as the forest is:
What if my leaves are falling like its own!
The tumult of thy mighty harmonies
Will take from both a deep autumnal tone,
Sweet though in sadness. Be thou, Spirit fierce,
My spirit! be thou me, impetuous one!
Drive my dead thoughts over the universe
Like withered leaves, to quicken a new birth;
And, by the incantation of this verse,
Scatter, as from an unextinguished hearth
Ashes and sparks, my words among mankind!
Be through my lips to unawakened earth
The trumpet of a prophecy! O Wind,
If Winter comes, can Spring be far behind?

Ozymandias

I met a traveller from an antique land
Who said: "Two vast and trunkless legs of stone
Stand in the desert. Near them on the sand,
Half sunk, a shattered visage lies, whose frown
And wrinkled lip and sneer of cold command
Tell that its sculptor well those passions read
Which yet survive, stamped on these lifeless things,
The hand that mocked them and the heart that fed.
And on the pedestal these words appear:
`My name is Ozymandias, King of Kings:
Look on my works, ye mighty, and despair!'
Nothing beside remains. Round the decay
Of that colossal wreck, boundless and bare,
The lone and level sands stretch far away.

English in 1819

An old, mad, blind, despised, and dying king, -
Princes, the dregs of their dull race, who flow
Through public scorn, -mud from a muddy spring, -
Rulers who neither see, nor feel, nor know,
But leech-like to their fainting country cling,
Till they drop, blind in blood, without a blow, -
A people starved and stabbed in the untilled field, -
An army, which liberticide and prey
Makes as a two-edged sword to all who wield, -
Golden and sanguine laws which tempt and slay;
Religion Christless, Godless -a book sealed;
A Senate, -Time's worst statute unrepealed, -
Are graves from which a glorious Phantom may
Burst, to illumine our tempestuous day.

To a Skylark

HAIL to thee, blithe Spirit!
Bird thou never wert,
That from Heaven, or near it,
Pourest thy full heart
In profuse strains of unpremeditated art.

Higher still and higher
From the earth thou springest
Like a cloud of fire;
The blue deep thou wingest,
And singing still dost soar, and soaring ever singest.

In the golden lightning
Of the sunken sun,
O'er which clouds are bright'ning,
Thou dost float and run;
Like an unbodied joy whose race is just begun.

The pale purple even
Melts around thy flight;
Like a star of Heaven,
In the broad daylight
Thou art unseen, but yet I hear thy shrill delight,

Keen as are the arrows
Of that silver sphere
Whose intense lamp narrows
In the white dawn clear
Until we hardly see -- we feel, that it is there.

All the earth and air
With thy voice is loud,
As, when night is bare,
From one lonely cloud
The moon rains out her beams, and Heaven is overflowed.

What thou art we know not;
What is most like thee?
From rainbow clouds there flow not
Drops so bright to see
As from thy presence showers a rain of melody.

Like a poet hidden

In the light of thought,
Singing hymns unbidden,
Till the world is wrought
To sympathy with hopes and fears it heeded not:

Like a high-born maiden
In a palace tower,
Soothing her love-laden
Soul in secret hour
With music sweet as love, which overflows her bower:

Like a glow-worm golden
In a dell of dew,
Scattering unbeholden
Its aërial hue
Among the flowers and grass, which screen it from the view:

Like a rose embowered
In its own green leaves,
By warm winds deflowered,
Till the scent it gives
Makes faint with too much sweet these heavy-wingèd thieves.

Sound of vernal showers
On the twinkling grass,
Rain-awakened flowers,
All that ever was,
Joyous, and clear, and fresh, thy music doth surpass:

Teach us, Sprite or Bird,
What sweet thoughts are thine:
I have never heard
Praise of love or wine
That panted forth a flood of rapture so divine.

Chorus Hymeneal,
Or triumphal chant,
Matched with thine would be all
But an empty vaunt,
A thing wherein we feel there is some hidden want.

What objects are the fountains
Of thy happy strain?
What fields, or waves, or mountains?

What shapes of sky or plain?
What love of thine own kind? what ignorance of pain?

With thy clear keen joyance,
Languor cannot be:
Shadow of annoyance
Never came near thee:
Thou lovest -- but ne'er knew love's sad satiety.

Waking or asleep,
Thou of death must deem
Things more true and deep
Than we mortals dream,
Or how could thy notes flow in such a crystal stream?

We look before and after,
And pine for what is not:
Our sincerest laughter
With some pain is fraught;
Our sweetest songs are those that tell of saddest thought.

Yet, if we could scorn
Hate, and pride, and fear;
If we were things born
Not to shed a tear,
I know not how thy joy we ever should come near.

Better than all measures
Of delightful sound,
Better than all treasures
That in books are found,
Thy skill to poet were, thou scorner of the ground!

Teach me half the gladness
That thy brain must know,
Such harmonious madness
From my lips would flow
The world should listen then -- as I am listening now

John Keats (1795–1821)

Ode on a Grecian Urn

Thou still unravish'd bride of quietness,
Thou foster-child of silence and slow time,
Sylvan historian, who canst thus express
A flowery tale more sweetly than our rhyme:
What leaf-fring'd legend haunts about thy shape
Of deities or mortals, or of both,
In Tempe or the dales of Arcady?
What men or gods are these? What maidens loth?
What mad pursuit? What struggle to escape?
What pipes and timbrels? What wild ecstasy?

Heard melodies are sweet, but those unheard
Are sweeter; therefore, ye soft pipes, play on;
Not to the sensual ear, but, more endear'd,
Pipe to the spirit ditties of no tone:
Fair youth, beneath the trees, thou canst not leave
Thy song, nor ever can those trees be bare;
Bold Lover, never, never canst thou kiss,
Though winning near the goal yet, do not grieve;
She cannot fade, though thou hast not thy bliss,
For ever wilt thou love, and she be fair!

Ah, happy, happy boughs! that cannot shed
Your leaves, nor ever bid the Spring adieu;
And, happy melodist, unwearied,
For ever piping songs for ever new;
More happy love! more happy, happy love!
For ever warm and still to be enjoy'd,
For ever panting, and for ever young;
All breathing human passion far above,
That leaves a heart high-sorrowful and cloy'd,

A burning forehead, and a parching tongue.
Who are these coming to the sacrifice?
To what green altar, O mysterious priest,
Lead'st thou that heifer lowing at the skies,
And all her silken flanks with garlands drest?
What little town by river or sea shore,
Or mountain-built with peaceful citadel,
Is emptied of this folk, this pious morn?
And, little town, thy streets for evermore

Will silent be; and not a soul to tell
Why thou art desolate, can e'er return.

O Attic shape! Fair attitude! with brede
Of marble men and maidens overwrought,
With forest branches and the trodden weed;
Thou, silent form, dost tease us out of thought
As doth eternity: Cold Pastoral!
When old age shall this generation waste,
Thou shalt remain, in midst of other woe
Than ours, a friend to man, to whom thou say'st,
"Beauty is truth, truth beauty,--that is all
Ye know on earth, and all ye need to know."

Ode to a Nightingale

My heart aches, and a drowsy numbness pains
My sense, as though of hemlock I had drunk,
Or emptied some dull opiate to the drains
One minute past, and Lethe-wards had sunk:
'Tis not through envy of thy happy lot,
But being too happy in thine happiness,--
That thou, light-winged Dryad of the trees
In some melodious plot
Of beechen green, and shadows numberless,
Singest of summer in full-throated ease.

O, for a draught of vintage! that hath been
Cool'd a long age in the deep-delved earth,
Tasting of Flora and the country green,
Dance, and Provençal song, and sunburnt mirth!
O for a beaker full of the warm South,
Full of the true, the blushful Hippocrene,
With beaded bubbles winking at the brim,
And purple-stained mouth;
That I might drink, and leave the world unseen,
And with thee fade away into the forest dim:
Fade far away, dissolve, and quite forget
What thou among the leaves hast never known,
The weariness, the fever, and the fret
Here, where men sit and hear each other groan;
Where palsy shakes a few, sad, last gray hairs,
Where youth grows pale, and spectre-thin, and dies;
Where but to think is to be full of sorrow
And leaden-eyed despairs,
Where Beauty cannot keep her lustrous eyes,
Or new Love pine at them beyond to-morrow.
Away! away! for I will fly to thee,
Not charioted by Bacchus and his pards,
But on the viewless wings of Poesy,
Though the dull brain perplexes and retards:
Already with thee! tender is the night,
And haply the Queen-Moon is on her throne,
Cluster'd around by all her starry Fays;
But here there is no light,
Save what from heaven is with the breezes blown
Through verdurous glooms and winding mossy ways.

I cannot see what flowers are at my feet,
Nor what soft incense hangs upon the boughs,
But, in embalmed darkness, guess each sweet

Wherewith the seasonable month endows
The grass, the thicket, and the fruit-tree wild;
White hawthorn, and the pastoral eglantine;
The murmurous haunt of flies on summer eves.

Darkling I listen; and, for many a time
I have been half in love with easeful Death,
Call'd him soft names in many a mused rhyme,
To take into the air my quiet breath;
Now more than ever seems it rich to die,
To cease upon the midnight with no pain,
While thou art pouring forth thy soul abroad
In such an ecstasy!
Still wouldst thou sing, and I have ears in vain--
To thy high requiem become a sod.
Thou wast not born for death, immortal Bird!
No hungry generations tread thee down;
The voice I hear this passing night was heard
In ancient days by emperor and clown:
Perhaps the self-same song that found a path
Through the sad heart of Ruth, when, sick for home,
She stood in tears amid the alien corn;
The same that oft-times hath
Charm'd magic casements, opening on the foam
Of perilous seas, in faery lands forlorn.

Forlorn! the very word is like a bell
To toll me back from thee to my sole self!
Adieu! the fancy cannot cheat so well
As she is fam'd to do, deceiving elf.
Adieu! adieu! thy plaintive anthem fades
Past the near meadows, over the still stream,
Up the hill-side; and now 'tis buried deep
In the next valley-glades:
Was it a vision, or a waking dream?
Fled is that music:--Do I wake or sleep?

On First Looking into Chapman's Homer

Much have I travell'd in the realms of gold,
And many goodly states and kingdoms seen;
Round many western islands have I been
Which bards in fealty to Apollo hold.
Oft of one wide expanse had I been told
That deep-brow'd Homer ruled as his demesne;
Yet did I never breathe its pure serene
Till I heard Chapman speak out loud and bold:
Then felt I like some watcher of the skies
When a new planet swims into his ken;
Or like stout Cortez when with eagle eyes
He star'd at the Pacific--and all his men
Look'd at each other with a wild surmise--
Silent, upon a peak in Darien.

I will give you a little politics. In every age there has been in England for some two or th[r]ee centuries subjects of great popular interest on the carpet: so that however great the uproar one can scarcely prophesy any material change in the government; for as loud disturbances have agitated this country many times. All civil[iz]ed countries become gradually more enlighten'd and there should be a continual change for the better. Look at this Country at present and remember it when it was even though[t] impious to doubt the justice of a trial by Combat - From that time there has been a gradual change - Three great changes have been in progress - First for the better, next for the worse, and a third time for the better once more. The first was the gradual annihilation of the tyranny of the nobles. when kings found it their interest to conciliate the common people, elevate them and be just to them. Just when baronial Power ceased and before standing armies were so dangerous, Taxes were few. kings were lifted by the people over the heads of their nobles, and those people held a rod over kings. The change for the worse in Europe was again this. The obligation of kings to the Multitude began to be forgotten - Custom had made noblemen the humble servants of kings - Then kings turned to the Nobles as the adorners of the[i]r power, the slaves of it, and from the people as creatures continually endeavouring to check them. Then in every kingdom therre was a long struggle of kings to destroy all popular privileges. The english were the only people in europe who made a grand kick at this. They were slaves to Henry 8th but were free-men under william 3rd at the time the french were abject slaves under Lewis 14th The example of England, and the liberal writers of france and england sowed the seed of opposition to this Tyranny - and it was swelling in the ground till it burst out in the french revolution -

that has had an unlucky termination. It put a stop to the rapid progress of free sentiments in England; and gave our Court hopes of turning back to the despotism of the 16 century. They have made a handle of this event in every way to undermine our freedom. They spread a horrid superstition against all inovation and improvement - The present struggle in England of the people is to destroy this superstition. What has rous'd them to do it is their distresses - Perpaps on this account the pres'ent distresses of this nation are a fortunate thing - tho so horrid in the[i]r experience. You will see I mean that the french Revolution but [*for* put] a tempor[a]ry stop to this third change, the change for the better - Now it is in progress again and I thing [for think] in an effectual one. This is no contest beetween whig and tory - but between right and wrong. There is scarcely a grain of party spirit now in England - Right and Wrong considered by each man abstractedly is the fashion. I know very little of these things. I am convinced however that apparently small causes make great alterations. There are little signs wherby we many [for may] know how matters are going on - This makes the business about Carlisle the Bookseller of great moment in my mind. He has been selling deistical pamphlets, republished Tom Payne and many other works held in superstitious horror. He even has been selling for some time immense numbers of a work call 'The Deist' which comes out in weekly numbers - For this Conduct he I think has had above a dozen [Prosecutions is crossed out] inditements issued against him; for which he has found Bail to the amount of many thousand Pounds - After all they are affraid to prosecute: they are affraid of his defence: it will would be published in all the papers all over the Empire: they shudder at this: the Trials would light a flame they could not extinguish. Do you not think this of great import? You will hear by the papers of the proceedings at Manchester and Hunt's triumphal entry into London - I[t] would take me a whole day and a quire of paper to give you any thing like detail - I will merely mention that it is calculated that 30.000 people were in the streets waiting for him - The whole distance from the Angel Islington to the Crown and anchor was lined with Multitudes. As I pass'd Colnaghi's window I saw a profil Portraict of Sands the destroyer of Kotzebue. His very look must interest every one in his favour - I suppose they have represented him in his college dress - He seems to me like a young Abelard - A fine Mouth, cheek bones (and this is no joke) full of sentiment; a fine unvulgar nose and plump temples. On looking over some Letters I found the one I wrote intended for you from the foot of Helvellyn to Liverpool-but you had sail'd and therefore It was returned to me. It contained among other nonsense an Acrostic of my Sister's name - and a pretty long name it is. I wrote it in a great hurry which you will see. Indeed I would not copy it if I thought it would ever be seen by any but yourselves - ... [This deleted section is a copy of the acrostic and other parts of his July 1818 Scottish letter to Tom.] I ought to make a large Q here: but I had better take the opportunity of telling you I have got rid of my haunting sore throat - and conduct myself in a manner not to catch another You speak of Lord Byron and me - There is this great difference between us. He describes what he sees - I describe what I imagine - Mine is the hardest task. You see the immense difference - The Edinburgh review are affraid to touch upom [*for* upon] my Poem - They do not know what to make of it - they do not like to condemn it and they will not p[r]aise it for fear - They are as shy of it as I should be of wearing a Quaker's hat - The fact is they have no real taste - they dare not compromise their Judgements on so puzzling a Question - If on my next Publication they should praise me and so lug in Endymion - I will address [them] in a manner they will not at all relish - The Cowardliness of the Edinburgh is worse than the abuse of the Quarterly.

Monday - This day is a grand day for winchester - they elect the Mayor. It was indeed high time the place should have some sort. of excitement. There was nothing going on - all asleep - Not an old Maids Sedan returning from a card party - and if any old women have got tipsy at christenings they have not exposed themselves in the Street - The first night tho' of our arrival here there was a slight uproar took place at about ten of the clock - We heard distinctly a noise patting down the high street as of a walking Cane of the good old dowager breed; and a little minute after we heard a less voice obse[r]ve 'what a noise the ferril made.' - it must be loose." Brown wanted to call the Constables, but I observed 't was only a little breeze and would soon pass over. The side-streets here are excessively maiden lady like - The door steps always fresh from the flannel. The knockers have a very staid ser[i]ous, nay almost awful qu[i]etness about them - I never saw so quiet a collection of Lions, and rams heads - The doors most part black with a little brass handle just above the key hole - so that you may easily shut yourself out of your own house - he! he! There is none of your Lady Bellaston rapping and ringing here - no thundering-Jupiter footmen no opera-trebble-tattoos - but a modest lifting up of the knocker by a set of little wee old fingers that peep through the grey mittens, and a dying-fall thereof - The great beauty of Poetry is, that it makes every thing every place interesting - The palatine venice and the abbotine Winchester are equally interesting - Some time since I began a poem call'd "the Eve of St Mark quite in the spirit of Town quietude. I th[i]nk it wlll give you the sensation of walking about an old county Town in a coolish evening. I know not yet whether I shall ever finish it - I will give it far as I have gone. Ut tibi placent!

letter to george/Thomas keats
http://englishhistory.net/keats/letters/georgekeatsseptember1819.html

Lesson 20

THE AMERICAN ROMANTICS

American Literature Review and Background Information

Prior to 1700 through 1776

The two poets you have read so far, Anne Bradstreet and Phyllis Wheatley, lived in New England, an area that would remain the primary center of American literature through the 1600 and 1700s. As far back as the settlements in Jamestown and Plymouth, you find Travel Journals. Primarily though, the writing of this period were theological in nature -- sermons, pamphlets which made public argument advocating or opposing some action or theological position. Roger Williams, the Quaker who founded the colony of Rhode Island, wrote a pamphlet which avocated religious tolerance. The First Great Awakening (1621-1649) initiated by Jonathan Edwards famous sermon, *Sinners in the Hands of an Angry God,* and spread throughout the Colonies.

The literature of The Revolutionary Age was dominated by the political essay as the colonies focused their energy and resources on the battle for Independence from Britain

Post Revolution 1776-1861:

In the Early National Period (1775-1828) we see an abundance of the kinds of material we typically think of as literature – novels, short stories, verse, as well as essays The most well-known of these included Washington Irving (*Sketchbook,* 1819-1820), James Fennimore Cooper (*Last of the Mohicans,*1826, *Deerslayer,* 1841), Nathaniel Hawthorne (*The Scarlett Letter*, 1850), Henry Melville (*Moby Dick*, 1851, Harriet Beecher Stowe, *Uncle Tom's* Cabin, 1852). Though we will not have time to read these for this course, it would be good for you to read them on your own. Most college lists of recommended reading for high school students will include these titles. (If you only have time to read one, you probably should read *The Scarlet Letter.*)

We will focus on the Transcendentalist writers, Emerson and Thoreau, then make a quick, small "drive-by" reading of the American Poets of the period who (for some reason I have yet to understand) are most widely read, The Fireside Poets.

General Overview of American Romanticism

from *An Outline of American Literature*

(info.state.gov)

The Romantic movement, which originated in Germany but quickly spread to England, France, and beyond, reached America around the year 1820, some 20 years after William Wordsworth and Samuel Taylor Coleridge had revolutionized English poetry by publishing *Lyrical Ballads*. In America as in Europe, fresh new vision electrified artistic and intellectual circles. Yet there was an important difference: Romanticism in America coincided with the period of national expansion and the discovery of a distinctive American voice. The solidification of a national identity and the surging idealism and passion of Romanticism nurtured the masterpieces of "the American Renaissance."

Romantic ideas centered around art as inspiration, the spiritual and aesthetic dimension of nature, and metaphors of organic growth. Art, rather than science, Romantics argued, could best express universal truth. The Romantics underscored the importance of expressive art for the individual and society. In his essay "The Poet" (1844), Ralph Waldo Emerson, perhaps the most influential writer of the Romantic era, asserts:

For all men live by truth, and stand in need of expression. In love, in art, in avarice, in politics, in labor, in games, we study to utter our painful secret. The man is only half himself, the other half is his expression.

The development of the self became a major theme; self-awareness a primary method. If, according to Romantic theory, self and nature were one, self-awareness was not a selfish dead end but a mode of knowledge opening up the universe. If one's self were one with all humanity, then the individual had a moral duty to reform social inequalities and relieve human suffering. The idea of "self" -- which suggested selfishness to earlier generations -- was redefined. New compound words with positive meanings emerged: "self-realization," "self-expression," "self-reliance."

As the unique, subjective self became important, so did the realm of psychology. Exceptional artistic effects and techniques were developed to evoke heightened psychological states. The "sublime" -- an effect of beauty in grandeur (for example, a view from a mountaintop) -- produced feelings of awe, reverence, vastness, and a power beyond human comprehension.

Romanticism was affirmative and appropriate for most American poets and creative essayists. America's vast mountains, deserts, and tropics embodied the sublime. The Romantic spirit seemed particularly suited to American democracy: It stressed individualism, affirmed the value of the common person, and looked to the inspired imagination for its aesthetic and ethical values. Certainly the New England Transcendentalists -- Ralph Waldo Emerson, Henry David Thoreau, and their associates -- were inspired to a new optimistic affirmation by the Romantic movement. In New England, Romanticism fell upon fertile soil.

(http://usinfo.state.gov/products/pubs/oal/lit3.htm)

Religious Influences:

Those who settled the New England Colonies are often refered to as Puritans. But there were two different groups of colonists. Though the two groups had much in common theologically, there were some significant differences. The group we call Pilgrims (1620) were Separatists. They believed that it was best to separate themselves from the Church of England, which they saw as a corrupted church. The group who settled the Massachusettes Bay Colony (1628), are refered to as Puritans. Though they agreed that the Church of England needed to be purified, they chose to remain in the Church of England and work toward reform from within. Doctrinally, however, there was not much difference between the two groups. Popularly, both groups are often refered to as Puritan.

In the 1730s and 1740s, the colonies experienced periods of spiritual revivals , which they called "Awakenings." The first of these seem to have begun in response to the preaching of Jonathan Edwards. This initial Awakening, sometimes call the Puritan Awakening, seemed to have called people away from a cold, largely intellectual adherence to doctrine, to a renewed sense of excitement for a personal experience of faith, and a renewed interest in things like personal Bible study ,

As might be expected, not everyone responded positively. In addition to some discomfort with the move from a more stoic, intellectual attitude toward religion, two doctrines were increasingly debated. Opponents of the Great Awakening argued in favor of Universal salvation (that is, that ALL mankind would be "saved") and against a Trinitarian (One God, Three Persons: Father, Son, and Spirit) view of God. Two very different worldview clashed in this debate. It was, however, not enough to say, "The Bible says…." as these questions were debated.

For the supporters of the Great Awakening, the revealed Word of God had the final say. But for their opponents, who believed that Reason was the key to all correct religious interpretation,

the doctrine of the Trinity was thoroughly unreasonable, for in this case, Revelation certainly seemed to contradict all Reason.

The conflict became even more problematic when the Unitarian tried to explain Jesus. Jesus could be a good moral teacher and operate within the confines of a closed system, Jesus could not, would not disturb the universe and its Law by coming in the world as the Virgin-born, Incarnate, Word made Flesh. The Unitarian and liberal Christian solution as to see

> the primitive religion of Jesus as the ideal expression of natural religion, and sought by purification of the church to return to that ideal. 'Is it not time,' said Bentley, 'to recur to the instructions of this wise friend of mankind, and to accept them uncorrupted by traditions, creedsor councils?' " (American Philosophic Addresses, 1700-1900. Contributors: Joseph L. Blau - editor.Columbia University Press. New York. 1946. p. 537.)

As a result, churches of New England divided themselves into two camps: Unitarian (belief in God as one Person) and Trinitarian (belief in One God in three Persons). Eventually the majority of New England churches were Unitarian. The American Romantic writers and American Transcendentalism came out of the Unitarian camp.

TENETS OF TRANSCENDENTALISM

Often Transcendentalism was described as a *miscellany,* or a collection of a variety of objects, beliefs, or styles. Transcendentalist put such an emphasis on the importance of the Individual, and individual experience, that specific lists of defining beliefs of Transcendentalism were never made.

There were however, some characteristics common to most Transcendentalists.

Transcendentalists would generally agree

There are Truths that *transcend* the physical world and the world of our senses, and the world of Reason. Intuition is a better guide that either our senses or our reason.

Every human spirit is Divine. God is all-encompassing, all-surrounding, and a part of all things. All things share in that all-encompassing Divinity. The Transcendentalists rejected the concept of a Universal Fall and so, did not believe that men needed to be redeemed. The more a person gave himself over to the Divine, the more of God, the universal Spirit, he would experience.

The natural world was embued with Divinity. As one experienced Nature, one experienced the Divine.

From *Outline of American Literature (USINFO.state.gov)*

"Transcendentalist movement was a reaction against 18th century rationalism and a manifestation of the general humanitarian trend of 19th century thought. The movement was based on a fundamental belief in the unity of the world and God. The soul of each individual was thought to be identical with the world -- a microcosm of the world itself. The doctrine of self-reliance and individualism developed through the belief in the identification of the individual soul with God.

"Transcendentalism was intimately connected with Concord, a small New England village 32 kilometers west of Boston. Concord was the first inland settlement of the original Massachusetts Bay Colony. Surrounded by forest, it was and remains a peaceful town close enough to Boston's lectures, bookstores, and colleges to be intensely cultivated, but far enough away to be serene. Concord was the site of the first battle of the American Revolution, and Ralph Waldo Emerson's poem commemorating the battle, "Concord Hymn," has one of the most famous opening stanzas in American literature:

By the rude bridge that arched the flood
Their flag to April's breeze unfurled,
Here once the embattled farmers stood
And fired the shot heard round the world.

"Concord was the first rural artist's colony, and the first place to offer a spiritual and cultural alternative to American materialism. It was a place of high-minded conversation and simple living (Emerson and Henry David Thoreau both had vegetable gardens). Emerson, who moved to Concord in 1834, and Thoreau are most closely associated with the town, but the locale also attracted the novelist Nathaniel Hawthorne, the feminist writer Margaret Fuller, the educator (and father of novelist Louisa May Alcott) Bronson Alcott, and the poet William Ellery Channing. The Transcendental Club was loosely organized in 1836 and included, at various times, Emerson, Thoreau, Fuller, Channing, Bronson

Alcott, Orestes Brownson (a leading minister), Theodore Parker (abolitionist and minister), and others.

"The Transcendentalists published a quarterly magazine, *The Dial*, which lasted four years and was first edited by Margaret Fuller and later by Emerson. Reform efforts engaged them as well as literature. A number of Transcendentalists were abolitionists, and some were involved in experimental utopian communities such as nearby Brook Farm (described in Hawthorne's *The Blithedale Romance*) and Fruitlands.

"Unlike many European groups, the Transcendentalists never issued a manifesto. They insisted on individual differences -- on the unique viewpoint of the individual. American Transcendental Romantics pushed radical individualism to the extreme. American writers often saw themselves as lonely explorers outside society and convention. The American hero -- like Herman Melville's Captain Ahab, or Mark Twain's Huck Finn, or Edgar Allan Poe's Arthur Gordon Pym -- typically faced risk, or even certain destruction, in the pursuit of metaphysical self-discovery. For the Romantic American writer, nothing was a given. Literary and social conventions, far from being helpful, were dangerous. There was tremendous pressure to discover an authentic literary form, content, and voice -- all at the same time. It is clear from the many masterpieces produced in the three decades before the U.S. Civil War (1861-65) that American writers rose to the challenge."

(http://usinfo.state.gov/products/pubs/oal/lit3.htm)

4 Georges (George 3) William, Victoria (Presidents Jefferson #3 – Chester Alan Arthur #21)

RALPH WALDO EMERSON (1803-1882)

Ralph Waldo Emerson (1803-1882)
From *Outline of American Literature* (USINFO.state.gov)

"Ralph Waldo Emerson, the towering figure of his era, had a religious sense of mission. Although many accused him of subverting Christianity, he explained that, for him "to be a good minister, it was necessary to leave the church." The address he delivered in 1838 at his alma mater, the Harvard Divinity School, made him unwelcome at Harvard for 30 years. In it, Emerson accused the church of acting "as if God were dead" and of emphasizing dogma while stifling the spirit.

"Emerson's philosophy has been called contradictory, and it is true that he consciously avoided building a logical intellectual system because such a rational system would have negated his Romantic belief in intuition and flexibility. In his essay "Self-Reliance," Emerson remarks: "A foolish consistency is the hobgoblin of little minds." Yet he is remarkably consistent in his call for the birth of American individualism inspired by nature. Most of his major ideas -- the need for a new national vision, the use of personal experience, the notion of the cosmic Over-Soul, and the doctrine of compensation -- are suggested in his first publication, *Nature* (1836). This essay opens:

> **Our age is retrospective. It builds the sepulchres of the fathers. It writes biographies, histories, criticism. The foregoing generations beheld God and nature face to face; we, through their eyes. Why should not we also enjoy an original relation to the universe? Why should not we have a**

> **poetry of insight and not of tradition, and a religion by revelation to us, and not the history of theirs. Embosomed for a season in nature, whose floods of life stream around and through us, and invite us by the powers they supply, to action proportioned to nature, why should we grope among the dry bones of the past...? The sun shines today also. There is more wool and flax in the fields. There are new lands, new men, new thoughts. Let us demand our own works and laws and worship.**

"Emerson loved the aphoristic genius of the 16th-century French essayist Montaigne, and he once told Bronson Alcott that he wanted to write a book like Montaigne's, "full of fun, poetry, business, divinity, philosophy, anecdotes, smut." He complained that Alcott's abstract style omitted "the light that shines on a man's hat, in a child's spoon." He was widely read in Hinduism, Confucianism, and Islamic Sufism. (http://usinfo.state.gov/products/pubs/oal/lit3.htm)

EMERSON'S DID NOT SEE GOD as a personal Being, but as a cosmic force, a spiritual essence that was a part of all things. All things are also a part of the oversoul. It is an Eastern concept, found similarly in Hindu and Buddhist thought. As such, there is no such thing as a fallen man in need of redemption or salvation. All men ARE divine and share in the Divine and need only to recognize the divinity already within.

In his work, *Nature* Emerson says the following about the nature of the soul.

> **We cannot describe the natural history of the soul, but we know that it is divine. I cannot tell if these wonderful qualities which house to-day in this mortal frame, shall ever reassemble in equal activity in a similar frame, or whether they have before had a natural history like that of this body you see before you; but this one thing I know, that these qualities did not now begin to exist, cannot be sick with my sickness, nor buried in any grave; but that they circulate through the Universe: before the world was, they were. Nothing can bar them out, or shut them in, but they penetrate the ocean and land, space and time, form and essence, and hold the key to universal nature. I draw from this faith courage and hope. All things are known to the soul. It is not to be surprised by any communication. Nothing can be greater than it. (Emerson, "The Method of Nature, http://rwe.org/works/Nature_addresses_4_The_Method_of_Nature.htm. accessed July 4, 2007),**

Go to **http://bellsouthpwp.net/k/e/kerjsmit/self_reliance/sr1-10.htm**
for an annotated text of *Self-Reliance* with vocabulary and other references linked to dictionary and background information.

Self-Reliance

"Ne te quasiveris extra."

"Man is his own star; and the soul that can
Render an honest and a perfect man
Commands all light, all influence, all fate;
Nothing to him falls early or too late.
Our acts our angels are, or good or ill,
Our fatal shadows that walk by us still."
--Epilogue to Beaumont and Fletcher's Honest Man's Fortune

Cast the bantling on the rocks,
Suckle him with the she-wolf's teat,
Wintered with the hawk and fox,
Power and speed be hands and feet.

I read the other day some verses written by an eminent painter which were original and not conventional. The soul always hears an admonition in such lines, let the subject be what it may. The sentiment they instil is of more value than any thought they may contain. To believe your own thought, to believe that what is true for you in your private heart is true for all men,--that is genius. Speak your latent conviction, and it shall be the universal sense; for the inmost in due time becomes the outmost,--and our first thought is rendered back to us by the trumpets of the Last Judgment. Familiar as the voice of the mind is to each, the highest merit we ascribe to Moses, Plato, and Milton is that they set at naught books and traditions, and spoke not what men, but what they thought. A man should learn to detect and watch that gleam of light which flashes across his mind from within, more than the lustre of the firmament of bards and sages. Yet he dismisses without notice his thought, because it is his. In every work of genius we recognize our own rejected thoughts: they come back to us with a certain alienated majesty. Great works of art have no more affecting lesson for US than this. They teach us to abide by our spontaneous impression with good-humored inflexibility then most when the whole Cry of voices is on the other side. Else, to-morrow a stranger will say with masterly good sense precisely what we have thought and felt all the time, and we shall be forced to take with shame our own opinion from another.

There is a time in every man's education when he arrives at the conviction that envy is ignorance; that imitation is suicide; that he must take himself for better for worse as his portion; that though the wide universe is full of good, no kernel of nourishing corn can come to him but through his toil bestowed on that plot of ground which is given to him to till. The power which resides in him is new in nature, and none but he knows what that is which he can do, nor does he know until he has tried. Not for nothing one face, one character, one fact makes much impression on him, and another none. This sculpture in the memory is not without preéstablishcd harmony. The eye was placed where one ray should fall, that it might testify of that particular ray. We but half express ourselves, and are ashamed of that divine idea which each of us represents. It may be safely trusted as proportionate and of good issues, so it be faithfully imparted, but God will not have his work made manifest by cowards. A man is relieved and gay when he has put his heart into his work and done his best; but what he has said or done otherwise shall give hint no peace. It is a deliverance which does not deliver. In the attempt his genius deserts him; no muse befriends; no invention, no hope.

Trust thyself: every heart vibrates to that iron string. Accept the place the divine providence has found for your the society of your contemporaries, the connection of events. Great men have always done so, and confided themselves childlike to the genius of their age, betraying their perception that the absolutely trustworthy was seated at their heart, working through their hands, predominating in all their being. And we are now men, and must accept in the highest mind the same transcendent destiny; and not minors and invalids in a protected corner, not cowards fleeing before a revolution, but guides, redeemers, and benefactors, obeying the Almighty effort, and advancing on **Chaos and the Dark. (1)**

What pretty oracles nature yields us on this text, in the face and behavior of children, babes, and even brutes! That divided and rebel mind, that distrust of a sentiment because our arithmetic has computed the strength and means opposed to our purpose, these have not. Their mind being whole, their eye is as yet unconquered, and when we look in their faces, we are disconcerted. Infancy conforms to nobody; all conform to it, so that one babe commonly makes four or five out of the adults who prattle and play to it. So God has armed youth and puberty and manhood no less with its own piquancy and charm, and made it enviable and gracious and its claims not to be put by, if it will stand by itself. Do not think the youth has no force, because he cannot speak to you and me. Hark! in the next room his voice is sufficiently clear and emphatic. It seems he knows how to speak to his contemporaries. Bashful or bold, then, he will know how to make us seniors very unnecessary.

The nonchalance of boys who are sure of a dinner, and would disdain as much as a lord to do or say aught to conciliate one, is the healthy attitude of human nature. A boy is in the parlor what the **pit (2)** is in the playhouse; independent; irresponsible, looking out from his corner on such people and facts as pass by, he tries and sentences them on their merits, in the swift, summary ways of boys, as good, bad, interesting, silly, eloquent. troublesome. He numbers himself never about consequences, about interests: he gives an independent, genuine verdict. You must court him: he does not court you. But the man is, as it were, clapped into jail by his consciousness. As soon as he has once acted or spoken with éclat, he is a committed person, watched by the sympathy or the hatred of hundreds, whose affections must now enter into his account. There is no **Lethe (3)** for this. Ah, that he could pass again into his neutrality! Who can thus avoid all pledges, and having observed, observe again from the same unaffected, unbiased, unbribable, unaffrighted innocence, must always be formidable. He would utter opinions on all passing affairs, which being seen to be not private, but necessary, would sink like darts into the ear of men, and put them in fear.

These are the voices which we hear in solitude, but they grow faint and inaudible as we enter into the world. Society everywhere is in conspiracy against the manhood of every one of its members. Society is a joint-stock company, in which the members agree, for the better securing of his bread to each shareholder, to surrender the liberty and culture of the eater. The virtue in most request is conformity. Self-reliance is its aversion. It loves not realities and creators, but names and customs.

Whoso would be a man, must be a nonconformist. He who would gather immortal palms must not he hindered by the name of goodness, but must explore if it he goodness. Nothing is at last sacred but the integrity of your own mind. Absolve you to yourself, and you shall have the suffrage of the world. I remember an answer which when quite young I was prompted to make to a valued adviser, who was wont to importune me with the dear old doctrines of the church. On my saying, What have I to do with the sacredness of traditions, if I live wholly from within? my friend suggested,--"But these impulses may be from below, not from above." I replied, "They do not seem to me to be such; but if I am the Devil's child, I will live then from the Devil." No law can be sacred to me but that of my nature. Good and bad are but names very readily transferable to that or this; the only right is what is after my constitution, the only wrong what is against it. A man is to carry himself in the presence of all opposition as if everything were titular and ephemeral but he. I am ashamed to think how easily we capitulate to badges and names, to large societies and dead institutions. Every decent and well-spoken individual affects and sways me more than is right. I ought to go upright and vital, and speak the rude truth in all ways. If malice and vanity wear the coat of philanthropy shall that pass? If an angry bigot assumes this bountiful cause of Abolition, and comes to me with his last news from **Barbadoes (4)** why should I not say to him, "Go love thy infant; love thy wood-chopper; be good-natured and modest: have that grace; and never varnish your hard, uncharitable ambition with this incredible tenderness for black folk a thousand miles off. Thy love afar is spite at home." Rough and graceless would he such greeting, but truth is handsomer than the affectation of love. Your goodness must have some edge to it,-- else it is none. The doctrine of hatred must be preached as the counteraction of the doctrine of love when that pules and whines. **I shun father and mother and wife and brother, when my genius calls me. (5) I would write on the lintels of the door-post, Whim. (6)** I hope it is somewhat better than whim at last, but we cannot spend the day in explanation. Expect me not to show cause why I seek or why I exclude company. Then again, do not tell me, as a good man did today, of my obligation to put all poor men in good situations. Are they my poor? I tell thee, thou foolish philanthropists that I grudge the dollar, the dime, the cent I give to such men as do not belong to me and to whom I do not belong. There is a class of persons to whom by all spiritual affinity I am bought and sold; for them I will go to prisons if need be; but your miscellaneous popular charities; the education at college of fools; the building of meeting-houses to the vain end to which many now stand; alms to sots; and the thousandfold Relief Societies;--though I confess with shame I sometimes succumb and give the dollar, it is a wicked dollar, which by and by I shall have the manhood to withhold.

Virtues are, in the popular estimate, rather the exception than the rule. There is the man and his virtues. Men do what is called a good action, as some piece of courage or charity, much as they would pay a fine in expiation of daily nonappearance on parade. Their works arc done as an apology or extenuation of their living in the world,--as invalids and the insane pay a high board. Their virtues are penances. I do not wish to expiate, but to live. My life is for itself and not for a spectacle. I much prefer that it should be of a lower strain, so it be genuine and equal, than that it should be glittering and unsteady. I wish it to be sound and sweet, and not to need diet and bleeding. I ask primary evidence that you are a man, and refuse this appeal from the man to his actions. I know that for myself it makes no difference whether I do or forbear those actions which are reckoned excellent. I cannot consent to pay for a privilege where I have intrinsic right. Few and mean as my gifts may be, I actually am, and do not need for my own assurance or the assurance of my fellows any secondary testimony.

What I must do is all that concerns me, not what the people think. This rule, equally arduous in actual and in intellectual life, may serve for the whole distinction between greatness and meanness. It is the harder, because you will always find those who think they know what is your duty better than you know it. It is easy in the world to live after the world's opinion; it is easy in solitude to live after our own; but the great man is he who in the midst of the crowd keeps with perfect sweetenss the independence of solitude.

4 Georges (Georges 3 & 4), William, Victoria
(Presidents James Monroe , # 5 to Lincoln # 16)

Lesson 21

HENRY DAVID THOREAU (1817-1862)

Thoreau is perhaps, "the most attractive* of the Transcendentalists today because of his ecological consciousness, do-it-yourself independence, ethical commitment to abolitionism, and political theory of civil disobedience and peaceful resistance." (Outline of Amercan Literature, USINFO.state.gov) In some ways, Thoreau can be seen as the quintessential Transcendentalist. He consistently attempted to live as simply as possible, and was ever the advocate of the absolute value of the individual. (*Attractive, in the sense of most appealing)

For much of his life Emerson functioned as a Mentor for the younger Thoreau, though they did not always agree, and their relationship was sometimes strained. Thoreau was educated at Harvard. He taught school for a short time, but was dismissed for opposition to the use of corporal punishment. For two years, two months and two days, he lived on a piece of property at Walden Pond which was owned by Emerson. His experiment was to see how simply and how deliberately he could live. The book, *On Walden Pond* was written about his two year stay there.

Thoreau's opposition both to the Mexican-American War and to paying taxes, landed him in jail for failure to pay his taxes. Much to his dismay, his aunt paid his tax for him and he was released after only one night. The essay, *On the Duty of Civil Disobedience*, was written out of this experience. Gandhi and Martin Luther King read and were greatly influenced by this essay and its call to peacefully resist unjust laws in their civil disobedience campaigns against the British in India in the first half of the twentieth century and for civil right in the South in the 1960s.

<u>PHYSICAL APPEARANCE:</u>

Nathaniel Hawthorne, though not a Transcendentalist, was a friend of Thoreau. In 1842, he described Thoreau this way:

> **He is a singular character — a young man with much of wild original nature remaining in him; and so far as he is sophisticated, it is in a way and method of his own. He is ugly as sin, long-nosed, queer-mouthed, and with uncouth and somewhat rustic, although courteous manners, corresponding very well with such an exterior. But his ugliness is of an honest and agreeable fashion, and becomes him much better than beauty. (http://ebooks.connect.com/author/336/96/33696.html) **

Emerson said of him,

> **He wore straw hat, stout shoes, strong gray trousers, to brave shrub-oaks and smilax, and to climb a tree for a hawk's or a squirrel's nest. He waded into the pool for the water-plants, and his strong legs were no insignificant part of his armor. (http://thoreau.eserver.org/images.html)**
>
> **His senses were acute, his frame well-knit and hardy, his hands strong and skillful in the use of tools. And there was a wonderful fitness of body and mind. (http://thoreau.eserver.org/images.html)**

THE MEXICAN-AMERICAN WAR AS VIEWED BY THOREAU:

Whether or not this assessment of the Mexican American War is accurate   Thoreau would have agreed with it:

> The war between the United States and Mexico in 1846 to 1848 was basically a struggle for land.
>
> The United States wanted the "frontier". The U.S. felt that it was its right to become a transcontinental country and expand to the west coast. More land was wanted to accommodate a growing population, and this desired land was also rich in natural resources.
>
> Mexico was on the defensive during the war. Its government claimed that the area that is now California, Nevada, Arizona, New Mexico, Wyoming, and Utah had long belonged to Mexico and that American settlers had no right to make their homes there.
>
> When the war ended and the Treaty of Guadeloupe Hidalgo had been signed, the United States had gotten its wishes and was substantially larger geographically. The result of the war was that for the first time, the United States encompassed the entire continent from sea to sea.
>
> (www.uen.org/themepark/liberty/mexicanamericanwar.shtml)

YOUR ASSIGNMENT:

1. Read *On the Duty of Civil Disobedience.*

2. From *Walden,* read the following chapters: "Economy," "Solitude," "Higher Laws," "Spring," and "Conclusion."

As you read, note any unfamiliar words and write the definitions down.

Take notes on the content of the essays. In each essay answer the following questions:

1. What is Thoreau's main point in *Civil Disobedience*? In each of the chapters in *Walden*?

2. What specific examples and illustrations does he use to support his point?

3. Underline those passages

- **which appear to be key to his argument**
- **that clearly typical of his general philosophy**
- **that you would like to be able to refer to or quote during class discussion**
- **that you just like**

4. How would you summarize Thoreau's views of God.

What is God like?

How does Thoreau describe His character of essential Nature?

Man: What is the nature of Man?

Is he basically good? fallen and flawed?)?

What is Man's relationship to other men?

What is Man's relationship to God?

What is Man's relationship to Nature?

Nature?

What is Nature's relationship to God?

What is Nature's relationship to Man?

Government: What should government be like? Why?

4 Georges, William, Victoria
(Jefferson #3 – Harrison #23)

Lesson 22

BOSTON BRAHMINS, AKA THE FIRESIDE POETS:

The Transcendentalist writers seemed to congregate in the area surrounding Concord Massachusettes. The more traditional, popular poets were from Boston. *The Outline of American Literature* describes them this way:

> **In their time, the Boston Brahmins (as the patrician, Harvard-educated class came to be called) supplied the most respected and genuinely cultivated literary arbiters of the United States. Their lives fitted a pleasant pattern of wealth and leisure directed by the strong New England work ethic and respect for learning.**
>
> **In an earlier Puritan age, the Boston Brahmins would have been ministers; in the 19th century, they became professors, often at Harvard. Late in life they sometimes became ambassadors or received honorary degrees from European institutions. Most of them travelled or were educated in Europe: They were familiar with the ideas and books of Britain, Germany, and France, and often Italy and Spain. Upper class in background but democratic in sympathy, the Brahmin poets carried their genteel, European-oriented views to every section of the United States, through public lectures at the 3,000 lyceums (centers for public lectures) and in the pages of two influential Boston magazines, the North American Review and the Atlantic Monthly.**
>
> **The writings of the Brahmin poets fused American and European traditions and sought to create a continuity of shared Atlantic experience. These scholar-poets attempted to educate and elevate the general populace by introducing a European dimension to American literature. Ironically, their overall effect was conservative. By insisting on European things and forms, they retarded the growth of a distinctive American consciousness. Well-meaning men, their conservative backgrounds blinded them to the daring innovativeness of Thoreau, Whitman (whom they refused to meet socially), and Edgar Allan Poe (whom even Emerson regarded as the "jingle man"). They were pillars of what was called the "genteel tradition" that three generations of American realists had to battle. Partly because of their benign but bland influence, it was almost 100 years before the distinctive American genius of Whitman,**

Melville, Thoreau, and Poe was generally recognized in the United States. (Outline of American Literature, USINFO.state.gov)

William Cullen Bryant

Thanatopsis

To him who in the love of nature holds
Communion with her visible forms, she speaks
A various language; for his gayer hours
She has a voice of gladness, and a smile
And eloquence of beauty; and she glides
Into his darker musings, with a mild
And healing sympathy that steals away
Their sharpness ere he is aware. When thoughts
Of the last bitter hour come like a blight
Over thy spirit, and sad images
Of the stern agony, and shroud, and pall,
And breathless darkness, and the narrow house,
Make thee to shudder, and grow sick at heart;--
Go forth, under the open sky, and list
To Nature's teachings, while from all around--
Earth and her waters, and the depths of air--
Comes a still voice. Yet a few days, and thee
The all-beholding sun shall see no more
In all his course; nor yet in the cold ground,
Where thy pale form was laid, with many tears,
Nor in the embrace of ocean, shall exist
Thy image. Earth, that nourished thee, shall claim
Thy growth, to be resolved to earth again,
And, lost each human trace, surrendering up

Thine individual being, shalt thou go
To mix forever with the elements,
To be a brother to the insensible rock
And to the sluggish clod, which the rude swain
Turns with his share, and treads upon. The oak
Shall send his roots abroad, and pierce thy mold.

Yet not to thine eternal resting-place
Shalt thou retire alone, nor couldst thou wish
Couch more magnificent. Thou shalt lie down
With patriarchs of the infant world -- with kings,
The powerful of the earth -- the wise, the good,
Fair forms, and hoary seers of ages past,
All in one mighty sepulchre. The hills
Rock-ribbed and ancient as the sun, -- the vales
Stretching in pensive quietness between;
The venerable woods -- rivers that move
In majesty, and the complaining brooks
That make the meadows green; and, poured round all,
Old Ocean's gray and melancholy waste,--
Are but the solemn decorations all
Of the great tomb of man. The golden sun,
The planets, all the infinite host of heaven,
Are shining on the sad abodes of death
Through the still lapse of ages. All that tread
The globe are but a handful to the tribes
That slumber in its bosom. -- Take the wings
Of morning, pierce the Barcan wilderness,
Or lose thyself in the continuous woods
Where rolls the Oregon, and hears no sound,
Save his own dashings -- yet the dead are there:
And millions in those solitudes, since first
The flight of years began, have laid them down
In their last sleep -- the dead reign there alone.

So shalt thou rest -- and what if thou withdraw
In silence from the living, and no friend
Take note of thy departure? All that breathe
Will share thy destiny. The gay will laugh
When thou art gone, the solemn brood of care
Plod on, and each one as before will chase
His favorite phantom; yet all these shall leave
Their mirth and their employments, and shall come
And make their bed with thee. As the long train
Of ages glides away, the sons of men--
The youth in life's fresh spring, and he who goes

In the full strength of years, matron and maid,
The speechless babe, and the gray-headed man--
Shall one by one be gathered to thy side,
By those, who in their turn, shall follow them.

So live, that when thy summons comes to join
The innumerable caravan, which moves
To that mysterious realm, where each shall take
His chamber in the silent halls of death,
Thou go not, like the quarry-slave at night,
Scourged to his dungeon, but, sustained and soothed
By an unfaltering trust, approach thy grave
Like one who wraps the drapery of his couch
About him, and lies down to pleasant dreams.

Yet one smile more, departing, distant sun!
One mellow smile through the soft vapory air,
Ere, o'er the frozen earth, the loud winds run,
Or snows are sifted o'er the meadows bare.
One smile on the brown hills and naked trees,
And the dark rocks whose summer wreaths are cast,
And the blue gentian-flower, that, in the breeze,
Nods lonely, of her beauteous race the last.
Yet a few sunny days, in which the bee
Shall murmur by the hedge that skirts the way,
The cricket chirp upon the russet lea,
And man delight to linger in thy ray.
Yet one rich smile, and we will try to bear
The piercing winter frost, and winds, and darkened air.

Henry Wadsworth Longfellow

(1807-1882)

Nature

As a fond mother, when the day is o'er,
Leads by the hand her little child to bed,
Half willing, half reluctant to be led,
And leave his broken playthings on the floor,
Still gazing at them through the open door,
Nor wholly reassured and comforted
By promises of others in their stead,
Which, though more splendid, may not please him more;
So Nature deals with us, and takes away
Our playthings one by one, and by the hand
Leads us to rest so gently, that we go
Scarce knowing if we wish to go or stay,
Being too full of sleep to understand

How far the unknown transcends the what we know

Mezzo Cammin

Half of my life is gone, and I have let
The years slip from me and have not fulfilled
The aspiration of my youth, to build
Some tower of song with lofty parapet.
Not indolence, nor pleasure, nor the fret
Of restless passions that would not be stilled,
But sorrow, and a care that almost killed,
Kept me from what I may accomplish yet;
Though, half-way up the hill, I see the Past
Lying beneath me with its sounds and sights, --
A city in the twilight dim and vast,
With smoking roofs, soft bells, and gleaming lights, --
And hear above me on the autumnal blast
The cataract of Death far thundering from the heights.

The Arsenal at Springfield

This is the Arsenal. From floor to ceiling,
Like a huge organ, rise the burnished arms;
But from their silent pipes no anthem pealing
Startles the villages with strange alarms.

Ah! what a sound will rise, how wild and dreary,
When the death-angel touches those swift keys!
What loud lament and dismal *Miserere*
Will mingle with their awful symphonies!

I hear even now the infinite fierce chorus,
The cries of agony, the endless groan,
Which, through the ages that have gone before us,
In long reverberations reach our own.

On helm and harness rings the Saxon hammer,
Through Cimbric forest roars the Norseman's song,
And loud, amid the universal clamor,
O'er distant deserts sounds the Tartar gong.

I hear the Florentine, who from his palace
Wheels out his battle-bell with dreadful din,
And Aztec priests upon their teocallis
Beat the wild war-drums made of serpent's skin;

The tumult of each sacked and burning village;
The shout that every prayer for mercy drowns;
The soldiers' revels in the midst of pillage;
The wail of famine in beleaguered towns;

The bursting shell, the gateway wrenched asunder,
The rattling musketry, the clashing blade;
And ever and anon, in tones of thunder
The diapason of the cannonade.

Is it, O man, with such discordant noises,
With such accursed instruments as these,
Thou drownest Nature's sweet and kindly voices,
And jarrest the celestial harmonies?

Were half the power, that fills the world with terror,
Were half the wealth bestowed on camps and courts,
Given to redeem the human mind from error,
There were no need of arsenals or forts:

The warrior's name would be a name abhorred!
And every nation, that should lift again
Its hand against a brother, on its forehead
Would wear forevermore the curse of Cain!

Down the dark future, through long generations,
The echoing sounds grow fainter and then cease;
And like a bell, with solemn, sweet vibrations,
I hear once more the voice of Christ say, "Peace!"

Peace! and no longer from its brazen portals
The blast of War's great organ shakes the skies!
But beautiful as songs of the immortals,
The holy melodies of love arise.

JOHN GREENLEAF WHITTIER
(1807-1892)

Barbara Frietchie

Up from the meadows rich with corn,
Clear in the cool September morn,

The clustered spires of Frederick stand
Green-walled by the hills of Maryland.

Round about them orchards sweep,
Apple and peach tree fruited deep,

Fair as the garden of the Lord
To the eyes of the famished rebel horde,

On that pleasant morn of the early fall
When Lee marched over the mountain-wall;

Over the mountains winding down,
Horse and foot, into Frederick town.

Forty flags with their silver stars,
Forty flags with their crimson bars,

Flapped in the morning wind: the sun
Of noon looked down, and saw not one.
Up rose old Barbara Frietchie then,
Bowed with her fourscore years and ten;

Bravest of all in Frederick town,
She took up the flag the men hauled down;

In her attic window the staff she set,
To show that one heart was loyal yet.

Up the street came the rebel tread,
Stonewall Jackson riding ahead.

Under his slouched hat left and right
He glanced; the old flag met his sight.

"Halt!" -- the dust-brown ranks stood fast.
"Fire!" -- out blazed the rifle-blast.

It shivered the window, pane and sash;
It rent the banner with seam and gash.

Quick, as it fell, from the broken staff
Dame Barbara snatched the silken scarf.

She leaned far out on the window-sill,
And shook it forth with a royal will.

"Shoot, if you must, this old gray head,
But spare your country's flag," she said.

A shade of sadness, a blush of shame,
Over the face of the leader came;

The nobler nature within him stirred
To life at that woman's deed and word;

"Who touches a hair of yon gray head
Dies like a dog! March on!" he said.

All day long through Frederick street
Sounded the tread of marching feet:

All day long that free flag tost
Over the heads of the rebel host.

Ever its torn folds rose and fell
On the loyal winds that loved it well;

And through the hill-gaps sunset light
Shone over it with a warm good-night.

Barbara Frietchie's work is o'er,
And the Rebel rides on his raids no more.

Honor to her! and let a tear
Fall, for her sake, on Stonewall's bier.

Over Barbara Frietchie's grave,
Flag of Freedom and Union, wave!

Peace and order and beauty draw
Round thy symbol of light and law;

And ever the stars above look down
On thy stars below in Frederick town!

Telling the Bees

Here is the place; right over the hill
Runs the path I took;
You can see the gap in the old wall still,
And the stepping-stones in the shallow brook.

There is the house, with the gate red-barred,
And the poplars tall;
And the barn's brown length, and the cattle-yard,
And the white horns tossing above the wall.

There are the beehives ranged in the sun;
And down by the brink
Of the brook are her poor flowers, weed-o'errun,
Pansy and daffodil, rose and pink.

A year has gone, as the tortoise goes,
Heavy and slow;
And the same rose blows, and the same sun glows,
And the same brook sings of a year ago.

There 's the same sweet clover-smell in the breeze;
And the June sun warm
Tangles his wings of fire in the trees,
Setting, as then, over Fernside farm.

I mind me how with a lover's care
From my Sunday coat
I brushed off the burrs, and smoothed my hair,
And cooled at the brookside my brow and throat.

Since we parted, a month had passed, --
To love, a year;
Down through the beeches I looked at last
On the little red gate and the well-sweep near.

I can see it all now, -- the slantwise rain
Of light through the leaves,
The sundown's blaze on her window-pane,
The bloom of her roses under the eaves.

Just the same as a month before, --
The house and the trees,
The barn's brown gable, the vine by the door, --
Nothing changed but the hives of bees.

Before them, under the garden wall,
Forward and back,
Went drearily singing the chore-girl small,
Draping each hive with a shred of black.

Trembling, I listened: the summer sun
Had the chill of snow;
For I knew she was telling the bees of one
Gone on the journey we all must go!

Then I said to myself, "My Mary weeps
For the dead to-day:
Haply her blind old grandsire sleeps
The fret and the pain of his age away."

But her dog whined low; on the doorway sill,
With his cane to his chin,
The old man sat; and the chore-girl still
Sung to the bees stealing out and in.

And the song she was singing ever since
  In my ear sounds on: --
"Stay at home, pretty bees, fly not hence!
  Mistress Mary is dead and gone!"

1858.

EDGAR ALLEN POE
1809-1949

Edgar Allen Poe is credited with being one of the earliest writers of the short story, as well as the father of mystery, crime, and science fiction genres. The cause of his death has never been specifically identified. All kinds of theories are out there: rabies, tuberculosis, brain fever, suicide, epilepsy, and diabetes among others. No autopsy was performed, so no one will ever know for certain. Unfortunately for Poe's American reputation, control of his literary estate fell into the control of an editor who hated him, Rufus Griswald. Griswald published a ficticious memoir of Poe soon after his death that presented a him as a grotesque and twisted character. As such, Poe's reputation in America was ruined. In France, however, he was and still his greatly honored and respected.

Enjoy!

The Cask of Amontillado

The thousand injuries of Fortunato I had borne as I best could, but when he ventured upon insult, I vowed revenge. You, who so well know the nature of my soul, will not suppose, however, that I gave utterance to a threat. At length I would be avenged; this was a point definitely settled--but the very definitiveness with which it was resolved, precluded the idea of risk. I must not only punish, but punish with impunity. A wrong is unredressed when retribution overtakes its redresser. It is equally unredressed when the avenger fails to make himself felt as such to him who has done the wrong.

It must be understood that neither by word nor deed had I given Fortunato cause to doubt my good will. I continued, as was my wont, to smile in his face, and he did not perceive that my smile now was at the thought of his immolation.

He had a weak point--this Fortunato--although in other regards he was a man to be respected and even feared. He prided himself on his connoisseurship in wine. Few Italians have the true virtuoso spirit. For the most part their enthusiasm is adopted to suit the time and opportunity-- to practise imposture upon the British and Austrian millionaires. In painting and gemmary, Fortunato, like his countrymen, was a quack-- but in the matter of old wines he was sincere. In this respect I did not differ from him materially: I was skillful in the Italian vintages myself, and bought largely whenever I could.

It was about dusk, one evening during the supreme madness of the carnival season, that I encountered my friend. He accosted me with excessive warmth, for he had been drinking much. The man wore motley. He had on a tight-fitting parti-striped dress, and his head was surmounted by the conical cap and bells. I was so pleased to see him, that I thought I should never have done wringing his hand.

I said to him--"My dear Fortunato, you are luckily met. How remarkably well you are looking to-day! But I have received a pipe of what passes for Amontillado, and I have my doubts."

"How?" said he. "Amontillado? A pipe? Impossible! And in the middle of the carnival!"

"I have my doubts," I replied; "and I was silly enough to pay the full Amontillado price without consulting you in the matter. You were not to be found, and I was fearful of losing a bargain."

"Amontillado!"

"I have my doubts."

"Amontillado!"

"And I must satisfy them."

"Amontillado!"

"As you are engaged, I am on my way to Luchesi. If any one has a critical turn, it is he. He will tell me--"

"Luchesi cannot tell Amontillado from Sherry."

"And yet some fools will have it that his taste is a match for your own."

"Come, let us go."

"Whither?"

"To your vaults."

"My friend, no; I will not impose upon your good nature. I perceive you have an engagement. Luchesi--"

"I have no engagement;--come."

"My friend, no. It is not the engagement, but the severe cold with which I perceive you are afflicted. The vaults are insufferably damp. They are encrusted with nitre."

"Let us go, nevertheless. The cold is merely nothing. Amontillado! You have been imposed upon. And as for Luchesi, he cannot distinguish Sherry from Amontillado."

Thus speaking, Fortunato possessed himself of my arm.

Putting on a mask of black silk, and drawing a roquelaire closely about my person, I suffered him to hurry me to my palazzo.

There were no attendants at home; they had absconded to make merry in honour of the time. I had told them that I should not return until the morning, and had given them explicit orders not to stir from the house. These orders were sufficient, I well knew, to insure their immediate disappearance, one and all, as soon as my back was turned.

I took from their sconces two flambeaux, and giving one to Fortunato, bowed him through several suites of rooms to the archway that led into the vaults. I passed down a long and winding staircase, requesting him to be cautious as he followed. We came at length to the foot of the descent, and stood together on the damp ground of the catacombs of the Montresors.

The gait of my friend was unsteady, and the bells upon his cap jingled as he strode.

"The pipe," said he.

"It is farther on," said I; "but observe the white web-work which gleams from these cavern walls."

He turned towards me, and looked into my eyes with two filmy orbs that distilled the rheum of intoxication.

"Nitre?" he asked, at length.

"Nitre," I replied. "How long have you had that cough?"

"Ugh! ugh! ugh!--ugh! ugh! ugh!--ugh! ugh! ugh!--ugh! ugh! ugh!--ugh! ugh! ugh!"

My poor friend found it impossible to reply for many minutes.

"It is nothing," he said, at last.

"Come," I said, with decision, "we will go back; your health is precious. You are rich, respected, admired, beloved; you are happy, as once I was. You are a man to be missed. For me it is no matter. We will go back; you will be ill, and I cannot be responsible. Besides, there is Luchesi--"

"Enough," he said; "the cough is a mere nothing; it will not kill me. I shall not die of a cough."

"True--true," I replied; "and, indeed, I had no intention of alarming you unnecessarily--but you should use all proper caution. A draught of this Medoc will defend us from the damps."

Here I knocked off the neck of a bottle which I drew from a long row of its fellows that lay upon the mould.

"Drink," I said, presenting him the wine.

He raised it to his lips with a leer. He paused and nodded to me familiarly, while his bells jingled.

"I drink," he said, "to the buried that repose around us."

"And I to your long life."

He again took my arm, and we proceeded.

"These vaults," he said, "are extensive."

"The Montresors," I replied, "were a great and numerous family."

"I forget your arms."

"A huge human foot d'or, in a field azure; the foot crushes a serpent rampant whose fangs are imbedded in the heel."

"And the motto?"

" Nemo me impune lacessit."

"Good!" he said.

The wine sparkled in his eyes and the bells jingled. My own fancy grew warm with the Medoc. We had passed through walls of piled bones, with casks and puncheons intermingling, into the inmost recesses of catacombs. I paused again, and this time I made bold to seize Fortunato by an arm above the elbow.

"The nitre!" I said; "see, it increases. It hangs like moss upon the vaults. We are below the river's bed. The drops of moisture trickle among the bones. Come, we will go back ere it is too late. Your cough--"

"It is nothing," he said; "let us go on. But first, another draught of the Medoc."

I broke and reached him a flagon of De Grave. He emptied it at a breath. His eyes flashed with a fierce light. He laughed and threw the bottle upwards with a gesticulation I did not understand.

I looked at him in surprise. He repeated the movement--a grotesque one.

"You do not comprehend?" he said.

"Not I," I replied.

"Then you are not of the brotherhood."

"How?"

"You are not of the masons."

"Yes, yes," I said; "yes, yes."

"You? Impossible! A mason?"

"A mason," I replied.

"A sign," he said, "a sign."

"It is this," I answered, producing a trowel from beneath the folds of my roquelaire.

"You jest," he exclaimed, recoiling a few paces. "But let us proceed to the Amontillado."

"Be it so," I said, replacing the tool beneath the cloak and again offering him my arm. He leaned upon it heavily. We continued our route in search of the Amontillado. We passed through a range of low arches, descended, passed on, and descending again, arrived at a deep crypt, in which the foulness of the air caused our flambeaux rather to glow than flame.

At the most remote end of the crypt there appeared another less spacious. Its walls had been lined with human remains, piled to the vault overhead, in the fashion of the great catacombs of Paris. Three sides of this interior crypt were still ornamented in this manner. From the fourth side the bones had been thrown down, and lay promiscuously upon the earth, forming at one point a mound of some size. Within the wall thus exposed by the displacing of the bones, we perceived a still interior recess, in depth about four feet in width three, in height six or seven. It seemed to have been constructed for no especial use within itself, but formed merely the interval between two of the colossal supports of the roof of the catacombs, and was backed by one of their circumscribing walls of solid granite.

It was in vain that Fortunato, uplifting his dull torch, endeavoured to pry into the depth of the recess. Its termination the feeble light did not enable us to see.

"Proceed," I said; "herein is the Amontillado. As for Luchesi--"

"He is an ignoramus," interrupted my friend, as he stepped unsteadily forward, while I followed immediately at his heels. In an instant he had reached the extremity of the niche, and finding his progress arrested by the rock, stood stupidly bewildered. A moment more and I had fettered him to the granite. In its surface were two iron staples, distant from each other about two feet, horizontally. From one of these depended a short chain, from the other a padlock. Throwing the links about his waist, it was but the work of a few seconds to secure it. He was too much astounded to resist. Withdrawing the key I stepped back from the recess.

"Pass your hand," I said, "over the wall; you cannot help feeling the nitre. Indeed, it is very damp. Once more let me implore you to return. No? Then I must positively leave you. But I must first render you all the little attentions in my power."

"The Amontillado!" ejaculated my friend, not yet recovered from his astonishment.

"True," I replied; "the Amontillado."

As I said these words I busied myself among the pile of bones of which I have before spoken. Throwing them aside, I soon uncovered a quantity of building stone and mortar. With these materials and with the aid of my trowel, I began vigorously to wall up the entrance of the niche.

I had scarcely laid the first tier of the masonry when I discovered that the intoxication of Fortunato had in a great measure worn off.

The earliest indication I had of this was a low moaning cry from the depth of the recess. It was not the cry of a drunken man. There was then a long and obstinate silence. I laid the second tier, and the third, and the fourth; and then I heard the furious vibrations of the chain. The noise lasted for several minutes, during which, that I might hearken to it with the more satisfaction, I ceased my labours and sat down upon the bones. When at last the clanking subsided, I resumed the trowel, and finished without interruption the fifth, the sixth, and the seventh tier. The wall was now nearly upon a level with my breast. I again paused, and holding the flambeaux over the mason-work, threw a few feeble rays upon the figure within.

A succession of loud and shrill screams, bursting suddenly from the throat of the chained form, seemed to thrust me violently back. For a brief moment I hesitated-- I trembled. Unsheathing my rapier, I began to grope with it about the recess; but the thought of an instant reassured me. I placed my hand upon the solid fabric of the catacombs, and felt satisfied. I reapproached the wall; I replied to the yells of him who clamoured. I re-echoed-- I aided-- I surpassed them in volume and in strength. I did this, and the clamourer grew still.

It was now midnight, and my task was drawing to a close. I had completed the eighth, the ninth, and the tenth tier. I had finished a portion of the last and the eleventh; there remained but a single stone to be fitted and plastered in. I struggled with its weight; I placed it partially in its destined position. But now there came from out the niche a low laugh that erected the hairs upon my head. It was succeeded by a sad voice, which I had difficulty in recognizing as that of the noble Fortunato. The voice said--

"Ha! ha! ha!--he! he! he!--a very good joke indeed--an excellent jest. We shall have many a rich laugh about it at the palazzo--he! he! he!--over our wine--he! he! he!"

"The Amontillado!" I said.

"He! he! he!--he! he! he!--yes, the Amontillado. But is it not getting late? Will not they be awaiting us at the palazzo, the Lady Fortunato and the rest? Let us be gone."

"Yes," I said, "let us be gone."

" For the love of God, Montresor!"

"Yes," I said, "for the love of God!"

But to these words I hearkened in vain for a reply. I grew impatient. I called aloud--

"Fortunato!"

No answer. I called again--

"Fortunato--"

No answer still. I thrust a torch through the remaining aperture and let it fall within. There came forth in reply only a jingling of the bells. My heart grew sick on account of the dampness of the catacombs. I hastened to make an end of my labour. I forced the last stone into its position; I plastered it up. Against the new masonry I re-erected the old rampart of bones. For the half of a century no mortal has disturbed them. In pace requiescat!

Lesson 23

BACK TO QUEEN VICTORIA'S ENGLAND

Queen Victoria reigned for sixty four years, from 1837 to 1901. During that time period, Britain saw slavery abolished and child labor laws enacted. It also saw the inventions of ice cream, telephones, voice recorders. During this time, Englishmen experienced the establishment of a nationwide railway system, public flushing toilets, post office boxes, and the establishment of a local police force in every town.

Philosophically, it was also the age of Darwin, Marx, and Freud. There was a sense of optimism. England expanded its borders, colonizing India and Africa and the obvious benefits to England of advances in Trade,the Industrial Revolution of the 1800's, the establishment of a national railway system, and the rise of an increasingly prosperous middle class added to this sense. The picture was not all that rosy, however. The business owners and managers may have done well, financially, but those who flocked to the city from the rural areas were often trapped in oppressive and abusive situations. Child labor laws were not enacted until later in the century, poor houses abounded, prostitution was widespread. Charles Dickens captures much of the social realities in his novels.

On the surface, Victorian England was a genteel place, and our perception of the time is often a bit skewed – afternoon tea where the women dressed in delicate spotless feminine lace dresses and the gentlemen gathered in the library in impeccably tailored suits, sipping their tea. Impropriety (sexual or otherwise) was banished. Queen Victoria was reported to have said, "We are not amused," whenever conversation strayed. Whether or not the Queen actually had a sense of humor, there was a cultural concern for propriety in all things. In Victorian England, below the surface, all things were not "sweetness and light." Much of Victorian literature picks up on this tension between appearance and reality below the surface: confusion of propriety/true piety, public virtue/private vices, and honesty/hypocrisy in general. This is particularly true of the late Victorian writers who are sometimes referred to as the *Anti-Victorians.*

Religious Influences

The Evangelical Party in England was especially active between 1789-1850. Their emphasis was on missionary work, formation of Bible societies, anti-slavery work, social reform (gambling, drinking, prostitution), and social relief on behalf of the poor and destitute. The Salvation Army was established during this period.

On the other end of the spectrum, the Victorian period saw a marked increase in interest in spiritualism and occultic religions – Madame Blavatsky and the Theosophist Society, Rudolph Steiner and the Anthroposophists, and various expressions of Rosicrusianism.

MUSICIANS OF THE PERIOD:
Ludwig Van Beethoven (1770-1827)
Frederic Chopin (1810-1849)
Franz Liszt (1811-1886)
Robert Schumann (1910-1856)
Peter Ilyich Tchaikovsky 1840-1893)
Gilbert (1836-1911) & Sullivan (1842-1900)
Georges Bizet (1838-1875)
Richard Wagner (1813-1883)
Claude Debussy (1862-1918)

PHILOSOPHY
John Stuart Mill
Charles Darwin
Karl Marx
Siegmund Freud

ARTISTS OF THE PERIOD

Pre-Raphaelites
Aesthetic Movement
Arts and Craft Movement
Impressionism
Realism
Post Impressionism
Symbolist Movement
James McNeill Whistler (1834-1903)
Dante Gabriel Rossetti (1826-1882)
John Singer Sargent (1856-1925)
Georges Seurat (1859-1891)
Jean-Francois Millet (1814-1875)
Auguste Rodin (1840-1917)
Aubrey Beardsley (1872-1898)
Gustave Courbet 1819-1877)
Honore Daumier (1808-1879)
Edouard Manet (1832-1883)
Paul Cezanne(1839-1906)
Lucien Pissarro (1863-1944)
Camille Pissarro (1830-1903)
Claude Monet (1840-1926)
Berthe Morisot (1841-1895)
Alfred Sisley (1839-1899)
Pierre-Auguste Renoir (1841-1919)
Edgar Degas (1834-1917)
Mary Cassatt (1844-1926)
Toulouse-Lautrec (1864-1901)
Francisco Goya (1746-1828)
Odilon Redon (1840-1916)
Gustave Moreau (1826-1898)
Vincent van Gogh (1853-1890)
Paul Gauguin (1848-1903

WRITERS OF THE PERIOD:

We will not have time to read all of the poets, playwrights, essayists, and novelist writing during this period. Choose from this list for your independent reading. Those we will read are marked with an *.

ENGLISH
Thomas Carlyle (essayist)
*Tennyson (poet)
Charles Dickens (novelist)
George Eliot (novelist)
Emily Bronte (novelist)
William Makepeace Thackeray (novelist)
Edward Fitzgerald (poet:, *The Rubaiyat of Omar Khayyam)*
*Robert Browning (poet)
*Thomas Hardy (novelist/poet)
*Gerald Manley Hopkins (poet)
Rudyard Kipling (novelist/poet)
*Oscar Wilde (playwright/novelist)
*Robert Louis Stevenson (novelist/poet)
Arthur Conan Doyle (novelist)
*A.E. Housman (poet)
Algernon Charles Swinburne (poet)
Sarah Orne Jewett
*Matthew Arnold
Lewis Carroll

EUROPEAN

Leo Tolstoy (Russia)
Anton Chekhov (playwright/short stories)
Charles Baudelaire (France)
Gustave Flaubert (France)
Henrik Ibsen (Sweden)

AMERICAN

Nathaniel Hawthorne
*Transcencentalists
  Emerson
  Thoreau
Harriet B. Stowe
*Fireside Poets
  Edgar A. Poe

Walt Whitman (Year 4)
Emily Dickenson (Year 4)
Henry Melville
Fredrick Douglas
Louisa May Alcott

Samuel Clemmons (Mark Twain) (Year 4)
Bret Harte
Henry James
Louisa May Alcott
Joel Chandler Harris
Sidney Lanier
Stephen Crane

English poets, Thomas Hardy, A. E. Housman, Gerard Manley Hopkins (along with Oscar Wilde) were writing at the end of the Victorian Period, and are often now grouped with a school of writers often refered to as the "Anti-Victorians." We will be reading them at the beginning of the Twentieth Century Literature course in the fourth year.

VICTORIAN POETS

Alfred Lord Tennyson

The Charge of the Light Brigade is one of Tennyson's best known poems. It was written during the Crimean War in response to news of the Light Brigade's charge against opposing Russian forces. You can read more about the background to the war at this website: http://home.freeuk.com/timarchive/html/crimean_war.htm

The following quotation gives an assessment of the caliber of the generals leading the army at this time:

"Good heavens! What generals then had charge of England's only army, and of her honour and fighting reputation! They were served to a large extent by incompetent staff officers as useless as themselves; many of them merely flaneurs 'about town,' who knew as little of war and its science as they did of the Differential Calculus! Almost all our officers at that time were uneducated as soldiers, and many of those placed upon the staff of the Army at the beginning of the war were absolutely unfit for positions they had secured through family or political interest. There were, of course, a few brilliant exceptions, but they made the incompetence of the many all the more remarkable." He added, "Before the Crimean War began there were few incentives for officers to study their profession scientifically. The great bulk of the staff at home, and most of those selected for staff work with the army sent to Turkey, were chosen for family reasons. However, that was soon changed, for they were found to be mostly incompetent for all practical work in the field. Clever educated professional soldiers took their places as vacancies occurred. I knew the officers well who were, as late as the fall of Sebastopol, the quarter-master-generals of two of our five divisions, and they were not men whom I would have entrusted with a subaltern's picket in the field. Had they been private soldiers I don't think any colonel would have made them corporals"

(Wolseley 1903, 95f, n. 100 as quoted at
http://www.victorianweb.org/history/crimea/beck/2.html)

The Charge of the Light Brigade

I

Half a league, half a league,
Half a league onward,
All in the valley of Death
Rode the six hundred.
`Forward, the Light Brigade!
Charge for the guns!' he said:
Into the valley of Death
Rode the six hundred.

II

`Forward, the Light Brigade!'
Was there a man dismay'd?
Not tho' the soldier knew
   Some one had blunder'd:
Their's not to make reply,
Their's not to reason why,
Their's but to do and die:
Into the valley of Death
Rode the six hundred.

III

Cannon to right of them,
Cannon to left of them,
Cannon in front of them
Volley'd and thunder'd;
Storm'd at with shot and shell,
Boldly they rode and well,
Into the jaws of Death,
Into the mouth of Hell
Rode the six hundred.

IV

Flash'd all their sabres bare,
Flash'd as they turn'd in air
Sabring the gunners there,
Charging an army, while
All the world wonder'd:
Plunged in the battery-smoke

Right thro' the line they broke;
Cossack and Russian
   Reel'd from the sabre-stroke
Shatter'd and sunder'd.
Then they rode back, but not
Not the six hundred.

V

Cannon to right of them,
Cannon to left of them,
Cannon behind them
Volley'd and thunder'd;
 Storm'd at with shot and shell,
While horse and hero fell,
They that had fought so well
Came thro' the jaws of Death,
Back from the mouth of Hell,
All that was left of them,
Left of six hundred.

VI

When can their glory fade?
O the wild charge they made!
All the world wonder'd.
Honour the charge they made!
Honour the Light Brigade,
Noble six hundred!

Ulysses

It little profits that an idle king,
By this still hearth, among these barren crags,
Match'd with an aged wife, I mete and dole
Unequal laws unto a savage race,
That hoard, and sleep, and feed, and know not me.
I cannot rest from travel: I will drink
Life to the lees: All times I have enjoy'd
Greatly, have suffer'd greatly, both with those
That loved me, and alone, on shore, and when
Thro' scudding drifts the rainy Hyades
Vext the dim sea: I am become a name;
For always roaming with a hungry heart
Much have I seen and known; cities of men
And manners, climates, councils, governments,
Myself not least, but honour'd of them all;
And drunk delight of battle with my peers,
Far on the ringing plains of windy Troy.
I am a part of all that I have met;
Yet all experience is an arch wherethro'
Gleams that untravell'd world whose margin fades
For ever and forever when I move.
How dull it is to pause, to make an end,
To rust unburnish'd, not to shine in use!
As tho' to breathe were life! Life piled on life
Were all too little, and of one to me
Little remains: but every hour is saved
From that eternal silence, something more,
A bringer of new things; and vile it were
For some three suns to store and hoard myself,
And this gray spirit yearning in desire
To follow knowledge like a sinking star,
Beyond the utmost bound of human thought.

This is my son, mine own Telemachus,
To whom I leave the sceptre and the isle,--
Well-loved of me, discerning to fulfil
This labour, by slow prudence to make mild
A rugged people, and thro' soft degrees
Subdue them to the useful and the good.
Most blameless is he, centred in the sphere
Of common duties, decent not to fail
In offices of tenderness, and pay

Meet adoration to my household gods,
When I am gone. He works his work, I mine.
Souls that have toil'd, and wrought, and thought with me--
That ever with a frolic welcome took
The thunder and the sunshine, and opposed
Free hearts, free foreheads--you and I are old;
Old age hath yet his honour and his toil;
Death closes all: but something ere the end,
Some work of noble note, may yet be done,
Not unbecoming men that strove with Gods.
The lights begin to twinkle from the rocks:
The long day wanes: the slow moon climbs: the deep
Moans round with many voices. Come, my friends,
'T is not too late to seek a newer world.
Push off, and sitting well in order smite
The sounding furrows; for my purpose holds
To sail beyond the sunset, and the baths
Of all the western stars, until I die.
It may be that the gulfs will wash us down:
It may be we shall touch the Happy Isles,
And see the great Achilles, whom we knew.
Tho' much is taken, much abides; and tho'
We are not now that strength which in old days
Moved earth and heaven, that which we are, we are;
One equal temper of heroic hearts,
Made weak by time and fate, but strong in will
To strive, to seek, to find, and not to yield.

The Eagle

He clasps the crag with crooked hands;
Close to the sun in lonely lands,
Ring'd with the azure world, he stands.

The wrinkled sea beneath him crawls;
He watches from his mountain walls,
And like a thunderbolt he falls.

Matthew Arnold

Dover Beach

The sea is calm to-night.
The tide is full, the moon lies fair
Upon the straits;--on the French coast the light
Gleams and is gone; the cliffs of England stand,
Glimmering and vast, out in the tranquil bay.
Come to the window, sweet is the night-air!
Only, from the long line of spray
Where the sea meets the moon-blanch'd land,
Listen! you hear the grating roar
Of pebbles which the waves draw back, and fling,
At their return, up the high strand,
Begin, and cease, and then again begin,
With tremulous cadence slow, and bring
The eternal note of sadness in.

Sophocles long ago
Heard it on the Ægean, and it brought
Into his mind the turbid ebb and flow
Of human misery; we
Find also in the sound a thought,
Hearing it by this distant northern sea.

The Sea of Faith

Was once, too, at the full, and round earth's shore
Lay like the folds of a bright girdle furl'd.
But now I only hear
Its melancholy, long, withdrawing roar,
Retreating, to the breath
Of the night-wind, down the vast edges drear
And naked shingles of the world.

Ah, love, let us be true
To one another! for the world, which seems
To lie before us like a land of dreams,
So various, so beautiful, so new,
Hath really neither joy, nor love, nor light,
Nor certitude, nor peace, nor help for pain;
And we are here as on a darkling plain
Swept with confused alarms of struggle and flight,
Where ignorant armies clash by night.

LESSON 24 FRANKENSTEIN!

The next three novels you will read are linked thematically. Mary Shelley's *Frankenstein,* was written during the Romantic Period, but relates thematically to the other two, Robert Louis Stevenson's, *The Unusual Story of Dr. Jekyll and Mr. Hyde* and Oscar Wilde's *The Picture of Dorian Gray.*

MARY SHELLEY

Mary Shelley was the second wife of Percy Bysche Shelley, the Romantic poet. Lord Byron challenged Mary, Percy, and their physician, John William Polidori to a contest. The winner would be the one could write the scariest story. She was only 19 years old at the time. The version that is most often read today is her third edition, published in 1831.

YOUR ASSIGNMENT: We are going to read *Frankestein* over two weeks. Read the first half for this week and the second half the following week.

As you read, as always, note any unfamiliar words. Look them up and write down their definitions.

Also, ask your basic observation questions (who,what,when,where,why and how) of the text as you read, and expect to find answers in the text. Underline or highlight (adding any marginal notes you like) passages that strike you as significant to theme, passages you will want to refer to during class discussion, or passages you just happen to like.

Answer the following questions.

1. The full title of the book is *Frankenstein: or, The Modern Prometheus.* Your first job, then, is to find out everything you can about Prometheus (hint: check out Greek Mythology). Write a quick summary of the Prometheus' story below. (As you read, be thinking about how Frankenstein might be a modern Prometheus.

2. List the things you learn about each of the following characters:

Frankenstein

Elizabeth

Justine

William

Robert Walton

The Monster

The family in the forest:

3. What motivates or influences Dr. Frankenstein at the beginning of the novel? What actions does he take because of these influences? Is there more than one influence, or contradictory influences?

4. What do you notice about the Monster's relationship with Frankenstein? What does he call Dr. Frankenstein? Why? Is he content with the quality of their relationship? How does his attitude toward Dr. F. change over the course of the story?

5. What do you notice about Dr. Frankenstein's attitude toward the Monster? Why does he feel this way? Does his attitude toward the Monster change over the course of the story? Why/why not?

6. Do you notice recurring ideas, symbols, themes running through the book? List them. Then tell what you notice about them. (Hint: What do you notice about Shelley's use of Light and Fire?)

7. What do you notice about the way people respond to the Monster?

8. Tell about the family that the Monster observes. In what way does Shelley use the descriptions of the Monster's observations to critique contemporary society? Be specific.

9. How would you describe the Monster's basic nature?

10. Does he change over the course of the story? What changes him? How is responsible for those changes?

11. In what way is Frankenstein a "modern Prometheus."

LESSON 25 *JEKYLL & HYDE*

ROBERT LOUIS STEVENSON

THE STRANGE CASE OF DR. JEKYLL AND MR. HYDE

YOUR ASSIGNMENT:
Read **Dr. Jekyll and Mr. Hyde** carefully this week.

As you read, as always, note any unfamiliar words. Look them up and write down their definitions.

Also, ask your basic observation questions (who,what,when,where,why and how) of the text as you read, and expect to find answers in the text. Underline or highlight (adding any marginal notes you like) passages that strike you as significant to theme, passages you will want to refer to during class discussion, or passages you just happen to like.

Answer the following questions in writing below:

1. List the characters in the story, and tell what you know about each one. If you need to use another sheet of paper, please do so.

Dr. Henry Jekyll

Mr. Edward Hyde

Mr. Gabriel John Utterson

Dr. Hastie Lanyon

Mr. Poole .

Mr. Enfield .

Mr. Guest

Sir Danvers Carew

2. Carefully note Stevenson's descriptions of Hyde. What adjectives does he use to describe him? What words does he use to describe his speech, his physical movements, his facial expressions. What overall picture is he trying to create in the reader's mind?

3. Also note Stevenson's descriptions of Jekyll. How are they different? How are they alike? What overall picture is he trying to create of Jekyll in the reader's mind?

3. Describe the main events in the story (plot). What is the first thing that happens? Second thing? Next thing? (List only the significant actions and events, not a detailed blow-by-blow recitation of every little thing that happens.)

3. How does Stevenson build the sense of the mysterious as the story progresses?

4. What appears on first reading to be a nice little horror story is more than that. Jekyll and Hyde has been described as a moral allegory. First, write the definition of *allegory*:

How might the book be interpreted as allegory? What might the various characters and actions represent?

5. Read Romans chapter 7. A duality describes the existence of two (generally conflicting) qualities or natures present together. Discuss the various dualities present in the story:

If Jekyll/Hyde are interpreted as representative of Mankind, what is Stevenson saying about Man?

If the work is interpreted as social commentary, what is Stevenson saying about Victorian Society?

About science?

6. Why does Dr. Jekyll set out to create a Mr. Hyde? What does he hope to accomplish?

7. What role does science play in the story? Compare/contrast the way Science is portrayed here with the way it is portrayed in *Frankenstein*.

LESSON 26
OSCAR WILDE, *The Picture of Dorian Gray*

Biography from the Modern Library website:

Oscar Wilde was born in Dublin in 1854. His father was a celebrated surgeon, his mother a supporter of Irish independence who presided over literary salons in Ireland and England. Although his brilliance as a classicist at Dublin's Trinity College won him a scholarship to Magdalen College, Oxford, Wilde failed in his attempts at an academic career. Instead he set his sights on the literary and artistic worlds of London. Fusing the influences of Ruskin, the Pre-Raphaelites, Walter Pater, and Gautier's l'art pour l'art, he made himself the most visible manifestation of the Aesthetic movement; by 1881 a burlesque of Wilde provided the protagonist for the Gilbert and Sullivan operetta Patience. It was to exploit the popularity of the operetta, in fact, that the producer D'Oyly Carte underwrote Wilde's immensely successful lecture tour of America. Married in 1884 to Constance Lloyd, Wilde worked briefly as a magazine editor while publishing poetry, plays, fairy tales, and essays.

The Picture of Dorian Gray was commissioned by J. M. Stoddardt, the Philadelphia publisher of Lippincott's Monthly Magazine. It appeared in the July 1890 issue and immediately gained a certain notoriety for being 'mawkish and nauseous,' 'unclean,' 'effeminate,' and 'contaminating.' When it was published as a book the following year, Wilde greatly revised and expanded the text, filling it out with a melodramatic subplot and adding a preface that defended his aesthetic philosophy. As for the book's value as autobiography, Wilde noted in a letter that the main characters are in different ways reflections of him: 'Basil Hallward is what I think I am: Lord Henry what the world thinks me: Dorian what I would like to be--in other ages, perhaps.'

In the early nineties, Wilde was at the center of an artistic milieu characterized by The Yellow Book, The Rhymers' Club, and the art of Aubrey Beardsley. Banned from performance in England, his poetic drama ***Salome*** (1892) was illustrated by Beardsley and finally produced in Paris in 1896. At the same time, Wilde achieved success as a popular playwright, writing in rapid succession ***Lady Windermere's Fan***, ***A Woman of No Importance***, ***An Ideal Husband***, and ***The Importance of Being Earnest***. In 1895, two of his plays were on the London stage simultaneously, and he was acknowledged as a pivotal figure in English literary life, admired for his wit and eloquence.

Since at least the mid-1880s, however, Wilde had lived a sexual double life, and in 1893 he distanced himself from his family by taking rooms at the Savoy Hotel. He had by then embarked on a passionate relationship with the considerably younger Lord Alfred Douglas, the English translator of Salome, whom he had met the year after he wrote ***The Picture of Dorian Gray***. In March 1895, Wilde undertook a libel action against the Marquess of Queensberry, Lord Alfred's father, who had denounced Wilde as a 'somdomite' (sic). Wilde withdrew the suit following damaging cross-examination by the marquess's defense attorney, a former classmate of Wilde's. (Question: 'Have you ever adored a young man madly?' Answer: 'I have never given adoration to anybody but myself.') Shortly thereafter, Wilde was arrested for homosexual offenses and underwent two trials before being sentenced to hard labor at Wandsworth Prison and Reading Gaol. A long recriminatory letter to Douglas written while in prison was eventually published as ***De Profundis***.

Released in 1897, Wilde left for France under the name Sebastian Melmoth, a pseudonym combining a martyred saint with a Faustian hero of Gothic romance. A poem based on his prison experience, ***The Ballad of Reading Gaol***, was published in 1898. His health destroyed, and bankrupted by his legal expenses, Wilde lived in Paris for three years, making a conversion to Roman Catholicism just before his death in November 1900. He is buried in the cemetery of Pere Lachaise.
(http://www.randomhouse.com/modernlibrary/catalog/display.pperl?isbn=9780679642091)

The Aesthetic Movement in Britain was initially associated with the writings of Oxford don, Walter Pater. The movement was also called the Decadent Movement. Pater advocated living so as to experience all things intensely, that pursuit of the intensity meant that you throw yourselves into full experience of all the senses and the pursuit of beauty. It was, by nature, hedonistic and sensual, which means that it represented a call to find meaning through pursuit of pleasure without regard for demands of morality, responsibility, or propriety. The young men who followed Pater lived, focused on the arts, on their appearance, dressing extravagantly with overly meticulous concern for every minute detail of dress and style. (see picture) You will find references to this lifestyle throughout *Dorian Gray*.

YOUR ASSIGNMENT:

READ: Divide your edition of Dorian Gray in half. Read the first half this week and the second half next week. Before you begin reading, look over the following questions. Some of them you will want to answer as you go, others you will want to keep in mind as you read, but actually write about at the end of the week or after you have finished the book.

1. As you read, list the things you learn about each of the following characters. Include passages from the text that are key to an understanding of each. Feel free to run out of space (and use addition sheets of paper to record your thoughts and observations.)

Dorian Gray

Lord Henry Wotton

Basil Hallward

Sibyl Vane

James Vane

Mrs. Vane

Alan Campbell

Lady Agatha

Lord Fermor

Duchess of Monmouth

Victoria Wotton -

Victor -

Mrs. Leaf

2. Summarize the plot. (You'll obviously do this over the two weeks. As you finish the first weeks work, summarize as much as you've read so far. Continue the next week.)

3. Discuss the relationships between the characters and the effects they have on each other.

4. Tell about the effect of Dorian's portrait on Basil, Henry, and Dorian.

5. Why does Dorian decide to put the portrait in a private and locked room? Why doesn't he want to see it? Why doesn't he want others to see it?

6. How does Dorian change of the years? (physically and spiritually?) How does the portrait change? The significance of these things?

7. At certain points in the story, Dorian reaches a crossroads in which his next choice will significantly affect his entire life – either for good or for evil. Look for these crossroads as you read. Mark them. Then list them here and comment on them. Tell. why are they significant.

8. Oscar Wilde wrote the following about *Dorian Gray:*

"Basil Hallward is what I think I am: Lord Henry what the world thinks of me: Dorian what I would like to be – in other ages, perhaps." (quoted in the 2004 Modern Library edition of *The Picture of Dorian Gray,* Oscar Wilde," p. vi.)

What do you think he meant?

9. At the beginning of the book, how would you describe Dorian's nature on a scale of 1 to 10, with 1 being innocent and 10 being thoroughly corrupt?

At the end of the book?

What accounts for the change? Is it something others do to him, or something he does to himself?

THINKING ABOUT *FRANKENSTEIN, JEKYLL AND HYDE,* AND *DORIAN GRAY* – COMMON THEMES

	FRANKENSTEIN	JEKYLL & HYDE	DORIAN GRAY
NATURE OF EACH			
CHANGES HOW?			
CAUSE OF CHANGE? INFLUENCES? INTERNAL OR EXTERNAL OR BOTH?			
NATURE AT END			
RESPONSE TO CHANGE?			
EFFECT OF CHANGE ON RELATIONSHIPS W/OTHERS			

EFFECTS OF CHANGE ON RELATIONSHIPS WITH OTHERS?			
HOW DOES EACH RESPOND TO SIN?			
ROLE OF SCIENCE?			N/A
OTHER OBSERVATIONS AND CONCLUSIONS			

This concludes our study of English and American literature for this year. Congratulations! You have read a lot of varied and challenging literature this year. The later part of the 1800's saw something of an explosion in American literature – work that was distinctively American. The Westward expansion also produced writers who were well removed from the New England establishment – Mark Twain, Bret Harte, Jack London among others.

We will being our study of 20th century literature next year with 19th century American writers who are seen as pre-cursers to 20th century American literature – Twain, Emily Dickinson, and Walt Whitman. Please read *The Adventures of Huckleberry Finn* over the summer. See you next year!

www.ingramcontent.com/pod-product-compliance
Lightning Source LLC
LaVergne TN
LVHW080308110826
845155LV00023B/92

* 9 7 8 1 8 8 2 5 1 4 4 6 5 *